KOLUSUWAKONOL

Peskotomuhkati-Wolastoqewi
naka
Ikolisomani
Latuwewakon

Philip S. LeSourd's

English
and
Passamaquoddy-Maliseet
DICTIONARY

Edited and Revised by
Robert M. Leavitt
University of New Brunswick
and
David A. Francis
Title IV-A Program
Pleasant Point, Perry, Maine

Second Printing
Passamaquoddy-Maliseet Bilingual Program
ESEA Title VII
Pleasant Point, Perry, Maine

1986

ISBN 0-920114-74-1

PREFACE

The production of KOLUSUWAKONOL has been, appropriately, an international effort.

Philip S. LeSourd originally created this dictionary for the Wabnaki Bilingual Education Program at Indian Township, Maine. It was first issued there in 1979 as a typed manuscript. Working in Maine and New Brunswick, LeSourd designed the format for Passamaquoddy entries which is used in this volume and compiled the original collection of words. The dictionary was circulated in Maine and New Brunswick.

In 1984 the Pleasant Point Title IV-A Program, under the direction of Joseph A. Nicholas, decided to expand and publish the dictionary as a resource for elementary school teachers and children, and for other speakers and students of the language. The Program asked the Micmac-Maliseet Institute at the University of New Brunswick to produce an updated edition of LeSourd's work.

In order that the dictionary could be continuously expanded, both in the vocabulary and in the types of entries included, and in order that the growing collection always be accessible to teachers and to students of the language, the Micmac-Maliseet Institute decided to store the dictionary in UNB's main-frame computer.

Bill Mersereau, Manager of User Services at the UNB Computing Centre, and Bonita Mockler and Brian Lesser, Programmer Analysts, have designed programs that will eventually allow for on-line searches as well as a straightforward way to add words, edit entries, and select words for language lessons and teaching materials. One of these programs has been used to create the English side of the dictionary from the original Passamaquoddy version. Future editions will take advantage of this expansion capability.

Robert M. Leavitt, of the Micmac-Maliseet Institute, and David A. Francis, of the Pleasant Point Title IV-A Program, took on the task of editing, amending, and cross-referencing the entries.

Susan Desormeau typed the original and new entries into the computer data-bank, ensuring a consistent format throughout.

Clearly, the greatest credit goes to those speakers of Passamaquody-Maliseet who have provided the words in the dictionary.

Veronica Atwin	Vickey Dana	Anna Harnois	George Sockabasin
Audrey Cote	David Francis	Estelle Neptune	Mary Ellen Socobasin
Albert Dana	Lorraine Gabriel	Wayne Newell	Eleanor Socoby
Charles Dana	Peter Gabriel	Joseph Nicholas	Aloysius Sopiel
Colleen Dana	Simon Gabriel	Peter Paul	Beverly Sopiel
Philomene Dana	Albert Harnois	Clara Polches	Maxine Tomah

INTRODUCTION

Who Speaks Passamaquoddy-Maliseet?

Passamaquoddy-Maliseet is an Algonquian language spoken along the St. Croix River in Maine and the St. John River in New Brunswick. Passamaquoddy communities are located at Pleasant Point (near Eastport) and at Indian Township (near Princeton), Maine. Maliseet communities are located in New Brunswick at St. Basile (near Edmundston), Tobique, Woodstock, Kingsclear, St. Mary's (in Fredericton), and Oromocto. There is also a band of Maliseets living at Houlton, Maine.

The differences between Passamaquoddy and Maliseet are comparable to those between British and North American English, chiefly a few vocabulary words, pronunciations, and "accent."

The languages closest to Passamaquoddy-Maliseet are Penobscot and Abenaki (Maine and Quebec) and Micmac (the Gaspe and Maritime Provinces, with communities in Newfoundland, northern Maine, and Boston).

What Kind Of Dictionary Is This?

KOLUSUWAKONOL is a "grammatical" dictionary. That is, it not only lists Passamaquoddy-Maliseet words with English translations (and vice-versa), but also gives sufficient information about each word to enable the user to construct desired forms. Without this information, for example, one could find out how to say "he comes toward here," *ckuhye*, but not "I come," *nuckuwi*, or "when they were coming," *weckuhyawolotihtit*. One could find out how to say "apple," *cikon*, but not "his apple," *'tahcikonemol*, or "on the apple," *cikonek*, or "little apple," *cikonehsis*.

It is evident that the present volume does not contain "every" Passamaquoddy-Maliseet word. The language has a potentially unlimited number of words that speakers can "invent" by combining various elements, such as preverbs, roots, finals, and theme-markers. The development of a method of presenting these elements in such a way that users can combine them to produce acceptable words is left to a future edition of this work.

The inflected forms of verbs are listed separately in a book of paradigms. See *Passamaquoddy-Maliseet Verb Paradigms* by R. M. Leavitt and D. A. Francis (Fredericton, Micmac-Maliseet Institute, 1984). A supplement with noun paradigms is planned.

What Does a Dictionary Entry Contain?

NOUNS AND PRONOUNS

Here are sample NOUN and PRONOUN entries, with a brief explanation of each part.

SAMPLE ENTRY 1

    akom (A) snowshoe
     plural: akomok
      poss: 'takomol
       loc: akomok
      dim: akomossis
      abs: akomokk (pl.)
      obv: akomol (sg.)

SAMPLE ENTRY 2

    wik (I) (dep.) his house; his home
     plural: wikol
      dim: wiksis
      loc: wikok

SAMPLE ENTRY 3

    wen (A) (PRO) who; someone
     plural: wenik
      dim: wenossis
      obv: wenil (sg.), wenihi, wenhi, weni (pl.)

    NOUN and PRONOUN entries contain information about the Passamaquoddy-Maliseet word and how it is used. In addition to the grammatical information shown here, many entries contain further notes about the word and/or sample sentences in which it appears in some form. The notes and sentences are self-explanatory and are not discussed here. Each NOUN or PRONOUN entry, then, has five parts:

A. The Passamaquoddy-Maliseet Word. For nouns, the entry form is singular (unless the word is found only in the plural), unpossessed (unless the noun is dependent). In sample entry 2, the word *wik*, "his house," occurs only in possessed (dependent) forms. To say "a house" one uses another word, *wikuwam*.

B. The Gender. All Passamaquoddy-Maliseet nouns and pronouns are either animate (A) or inanimate (I). The designation (A, I) means that the same entry form is used for both an A and an I noun. For example--

    piley (A, I) new one

Note that for any word of this type the animate plural is not the same as the inanimate plural (pileyak, A; pileyal, I).

C. Inflected and Derived Forms of the Noun. Alternatives may be shown for each.

(1) plural (of a noun or pronoun): more than one.
(2) possessed form (of a noun): his _____.
(3) locative form (of a noun): on the _____, in the _____, at _____, etc.
(4) diminutive form (of a noun or pronoun): a small _____.
(5) absentative form (of a noun or pronoun): a dead or absent _____; one that was here before, but isn't now.
(6) obviative form (of an animate noun or pronoun): "fourth person" form.

These forms are not necessarily predictable from the entry form (or in turn, from the plural).

D. Further Information about the Noun or Pronoun.

E. Sample Sentences Showing How The Noun Or Pronoun Is Used.

LOCATIVE NOUNS

Here is a sample LOCATIVE NOUN entry, together with a brief explanation.

SAMPLE ENTRY 4

Mihkomahkik land of the Micmacs (Locative)

Entries like sample entry 4 are place-names, nouns which almost always in locative form. These locatives do not have the other inflected or derived forms listed in noun entries. Place-names, depending upon the sentence in which they are used, may have a translation like one of the following (using sample entry 4)--

Mihkomakik to the land of the Micmacs;
in, from, by way of, toward, through, along the coast of (etc.), the land of the Micmacs.

VERBS

Here are sample VERB entries, with a brief explanation of each part.

SAMPLE ENTRY 5

mosonal (TA) he catches him; he gets it (an.)

Stem 1a: -moson-
Stem 1b: pson-
Stem 2: meson-
Stem 3: mson-

SAMPLE ENTRY 6

peciye (AI) he arrives

plural: peciyawolotuwok
Stem 1: -peciy(a)-

Each verb entry shows:

A. The Passamaquoddy-Maliseet Word. For verbs, the entry form is the Independent, third person singular (with a singular object if the verb is transitive). That is, it is the form that means he _____s, or he _____s it, or he _____s it (an.), or he _____s him. For example--

mosonal (TA) he catches him
peciye (AI) he arrives

Some words take only dual or plural subjects, or only plural objects (they _____, he _____them). In that case, the "they" form is used. For example--

mawona (TA) he gathers them
macehkawotuwok (AI) they (dual) walk away

When a verb is marked (AI, II), this means that the same entry form is used for both the AI and the II verb. Other forms of the two verbs will differ. The plural form shown for such a verb is the AI plural. When a verb is marked (AI, AI + OBJ), this means that the verb may be used in both ways. AI + OBJ forms are AI forms with (sometimes) additional inflection. (See paradigms.)

B. The Type of Verb. There are six types of Passamaquoddy-Maliseet verbs.

(AI)	Animate Intransitive (animate subject)
(AI + OBJ)	Animate Intransitive, but with grammatical object
(II)	Inanimate Intransitive (inanimate subject)
(TA)	Transitive Animate (animate object)
(TI)	Transitive Inanimate (inanimate object)
(DOV)	Double Object Verb ("direct" and "indirect" objects--only the direct object may be inanimate)

C. The English Translation or Translations of the Entry Word. For consistency, the pronouns "he" and "him" have been used in the translations, whenever appropriate. In Passamaquoddy-Maliseet there is no distinction made between "he" and "she"; both are translated by *nekom*. "He" and "him" are not used in the translations when the subject or object of the verb must be female or when the subject or object is best expressed as "it." Alone, "it" refers to an inanimate noun; "it (an.)" refers to an animate noun, which may be something other than a person or animal. According to the sentence in which a verb is used, "he," "she" and "it (an.)" may be freely interchanged. For example--

> nomiyal (TA) he sees him, he sees her,
> she sees him, she sees her,
> he sees it (an.), she sees it (an.)
> (but usually not: it (an.) sees him,
> or her)

D. The Plural Form of the Verb, third person (*nekomaw*) AI and some TI verbs only. The infix (theme-marker) used in AI and some TI verbs to show a plural subject *(more than two)* is not predictable from the entry form of the verb. Some verbs may take one or another infix (or even a combination), according to the speaker or the community. Without the infix, the "plural" forms of AI verbs generally show *dual* subjects, although some such forms may be used as true plurals.

Common plural infixes seen in the plural forms are *-aht(i)-, -awolot(i), -awot(i)-, -hot(i)-, -iy(a)-, -olot(i)-, -uht(i)-, -ult(i)-*. The plural form in sample entry 6, *peciyawolotuwok*, uses *-awolot(i)-*.

E. The Verb Stem or Stems. These stems are used in the paradigms for various forms of the verbs.

Stem 1a is the stem used with personal prefixes.

Stem 1b is the stem used without personal prefixes and without "initial change." (Note: If stem 1a and stem 1b are the same, the stem is called *Stem 1*). Some speakers may use stem 1b (stem 1) throughout the paradigms.

Stem 2 is the stem with "initial change"; that is, a vowel in the first syllable of the stem changes to *e*. (Note: If no change occurs, stem 2 is the same as stem 1, and it is not listed.) This stem is also referred to as the "neke" form because it is used with that word.

Stem 3 is the stem used with preverbs. (Note: If stem 3 is the same as stem 1b (stem 1), it is not listed.)

F. Further Information About The Verb.

G. Sample Sentences Showing How The Verb Is Used.

VERB ROOTS

Here is a sample VERB ROOT entry, with a brief explanation.

SAMPLE ENTRY 7

-ahk(e)- throw; drop; release
(forms AI and AI+OBJ verb stems)

This type of entry, more of which will be added to future editions, shows a verb root to which a preverb, and perhaps other elements, must be added in order to form a complete stem. For example--

tolahke (AI) he is throwing
kisahkewan (AI+OBJ) he threw it to him
'qasahkan (AI, AI+OBJ) he throws it away
'kossiyahkan (AI, AI+OBJ) he throws it into (a room, window, etc.)

A current dictionary project is finding a way to present components of Passamaquoddy-Maliseet words so that users can make--or interpret--new combinations. The limited number of verb root entries in this edition is the beginning of this effort. Noun roots will also be added.

PREVERBS AND PRENOUNS

Here is a sample PREVERB entry, with a brief explanation of each part. PRENOUN entries follow the same format, but prenouns are used with nouns and so do not have a *neke* (stem 2) form. Some entries are used as both prenouns and preverbs.

SAMPLE ENTRY 8

ckuwi (ckuw-, ckuh-) (PV) toward here

prefixed form: -uckuwi (-uckuw-, -uckuh-)
neke form: weckuwi (weckuw-, weckuh-)

Each PREVERB or PRENOUN entry shows:

A. The Preverb. The entry form is the "complete" form of the preverb, used before any other preverbs, and used when the preverb does not combine with the verb. For example--

ckuwi motapehe (AI) he comes downhill toward here
ckuwi qasku (AI) he runs toward here

The form or forms in parentheses are those used in combination with a verb. For example--

ckuwame (AI) he fishes toward here

ckuhqepu (AI) he sits facing toward here

B. Other Forms of the Preverb (if they occur).

The prefixed form is that used with a personal prefix; for example, *kuckuwi qasq,* "you (sg.) run toward here." (Compare stem 1a of a verb.)

The neke form is the form with "initial change"; that is, a vowel in the first syllable of the preverb changes to e; for example, *weckuwi qasqiyin,* "when you (sg.) run toward here." (Compare stem 2 of a verb.)

(Note: If the prefixed form or the *neke* form is the same as the entry form, it is not listed.)

C. Further Information about the Preverb or Prenoun.

D. Sample Words Showing How the Preverb or Prenoun is Used.

PARTICLES

Here is a sample PARTICLE entry, with a brief explanation.

SAMPLE ENTRY 9

naka (P) and; with

Particles are complete words that are not nouns, pronouns, verbs, preverbs or prenouns. Generally, particles have only one form; they are not inflected As a part of speech, particle corresponds to the English adverb, conjunction, interjection, or counting number. (Note that many English adverbs occur as Passamaquoddy-Maliseet preverbs.)

For counting numbers, some entries show "nominal" forms; that is, those used as nouns. For example--

new (P) four, (in counting)

newwok (four animates); obviative: newu
newonul (four inanimates)

ABBREVIATIONS USED IN THE DICTIONARY

abs.	absentative
an.	animate
dep.	dependent
dim.	diminutive
dual	subject is two persons, animals, etc.
inan.	inanimate
loc.	locative
neke	showing "initial change"
obv.	obviative
pl.	plural
poss.	possessed form
prox.	proximate (third person, non-obviative)
sg.	singular

A	Animate Noun
AI	Animate Intransitive verb
AI+OBJ	Animate Intransitive verb with Object
DOV	Double Object Verb
I	Inanimate noun
II	Inanimate Intransitive verb
P	Particle
PRO	Pronoun
PN	Prenoun
PV	Preverb
TA	Transitive Animate verb
TI	Transitive Inanimate verb

PRONOUNCING PASSAMAQUODDY-MALISEET

VOWELS

Passamaquoddy-Maliseet Letter	English Example	Passamaquoddy-Maliseet Examples	English Translation
a	father	ahahs	horse
e	bed	epit	sitting
eh	tack	ehpit	woman
o	apron	opos	tree (stick)
u	tune	uten	town

BLENDS

Passamaquoddy-Maliseet Letter	English Example	Passamaquoddy-Maliseet Examples	English Translation
aw	how	ahtulhaw	shirt
ew		new	four
iw	few	lamiw	within
ay	aye	sepay	this morning
ey	grey	piksey	pork

CONSONANTS

l, m, n, w, y, have the same sounds as in English. h is pronounced before a vowel, silent before a consonant.

Other consonants:

Passamaquoddy-Maliseet Letter	When next to vowels or first-person initial n, is voiced, sounds like English letter...	When next to consonant or apostrophe, is voiceless, sounds like English...
c	j	ch
k	g	k
p	b	p
q	gw	kw
s	z	s
t	d	t

APOSTROPHE

Apostrophe (') indicates a missing initial consonant that used to be pronounced in an older form of the word.

PESKOTOMUHKATI - WOLASTOQEWI

KOLUSUWAKONOL

A

acaqaluhs, aqacaluhs (A) yellow perch
  plural: acaqaluhsuwok, aqacaluhsok
  poss: 'tacaqaluhsumol,
            'tacaqaluhsomol, etc.
  dim: acaqaluhsis
accossu (AI) he changes color; he turns red
  plural: accossultuwok
  stem 1:   -accoss(i)-
't-acehlal (TA) he changes him
  stem 1:   -acehl-
  Qeni yaliyat skitkomiq mecimiw, kisi mili acehlosu. When he used to roam the earth, he could change himself into many forms.
't-acehtun (TI) he changes it
  stem 1:   -aceht-
acessu (AI, II) he, it moves to a different location
  plural: acessultuwok
  stem 1:   -acess(i)-
aciye (AI) he moves to a different location
  plural: aciyawolotuwok (AI)
  stem 1:   -aciy(a)-
  Skinuhsisok kisi acihhik sitomok tokkiw elomocokek. The boys (dual) moved from the shore to the bog.
aciye (II) it moves to a different location; it is... o'clock
  stem 1:   aciy(a)-
  Tan kehs aciye? What time is it?
  Mehsi conessok psi te kolahkol etuceyik esqonatek aciyak? Why did all the clocks stop at nine o'clock?
acomu (AI) he tells (a story)
  plural: acomultuwok, acomuhtuwok
  stem 1:   -acom(i)-
  Kisacomu wikuwak. He told a story at his house.
  Kisacomuhtihtit eci assokitahasi. When they (pl.) told stories, I was surprised.
  Tokec op acomit If he tells a story...
  Neke acomiyan When I told a story...
acomuwakon (I) story-telling; story; statement
  plural: acomuwakonol
  poss: 'tacomuwakonum
  dim: acomuwakonossis
  Wikhomun acomuwakon. Write down the story.
aha (P) yes (indicates agreement: compare cu, haw)
  Knonuwa?--Aha, nonuwa. Do you (sg.) know her?--Yes, I know her.
ahaciw (P) gradually; more and more
  Ahaciw olu olomi apsitome (cinitome). However, it gets more and more shallow.
  Ahaciw pomolamson, kospon te neke peciwehse. More and more the wind blew, until at last it gusted and brought on a storm.

Ahaciw olomi millukhotuwok skinuhsisok. The boys are doing more and more things that cause trouble.
  Ahaciw olomi nawtaqsu. His voice gets fainter and fainter as he goes away.
ahahs (A) horse
  plural: ahahsuwok
  poss: 'tahahsumol
  dim: ahahsis
  (from English, horse)
  Ahahsuwok qaskultuwok. The horses are running.
  'Tahahsumol wapeyuwol. His horse is white.
ahahs elsewet (I) harness
  plural: ahahsuwok elsewhotihtit
  (literally, "the way a horse is dressed")
  Ahahs elsewet piley. The harness is new.
ahahsuwipis (I) horse whip
  plural: ahahsuwipisiyil
  poss: 'tahahsuwipisim
  loc: ahahsuwipisik
  dim: ahahsuwipisis
  Ahahsuwipis nokatomon ahahs. The horse is afraid of the horse whip.
't-ahcikonemol (A) his apple; his adam's apple
  (See cikon "apple.")
ahcuwi
  (See cuwi.)
't-ahcuwyal, 'cuwyal (TA) he hires him
  stem 1a: -ahcuwy-, -cuwy-
  stem 1b: cuwy-: cuwya he is hired
  stem 2:   ehcuwy-, cuwy-: ehcuwyut, cuwyut when he was hired.
  stem 3:   -hcuwy-: 'totolihcuwyal he is hiring him
  (Note: Stem-final y may be changed to h before i: ktahcuwhi you (sg.) hire me.)
-ahke- throw
  (forms AI and AI+OBJ verbs)
  'tolahkan (AI, AI+OBJ) he throws it
  'qasahkan (AI, AI+OBJ) he throws it away, he discards it
  kakawahke (AI) he throws fast
't-ahkihkan (I) his garden
  plural: 'tahkihkanol
  poss: 'tahkihkanom, 'tahkihkan
  loc: 'tahkihkanok
  dim: 'tahkihkanossis
  (See kihkan "garden.")
  Skitap ulankeyutomon 'tahkihkan. The man takes good care of his garden.
ahkiq (A) seal (animal)
  plural: ahkiqok, ahkiqiyik
  poss: 'tahkikumol
  dim: ahkiqsis
  Olomomu pahq pahkamok ahkiq. An arrow is stuck in the seal's back.
ahkiqewi (ahkiqew-) (PN) seal; seal's
  Skicin 'poskuwa ahkiqewi olonakson. The Indian is wearing sealskin moccasins.
ahkiqqe (AI) he hunts seals
  plural: ahkiqqahtuwok
  stem 1:   -ahkiqq(e)-

ahkiqsiske (AI) he hunts pup seals
plural: ahkiqsiskahtuwok
stem 1: -ahkiqsisk(e)-
Skicin api ahkiqsiske. The Indian has returned from hunting pup seals.
Totoli ahkiqsiske. He is hunting pup seals.

't-ahkuhkol (A) (dep.) his buttocks
ntahkuhk my buttocks

ahp (A) fish net
plural: ahpiyik
poss: 'tahpimol
loc: ahpik
dim: ahpehsis, ahpossis
Kolomu ahpik nomehs. The fish is trapped in the net.
Pesq ahp piyemkil katok kotokik. One fish net is bigger than the others.
Pqishan not ahp! Mend that fish net!

ahpap (A) rope
plural: ahpapiyik, ahpapihik
poss: 'tahpapimol
loc: ahpapik
dim: ahpapossis string
Siyatokessu ahpap. The rope unravelled.
'Ciqolatokessu ahpap. The rope tangled.

ahsaksitehe, sahsaksitehe (AI) he is barefoot
plural: ahsaksitahawolotuwok
stem 1: -ahsaksit_h(a)-
Wasis yali ahsaksitehe. The baby is going around barefoot.
Psite wen ahsaksitehe. Everybody is barefoot.

't-ahsihpilal (TA) he gives him medicine
stem 1a: -ahsihpil-: ntahsihpila I give him medicine
stem 1b: sihpil-: sihpilat if he gives him medicine
stem 2: ehsihpil-: ehsihpilat when he gives him medicine
Ehpit 'tahsihpilal nicanol. The woman gave medicine to her child.
Skinuhsis 'tahsihpilkul wikuwossol. The boy's mother gave him medicine.

't-ahskihkipolomon, uskihkipolomon (TI) he tramples it
plural: uskihkipolomultiniya, uskihkipolomuhtiniya
stem 1a: -ahskihkipolom-, -uskihkipolom-
stem 1b: skihkipolom-
stem 2: eskihkipolom-, weskihkipolom-: eskihkipolok, weskihkipolok when he trampled it

't-ahsomal (TA) he feeds him
stem 1a: -ahsom-: ntahsoma I feed him
stem 1b: 'som-: 'somat if he feeds him
stem 2: ehsom-, ahsom-: ehsomat, ahsomat when he fed him
Skitap 'tahsomal 'qossisol. The man feeds his son.
Skitap 'tahsoman 'qossisol otuhkey. The man feeds his son deer meat.

ahsuhun, ahsuwun (I) blanket
plural: ahsuhunol
poss: 'tahsuhunom
loc: ahsuhunok
dim: ahsuhunsis
Ehpit 'totoli cikonekisomon ahsuhun. The woman is ironing the blanket.
Susehp! Natekhut ahsuhun! Joseph! Go hang up the blanket!

ahsusuwon (I) hat
plural: ahsusuwonol
poss: 'tahsusuwon
loc: ahsusuwonok
dim: ahsusuwonossis, ahsusuwonsis (also: ahsosuwon)
'Samkihqon not skinuhsis 'tahsusuwon. That boy's hat is too big.
Skinuhsis peskok 'somakonossuwey ahsusuwon. The boy is wearing a soldier hat.
Susehp yali psihkok piyehsuwey ahsusuwon. Joseph is wearing a fur hat.

ahsuwekopolikon (I) window shade; curtain
plural: ahsuwekopolikonol
poss: 'tahsuwekopolikonum
loc: ahsuwekopolikonok
dim: ahsuwekopolikonossis
Ahsuwekopolikonol ntahcuwi kospahtunennul. We (nilun) have to wash the blinds.

ahsuwun (I) blanket
(See ahsuhun.)

't-ahtapiyil (A) his bow
plural: 'tahtapiyik
poss: 'tahtapimol; also 'tahtapiyil
loc: 'tahtapik
dim: 'tahtapossis
(See tap.)
Skinuhsis 'tahtapiyil pileyal. The boy's bow is new.

't-ahtim (I) his tea
(See ti.)

ahtoli (ahtol-) (PV) over and over; again and again; keeps on...
ahtoli ikotohom (AI) he keeps on yawning

't-ahtolotutuwatomon (TI) he keeps it burning
stem 1: -ahtolotutuwatom-
Ntahtolotutuwatomon papskot weci skat tkeyinuhk lamikuwam. I keep the fire burning in the stove so that it will not be cold in the house.

't-ahtoptahal (TA) he hits him by luck
stem 1: -ahtopt_h-

't-ahtoptehmon (TI) he hits it by luck
stem 1: -ahtoptehm-; but: ahtoptohok when he hits it by luck

't-ahtoptelomon (TI) he shoots at it and hits it by luck
stem 1: -ahtoptelom-

't-ahtopteluwal (TA) he shoots at him and hits him by luck
stem 1: -ahtopteluw-

ahtulhaw (A) shirt
plural: ahtulhawiyik
poss: 'tahtulhawiyil

loc: ahtulhawek
dim: ahtulhawehsis

Nahsonan not mehqekit ahtulhaw! Put on that red shirt!

ahtulhawekon (I) rag
plural: ahtulhawekonol
poss: 'tahtulhawekonum
loc: ahtulhawekonok
dim: ahtulhawekonossis

Musa macahahkoc qeni alcoktek ahtulhawekonol tuhsanok. Don't (sg.) leave while there are dirty rags lying around in the shed.

Milin yet ahtulhawekon! Give me that rag over there!

akalhike (AI) he shovels snow
plural: akalhikotuwok
stem 1: -akalhik(e)-
(See also okalhike.)

akawhu (A) tent caterpillar
plural: akawhuwiyik
poss: 'takawhuwemol
loc: akawhuwek
dim: akawhuwehsis

Akawhu etolotok mip. The caterpillar is eating a leaf.

akim (P) as many as; exactly

Api kotunket, akim nehpahacihi nanu otuhk. When he returned from hunting, he had killed as many as five deer.

akiyahq (A) stucco; plaster; lime
plural: akiyahqok
poss: 'takiyahqomol
loc: akiyahqok
dim: akiyaqsossis

Kil mawcokhan akiyahq. You (sg.), mix the plaster!

akiyaqhasu (II) it is stuccoed, plastered
stem 1: -akiyaqhas(i)-

Totoli akiyaqhasu. It is being stuccoed.

Tayuwek akiyaqhasu kik? When is your (sg.) house going to be stuccoed?

akiyaqhike (AI) he stuccoes; he plasters
plural: akiyaqhikhotuwok
stem 1: -akiyaqhik(e)-

't-akiyaqhomon (TI) he stuccoes it; he plasters it
stem 1: -akiyaqhom-

akocu
(See okocu.)

akom (A) snowshoe
plural: akomok
poss: 'takomol
loc: akomok
dim: akomossis
abs: akomokk (pl.)
obv: akomol (sg.)

Naciptuwin kotok akom tuhsanok. Go get me the other snowshoe in the shed.

Psi te wen mecimi te 'tiywaponihi akom. Everybody used to have snowshoes.

akomahq (A) white ash
plural: akomahqok
poss: 'takomahkumol
loc: akomahqok

dim: akomaqsis

Wot akomahq eci kiyahqinahat. This white ash splits straight.

akomawt (I) snowshoe path
plural: akomawtiyil
poss: 'takomawtim
loc: akomawtik
dim: akomawtossis

Akomawt eci sakolipolasik. The snowshoe path is beaten down hard.

akomihom (AI) he goes by snowshoe
plural: akomihomultuwok
stem 1: -akomihom(o)- type A
(See akomohom.)

akomiw (AI) he has snowshoes
(See 'takomiw.)

akomohom (AI) he wears snowshoes
plural: akomohomuhtuwok
stem 1: -akomohom(o)- type A
(See akomihom)

akonutomakon (I) story; account; narrative
plural: akonutomakonol
poss: 'takonutomakonum
loc: akonutomakonok
dim: akonutomakonossis

Skicin 'takonutomakon nsekpawolokunen. The Indian's story scared us (nilun).

akonutome (AI) he talks; he tells a story; he reports news
plural: akonutomahtuwok
stem 1: -akonutom(a)-

Mali mihtaqsol wisokiluwehe skat Piyelol akomutomalihq. Mary's father was angry because Peter did not tell a story.

't-akonutomon (TI) he tells it (e.g., a story)
stem 1: -akonutom-

't-akonutomuwal (TA) he tells him a story
stem 1: -akonutomuw-

akotalahq (A) alligator
plural: akotalahqok
poss: 'takotalahqomol
dim: akotalaqsis
abs: akotalaqqol (obviative, sg.): Nomiyakkol akotalaqqol. He also saw an alligator (but he didn't shoot it).

Tehpu akotalahq sakhahtek wihton tehsahqiw 'samaqanok. Only the alligator's nose shows on top of the water.

-akson-, -koson- shoe

kinaksone, kinkosone (AI) he has big shoes

maskakosone (AI) he has smelly shoes; he has fancy shoes

puskosone (AI) he has wet shoes

akun (P) it's a good thing

Akun nit nil ntotoli peciyan. It's a good thing I came.

akuwahtihikon (I) umbrella; sun shade (e.g. a roof supported by four poles); canopy
plural: akuwahtihikonol
poss: 'takuwahtihikonum
loc: akuwahtihikonok
dim: akuwahtihikonossis

Nitap nisuwehkanen akuwahtihikon peci wiskolak. My friend and I shared the umbrella when it started to rain hard.

akuwahtuhusut (I) umbrella
> *plural:*   akuwahtuhusutiyil
> *poss:*   'takuwahtuhusut,
>   'takuwahtuhusutim,
>   'takuwahtuhusutom
> *loc:*   akuwahtuhusutik
> *dim:*   akuwahtuhusutsis

Tollan ehpicik 'takuwahtuhusutimuwak. It is raining on the women's umbrellas.

Akuwahtuhusut kisi sipelekessu. The umbrella can be spread out.

akuwi (akuw-) (PV) behind (something); in back; out of view
> akuwiphuwe (AI) he runs behind
> akuwitutom (AI) he tries to hide behind; he tries to escape notice
> akuwuhucin (AI) he bends down behind to hide
> akuwuhse (AI) he walks out of view
> akuwuhqehtehsin (AI) he quickly hides his head behind

akuwiw (P) behind; in back; out of view

Akuwiw luhsane natamotinen tolehpok. Let's (dual) walk out back and play cards.

al (P) (indicates uncertainty, vagueness; approximation)
> (See ali, yali.)

Skitapiyik al te olkiluhtuwok. They (pl.) are about as big as men.

Natsakiyal 'tantimol, kosona al wenil. He goes to see his aunt, or somebody like that.

alahkahamu (AI) he limps
> *plural:*   alahkahamultuwok
> *stem 1:*   -alahkaham(i)-

alahket (A) fry bread
> *plural:*   alahketok
> *poss:*   'talahketomol, 'talahketumol
> *loc:*   alahketok
> *dim:*   alahketsis

(Tobique Maliseet)

Alahket wolihpuksu wiciw molahsoss. Fry bread tastes good with molasses.

alakomasu (AI) he snowshoes around
> *plural:*   alakomasultuwok
> *stem 1:*   -alakomas(i)-

Skicin 'qocipun te alakomasu. The Indian snowshoed around all winter.

alaku (AI) he glides (on wings)
> *plural:*   alakultuwok
> *stem 1:*   -alak(i)-
> ali suwwaku (AI) he glides

alalikonike (AI) he walks around in deep snow (without snowshoes)
> *plural:*   alalikonikhotuwok
> *stem 1:*   -alalikonik(e)-

alamehe (AI) he zigzags through the water; he swims around underwater
> *plural:*   alamahawolotuwok
> *stem 1:*   -alam__h(a)-

alamkuhusu (AI) he poles himself around (in a boat)
> *plural:*   alamkuhusultuwok
> *stem 1:*   -alamkuhus(i)-

Alamkuhusu etoli cinitomek. He poled himself around in shallow water.

alapasuwok (AI) they (pl.) walk around
> *plural:*   also: aluhsahtuwok (esp. Maliseet)
> *stem 1:*   -alapas(i)-

(This stem is used only with plural subjects. For singular and dual subjects, see aluhse.)

Kotunkewinuwok alapasuwok kcihkuk. The hunters are walking around in the woods.

't-alaphal ('t-iyalaphal) (TA) he tracks him around
> *stem 1:*   -alaph-

'Talaphal 'kekiw. He tracks him all day.

alaptahsu (AI) he tracks (an animal) around
> *plural:*   alaptahsultuwok
> *stem 1:*   -alaptahs(i)-

Wikuwaci alaptahsu kcihkuk. He likes to go around tracking in the woods.

alaptu (AI) he leaves tracks around
> *plural:*   alaptuhtuwok
> *stem 1:*   -alapt(u)-

Mahtoqehs alaptu pahkak nikonuk. The rabbit left its tracks behind my house.

alaputihike (AI) he looks around with a telescope; he looks around with binoculars
> *plural:*   alaputihikhotuwok
> *stem 1:*   -alaputihik(e)-

Skinuhsis alaputihike kisahqew. The boy is looking around with binoculars up on the hill.

alasuke (AI) he wades around
> *plural:*   alasukhotuwok,
>   alasukolotuwok
> *stem 1:*   -alasuk(e)-

Wasis alasuke sipuhsisok. The child is wading around in the little brook.

Pilsqehsis alasuke sonuciw sitomok. The girl is wading around along the edge of the shore.

alhom (AI) he swims around
> *plural:*   alhomultuwok, alhomuhtuwok
> *stem 1:*   -alhom(o)- type A

Akiyan yat alhok. Look at him swimming around.

Alhom sipuhsisok. He is swimming around in the brook.

't-alhulal (TA) he guides him around in a boat
> *stem 1:*   -alhul-

Skitap 'talhulal muhsumsol. The man guides his grandfather around.

ali (al-) (PV) around; within an area; (direction and location vague, unspecified or uncertain)
> (See yali.)

Ali ksona wasis. The child is going around being hurt.

Naci ali wewisultine. Let's (pl.) go nose around.

alihpu (AI) he eats around (in various places)
plural: alihpultuwok
stem 1: -alihp(i)-
(also: yalihpu)
Otuhk alihpu sonuciw pemskutek. The deer is eating around the edge of the field.
Wasis alihpu apcuhset. The child is eating around while walking.

alikhahsu (AI) he looks around (for something)
plural: alikhahsultuwok
stem 1: -alikhahs(i)-
(also: yalikhahsu)
Ntemis alikhahsu keq. My dog is looking around for something.
Ntemis alikhahsu wenil. My dog is looking around for someone.

alikopomu (AI) he skates; he rides a bike
plural: alikopomultuwok
stem 1: -alikopom(i)-
Nomiya Sistoss alikopomit pqomik. I saw Sister skating around on the ice.

alinaqsu (AI) he is seen around (in various places within an area)
plural: alinaqsultuwok
stem 1: -alinaqs(i)-
Nekom alinaqsu etoli putuwosimok. He is seen around at meetings.

't-aliphal (TA) he carries him around; he drives him around in a vehicle
stem 1: -aliph-
(also: 't-iyaliphal)
Skitap 'taliphal muhsumsol utapakonok. The man drove his grandfather around in his car.

alipokomu (AI) he skates; he rides a bike
plural: alipokomultuwok
stem 1: -alipokom(i)-
(variant of alikopomu)
Pilsqehsis alipokomu pqomik. The girl is skating around on the ice.
Skinuhsis alipokomu awtik. The boy is riding a bike on the road.

alitahasu (AI) he is always thinking
plural: alitahasultuwok
stem 1: -alitahas(i)-
(See also: tpitahasu.)
Sakom cuwi alitahasu. The governor always has to be thinking.
Ehpit mate keq itomu, tehpu alitahasu. The woman does not say much, only thinks a lot.

alitahasuwin (A) wise person; thinker
plural: alitahasuwinuwok
Qecimulan alitahasuwin. Ask the thinker.
Itom alitahasuwin, "Katop kisi leyiw."
The wise person said, "It can't happen."

alitahasuwinuwiw (AI) he is a wise person; he is a thinker
plural: alitahasuwinultuwok
stem 1: -alitahasuwinuw(i)- type B

alonocis, alinocis (I) orange (fruit)
plural: alonocisol
poss: 'talonocisom

loc: alonocisok
dim: alonocossis, alonocisossis
Ma te tahkomonsiwiyil alonocisol lamiw. The oranges aren't seedy inside.
Alonocis kis kisocihte. The orange is already ripe.

aloq
(See waloq.)

alossin (AI) he lies around
plural: alossinultuwok, alossinuhtuwok
stem 1: -alossin(o)- type B
Skitap eci maleyit tehpu alossin. The man is so lazy he just lies around.
Psuwis alossin kuhutihihkuk. The cat lies around on beds.

alosu (AI) he sweats
plural: alosultuwok
stem 1: -alos(i)-
Wen ktanaqalosit, cuwitpotuhpon micin kehtenaqahk salawey. If somebody sweats a lot, he should eat a lot of salt.
Etutalosultihtit, nkosicihtun eli wisokihpotek. They are sweating so much that I know it is very hot.

alqepu (AI) he sits around
plural: alqepultuwok
stem 1: -alqep(i)-
Skitap mate keq elluhket tehpu alqepu. The man has nothing to do but sit around.
Sipsis alqepu stahqonuk. The bird is sitting around in the tree.

altehkasu (AI, II) it is kicked around
plural: altehkasuwok (AI); altehkasuwol (II)
stem 1: altehkas(i)-
(Altehkasu is the indefinite subject form of 'taltehkomon (TI). It can be used with an. or inan. subjects.)
Epeskomakon altehkasu etolamotultimok. The ball is being kicked around at the game.
Skitap 'pokuhulakon altehkasu. The man's drum is being kicked around.

't-altehkomon (TI) he kicks it around
stem 1: -altehkom-
(also: 't-iyaltehkomon)
Skinuhsis 'taltehkomon 'tahsusuwon. The boy is kicking his (own) hat around.
Pilsqehsis 'taltehkomon pocetes. The girl is kicking the potato around.

't-altehkuwal (TA) he kicks him around; he kicks it (an.) around
stem 1: -altehkuw-
(also: 't-iyalehkuwal)
Ntaltehkak. I am kicked around.
Neke altehkuhut (altehkuwut)... When he was kicked around

altestakon (A) wooden dish used in a traditional dice game; the traditional dice game
plural: altestakonok
poss: 'taltestakonol
loc: altestakonok
dim: altestakonossis

(also: waltestakon)

Nisuwok kosqehsuhsok etolamoticik altestakon. Two old women are playing the traditional dice game.

aluhk (I) cloud
plural: aluhkol
poss: 'taluhkom
loc: aluhkok
dim: aluksis, aluhkis
Sipsisok pisituwiyawolotuwok aluhkok. The birds are flying into the cloud.

aluhkot (II) it is cloudy
stem 1: aluhkot(o)-
Skat aluhkotunuhk. If it is not cloudy.
Aluhkahk. When it was cloudy.
Ma te aluhkotu. It is not cloudy.

aluhse (AI) he walks around
plural: alapasuwok, aluhsawolotuwok
stem 1: -aluhs(e)-
(See alapasuwok.)
Skinuhsis aluhse naka 'temisol. The boy is walking around with his dog.
Kiyahq aluhse elomococek. The gull is walking around on the mud flats.

't-aluwihtun (TI) he tries to make it and fails; he tries in vain to make it
stem 1: -aluwiht-
Ma 'taluwihtuwon tan tehpu keqsey. He never fails, no matter what he tries to make.

't-aluwimal (TA) he asks (or tells) him in vain to do something
stem 1: -aluwim-

amakehs (A) butterfly
plural: amakehsuwok
poss: 'tamakehsumol
dim: amakehsis
Amakehs kelomit pesqahsuweskik. The butterfly clings to the flower.

amalhi (amalh-) (PV) fancy
amalhikon (II) it is fancy

amalhiwisu (AI) he has a nickname
plural: amalhiwisultuwok
stem 1: -amalhiwis(i)-

't-amalhiwiyal (TA) he nicknames him
stem 1: -amalhiwiy-
Skitap mecimite 'tamalhiwiyal 'qossol. The man always calls his son by his nickname.
Keq olu oli amalhiwiya? What is his nickname?

amalhotokku (AI) he jumps fancily; he does acrobatics
plural: amalhotokkultuwok
stem 1: -amalhotoqq(i)-: nil ntamalhotoqq I jump fancily
(also: amalhotkuhu)
tokec op nekom amalhotoqqit if he jumped fancily
Wasis eci wolitahasit cel olomi amalhotokku. The child was so happy he jumped forward fancily.
Pilsqehsis amalhotokku metokehkitimok. The girl jumped fancily when the school was over.

't-amalhuwikhomon (TI) he writes it fancily; he makes it with fancy designs or colors; he decorates it
stem 1: -amalhuwikhom-
Ehpit 'tamalhuwikhomon 'toposonut. The woman made fancy designs on her basket.
Wasis 'tamalhuwikhomon wisuwon. The child fancily wrote her name.

amalomeq (A) mackerel
plural: amalomeqok
poss: 'tamalomekumol
loc: amalomeqok
dim: amalomeqsis
Amalomeq wolihpuksu 'sami tahk ksi skonisiw. Mackerel tastes good, but it's too bony.

ame (AI) he fishes
plural: amhotuwok, amahtuwok
stem 1: -am(e)-: nil ntam I fish
'Kekiw te amewin ame. All day the fisherman fished.
Skinuhsis 'kekiw te ame, tehpu pethacil supeqihponol. The boy fished all day but he only caught a sea urchin.

amewin (A) fisherman
plural: amewinuwok
poss: 'tamewinumol
dim: amewinuhsis
Amewin kehsiptahat peskotom. The fisherman caught many pollock.

amihkessu (AI) he gets up (from a sitting position)
plural: amihkessultuwok
stem 1: -amihkess(i)-
Psi te wasisok amihkessultuwok pskihqihkuk naka naci tkahsomultiniya. All of the children got up from the grass and went swimming.
Wasis amihkessu wikuwossol kakalumiht. The child got up when her mother called her.

amihku (AI) he gets up
plural: amihkultuwok
stem 1: -amihk(i)-
Mesq amihkultihtihq wasisok kutoputihkuk, kil kmacahan. Before the children (pl.) get up from the chairs, you (sg.) should go.
Skinuhsis amihku tuhkiyat. The boy got up when he woke up.

't-amihkuhtuwal (TA) he throws him off (in wrestling)
stem 1: -amihkuhtuw-: neke amihkuhtuhut when he was thrown off

amikotokku (AI) he jumps up
plural: amikotokkultuwok
stem 1: -amikotoqq(i)-: tokec op nekom amikotoqqit if he jumps up

amkakon (A, I) game (I); die (A)
plural: amkakonol (I); amkakonok (A) dice

amke (AI) he plays a game; he runs for an office
plural: amkahtuwok
stem 1: -amk(e)-: nil ntamk I play a game
On 'qossol 'tamkalin sakomawey. And her son was running for (tribal) governor (Maine) or chief (New Brunswick).
Nqoss ona amke sepawonuk. My son also plays tomorrow.
Kil ona qoss amke? Is your son also playing?

amoniw (P) detouring (avoiding something); around (circling)
(Second meaning used at St. Mary's Reserve, Fredericton; compare wiwoniw.)

amoqalokehs (A) whistler (duck)
plural: amoqalokehsuwok
poss: 'tamoqalokehsumol
loc: amoqalokehsuk
dim: amoqalokehsis
Amoqalokehs tomilqone. The whistler has a broken wing.

amsqahs (P) first; at first
Wolitahasu amsqahs. He is happy at first.
Amsqahs tetomihkuwacil wikuwossol. The first one he overtakes is his mother.

amsqahsewey (A, I) first; the first one
plural: amsqahseweyak, amsqahseweyal

amsqahsukonohom (II) it is the first day of the month
stem 1: amsqahsukonehm(o)-, amsqahsukonahm(o)- type A; but: without ending amsqahsukonohom; neke form amsqahsukonohok
Amsqahsukonohom pemkiskahk July. Today is the first day of July.
Amsqahsukonahmuhpon (amsqahsukonehmuhpon) wolaku. Yesterday was the first day of the month.

amsqocehkan (A) doll
plural: amsqocehkanok
poss: 'tamsqocehkanol
loc: amsqocehkanok
dim: amsqocehkansis
Amsqocehkan kisi piskiqewu naka kisotemu. The doll can close its eyes and can cry.

amucalu (A) fly
plural: amucaluwiyik
poss: 'tamucaluwemol
dim: amucaluwehsis
Amucalu kolhuke amushopihkewi ahpapik. The fly is trapped in the spider web.

amushopihk (A) spider
plural: amushopihkiyik
poss: 'tamushopihkemol
dim: amushopihkehsis
Amushopihk 'kolhal amucaluwiyil 'tahpapimok. The spider caught a fly in its web.
(also: amussopihk)

amuwes (A) bee
plural: amuwesok

amuwyahsu (AI) he acts a little bit crazy
plural: amuwyahsultuwok
stem 1: -amuwyahs(i)-
Nehtaw amuwyahsultihtit yut pomawsuwinuwok wikuhticik, ma nil nwikiwon. If the people who are living here act crazy, I will not live here.

amuwye (AI) he is crazy
plural: amuwyawolotuwok, amuwyahtuwok
stem 1: -amuwy(a)-: with no ending: -amuwi: nil ntamuwi I am crazy
Mus wolamsotuwahkoc, amuwye not! Don't believe him, he's crazy!
Skitap amuwye oposihtahat nican. A man is crazy who beats his children with a stick.
Amuwye yat skitap sehket, 'sami ntiyukun nmihtaqs welaqik. (I know that) that man standing over there is crazy, because my father told me last night.

amuwyessu (AI) he goes crazy
plural: amuwyessultuwok
stem 1: -amuwyess(i)-
Skitap amuwyessu keskahlat 'qossol. The man went crazy when he lost his son.
Nehtaw amuwyessultihtit weyossisok kcihkuk, cu peci qaskultuwok Motahkomikuk naka kmatonokunen. If the animals in the woods go crazy, they will come running to Peter Dana Point, Maine, and fight us.

aneqehs (A) flounder
plural: aneqehsuwok
poss: 'taneqehsumol
dim: aneqehsis
Wahka nkisi monehtun pkihkon aneqehs 'tunok. I could hardly take the hook off the flounder's mouth.

aneqehsuhke (AI) he spears flounder; he fishes for flounder
plural: aneqehsukhotuwok
stem 1: -aneqehsuhk(e)-
Ntatat toli aneqehsuhke. My father is spearing flounder.
Susehp olomi naci aneqehsuhke. Joseph has gone to spear flounder.

't-ankeyutomon (TI) he takes care of it
stem 1: -ankeyutom-: ankeyutok when he took care of it
'Totoli ankeyutomon. He is taking care of it.
Skitap 'tankeyutomon wikuwam tokkiw sepawonu. The man is taking care of the house until tomorrow.
Nekomaw 'tankeyutomoniya psite man. They take care of all the money.

't-ankeyuwal (TA) he takes care of him
stem 1: -ankeyuw-: ntankeyaq he takes care of me
Ehpit 'keki te 'tankeyuwal wasisol. The woman took care of the child all day.

Skitap 'tankeyuwal wasisol skat miyawtehkuwawon. The man was careful not to hit the child.

ankusu (AI) he buys; he sells
plural: ankusultuwok
stem 1: -ankus(i)-
Ankusu eli tpeltok. He sold his belongings.

ankuwacomu (AI) he relays a message; he brings a report of; he interprets (translates)
plural: ankuwacomultuwok,
ankuwacomuhtuwok
stem 1: -ankuwacom(i)-
Sakom kisi ankuwacomu putuwossimok. The governor interpreted at the meeting.
Ehpit ma 'tawi ikolisomanatuwew. Cuwi wen ankuwacomu. The woman can't speak English. Someone has to translate.

't-ankuwacomuwewal (TA) he interprets for him
stem 1: -ankuwacomuwew-:
ankuwacokmuwewosk the one who interprets for you
Skitap cuwi ankuwacomuwewa. The man has to be interpreted for.

ankuwakhucu (AI) he stops for a while (ends a stage in a trip)
plural: ankuwakhucultuwok
stem 1: -ankuwakhuc(i)-: nil ntankuwakhuc I make stops along my journey
'Sami siktehsonu cuwi ankuwakhucu. She was so tired she had to stop along her journey.

ankuwaqtihikon (A) second length of pounding-ash (from a single tree)
plural: ankuwaqtihikonok
poss: 'tankuwaqtihikonumol
loc: ankuwaqtihikonok
dim: ankuwaqtihikonossis
Skicin 'kisuwehkahal psite eli qonaqsit ankuwaqtihikon. The Indian can use all of the second length of the pounding-ash.

't-ankuwehtun (TI) he sells it
stem 1: -ankuweht-: ankuwehtaq if he sold it
Amewin 'tankuwehtun 'toqitonum. The fisherman is selling his canoe.
Ehpit tankuwehtun piley te mahkut. The woman is selling a brand new dress.

't-ankuwekhal (TA) he sells it (an.)
stem 1: -ankuwekh-
Nitap 'tankuwekhal 'temisol. My friend is selling his dog.

ankuwi- (ankuw-) (PV) further; a little further; beyond

ankuwiposehehs, ankuwiposiyehs (A) robin
plural: ankuwiposehehsuwok
poss: 'tankuwiposehehsumol
dim: ankuwiposehehsis
Malomote ankuwiposehehs 'tetoqi wiqtokehlal wetossisol ktahkomikuk. Finally the robin pulled the little worm all the way out of the ground.

ankuwiw (P) a little further
Mahkiyewoss eluhsiyin ankuwiw nittehc kpecuhsan wikit Susehp. In no time by walking a little further, you will come to where Joesph lives.

ankuwotkuhu (AI) he jumps from place to place
plural: ankuwotkuhultuwok
stem 1: -ankuwotq_h(i)-: nil ntankuwotqihi I jump from place to place
(Note: q changes to k before u.)
Skinuhsis olomi ankuwotkuhu ponapsqihkuk. The boy jumped along amonst the rocks.
Mihku ankuwotkuhu stahqonihkuk. The squirrel jumped from tree to tree.

anqoc (P) sometimes
Anqoc nit leyu. Sometimes it happens.

anqotuwa (A) boil; carbuncle
plural: anqotuwak
poss: 'tanqotuwamol
loc: anqotuwawok
dim: anqotuwahsis
Tamahc anqotuwa 'sakhapskessit skitap hokek. Different places, a boil would lump up on a man's body.

ansa (P) like; truly; really
'Samaqan ansa wapinaqot. The water really looks white.
Ansa te woli piyemhantuwikotuwok. They are truly outdone.
Ntolinuwa ansa mihtaqsol. He looks like his father to me.

-ap(i)- look
(forms AI verb stems)
sehtayapu (AI) he looks back
pisapu (AI) he looks inside (something)

apaci (apac-, apat-) (PV) coming back; returning
(Compare wesuwe.)
Apaciye wolaku. He returned yesterday.
Apacikpenan sehkomicik ktoposonutek. Bend back the stander ends of your basket.
Apatawsuwa. He came back to life.

apaciye (AI) he returns
plural: apaciyawolotuwok,
apaciyahtuwok
stem 1: -apaciy(a)-: apaciyat when he returned
Nekom ona koti apaciye? Is he planning to come back?
Sakom 'ci apaciye 'ciw Wasihtonok. The governor returned from Washington.

apacuhse (AI) he walks back
plural: apatapasuwok
stem 1: -apacuhs(e)-; plural stem -apatapas(i)-
(The stem -apacuhs(e)- is used for singular and dual forms only.)
Skinuhsis kotha, 'cuwi apacuhse. The boy missed his ride, he had to walk back.

Skitap macewse Muselenk naka apc ote cuwi apacuhse. The man walked to Eastport, Maine, and he had to walk back.

't-apaphal (TA) he went and tracked him (and came back)
> *stem 1:*   -apaph-

Olomuss 'tapaphal qaqsossol kcihkuk. The dog went and tracked a fox in the woods.

apaptahsu (AI) he has been out tracking
> *plural:*   apaptahsultuwok
> *stem 1:*   -apaptahs(i)-

Susehp apaptahsu wolaku. Joseph went tracking yesterday.

-apas(i)- walk (pl. only)
> (forms AI verb stems, with plural meanings only)

ckuwapasuwok (AI) they (pl.) walk toward here

apatawsu (AI) he comes back to life
> *plural:*   apatawsultuwok
> *stem 1:*   -apataws(i)-: nil ntapataws I came back to life

'Skitap apatawsu kisi ehqolatok. The man came back to life after he had stopped breathing.

Otuhk kisi peskhuk apc ote apatawsu. After I shot the deer he came back to life.

apc (P) again; else; next

Apc wen keselomot naka Pal? Whom else do you love besides Paul?

Musa apc nit oluhkehkoc! Don't ever do that again!

apcituwiye (AI) he is flying; he is on the wing; he continues to fly
> *plural:*   apcituwiyawolotuwok
> *stem 1:*   -apcituwiy(a)-: nil ntapcituwi I continue to fly

Sipsis apcituwiye meyawteluwut. The bird was shot while flying.

Amucalu apcituwiye kelhuket. The fly was trapped while flying.

-apektuhus(i)- play a stringed instrument
> (forms AI verb stems)

'tawapektuhusu (AI) he knows how to play a stringed instrument

apenke (AI) he pays
> *plural:*   apenkahtuwok
> *stem 1:*   -apenk(e)-

Skitap apenke kisolumut. The man paid after he was judged.

Skitap apenke elocanomahsit. The man paid what he owed.

't-apenkotuwewal (TA) he pays (for something) for him
> *stem 1:*   -apenkotuwew-

Skitap 'tapenkotuwewal witapiyil elocanomahsilit. The man paid what his friend owed.

't-apenkuwal (TA) he pays him
> *stem 1:*   -apenkuw-: ktapenkakepon we (kilun) get paid

Skitap 'tapenkuwal 'toluhketomol ketuwahsonotek. The man pays his worker on Saturday.

Ehpit 'tapenkuwal nuci ksonuwikelicil. The woman pays the babysitter.

't-apenkuwan (DOV) he pays him with it
> *stem 1:*   -apenkuw-

'Tapenkuwan posonut witapihil. He paid his friend with a basket.

Ehpit 'tapekuwan man nuci ksonuwikelicil. The woman paid her babysitter in money.

apeq (P) although

Qaqoss nutuwal apeq pihcetu. The fox hears him, although it is far.

api (ap-) (PV) having gone to do X and returned; be back from doing X
> (X is the action described by the verb used with api.)

'tapiptun (TI) he went and got it (and came back)

apsoqe (AI) he went to check traps (and came back)

api witimiye (AI) he went to church (and came back)

apikcilu (A) skunk
> *plural:*   apikciluwiyik, apikciluwihik
> *poss:*   'tapikciluwemol
> *loc:*   apikciluwek
> *dim:*   apikciluwehsis

Piyel 'tapikciluwem macephuwiyi. Peter's skunks ran away.

Apikcilu nutehe nipayiw. The skunk goes out at night.

apiqosikon (A) lynx
> *plural:*   apiqosikonok
> *poss:*   'tapiqosikonumol
> *dim:*   apiqosikonossis

Apiqosikon ahqalomu. The lynx is crafty.

apiqsehs (A) rat
> *plural:*   apiqsehsuwok
> *poss:*   'tapiqsehsumol
> *dim:*   apiqsehsis: small rat; mouse (Maine)

Apiqsehs kolhuke. The rat is trapped.

apolahsatpe (AI) he is bald
> *plural:*   apolahsatpawolotuwok
> *stem 1:*   -apolahsatp(a)-: nil ntapolahsatp I am bald

Skitap miyahsi apolahsatpe. The man is prematurely bald.

Skitap mace apolahsatpe. The man is starting to get bald.

apolahsomuwehs (A) whirlwind
> *plural:*   apolahsomuwehsuwok
> *poss:*   'tapolahsomuwehsumol
> *loc:*   apolahsomuwehsuk
> *dim:*   apolahsomuwehsis

Mipiyil alituwiyetul apolahsomuwehsuk. The leaves are flying around in the whirlwind.

-apom- look at
> (forms TA verb stems)

'kisapomal (TA) he looked at him

'tahtolapomal (TA) he keeps looking at him; he looks at him again and again

apote (apotiy-) (PV) leaning

'**t-apotehsinon** (AI, AI+OBJ) he stands leaning against it; he leans on it
    stem 1:   -apotehsin(o)- type B: apotehsit when he stood leaning against it
    Ntapotehsinnok oposiyik. I am leaning against the trees.
    'Tapotehsinon 'tapotuhun. She leans on her cane.

'**t-apotepin** (AI, AI+OBJ) he sits leaning against it;
    stem 1:   -apotep(i)-

-apotom- look at
    (forms TI verb stems)
    milapotomon (TI) he looks at it curiously

apotuhun (I) cane; walking stick
    plural: apotuhunol
    poss: 'tapotuhun
    loc: apotuhunok
    dim: apotuhunsis
    Ktaqhomuhs 'kisaqsal cihpolakonol apotuhunok. The old man carved an eagle on the cane.

'**t-apotukonapin** (AI+OBJ) he sits against it with his knees raised
    stem 1:   -apotukonap(i)-

'**t-apqasokahal** (TA) he lets him out by unlocking a door, etc.
    stem 1:   -apqasok_h-

'**t-apqasokahmon** (TA) he unlocks it
    stem 1:   -apqasokahm-; but: apqasokohok when he unlocks it

apqasokihike (AI) he unlocks (something)
    stem 1:   -apqasokihik(e)-

apqasokihikon (I) key
    plural: apqasokihikonol
    poss: 'tapqasokihikon
    loc: apqasokihikonok
    dim: apqasokihikonossis
    'Koskahtuniyal 'tapqasokihikonumuwal. They lost their keys.

'**t-apqotehmuwan** (DOV) he opens it for him
    stem 1:   -apqotehmuw-

'**t-apqotehtun** (TI) he opens it
    stem 1:   -apqoteht-

'**t-apqotiyaqhomon** (TI) he props it open with a stick
    stem 1:   -apqotiyaqhom-

apsalokosu (AI) it (an.) has a small hole in it
    stem 1:   -apsalokos(i)-

apsaskute (II) it is a small field
    stem 1:   apsaskut(e)-

apsatokosossu (AI) he is thin (said of a snake, a string, etc.); he is skinny (said of a person)
    stem 1:   -apsatokososs(i)-
    'Sami apsatokosossu ahpap, ma te nkisapekiyaw. Because the rope is too thin, I can't swing.
    Psi te 'qoss apsatokosossultu. All her sons are skinny.

'**t-apseksal** (TA) he slices it (an.) into thin pieces
    stem 1:   -apseks-

'**t-apseksomon** (TI) he slices it into small pieces
    stem 1:   -apseksom-

'**t-apsihtahal** (TA) he chops it (an.) into small pieces
    stem 1:   -apsiht_h-

'**t-apsihtehmon** (TI) he chops it into small pieces
    stem 1:   -apsihtehm-; but: apsihtohok when he chops it into small pieces

apsiqe (AI) he has a small face
    stem 1:   -apsiq(a)-

apskapu (AI) his eyes are open
    Isikonapskapu. He has one eye open.

apsokil (AI) he is small
    plural: apsokilultuwok, apsokiluhtuwok, apsokilhotuwok
    stem 1:   -apsokil(o)-
    Nit nuhkomoss pihce elakonutomuwitpon nil apsokilan. That's what my grandmother told me a long time ago, when I was small.
    Motewolon 'kisehtuwan 'tapsokilulin mahtoqehsuwol. The motewolon made the rabbit small.

aptelomultineweyal (I) (pl.) rice

'**t-aptomimal** (TA) he went to hire him (and came back)
    stem 1:   -aptomim-

apuciqaha (A) dragonfly
    plural: apuciqahak

apuciyaskuwakon (I) see-saw
    plural: apuciyaskuwakonol

apuckoliye (AI) he falls over backwards
    plural: apuckoliyawolotuwok
    stem 1:   -apuckoliy(a)-
    Ktaqhomuhs etucossomit, on 'tapuckoliyan. The old man got very drunk and fell over backwards.
    Nehtaw apuckoliyayan, knihtuphin. If I fall over backwards, catch (sg.) me.

apuckolopu (AI) he is upside down

apuckolte (II) it is upside down

aqacaluhs (A) yellow perch
    (variant of acaqaluhs)

aqami (aqam-) (PV) more
    Aqami cipinaqot katok kotok. It is more hideous than the other one.
    On 'taqami pisoluhkalin pahqihil hokek. And the arrow worked further into his body.

aqamkihqon (II) it is larger
    Aqamkihqon wikuwawihkuwa muwiniyik katok nilun. The bears' house is larger than ours (nilun).

aqamok, aqamk (P) more; more than; anymore
    Pemikhoticik aqamok 'qotatq wikuwamol. Those living there number more than one hundred wigwams.
    Nekomaw olu kotama aqamk 'kisikapuwihtomuwoniya. They, however, cannot stand it anymore.

-aqos- cook; burn
    (forms TA verb stems)

motiyaqosal (TA) he is heard cooking it (an.)

asahqahahsis (A) acorn
plural: asahqahahsisok
poss: 'tasahqahahsisomol
loc: asahqahahsisok
dim: asahqahahsossis
Mihkuwiyik mahawa asahqahahsis. Squirrels eat acorns.

asakuwahq (A) chipmunk
plural: asakuwahkuk, asakuwahqiyik
poss: 'tasakuwahkumol, tasakuwahqemol
dim: asakuwaqsis, asakuwahqehsis, asakuwahqis
Ma te kisi tpelomaw asakuwahq, 'sami Keluwosit nihtol 'topelomal. You (sg.) cannot own a chipmunk, because God owns him.

't-asihtuwal (TA) he brings bad luck by magic
stem 1: -asihtuw-

asit (P) behind, in back; at the rear;
Opin asit. Sit (sg.) in the back seat (in a car).

't-asitehmuwal (TA) he replies to him; he answers him
stem 1: -asitehmuw-

't-asitehtahal (TA) he hits him back
stem 1: -asiteht_h-

't-asitemal (TA) he answers him
stem 1: -asitem-
Nit tehc etolaskuwasultihtit tokkiw asitemut. Then they (pl.) wait until they are answered.

asitewtom (AI) he answers
stem 1: -asitewtom(o)- type A

't-asitewtomon (TI) he answers it
stem 1: -asitewtom-

't-asitewtomuwan (DOV) he answers something of his
'Tasitewtomuwanol 'tahtuwikhikonol. He answers his letters.

asitiw (P) in the distant past

askomawsu (AI) he lives forever
Eli te nokolatpon, nit te apc elimskuwat, Wocawson ipocol askomawsu. He found him just as he had left him, for Wocawson lives forever.

askomi (askom-) (PV) forever

askomiw (P) forever

't-askuwatomon (TI) he waits for it
stem 1: -askuwatom-

't-askuwyal (TA) he waits for him
stem 1: -askuwy-
(Stem-final y may change to h before i: Askuwhin! Wait for me!)

assihkawe (AI) he meets someone
stem 1: -assihkaw(e)-

assihkawotuwok (AI) they (dual) meet

't-assihkuwal (TA) he meets him
stem 1: -assihkuw-: ntassihkaq he meets me

assiye (AI) she (a bitch dog) is going into heat
stem 1: -assiy(a)-

assokeyu (AI) he has strange ways
stem 1: -assokey(i)-

astuwokak (AI) they (dual) dance toward each other and then apart (part of the welcome dance)
stem 1: -astuwok(a)-

asups (A) devil diver (bird species.)
plural: asupsok

't-asuwi psihkomon (TI) he wears it at an angle
'Tasuwi psihkomon 'tahsusuwon. He wears his hat at an angle.

't-asuwihtahkusin (AI, AI + OBJ) he wears it over one shoulder and diagonally across his body to the opposite hip
stem 1: -asuwihtahkus(i)-

asuwikon (I) crooked thing
plural: asuwikonol

asuwiw (P) crooked; at an angle; obliquely

asuwocokahte (II) it has slid over to one side; it has flopped over to one side
stem 1: asuwocokaht(e)-
Asuwocokahtetul 'tahsuhunol. His blankets have slipped over to one side (of the bed).

athusoss (A) snake
plural: athusossok
poss: 'tathusossomol
dim: athusossis
Nomiya etolatokiyat athusoss psihqihkuk. I see a snake wriggling in the grass.

atkiqe (AI) he has wrinkles on his face

atkuhkakon (I) story; legend
plural: atkuhkakonol
poss: 'tatkuhkakon
loc: atkuhkakonok
dim: atkuhkakonossis

atkuhke (AI) he tells an old story; he tells a legend
plural: atkukhotuwok, atkuhkahtuwok
stem 1: -atkuhk(e)-
Atkukhotuwok skicinuwok mecimiw puniw. The Indians always used to tell stories in the winter.

atkuwessoss (A) wriggler (mosquito larva); water-strider
plural: atkuwessossok
(literally, "little wave-maker")

atomupil (I) car
plural: atomupilol
poss: 'tatomupilom, 'tatomupil
loc: atomupilok
dim: atomupilsis
(from English, automobile)

atpahqonikehs (A) caterpillar; inch-worm
plural: atpahqonikehsuwok

atpe (II) the water level changes
stem 1: atp(e)-

atpehe (II) the tide changes
stem 1: atp_h(a)-

-atuw(e)- climb
1) Stems ending in -atuw(e)- are AI stems. They form plurals in -aht(i)-, -awolot(i)-,

-ult(i)-, and -uht(i)-: olomatuwahtuwok, olomatuwawolotuwok "they (pl.) climb away."

2) Some speakers change the w of -atuw(e)- to h when it comes before u: olomatuhuhtuwok "they (pl.) climb away."
   olomatuwe (AI) he climbs away
   poneqatuwe (AI) he climbs down
-atuw(e)- speak a language
   (forms AI verb stems)
   ikolisomanatuwe (AI) he speaks English
atuwe (AI) he (an animal) sheds his hair
   stem 1:   -atuw(e)-
awahsihikon (I) small hand-held fan
awonehe (P) instead
   Awonehehp nil skat ntahcuwyukuwon, 'tahcuwyal kotokil pilsqehsisol. Instead of hiring me, he hired another girl.
awotu (AI, II) he, it is worth something
   stem 1:   -awot(i)-
-aws(i)- live
   (forms AI verb stems)
   sipkawsu (AI) he lives a long time
   siqonawsu (AI) he survives until spring (he lives through hard times)
't-awskahqahal (TA) he stirs it (an.)
   stem 1:   -awskahq_h-
't-awskahqehmon (TI) he stirs it
   stem 1:   -awskahqehm-; but:
             awskahqohok when he stirs it
awt (I) road; path
   plural: awtiyil, awtihil
   poss: 'tawtim
   loc: awtik
   dim: awtossis
ayut (P) and even; and besides; including even
   Yut ehkosqenahtit ayut wecemahtit. They hugged him and even kissed him.

C

cahahq (A) butt of a tree
   plural: cahahqok
   dim: cahaqsis
cahlak (A) nasal mucus
cahlakiw (AI) he has nasal mucus on him
calokoss (I) ear
   plural: calokossiyil, calokossihil, calokoshil
   poss: 'calokoss
'calokossewine (AI) he has an earache
cals (A) grasshopper
   plural: calsok
   poss: 'calsomol
   dim: calsis, calsossis
caqahk (I) rust
caqahkiye (AI, II) it is rusty
   plurual: caqahkiyawolotuwok (AI)
   stem 1:   -caqahkiy(a)-

cehcis (A) vein
   plural: cehcisok
cehcoloqs (A) gland
   plural: cehcoloqsok
cehkit (A) jacket
   plural: cehkitok
   poss: 'cehkitomol
   (from English, jacket)
cehqoniw (P) at dawn
cehqonoluhke (AI) he works until dawn
   stem 1:   -cehqonoluhk(e)-
'cehtu (AI) he hemorrhages through the nose and mouth
cel (P) and besides; and even
   Mali macehe, cel ona Piyel. Mary is leaving, and Peter too.
   Kmillon piksey-- 'qoci tkihqon cel epahsiw. I will give you (sg.) pork-- a pound and a half.
   Skitap wapatpe cel kinapskosu. The man has white hair, and he's fat.
   (Compare: Skitap wapatpe naka 'kinapskosin. The man has white hair and is fat.)
celkahq (A) roof of the mouth
   poss: 'celkahkumol
cepi (cep-) (PV) separately; apart
   (See cocepi "separately, apart.")
cepiw, cocepiw (P) separately; apart
cepiye, cocepiye (AI) he is separated from his spouse
   plural: cepiyawolotuwok
   stem 1:   -cepiy(a)-
   Kisihponoltihtit, nit te 'cepiyaniya. After they (dual) fought, they separated.
   Mec ote cepihhik nekomaw. They (dual) are still separated.
ceposkehtehson, cocoposkehtehson (II) it becomes dislocated (of a bone)
ceposkessu, cocoposkessu (II) it becomes dislocated (of a bone)
   (See coceposkessu.)
'cepsomon, 'cocepsomon (TI) he cuts it apart
   stem 1:   -cepsom-
cepte, cocepte (II) it is separate; it is disassembled
   stem 1:   cept(e)-
   Nohonul qotoputihil ceptetul. The three chairs are separate.
   'Tapakonossis cepte. The toy wagon is disassembled.
cess (P) as if
   On yaq cess te wen yahat, "Ipa lapotomun ktahtuwiput." And then, they say, it was just as if someone told her, "Hey, look (sg.) at your table."
'cey (A) someone from there
   plural: 'ceyak
   obv: 'ceyal (sg.); 'ceya (pl.)
   Nmihtaqs Qonasqamkuk 'cey. My father is from St. Andrews, New Brunswick.
   Wikuwossol Sipayik 'ceyal. Her mother is from Pleasant Point, Maine.

Nikihku utenek 'ceya. Her parents are from town.

'ci ('c-, 't-) (PV, PN) from; out of; on account of

(See weci "in order that.")
prefixed form: -uci (-uc-, -ut-)
neke form: weci (wec-, wet-)

cihcihke (AI) he paddles in the back of a canoe (steers)

cihcin (I) thumb
  plural: cihcinol
  poss: 'cihcin

'cihkehmon (TI) he sweeps it away
  stem 1: -cihkehm-; but: cihkohok when he sweeps it away

cihkihike (AI) he sweeps
  plural: cihkihikhotuwok
  stem 1: -cihkihik(e)-

cihkihikon (A) (I for some speakers) broom
  plural: cihkihikonok (cihkihikonol)
  poss: 'cihkihikonumol ('cihkihikonum)
  loc: cihkihikonok
  dim: cihkihikonossis

'cihtasu (II) it is made of (something)
  stem 1: 'cihtas(i)-
  stem 2: wecihtas(i)-: wecihtasik what it is made of

'cihtasu is the indefinite subject form of ucihtun (TI) he makes it out of (something)

'Cihtasu akomahqey tomhikonahtoq. An axe handle is made of white ash.

'cihtihike (AI) he wins
  plural: 'cihtihikhotuwok
  stem 1a: -uttihik(e)-: nuttihik I win
  stem 1b: 'cihtihik(e)-
  stem 2: wettihik(e)-: wettihiket winner

cika (P) even if

Cika te tomiqehtuhukiyin, mec otehc kpomaws. Even if you (sg.) are beheaded, you will still live.

'cikawi nutehkuwal (TA) he forces him to move out

'cikawi nutehlal (TA) he forces him to go out

'cikawiyal (TA) he teases him
  stem 1: -cikawiy-

cikcahkehe (AI) he goes downhill
  plural: cikcahkahawolotuwok
  stem 1: -cikcahk_h(a)-

cikcahkew (P) at the bottom of a hill

cikcahkiw (P) downhill

'cikihtomon (TI) he leaves it alone
  stem 1: -cikihtom-

'cikihtuwal (TA) he leaves him alone
  stem 1: -cikihtuw-

cikon (A) apple
  plural: cikoniyik, cikonihik
  poss: 'cikonemol, 'tahcikonemol
  loc: cikonek
  dim: cikonesis, cikonehsis

Musa mahahkoc nikt cikonihik tokkiw yaka sepawonu. Don't (sg.) eat those apples until tomorrow.

  'tahcikonemol (A) (dep.) his adam's apple

cikoniyahqemus (A) apple tree
  plural: cikoniyahqemusiyik

cikopu (AI) he is silent; he sits silently
  plural: cikopultuwok, cikopihhik, cikopiyahtuwok, cikopiyawolotuwok
  stem 1: -cikop(i)-

'ciksotomon (TI) he listens to it; he heeds it
  stem 1: -ciksotom-

'ciksotuwal (TA) he listens to him; he heeds him
  stem 1: -ciksotuw-

cikte (II) it is quiet it is silent
  stem 1: cikt(e)-

cilkatokosu (AI) it (an.) is short (said of something string-like)
  plural: cilkatokosultuwok
  stem 1: -cilkatokos(i)-

cilkatokot (II) it is short (said of something string-like); it is short (said of a story, film, etc.)
  stem 1: -cilkatokot(o)-

cilkenskosu (AI) he is short (standing up)
  plural: cilkenskosultuwok
  stem 1: -cilkenskos(i)-

Nusami cilkenskos ma te keq nmemonomuhwon tehsaqtihikonok. I am too short to reach anything on the shelf.

Skat cilkenskosiwon, ma te kcuwi qotoputik sehkew. If you (sg.) are not short, you do not need to stand on the chair.

cilkeyu (AI, II) it is short
  plural: cilkeyultuwok, cilkeyuhtuwok (AI)
  stem 1: -cilkey(i)-

Neke cilkeyit opos, etuci wolankeyuhuk. When the tree was short, I took very good care of it.

Cilkeyic opos peciptuwon. Have the stick be short when you (sg.) bring it.

cilkokiskot (II) it is a short day
  stem 1: -cilkokiskot(o)-

'cilomomal (TA) he receives a sign from him; he is haunted by him
  stem 1: -cilomom-

Cipotu te nican 'cilomomku tokec ktaqhomuhs koti mehcinet. Perhaps his children will receive a sign from him if the old man is going to die.

cilomotome, cilomotoma (AI) he receives a sign; he is haunted; he receives an omen
  plural: cilomotomahtuwok
  stem 1: -cilomotom(a)-

Tokec ksiyutihin nit wikuwamok, cu kcilomotom. If you (sg.) move into that house, you will be haunted.

'cilomotomon (TI) he receives a sign through it; he is haunted through it
  stem 1: -cilomotom-

Tokec cilomotomon qotoput, woli te knutiyahkan. If you receive a sign through that chair, just throw it out.

cilonasit (A) haddock
plural: cilonasicik
poss: 'cilonasitomol
dim: cilonasossit

'cimaciw, 'cimacihiw (P) from... on (time)
Tokec 'cimaciw, kisihc pomaws 'samaqanok. From now on, you (sg.) will be able to live in the water.
Neke 'cimaciw kotama tutclamsonihkew tahalu pihce. From then on the wind did not blow as hard as it had long ago.

cimqaha (A) bird species (American bittern?)
plural: cimqahak

cinituwiye (AI) he flies low
stem 1:   -cinituwiy(a)-

'cinituwiyemuhtuwal (TA) he flies low at him
stem 1:   -cinituwiyemuhtuw-

cipi (cip-) (PV.PN) ugly; evil-looking; hideous
cipinaqsu (AI) he looks ugly, evil

'cipilqe (AI) he has epilepsy
plural: 'cipilqahtuwok,
            'cipilqawolotuwok
stem 1a: -ucipilq(e)-: nucipilq I have epilepsy
stem 1b: 'cipilq(e)-
stem 2:   wecipilq(e)-: wecipilqet epileptic

'cipiluwehs (A) pleurisy; epilepsy; muscle spasms
'Cipiluwehsuwol matonokul. He is suffering from pleurisy. (Literally, "Pleurisy is fighting him.")

'cipimal (TA) he startles him by talking
stem 1:   -cipim-

cipiyahtoq (A) cross; crucifix
plural: cipiyatkuk
poss: 'cipiyatkumol
loc: cipiyatkuk
dim: cipiyatqis, cipiyatkuhsis

cipokalokotune (AI) he is a loud-mouth
stem 1:   -cipokalokotun(a)-

cipoki (cipok-) (PV) loud

cipokihtaqot (II) it is noisy; it is loud
stem 1:   cipokihtaqot(o)-

cipokihtaqsu (AI) he yells
stem 1:   -cipokihtaqs(i)-

'cipokihtaqsuwamal (TA) he talks very loudly to him
stem 1:   -cipokihtaqsuwam-

cipotu, cipotuk (II (?)) it is possible; maybe; perhaps
Cipotu te kmonuhmulon ktul. Maybe I'll buy your (sg.) canoe.

cipqahsin (AI) he has a nightmare
stem 1:   -cipqahsin(o)- type B

cipqam (AI) he has a nightmare of falling; he jumps in his sleep or when dozing
stem 1:   -cipqam(o)- Type A: cipqak when he has a nightmare of falling

'ciptinessu (AI) he makes a hand print
stem 1a: -uciptiness(i)-
stem 1b: 'ciptiness(i)-
stem 2:   weciptiness(i)-

cipuhtes (A) clown
plural: cipuhtesok

ciqolatokopu (AI) it (an.) is tangled up
stem 1:   -ciqolatokop(i)-

ciqoleqsu (AI) he snores
plural: ciqoleqsultuwok,
            ciqoleqsuhtuwok
stem 1:   -ciqoleqs(i)-

'cishal (TA) he scrapes him
stem 1:   -cish-

cituwessu (AI) he bends over
plural: cituwessultuwok
stem 1:   -cituwess(i)-
Cituwessit, on 'pokossinon. When he bent over, he fell down.

'ciw (P) about; for
(also: uhc)

ciwciye (AI) it (an.) leaks
plural: ciwciyawolotuwok
stem 1:   -ciwciy(a)-
Ciwciyat wapahkuhs, musa wehkahahkoc. If the pail leaks, don't use it.

ciyahkehs (A) mink

ciyahkehsuhke (AI) he hunts (or traps) mink
plural: ciyahkehsukhotuwok,
            ciyahkehsuhkahtuwok
stem 1:   -ciyahkehsuhk(e)-

'ciye (AI) he comes back from there; he has been there
plural: 'ciyahtuwok; 'ciyawolotuwok
stem 1a: -uciy(a)-: nuciyan I have been there (Relative)
stem 1b: 'ciy(a)-: 'ciyat if he has been there
stem 2:   weciy(a)-: weciyat when he was coming back from there
Weciyat utenek, nit te etoli wekinewik utapakon. When he was coming back from town, his car broke down.
Tama kuci? Where have you (sg.) been?

ckuhpehe (II) the tide is coming in
stem 1:   ckuhp_h(a)-
stem 2:   weckuhpah(a)-: weckuhpahak when the tide is coming in

ckuhqepu (AI) he sits facing this way
stem 1a: -uckuhqep(i)-
stem 1b: ckuhqep(i)-
stem 2:   weckuhqep(i)-: weckuhqepit he is sitting and facing this way

ckuhtaqot, ckuwihtaqot (II) it sounds as if it is coming toward here; it (a sound) approaches
stem 1:   ckuhtaqot(o)-
stem 2:   weckuhtaqot(o)-: weckuhtaqahk when it (a sound) approaches

ckuwahkuhucin (AI) he is bent over (rear end facing this way)

ckuwapon (II) it is dawn; dawn approaches; dawn arrives
stem 1:   ckuwapon(o)- type A
stem 2:   weckuwapon(o)-: weckuwapok as dawn arrives

ckuwi (ckuw-, ckuh-) (PV) toward here
  prefixed form: -uckuwi (-uckuw-, -uckuh-)
  neke form: weckuwi (weckuw-, weckuh-)
  ckuwiqehe (II) it rolls toward here
  ckuwuhse, ckuhuhse (AI) he walks toward here
  ckuhqepu (AI) he sits facing toward here
ckuwihtaqot
  (See ckuhtaqot.)
ckuwinuwe (II) the wind is coming up over the water
  stem 1: ckuwinuw(e)-
  stem 2: weckuwinuw(e)-:
          weckuwinuwek when the wind was coming up over the water
ckuwoqotehe (AI) he swims toward here under the water
  plural: ckuwoqotahawolotuwok, ckuwoqotahahtuwok
  stem 1a: -uckuwoqot_h(a)-type A
  stem 1b: ckuwoqot_h(a)-
  stem 2: weckuwoqot_h(a)-
ckuwye (AI, II) he, it comes toward here
  plural: ckuwyawolotuwok, ckuwyahtuwok, ckuwyawotuwok
  stem 1a: -uckuwy(a)- (Without ending: -uckuwi: nuckuwi I come toward here)
  stem 1b: ckuwy(a)-: ckuwyat if he comes toward here (But: ckuwi come (sg.) here!)
  stem 2: weckuwy(a)-: weckuwyat he is coming toward here
  stem 3: ckuwy(a)-: koti ckuwye he is going to come toward here (Without ending: ckuwi: nkoti ckuwi I am going to come toward here)

  Kuckuwiyawolotipa na kiluwaw sepawonu? Are you (pl.) coming here tomorrow?

  Neke weckuwyat, kisi nimskehe wikuwossok. When he was coming here, he stopped in at his mother's.

  Nit weckuwyak keq. There is something coming.

cocepi (cocep-) (PV) separately; apart
  cocepi is now often reduced to cepi (cep-). See entries under cep-.
  neke form: cecepi (cecep-)
  cocepiye (AI) he is separated from his spouse
coceposkehtehson (II) it becomes dislocated (of a bone)
  stem 1: coceposkehtehson(o)- type A
  stem 2: ceceposkehtehson(o)-
cokahk (P) (interjection indicating surprise, shock, disgust)
coke (P) here; let me see (indicates interest in something near the person spoken to); hmm, let me think; well, now...

  Coke, milin ktahtuwikhikon. Here, give me your (sg.) book.

cokiqis (A) wart; decorative loop woven into the side of a basket
  plural: cokiqisok
'colokehlal (TA) he presses it (an.)
  stem 1: -colokehl-
  stem 2: celokehl-
'colokonal (TA) he squeezes him, it (an., something soft)
  stem 1: -colokon-
  stem 2: celokon-
'conehlal (TA) he stops him
  stem 1: -conehl-
  stem 2: cenehl-
conehtasu (II) it is stopped
  stem 1: -conehtas(i)-
  stem 2: cenehtas(i)-
  (indefinite subject form of 'conehtun)
'conehtun (TI) he stops it
  stem 1: -coneht-
  stem 2: ceneht-
conesson (II) it stops; it comes to a stop
  stem 1: conesson(o)- type A
  stem 2: cenesson(o)-
  'Tatomupilomuwal conessonul awtik. Their cars stopped on the road.

  Mehsi conessok psi te kolahkol eci tuceyik esqonatek aciyak? Why did all the clocks stop at nine o'clock?
conessu (AI) he stops; he comes to a stop
  plural: conessultuwok
  stem 1: -coness(i)-
  stem 2: ceness(i)-
  Skitapiyik conessultuwok Pitok. The men (pl.) stopped at the Pit.

  Coness! Stop! (message on a stop sign)
conpekiw (II) the motion of the tide stops (when it is about to change)
  stem 1: conpek(i)- type B
  stem 2: cenpek(i)-: cenpekik when the motion of the tide stopped
conte (II) it is parked (of a vehicle)
  stem 1: cont(e)-
  stem 2: cent(e)-
copkatom (AI) he is married
  (variant of cpahkatom)
coqahk, cu kahk (P) sure; of course (always used with another particle)
  coqahk al, cu kahk al of course
  coqahk oc, cu kahk oc of course + future (of course he will, etc.)
  coqahk op, cu kahk op of course + potential (of course he would, etc.)
coqols (A) frog
  plural: coqolsok
  poss: 'coqolsomol
  dim: coqolsis
coqolsuwi (coqolsuw-) (PN) frog; frog's
  coqolsuwi akuwahtuhusut (I) toadstool
  coqolsuwotekon (I) frog skin
'coskuwalal (TA) he is jealous of him
  (variant of 'kocoskuwalal)
coskuwe (AI) he is jealous
  (variant of kcoskuwe)

cossakon (I) awl
plural: cossakonol
cossikon (I) dye
plural: cossikonol
cossinaqsu (AI) he is bothersome; he is a nuisance
plural: cossinaqsultuwok
stem 1: -cossinaqs(i)-: ncossinaqsipon we (nilun, dual) are bothersome
stem 2: cessinaqs(i)-: cessinaqsit pest
Komac wot skinuhsis cossinaqsu eci milehtakeskit. This boy is really a nuisance because he is always getting into everything.
cossokhikon (I) nail
plural: cossokhikonol
poss: 'cossokhikonumol
loc: cossokhikonok
dim: cossokhikonossis
cossu (A) mosquito
plural: cossuwiyik, cossuwihik
poss: 'cossuwemol
dim: cossuwesis
cossuwan (I) bullet
plural: cossuwanol
cossuwewekon (I) mosquito net; gauze
plural: cossuwewekonol
cossuwewihke (II) there are a lot of mosquitoes out
stem 1: cossuwewihk(e)-
stem 2: cessuwewihk(e)-
costaqsu (AI) he talks constantly; he talks and talks
plural: costaqsultuwok, costaqsuhtuwok
stem 1: -costaqs(i)-
stem 2: cestaqs(i)-
(Note: Absentative Independent forms and Imperative forms may mean "be quiet, shut up": costaqsuwa "he has shut up"; costaqs! "You shut up!")
Olomihkawotukk cestaqsicikk. The (two) people who were talking constantly went away.
Costaqsic not wasis. Make that child be quiet.
cpahkatom, copkatom (AI) he is married
plural: cpahkatomultuwok, cpahkatomuhtuwok, copkatomultuwok, copkatomuhtuwok
stem 1a: -copkatom(o)- type A
stem 1b: cpahkatom(o)-, cpahkatomuk, they (dual) are married
stem 2: cepkatom(o)-: cepkatok when he was married
Mehsi skat cpahkatomuhk? Why wasn't he married?
Kilun kcopkatomupon. You (sg.) and I are married.
cu (P) yes, why yes; for sure; (when the answer "no" is expected or disbelief expressed) on the contrary; for sure

(Compare aha "yes"; kotama, ma "no.")
Cu te lu it is too!; yes, it is true: Cu te lu, uhkomi, nomiya nikuwoss. Yes, grandmother, I do see my mother.
(tokec)... cu if... then: Tokec kisaciyin, cu kmacephul. If you (sg.) are ready, I'll take you.
Ma te knonuwaw? ---Cu. Don't you (sg.) know her? ---Yes, I do.
Cu peciye temonuk. She'll come later for sure.
Skat wasisok kahsihpulsuhtihtihq, cu ksinukhotuwok. If the children (pl.) don't dry themselves off, they will get sick.
cuhpi (cuhp-) (PV) in (or into) water
(See cuwahpi "in (or into) water.")
cuhpiye (AI, II) he, it falls into the water
plural: cuhpiyawolotuwok, cuhpiyahtuwok, cuhpiyawotuwok
stem 1: -cuhpiy(a)-: cuhpiyat when he fell into the water
cuhponapsqakon, cuwahponapsqakon (I) anchor
plural: cuhponapsqakonol
poss: 'cuhponapsqakonum
cuppu (AI) he sits in the water
stem 1: -cupp(i)-
cuspes (A) porpoise
plural: cuspesok
poss: 'cuspesomol
dim: cuspesis
cuspeske (AI) he hunts porpoise
plural: cuspeskahtuwok
stem 1: -cuspesk(e)-
cuwahpi (cuwahp-, cuwap-) (PV) in (or into) water.
(See cuhpi "in (or into) water.")
cuwahpiye (AI, II) he, it goes (or falls) into the water
plural: cuwahpiyawolotuwok, cuwahpiyahtuwok, cuwahpiyawotuwok
stem 1: -cuwahpiy(a)-
stem 2: cuwahpiy(a)-, cewahpiy(a)-: cewahpiyat when he fell into the water
Neke cuwahpiyayan, psi te npuccokp. When I fell into the water, I got all wet.
cuwapotokku (AI) he jumps into the water
cuwi, ahcuwi (PV) must; should; have to
prefixed form: -cuwi, -ahcuwi: nil ncuwi, nil ntahcuwi I have to...
neke form: cuwi, ehcuwi
(Does not combine with verb stems; must be followed by a complete verb: cuwi opu he has to sit; cuwi laqote it has to cook thus.)
cuwitpot (II) it should be
Kat cuwitpotu knoqtuhkanin. You (sg.) should not live alone.
'cuwyal (TA) he hires him
(See 't-ahcuwyal)

E

eci (PV) very; when
(variant of etuci)
(Note: eci is used only in neke forms.)
(Does not combine with verb stems; must be followed by a complete verb: eci kotuhpit he is very hungry.)
Ecihc wikuwaceyik. It will be a lot of fun.
Eci pilsqehsis wolinaqahk hok. The girl's body is very beautiful.

ehcuwi (PV) must; should; have to
(See cuwi.)

ehecinaqsu (AI) he is hard to see
plural: ehecinaqsultuwok
stem 1: -ehecinaqs(i)-
Ehecinaqsu mahtoqehs weckuhqepit 'toputossok. A rabbit is hard to see when he is sitting in his hiding place.

ehem (A) chicken
plural: ehemuwok
poss: 'tehemumol
dim: ehemuhsis

ehemuhke (AI) he hunts chickens
stem 1: -ehemuhk(e)-
Espons ali ehemuhke. A raccoon went around hunting chickens.

ehemuwikuwam (I) chicken coop
plural: ehemuwikuwamol

ehetsu (AI) he hesitates
plural: ehetsultuwok
stem 1: -ehets(i)-: ntehetsipon we (nilun, dual) hesitate; ehetsit one who hesitates
Skat op tuci ehetsihq, pihcehp 'kiskatomon. If he had not hesitated for so long, he would have gotten married long ago.

ehetuwiw (P) on both sides
Sitektehmun ehetuwiw khakonok. Nail (sg.) them (inan.) up on both sides of the door.

ehetuwosqone (AI) he can pitch (in baseball) with either arm (literally, with either elbow); he is ambidextrous
plural: ehetuwosqonawolotuwok
stem 1: -ehetuwosqon(a)-

't-ehkosqenal (TA) he hugs him
stem 1: -ehkosqen-

-ehl- do to
(forms TA verb stems)
'sakhehlal (TA) he brings it (an.) into view; 'kisehlal (TA) he finishes him, it (an.); he rescues him; he makes him (do something)

ehpit (A) woman
plural: ehpicik
poss: 'tehpitemol
dim: ehpitsis
obv: ehpilicil (sg.); ehpilicihi, ehpilici (pl.)
Nomiya ehpilicihi. He sees the women.

Ehpit eci paliqewit epit. The woman is sitting and looking happy.

ehpituwehlosu (AI) he turns himself into a woman
stem 1: -ehpituwehlos(i)-

ehqamkole (II) it stops burning
stem 1: ehqamkol(e)-
Pol ehqamkolec on yaka kossahan. Let the fire go out first before you (sg.) go in.

ehqi (ehq-, eq-) (PV) stop; cease
(ehq- changes to ehk- before u)
ehqi kolusku (AI) he stops lying
ehqoluhke (AI) he stops working
ehkuwikhike (AI) he stops writing
eqotemu (AI) he stops crying

ehta (P) (emphatic)
Etuci ehta ktomakeyi. I am so very poor.
Milin ehta. Give (sg.) it to me!

ehtahs (P) every; every time; time after time
ehtahs te likotok every year

ehtahsikiskot (II) it is once a day
stem 1: ehtahsikiskot(o)-
Ehtahsikiskahk wocawson. Every day the wind blows.

ekhucaloss (A) uvula
plural: ekhucalossok

ekhucossit (A) uvula
plural: ekucossicik

ekhucuwole (AI) he hangs clothes out to dry
plural: ekhucuwolhotuwok, ekhucuwolahtuwok
stem 1: -ekhucuwol(e)-
Nit te eli mehtekhucuwoli, nit te macelan. Just as I finished hanging the clothes out to dry, it started to rain.

ekhute (II) it hangs down
stem 1: ekhut(e)-

-eks- slice
(forms TA verb stems)
'pipuweksal (TA) he slices it (an.) thin

eksku (AI) he sneezes
plural: ekskultuwok
stem 1: -eksq(i)-: nteksqinen we (nilun, dual) sneeze (Relative)
(Note: stem q changes to k before u.)
Tehpisewey nkisehtakunen nteksqinen. The pepper made us (nilun, dual) sneeze.
Toli ekskultuwok 'sami keckuluwultuwok. They (pl.) are sneezing because they have colds.

el (A) doe
plural: eliyik

elinaqahk (II) there is a lot of it; there are a lot of them (inan.)
(See linaqot "it looks thus.")
Elinaqahk posonutiyil. There are a lot of baskets.

elinaqsit (AI) there is a lot of it (an.); there are a lot of them (an.)
elinaqsihtit there are a lot of them (an.)
(See linaqsu "he looks thus.")
Elinaqsit cossuwihik. There are a lot of mosquitoes.

Elisomen (A) Irishman
   plural: Elisomenok
-elom(i)- laugh, smile
   (forms AI verb stems)
   siktiyelomu (AI) he laughs very hard
   skewelomu (AI) he laughs easily
elomelkimok (II) so many yards; so many
paces (land measure)
   (See olomelku "he paces off so much.")
elomocokek (I) bog, mudflat
   plural: elomocokekil
eluwe (P) almost; nearly (indicates final state,
activity completed--compare keka)
   Eluwe te psiw 'tihiniya piluwitposuwakon.
Almost all have magical power.
   Eluwe te mehcine. He almost died.
   Eluwe te kis psi wen peciye. Almost
everyone had arrived.
eluwehkal (P) of course; must be; maybe
   Eluwehkal te Koluskap nicalkul. He must
be Koluskap's uncle.
emehkew (P) down below; downstairs
emekte (II) it is down below
   stem 1:   -emekt(e)-: emektek something
               which is below
emqan (A) spoon
   plural: emqanok
   poss: 'temqanomol
   loc: emqanok
   dim: emqansis teaspoon
enehtawe (AI) he is deaf and dumb
   plural: enehtawhotuwok
   stem 1:   -enehtaw(e)-: enehtawet one
               who is deaf and dumb
eniqs (A) ant
   plural: eniqsok
   dim: eniqsis
't-enkamhal (TA) he challenges him (to a race)
   stem 1:   -enkamh-
enuwaqhomakon (I) lever stick (placed over
one shoulder and under a log one is carrying
over the other shoulder, thus helping to
distribute the log's weight)
   plural: enuwaqhomakonol
   poss: 'tenuwaqhomakon
   loc: enuwaqhomakonok
't-enuwaqhomuwal (TA) he assists him
   stem 1:   -enuwaqhomuw-:
               ntenuwaqhomaq he assists me
enuwiye (AI) he comes to; he regains
consciousness
   stem 1:   -enuwiy(a)-
epahsahkiw (P) halfway up (or down) a hill
epahsahsu (AI) it (an.) is half-illuminated
   stem 1:   -epahsahs(i)-
epahsakisu (A) half dollar
   plural: epahsakisuwok
epahsakom (P) in the middle of a lake
epahsaskutew (P) right in the middle of a field
epahsasokiw (P) right in the middle of the
floor
epahsi (epahs-, epas-) (PV) half, halfway; in
the middle; in two, in half

't-epahsiksal (TA) he saws it (an.) in two; he
saws it (an.) in half
   stem 1:   -epahsiks-
't-epahsiksomon (TI) he saws it in two; he saws
it in half
   stem 1:   -epahsiksom-
epahsitpuhkot (II) it is midnight; it is the
middle of the night
   stem 1:   epahsitpuhkot(o)-:
               epahsitpuhkahk at midnight;
               in the middle of the night
epahsiw (P) halfway; in the middle
   Nehtaw opos 'samkihqahk, tomosomun
epahsiw. If the stick is too long, cut (sg.) it
in half.
   Epahsiw iyu skonimin cikonek. The seed
is in the middle of the apple.
epahsiyahsu (AI) he is a little crazy
   stem 1:   epahsiyahs(i)-
epahsiye (AI) he is foolish; he is crazy
   plural: epahsiyawolotuwok,
               epahsiyahtuwok
   stem 1:   -epahsiy(a)-
epaspe (AI, II) it is half full (of liquid)
   stem 1:   -epasp(e)-
epeskocossis (A) barn swallow
   plural: epeskcocossisok
epeskomakon (A) ball
   plural: epeskomakonok
   poss: 'tepeskomakonumol
   loc: epeskomakonok
   dim: epeskomakonossis
epeskome (AI) he plays ball
   plural: epeskomhotuwok,
               epeskomahtuwok,
               epeskomawolotuwok
   stem 1:   -epeskom(e)-
   Calsok alotokkultuwok ihtoli
epeskomhotimok. Grasshoppers are jumping
around on the ballfield (literally, where they
usually play ball).
eqhike (AI) he stops shooting
eqopu (AI) he stops being able to sit up
   stem 1:   -eqop(i)-
eqotemu (AI) he stops crying
   stem 1:   -eqotem(i)-
eqotokku (AI) he stops jumping
   stem 1:   -eqotoqq(i)-
eqqa (AI) he stops dancing
   stem 1:   -eqq(a)-
eqtaqsu (AI) he stops making noise (by
mouth)
   stem 1:   -eqtaqs(i)-
eqtihike (AI) he stops pounding; he stops
knocking
eqtokot (II) it ends (said of the length of
something)
esansu (AI) she wears something one can see
through
   plural: esansultuwok
   stem 1:   -esans(i)-
eskitaqotek (I) bean cooked on stove top
   plural: eskitaqotekil

espons (A) raccoon
  plural: esponsok
  poss: 'tesponsomol
  dim: esponsis
    Espons 'posqentun tahalu tehp skat wetomitahamahq Muwiniyil. Raccoon bursts into song as if he were not worried about Bear at all.

esponsuwehlosu (AI) he turns himself into raccoon
  stem 1:   -esponsuwehlos(i)-

esqonatek (P) nine

ess (A) clam
  plural: essok
  poss: 'tessumol
  loc: essok
  dim: essis
    Naciphane essok sopayiw supekuk. Let's go get clams along the seashore.

esuwapilom (AI) he goes back and forth fetching water
  stem 1:   -esuwapilom(o)- type A

esuwessu (AI, II) he, it goes back and forth
  stem 1:   -esuwess(i)-

esuwi (esuw-) (PV) back and forth
  esuwacqessu (AI) he slides back and forth
  esuwuhse (AI) he walks back and forth

esuwiw (P) back and forth

etoli (etol-) (PV) (See toli "is ...-ing.")

etuci (etuc-, etut-) (PV) very; to an extreme; at that point
  (See tuci.)
    Etuci kotuhpit espons. The raccoon is very hungry.
    Apc etuci apqotehmuhtit wikuwam. At that point they opened the house again.
    Etutapskosit. He is very fat.

't-ewahsehmon (TI) he fans it (a fire)
  stem 1:   -ewahsehm-: neke ewahsohok when he fanned it

ewecitu (P) previously
    Pokosson eyikpon ewecitu. It landed where it had been previously.

ewepamu (AI) he moves rapidly upward (involuntarily)
  stem 1:   -ewepam(i)-

ewepaqhikon (A) clothes pole
  plural: elopaqhikonok
  (also: spiqaqhikon)

't-ewepehlal (TA) he lifts him
  stem 1:   -ewepehl-

't-ewepehtun (TI) he lifts it
  stem 1:   -ewepeht-

ewepi (ewep-) (PV) upward; up above

ewepikonatutom (AI) he has his leg propped up; he holds his leg up
  plural: ewepikonatutomultuwok, ewepikonatutomuhtuwok
  stem 1:   -ewepikonatutom(o)- type A

ewepikonawu (AI) he holds his (own) leg up
  plural: ewepikonawultuwok
  stem 1:   -ewepikonaw(i)-: Ewepikonaw! Hold your leg up!

ewepiw (P) up; up above

't-eweponal (TA) he holds him up; he lifts him up
  stem 1:   -ewepon-

't-eweponomon (TI) he holds it up; he lifts it up

ewepotokku (AI) he jumps up
  plural: ewepotokkultuwok
  stem 1:   -ewepotoqq(i)-: ktewepotoqq you (sg.) jump up
  (Note: qq changes to kk before u.)
    Eci tehpisewey kisehtuwit nteksqin, ktewepotoqq. When the pepper made me sneeze, you (sg.) jumped up.
    Neke ewepotoqqit, ntokomokun ewehket 'pihtin. When he jumped up, he hit me with his hand.

eweppu (AI) he sits up
  stem 1:   -ewepp(i)- (Without ending: -ewepop)
    Ewepop! Sit (sg.) up!

ewepte (II) it is up

-ewest(u)- speak; talk
  (See lewestu "he speaks," tolewestu "he is speaking.")

-ewot- arrange
  (forms TI verb stems)
  wolewotun (TI) he arranges it well, nicely

ewot-, awot- (PV) back and forth

ewotapilom, awotapilom (AI) he goes back and forth fetching water
  stem 1:   -ewotapilom(o)-, -awotopilom(o)-

't-ewotewolal (TA) he goes back and forth bringing it (an.) out
  stem 1:   -ewotewol-

't-ewotewotun (TI) he goes back and forth bringing it out
  stem 1:   -ewotewot-

ewotonike (AI) he goes back and forth fetching (or bringing out) wood
  stem 1:   -ewotonik(e)-

't-ewotuhulal (TA) he goes back and forth ferrying him
  stem 1:   -ewotuhul-

H

-h(a)- go
  (See -y(a)-.)

haw (P) sure; yes, go ahead
  (Compare aha "yes.")

hesis (A) older brother
  plural: hesisok
  poss: hesisol
  dim: hesossis
    Oliye hesisk. He is going to his older brother's house.
    Hesisol 'kosi iyakul. His older brother likes him.

Hesiskol wikuponil Motahkomikuk. His (deceased) older brother used to live at Indian Township.

hesisuwiw (AI) he is an older brother

-hk from then (or now) on

Katamahk apc nit leyiw. That won't ever happen again.

Nmiyawomols ote tanehk nmace wihqonomonehk nit 'pisun. I have felt better ever since I started to take that medicine.

Musahk koluskakonutomuwahkoc witawsumot. Thou shalt not bear false witness against thy neighbor.

-hkom-, -kom- drive

(forms TI verb stems)

pomkomon he drives it (e.g. a car) along

macehkomon he starts to drive it

hok (I) body

plural: hokiyil, hokihil

poss: hok (may be whok after a vowel)

loc: hokek

dim: hokehsis

Muskessu nhok. I'm breaking out in a rash.

Eci pilsqehsis wolinaqahk hok. The girl's body is very beautiful.

Psi te kisaqote whok. His body was burned all over.

-hom(o)-, -ohom(o)- swim

(forms AI verb stems, type A)

pethom (AI) he approaches by swimming

sakhohom (AI) he swims into view

-hsin(o)- lie down; be lying down

(forms AI verb stems, type B, after preverbs ending in a or e; changes to -ossin(o)- after other preverbs)

ksokahsin (AI) he lies across (something)

lossin (AI) he lies down; he is lying down

-ht_h-, -t_h- hit; strike; chop

(forms TA verb stems)

mattahal (TA) he spanks him; he beats him (in a fight); he hits it (an.) along

-htehm-, -tehm- hit; strike; chop

(forms TI verb stems)

'suhkamkihtehmon (TI) he smashes it to smithereens

-htihik(e)-, -tihik(e)- hit; strike; chop

(forms AI verb stems)

totolihtihike (AI) he is chopping (wood)

hustiwin (A) host (altar bread)

plural: hustiwinok

(variant of ustiwin)

I

't-ihin (TI) he has it

plural: 'tiyultiniya, 'tiyuhtiniya

stem 1: -ih(i)-: ntihinen we (nilun) have it; ihit if he has it

stem 2: ey(i)-: eyit when he had it

(Note: Stem h changes to y before u in plural forms: ktiyultinen we (kilun) have it.)

't-ihkaskuwal (TA) he does not correct him (a child); he does not discipline him (a child)

stem 1: -ihkaskuw-

't-ihkasumal (TA) he does not correct him (a child); he does not discipline him (a child)

stem 1: -ihkasum-

Tokec op skat ihkasumahq, kat op nit 'toleyiwon. If he had not failed to discipline him, he would not have been that way.

't-ihmuwan (DOV) he has something of his (someone else's)

stem 1: -ihmuw-: ihmaht if he (obv.) has something of his (prox.)

stem 2: eymuw-: eymuwit when he had something of mine

Mihtaqsol eymaht 'tapqasokihikonol, ma kisi ksehew wikuwak. When his father had his keys, he couldn't get into his house.

ihtolahte (II) it is always there

stem 1: -ihtolaht(e)-

Ihtolahte 'tul sitomok. His canoe is always on the shore.

ikahawqe (AI) he gets sick

stem 1: -ikahawq(e)-

ikolisoman (A) white man; Englishman

plural: ikolisomanok

(from English, Englishman)

ikolisomanatuwe (AI) he speaks English

stem 1: -ikolisomanatuw(e)-: ntikolisomanatu I speak English

ikotahma, ikotehma, ikotohom (AI) he yawns

plural: ikotahmultuwok, ikotahmuhtuwok, ikotehmultuwok, ikotehmuhtuwok

stem 1: -ikotahm(o)-, -ikotehm(o)-

(without ending: -ikotohom)

(Note also: ikotohok if he yawns, when he yawned; ikotohoc have him yawn.)

Ntotoli ikotohom 'sami ma te nkisqahsinu welaqik. I am yawning because I did not sleep last night.

Ikotahmuk weci litahasit kotuksultipon. Yawn (you two), so he will think that we (kilun, pl.) are sleepy.

imiyakonok (A (pl.)) rosary beads

imiye (AI) he prays

plural: imiyahtuwok

stem 1: -imiy(a)-

stem 3: -miy(a)-: macemiye he begins to pray; nokosamiye he prays quickly

imiyewakon, imiyakon (I) prayer

plural: imiyewakonol, imiyakonol

imiyewikuwam (I) church

plural: imiyewikuwamol

poss: 'timiyewikuwam

loc: imiyewikuwamok

dim: imiyewikuwamsis

Wapilomonhasu ktimiyewikuwamon. Our (kilun) church is painted white.

imiyewissul (A) religious medal
  plural: imiyewissulok
imiyewp (I) holy water
ipa (P) hey!; listen!; look!
  Ipa, pesq mahkuwiyiq. Hey, lend (pl.) me one.
ipis (I) switch (slender, flexible stick); whip
  plural: ipisiyil
  poss: 'tipisim
  loc: ipisik
  dim: ipisis
  Sipsis tehsaqopu ipisik. The bird is sitting on the switch.
  'Kisi qasahkanol ipisiyil. He threw away the switches.
ipocol (P) because; because of course
  Tehpu npahpuwi nuhsuhkuwa, ipocol nmuhsacin. I am only chasing him in jest, because I like him.
  ...mahtoqehs ipocol wapeyu ...because after all a rabbit is white
isikoni- (isikon-) (PV) on one side (only)
  Isikoni sahsaksitehe. He has one shoe off, one shoe on.
isikoniw (P) on one side (only)
isomeqehs A fish hawk; osprey
  plural: isomeqehsuwok
itom (AI) he says
  plural: itomultuwok, itomuhtuwok
  stem 1:   -itom(o)-: itok what he says
  Wasisok ehta nikk itomuk nekomaw wekihtuhtit possiyantehsok. Those kids said they broke the window.
  Keq kitap itom? What did your friend say?
  Wen itok koti macehe? Who said he was going to leave?
't-itomon (TI) he says it
  stem 1:   -itom-
't-iyal (TA) he tells him
  stem 1a: -iy-: ntiyahpon I had told him
  stem 1b: y__h-: yahat if he tells him; yihin tell (sg.) me!
  stem 2:   y__h-: yahat when he told him; yuhut when he was told
  stem 3:   y__h-: nkisi yohoq he told me
  Wen yuhusk koti macehe? Who told you (sg.) he was going to leave?
't-iyalaphal (TA) he tracks him around
  stem 1a: -iyalaph-
  stem 1b: yalaph-
  stem 2:   yalaph-
  (See 't-alaphal.)
iyap (A) buck deer
  plural: iyapihik
  (variant of yap)
iyu (AI, II) he,it is there (or is here)
  plural: iyultuwok, iyuhtuwok (AI)
  stem 1:   -iy(i)-: nti I am here
  stem 2:   ey(i)-: eyit when he was there
  (Note: In stem 1, y may be changed to h before i.)
  Keqsey mehsi skat ihihq wikuwak? Why isn't he at home (literally, at their house)?

Meskat na nekomaw yut iyultihtihq? Why aren't they (pl.) here?
't-iywal (TA) he has him; he has it (an.)
  stem 1:   -iyw-: iywat if he has him
  stem 2:   eyw-: eywat when he had him
  (Note: The stems of 'tiywal undergo the same contractions as stems ending in -uw: eyaht "when he (obv.) had him (prox.).")
  Mihtaqsol iyahc. Let his father have him.

K

-k(i)- look; be of a kind or nature (forms AI verb stems)
  mociku (AI) he is evil
  ksiku (AI) he is ugly
'kaciptun (TI) he takes it by hiding it
  stem 1:   -kacipt-
kaciw (P) secretly; hidden
'kahakonum (I) his door
  (See khakon.)
kahk (P) but; however (emphatic; singles out the preceding word)
  Yut kahk kil 'sami koluwot kmicin. This is too good for you to eat.
  Kotokik ketunkahtihtit, nekom kahk lossin wikok. When the others go out hunting, he lies in his house.
  Tan kahk wen piluwitposit, nokomasitahatomon. But one who has magic powers thinks it easy.
  Nikt kahk nomihqosultuponik nipayiw. Kil spotewi wasis. Those were born at night. You (sg.) are a child of the day.
kahkakomahq (A) brittle white ash (tree)
kahkakuhs (A) crow
  plural: kahkakuhsok
  poss: 'kahkakuhsumol
  dim: kahkakuhsis
kahkeyu (II) it is brittle
  stem 1:   kahkey(i)-
kahpe (I) coffee
  plural: kahpewol
  (from French or English, café, coffee)
kahpehsis (A) coffee pot
  plural: kahpehsisok
kahpotassu (AI) he steps out; he gets off
  stem 1:   -kahpotass(i)-
'kahsapawolal (TA) he rinses it (an.)
  stem 1:   -kahsapawol-
  'Kahsapawola waloti. He rinses the dishes.
kahsicukhike (AI) he wipes dishes
  stem 1:   -kahsicukhik(e)-
'kahsihpulal (TA) he dries him off; he wipes him dry
  Skat wasisok kahsihpulsuhtihtihq, cu ksinukhotuwok. If the children (pl.) do not dry themselves off, they will get sick.
'kahsihputun (TI) he dries it off; he wipes it dry

Kahsihput tuwihput. Dry (sg.) off the table.

kahsiye (II) it fades
stem 1:   kahsiy(a)-

kahtopassu (AI) he gets out of the water
plural: kahtopassultuwok
stem 1:   -kahtopass(i)-

'kakaluwamal (TA) he calls him; he yells to him
stem 1:   -kakaluwam-

kakaluwe (AI) he hollers; he calls out
stem 1:   -kakaluw(e)-: nuci kakaluwet herald

'kakawahkan (AI, AI+OBJ) he throws it fast
stem 1:   -kakawahk(e)-

kakawatqin (II) the water is rough
stem 1:   kakawatqin(o)- type B

kakawessu (AI, II) he, it goes fast
stem 1:   -kakawess(i)-

kakawi- (kakaw-) quickly; fast
kakawwikhike (AI) he writes quickly

kakawiw (P) quickly; fast

kakawiyewiw (II) it goes fast
stem 1:   kakawiyew(i)- type B

kakehsukoniw (P) for many days; for several days

Kakehsukoniw mawe putuwosiniya. For many days they hold a great council meeting together.

kakskus (A) cedar
plural: kakskusiyik
poss: 'kakskusimol
loc: kakskusik
dim: kakskusis

'kalal (TA) he hides him
stem 1:   -kal-: kallopa I hide you (pl.)
                kalsu he hides (himself)

kaltolu (A) quarter dollar
plural: kaltoluwok
(from English, quarter)

kaluhs (A) diamond (in cards)
plural: kaluhsok
(Maliseet)
(from French, carreau)

kamahcin (P) six

kamkamoss (A) barn owl
plural: kamkamossok

kamot op (P) it would be better...

Kamot op nil ntotoliwtoman nikok. It would be better for me to stay home and smoke. (Literally, to be smoking at my home.)

Kamot op knukcoktihiniya kat op kcuwahpahkaliniya. It would be better for you (pl.) to chop me up than for you to throw me in the water.

kamotu (P) all of a sudden
(See komotu.)

'kansuhs (A) old person; person who lived long ago
plural: 'kansuhsuwok
old form: nkansuhs

'kapu (AI) he is blind
(See khapu.)

-kapuw(i)- stand

1) Stems ending in -kapuw(i)- are AI or AI+OBJ stems. They form plural stems in -ult(i)-, -uht(i)-, -iy(a)-, and -iyaht(i)-.

2) The w of -kapuw(i)- is changed to h by some speakers when it is followed by u: tehsahqikapuwu, tehsahqikapuhu "he stands on top."

'tehsahqikapuwin (AI, AI+OBJ) he stands on top of it

'toqcikapuwin (AI, AI+OBJ) he stands on it

uskicikapuwin (AI, AI+OBJ) he stands on the surface of it

usqicikapuwin (AI, AI+OBJ) he straddles it

kaskimikikone (AI) he has chest pains

kaskolosihil (I) (pl.) kelp

kat (A) eel
plural: katiyik, katihik
poss: 'katimol
dim: katehsis
misselihkat (A) sand-worm (found in clam-flats)

Nomiya katihi alamahawolotihtit qospemok. He saw eels zigzagging through the water in the lake.

kat (I) leg (including the foot)
plural: katol
poss: 'kat, 'qat his leg
dim: katsis
Eliksok 'qatsisol. His little legs are cute.
Ntokotomuwan 'kat. I hit his leg.
Kat kat! Hide your (sg.) leg!

kat (P) not (used to deny an identification; compare ma, kotama "not")

kat te not at all: Kat te keq lawotiw. He is not worth anything at all.

kat op will not, would not
Kat op apc nkisi monessiw. I will not be able to get off of here again.

Kat op keq ktolessiw. Nothing will happen to you (sg.)

Kat nihtol 'temisol. That is not his dog.

Kat not kil kikuwoss. That is not your (sg.) mother.

kat cipotu, kat cipotuk, kat cuwitpotu (II (?)) it should not be; it had better not be
(See cipotu "it could be; maybe; perhaps.")
Kat cuwitpotu 'peciyanehpon not ehpit. That woman should not have come here.

kat olu (P) of course
Wen nit eli npakotask? ---Kat olu Piyel. Who fibbed to you? ---Peter of course.

katama (P) no; not
(See "kotama".)

katekon (P) not at all
Katekon wolitahatomuwon. He does not like it at all.

kathucin (AI) he ducks (to hide)
plural: kathucinuhtuwok

stem 1:   -kathucin(o)-: kathucinuk they (dual) duck; kathucit when he ducked

kathucu (AI) he ducks (to hide)
plural: kathucultuwok
stem 1:   -kathuc(i)-: nkathucipon we (nilun, dual) duck; kathucit when he ducked

katkuhk (A) cooking pot
plural: katkuhkok
poss: 'katkuhkomol, 'katkuhkol, 'tahkatkuhkomol
loc: katkuhkok
dim: katkuksis

katok (P) than
Nisokehs oli seskapewiw katok op sakom. He is twice as handsome as a chief would be. (Literally, he is two times more handsome-looking than a chief would be.)

katte (II) it is hidden
stem 1:   katt(e)-: kattetul they (inan.) are hidden

'katun (TI) he hides it
stem 1:   -kat-
Ehqi katuk otuhkey. Stop hiding (pl.) the deer meat.

'katuwan (DOV) he hides it from him; he hides something of his (someone else's)
stem 1:   -katuw-
Nit kikuwosson katakun kuthakon. Our (kilun) mother will hide your (sg.) paddle.

kaw (A) porcupine quill
plural: kawiyik

kawatokup (I) spruce beer

kawatoq (A) skunk spruce
plural: kawatokuk
poss: 'kawatokumol
loc: kawatokuk
dim: kawatoqis, kawatokuhsis

kaweyu (AI, II) it is rough
stem 1:   -kawey(i)-

kawihuke (AI) he has porcupine quills on him
stem 1:   -kawihuk(e)-

kawis (A) burdock (plant or seed pod)
plural: kawisok
poss: 'kawisomol, 'kawisumol
loc: kawisok
dim: kawisossis

-kawot(i)- walk (of two individuals)
(See -hkawot(i)-.)
pomkawotuwok (AI) they (dual) walk along

kceyawi (kceyaw-) (PV) much; many
prefixed form: -kihceyawi (-kihceyaw-)
neke form: kehceyawi (kehceyaw-)

kceyawiw (AI, II) there is a lot of it
stem 1a: -kihceyaw(i)- type B
stem 1b: kceyaw(i)-
stem 2:   kehceyaw(i)-: kehceyawik when there was a lot of it
kceyawiwol there are many of them (inan.)
kceyawiwok there are many of them (an.)

kci kakak (A) raven
plural: kci kakakok

kci (kc-, kt-) (PV, PN) big; great; old
prefixed form: -kihci- (-kihc-, -kiht-)
neke form: kehci- (kehc-, keht-)
Sepawonu koti kci mawi epeskomhotin. Tomorrow there is going to be a big general ball game.
Moskuwan 'kihci sakomal. He found his great chief.

kci kotqesit (I) big toe
poss: 'kihci kotqesit

Kci Skehewahtoq (I) Good Friday

kcihq (I) woods; forest
plural: kcihkul, kcihqiyil
poss: 'kihcihkum, 'kihcihqem
loc: kcihkuk, kcihqek
dim: kcihkuhsis, kcihqehsis

kcikotone (AI) he is old
plural: kcikotonhotuwok
stem 1a: -kihcikoton(e)-: nkihcikoton I am old
stem 1b: kcikoton(e)-: kcikotonet if he is old
stem 2:   kehcikoton(e): kehcikotonet when he was old
Tokec op pomawsitsopon neke, kis op kcikotoniya. If he was alive then, he was old.

kcimkatoke (II) there is thick growth
stem 1:   kcimkatok(e)-
stem 2:   kehcimkatok(e)-

kciqaha (A) head (of a business, office, etc.)

kcitqihikon (A) bread cooked directly in coals
plural: kcitqihikonok

kcoci (P) all alike; nothing but
Kcoci te yut sahthil eyik. There is nothing but blueberries here.
Kcoci te yukk skicinuwok, ma te wapeyicik. These are all Indians, not white men.

kcoskuwesu (AI) his hair burns off
stem 1a: -koccoskuwes(i)-
stem 1b: kcoskuwes(i)-
stem 2:   keccoskuwes(i)-

kcoskuwete (II) its hair burns off
stem 1:   kcoskuwet(e)-
stem 2:   keccoskuwet(e)-

kecalokiqat (AI) the edge of his eye
kecalokiqay the edge of my eye
Nkocalokiq. I think I have something in the corner of my eye.

'keccopskahal (TA) he uproots it (an.)
stem 1:   -keccopsk_h-

'keccopskehlal (TA) he uproots it (an.)
stem 1:   -keccopskehl-

'keccopskehtun (TI) he uproots it
stem 1:   -keccopskeht-

keckuluwiw (AI) he has a cold; he catches a cold
stem 1:   -keckuluw(i)- type B
(from English, catch cold)

kehci (kehc-, keht-) (PV) big; great; old
(See kci.)

kehkimsu (AI) he teaches himself
plural: kehkimsultuwok
stem 1a: -okehkims(i)-
stem 1b: kehkims(i)-
stem 2: ekehkims(i)-
(See 't-okehkimal "he teaches him.")
kehsahqonasu (II) it is so many yards (cloth measure)
stem 1: kehsahqonas(i)-
kehsalke (AI) he digs so much
stem 1: -kehsalk(e)-
(See walke "he digs.")
kehsalokamqahk (P) millions
kamachin kehsalokamqahk six million
kehsatokot (II) it is so long (said of something string-like)
stem 1: kehsatokot(o)-
kehsi (kehs-, kes-) (PV) X much, X many
(X represents a number or quantity.)
Tan tehc kehsalkiyin naka tan kehsi ksomonot wot opos, kat tehc kmosoniw. However much you (sg.) dig and however much you push on this tree, you (sg.) will not catch me.
Oluwikonok kehsuwok (kehsiwok) etololukhoticik. There are seven of them working.
kehsikotonewiw (II) it is so many years old
stem 1: kehsikotonew(i) type B
kehsintu (AI) he sings so much
stem 1: -kehsint(u)-
kehsuhsalqot (II) it is so many miles (land measure)
stem 1: kehsuhsalqot(o)-
Yut olu te 'ci macahat tokki utenek, oluwikonok kehsuhsalqot. When one goes from here to town, it is seven miles.
kehtahqehe (AI) he is dizzy
stem 1: -kehtahq_h(a)-
(variants: kiltahqehe; kiwtahqehe; kihtalqehe; kiltalqehe; kiwtalqehe)
kehtaqs (A) ghost
plural: kehtaqsuwok
poss: 'kehtaqsumol
dim: kehtaqsossis
kehtepsulu (AI) he hiccups
stem 1: -kehtepsul(i)-: nkehtepsul I hiccup
keka (P) almost, nearly; soon; practically, all but;
(Note: Indicates something still incomplete--action is still going on. Compare eluwe.)
Keka knehpihi. You (sg.) are almost killing me.
Keka te mehcine. He is almost dead.
Keka te nis aciye. It is almost two o'clock.
Keka te psi wen pomoka. Almost everyone has danced (so far).
kekesk (P) a little; slightly
kekeskossis a very little; very slightly
Kekesk apskapu. He opens his eyes a little.
Milin kekesk. Give (sg.) me a little bit.

'kekiw (P) all day
'kekoluhke (AI) he works all day
stem 1a: -nokkekoluhk(e)-: nokkekoluhk I work all day
stem 1b: 'kekoluhk(e)-
stem 2: nekkekoluhk(e)-: nekkekoluhket one who works all day
(Compare 'kekiw all day.)
Kelisk Calais, Maine (Locative)
Kelusit
(See Keluwosit.)
Keluwosit, Kelusit (A) God
obv: Keluwosilicil, Kelusilicil
kenoq, kenuk, qenoq (P) but; however
Pal nomiyal muwinuwol, kenoq ma te nomiyawiyil Mali. Paul saw a bear, but Mary did not see it.
keq, keqoss, keqsey (I) (PRO) what; something
Keq leyu? What happened?
Keq nit? What is that (inan.)?
Keqoss oc eleyik cuwi leyu tehc na nokosayiw. What is to happen should happen right away.
Keq ktotoli oluhk? What are you doing?
'keskuhtehkuwal (TA) he comes upon him
stem 1: -keskuhtehkuw-
kespiw (P) accidentally
kespoqsu (AI) he oversleeps
stem 1: -kespoqs(i)-
kesq (P) while; as
Kesq etolihpultihtit, macelan. While they (pl.) were eating, it started to rain.
'kessal (TA) he cuts so much of it (an.); he cuts it (an.) into so many pieces
stem 1: -kess-
Kis nihtol sukolopanol kamahcin 'kessal. He has already cut the cake into six pieces.
'kessomon (TI) he cuts so much of it; he cuts it into so many pieces
stem 1: -kessom-: neke kessok when he cut it into so many pieces.
Tan 'kessomon wiyuhs? How much meat did he cut?
kestokot (II) it is so long (said of something string-like)
'ketapitehlal (TA) he extracts his (someone else's) tooth
stem 1: -ketapitehl-
kete (P) for example
Anuwit kete mehtoluhke. Anna, for example, has stopped working.
ketkosewe (AI) he unloads a gun
stem 1: -ketkosew(e)-
ketolaskessu (AI) it (an.) slips off
stem 1: -ketolaskess(i)-
Ktopinuwan te eli ketolaskessilit epeskomakonol 'pihtinok. Watch (sg.) the way the baseball slips off his hand.
ketsewe (AI) he undresses
plural: ketsewhotuwok, ketsewahtuwok
stem 1: -ketsew(e)-

'ketsewhutolal (TA) he undresses him
  stem 1: -ketsewhutol-
'kettahal (TA) he chops it (an.) off
  stem 1: -kett_h-
'kettehmon (TI) he chops it off
  stem 1: -kettehm-
  bare stem -kett_h-: kettohok when he chops it off
  without ending kettem: neke kettem long ago when I chopped it off
khakon (I) door
  plural: khakonol
  poss: 'kahakonum
  loc: khakonok
  dim: khakonossis
khapu, 'kapu (AI) he is blind
  plural: khapultuwok, 'kapultuwok
  stem 1a: -nikhap(i)-, -nihkap(i)-: nikhap, nihkap I am blind
  stem 1b: khap(i)-, 'kap(i)-: khapit, 'kapit if he is blind
  stem 2: nekhap(i)-, nehkap(i)-: nekhapit, nehkapit when he was blind
  stem 3: -nkhap(i)-, -nkap(i)-
Kakawi nkhapuhpon ewasisuwit. He was more nearly blind when he was young.
-kihci (-kihc-, -kiht-) (PV, PN) big; great; old
  unprefixed form: kci (kc-, kt-)
  neke form: kehci (kehc-, keht-)
  (See kci.)
'kihka ('kihkay-)
  (See -nokka)
kihkan (I) garden
  plural: kihkanol
  poss: 'tahkihkan
  loc: kihkanok
  dim: kihkansis
'kihkane (AI) it (an.) is completely dead; he dies completely
  plural: 'kihkanhotuwok, 'kihkanahtuwok they (an.) are all dead
  stem 1a: -nokkan(e)-: nokkanan it (an.) dies completely (Relative)
  stem 1b: 'kihkan(e)-
  stem 2: nekkan(e)-: nekkanet when it (an.) died completely
'Kihkanhotossultu nicankokk. All his poor little children are dead.
'kihkaqosu (AI) he burns himself
  (See 'kihkayaqosu.)
'kihkaqote (II) it gets burned
  (See 'kihkayaqote.)
'kihkayaqosu (AI) it (an.) burns up
  stem 1a: -nokkayaqos(i)-
  stem 1b: 'kihkayaqos(i)-
  stem 2: nekkayaqos(i)-
  stem 3: nkihkayaqos(i)-
'kihkayaqote (II) it burns up
  stem 1: 'kihkayaqot(e)-
  stem 2: nekkayaqot(e)-
  stem 3: nkihkayaqot(e)-

kihke (AI) he plants
  plural: kikhotuwok, kihkahtuwok
  stem 1a: -ahkihk(e)-: ntahkihk I plant
  stem 1b: kihk(e)-
  stem 2: ekihk(e)-: ekihket when he was planting
  stem 3: -ahkihk(e)-, -kihk(e)-: kisahkihke, kiskihke he planted
Ekihket on 'peci ksinuhkan. When he was planting, he got sick.
'kihtomatomon (TI) he does not feel like doing it; he is disinclined to do it
  stem 1a: -kihtomatom-
  stem 1b: ktomatom-
  stem 2: kehtomatom-: kehtomatok when he did not feel like doing it
Skat 'sami ktomatomuwan, ntolluhkanc. If I'm not too tired to want to do it, I'll do it.
'kikahal (TA) he heals him
  stem 1: -kik_h-
kikcokapitehe (AI) he is teething
  stem 1: -kikcokapit_h(a)-
kikcokapskotiyehputikon (A) sculpin
  plural: kikcokapskotiyehputikonok
kikcokiye (AI) he itches
  plural: kikcokiyahtuwok
  stem 1: -kikcokiy(a)-
kikehtahsu (AI) he heals (someone)
  plural: kikehtahsultuwok
  stem 1: -kikehtahs(i)-
'Tapsakiyal nuci kikehtahsilicil. He went to see the doctor (literally, the healer).
kikehtasu (II) it is healed
  stem 1: kikehtas(i)-
'kikehtun (TI) he heals it
  stem 1: -kikeht-
kikihike (AI) he heals (someone)
  stem 1: -kikihik(e)-
'kikimapomal TA he looks at him secretly
  stem 1: -kikimapom-
kikimi (kikim-) (PV) secretly; stealthily; silently
  kikimi macephuwe (AI) he runs away without making any noise
kikimskahsu (AI) he moves along without making any noise
  plural: kikimskahsultuwok
  stem 1: -kikimskahs(i)-
kikimuwasu (AI) he whispers
  plural: kikimuwasultuwok, kikimuwasuhtuwok
  stem 1: -kikimuwaş(i)-
kikociw (P) in the corner; at the corner
kil (A) (PRO) you (sg.); your, yours (sg.)
  plural: kiluwaw you (pl.); kilun we (including you)
  kila you (sg.) (emphatic)
kilun (A) (PRO) we, us (including you); our, ours (including you)
  (Compare nilun.)

'kiluwahal (TA) he looks for him
　　(See 'qiluwahal.)
'kiluwapomal (TA) he looks for him (with his eyes); he tries to catch sight of him
　　(See 'qiluwapomal.)
kiluwaw (A) (PRO) you (pl.); your, yours (pl.)
kinahant (A) devil; fearless person
　　plural:　　kinahantuwok
kinahqisomuwe (AI) he has big antlers
　　stem 1:　　-kinahqisomuw(e)
kinalokiqe (AI) he has big eyes
　　plural:　　kinalokiqahtuwok,
　　　　　　　　kinalokiqawolotuwok
　　stem 1:　　-kinalokiq(a)-
　　Elomi motapewset puskonikonihkuk, on nomiyan kinalokiqalicil coqolsol. When he was walking down the hill by the graveyard, he saw a big-eyed frog.
kinapiw (AI) he is brave
　　stem 1:　　-kinap(i)- type B
kinapskosu (AI) he is fat
　　plural:　　kinapskosultuwok,
　　　　　　　　kinapskosuhtuwok
　　stem 1:　　-kinapskos(i)-
　　'Sami kinapskosuhtu nicanuwa, 'cuwi monuhmoniya piley utapakonuwa. Because their children were fat, they had to buy a new car.
kinhoke (AI) she is pregnant
　　plural:　　kinhokahtuwok,
　　　　　　　　kinhokawolotuwok
　　stem 1:　　-kinhok(a)-
　　Eci kinhokat ehpit, eci mili kotuhtok. When a woman is pregnant, she is always craving some kind of food.
kini (kin-) (PV) big
　　kinahqot (II) it is big around
　　kinaksone, kinkosone (AI) he has big shoes;
　　kintune (AI) he has a big mouth
　　kintaqsu (AI) he talks big
'kinikonomon (TI) he grows it bigger
　　stem 1:　　-kinikonom-
kinkihqon (II) it is big
　　stem 1:　　kinkihqon(o)-
kinkil (AI) he is big
　　plural:　　kinkilultuwok, kinkiluhtuwok
　　stem 1:　　-kinkil(o)-
　　Kinkilul musuwol nehpahacil. The moose that he killed is big.
　　Nomiya kinkilok otuhk. I see a big deer.
kinskute (II) it is a big field
　　stem 1:　　kinskut(e)-
kinskutenoma (AI) he has a big field
　　plural:　　kinskutenomahtuwok
　　stem 1:　　-kinskutenom(a)-
kinsonu (AI) he is strong
　　stem 1:　　-kinson(i)-
'kinuwehlal (TA) he notifies him; he makes it (an.) in his own special way
　　stem 1:　　-kinuwehl-
kinuwehlosuwiw (II) it announces itself
　　stem 1:　　-kinuwehlosuw(i)- type B

　　Kat olu ktahkomiq oli kinuwehlosuwiw tahalu tap elakiyat. Land announces itself, as you know, like the curve in a bow.
kinuwehtahsu (AI) he delivers a message
　　plural:　　kinuwehtahsultuwok
　　stem 1:　　-kinuwehtahs(i)-
kinuwehtahsuwin (A) messenger
　　plural:　　kinuwehtahsuwinuwok
　　Ktoluwehkuhu¹pahc kotunkewinuwok naka kinuwehtahsuwinuwok. I will use you as hunters and messengers.
'kinuwehtun (TI) he announces it; he does it in his own special way
　　stem 1:　　-kinuweht-
'kinuwehtuwal (TA) he informs him
　　stem 1:　　-kinuwehtuw-
kinuwitpiye (II) it happens sometimes
　　stem 1:　　kinuwitpiy(a)-
kinuwosu (AI) he is a certain one; he is a particular one
　　plural:　　kinuwosultuwok,
　　　　　　　　kinuwosuhtuwok
　　stem 1:　　-kinuwos(i)-
　　Kinuwosu litposuwin eliyat Sipayik. A particular council member is going to Pleasant Point, Maine.
kinuwot (II) it is a particular one
　　stem 1:　　kinuwot(o)- type A
kipiye (AI) he falls over
　　stem 1:　　-kipiy(a)-
　　Espons 'kocicihtun elihc opos kipiyat, nit te na nekom macahan. Raccoon knows that the tree will fall over, and then he will leave.
kiposs (A) orphan (one or both parents dead)
　　plural:　　kipossok
　　dim:　　kipossis
kis (P) already; yet
　　Kis nomihtasu ktahkomiq? Can land be seen yet?
　　Peciyat wikihtitpon, tehpu meskok sqotewamq; naka cel kis tkiye. When he comes to where they had lived, he finds only ashes; and they have already become cold, too.
　　Kis kisuhs? Can you (sg.) walk already?
'kisahkan (AI, AI + OBJ) he threw it; he can throw it
　　stem 1:　　-kisahk(e)-
　　Nkisahkanok cikoniyik pskihqihkuk. I threw the apples onto the grass.
　　Nutahket 'kisahkanol epeskomakonol, kenoq ma te nihtuphawiyil nuci ntuptasit. The pitcher threw the ball, but the catcher did not catch it.
'kisahkewan (DOV) he threw it for him; he threw it to him
kisahqew (P) uphill
　　Kisahqew olomihkawotuwok. They (dual) have walked up the hill.
'kisahsomal (TA) he fed him
　　(See 't-ahsomal "he feeds him.")
　　(variant of 'kissomal)

'kisamihkuhtuwal (TA) he threw him off (in wrestling); he can throw him off (in wrestling)
  stem 1:   -kisamihkuhtuw-
kisamikotokku (AI) he jumped up; he can jump up
  stem 1:   -kisamikotoqq(i)-
  (Note: qq changes to kk before u.)
'kisamoqehlal (TA) he wronged him
  stem 1:   -kisamoqehl-
'kisaqsal (TA) he carved it (an.)
  'Kisaqsal weyossisol 'tahakonok. He carved a little animal on a paddle.
'kisehtun (TI) he did it; he can do it
  stem 1:   -kiseht-
'kisehtuwan (DOV) he made him do it
'kisekehlal (TA) he spread (an., sheetlike) it out
  stem 1:   -kisekehl-
'kiseltomuwal (TA) he lets him; he allows him; he permits him
kishike (AI) he shot
  plural: kishikhotuwok, kishikahtuwok
  stem 1:   -kishik(e)-
kisi (kis-) (PV) (indicates completion or past time)
  kiskihke, kisahkihke (AI) he planted
kisi (kis-) (PV) can; be able to
  kiskihke, kisahkihke (AI) he can plant
'kisihtun (TI) he made it; he can make it
  stem 1:   -kisiht-
'kisikapuwehlal (TA) he stood him; he erected it (an.)
  stem 1:   -kisikapuwehl-
kisikon (II) it is full grown; it is mature
  stem 1:   kisikon(o)-
kisiku (AI) he is full grown
  stem 1:   -kisik(i)-
'kisisol (A) (dep.) his aunt
  nkisis my aunt
'kisitahatomon (TI) he decides on it
  'Kocoskuwalawal Koluskapiyil, on 'kisitahatomoniya nehpahaniya. They were jealous of Koluskap, and they decided to kill him.
'kisiyal (TA) he made it (an.); he can make it (an.)
  stem 1:   -kisiy-
kiskatom (AI) he got married
  stem 1:   -kiskatom(o)- type A
kiskot (II) it is low tide
  stem 1:   kiskot(o)-
kisolan (II) it rained
  stem 1:   kisolan(o)-: kisolak when it rained
'kisolumal (TA) he decided about him
  stem 1:   -kisolum-
'kisonuhmon (TI) he bought it
  (See monuhmon "he buys it.")
'kisonuhmuwewan (DOV) he bought it for him; he can buy it for him
kisotemu (AI) he cried; he can cry
  plural: kisotemultuwok, kisotemuhtuwok
  stem 1:   -kisotem(i)-

'kispekehlal (TA) he sprinkled him; he can sprinkle him
  stem 1:   -kispekehl-
  Ehpit yaq mace wolehlan weci kispekehlut naka 'punan kuhutik. The woman, they say, prepared him to be sprinkled (with holy water), and put him on the bed.
'kispekehlal (TA) he sprinkled him; he can sprinkle him
  Ehpit yaq mace wolehlan weci kispekehlut naka 'punan kuhutik. The woman, they say, started to prepare him (a dead man) so that he could be sprinkled (with holy water), and she put him on the bed.
kisq (I) day
  plural: kiskul
  poss: 'kiskum
  Sitan 'kiskum pemkiskahk. Today is the Feast of St. Ann.
'kissihpilal (TA) he gave him medicine
  (See 't-ahsihpilal "he gives him medicine.")
kiste (II) it is finished; it is ready
  stem 1:   kist(e)-
  Kiste wtoposonut. Her basket is finished.
kistehsin (AI) he fell; he got into an accident
  plural: kistehsinultuwok, kistehsinuhtuwok
  stem 1:   -kistehsin(o)-
  Toli kistehsinuk Sipayik ali wiwoniphut atomupilok. They (dual) got into an accident at Pleasant Point, Maine, when they were riding around in a car.
kistehsu (AI) he fell; he got into an accident
  plural: kistehsultuwok
  stem 1:   -kistehs(i)-
  Tama toli kistehsu nekom? Where did he fall down?
  Nkosiciyak eli kistehsihtit kisahqew. I know that they (dual) got into an accident up the hill.
kisuhs (A) sun; moon; month
  plural: kisuhsok
  poss: 'kisuhsomol
  loc: kisuhsok
  dim: kisuhsis
  Etutahsit kisuhs pemkiskahk. The sun is very hot today.
kisuwupeq (I) warm spring (of water)
  plural: kisuwupeqol
  loc: kisuwupekuk
kittakon (A) file (for working wood or metal)
  plural: kittakonok
'kiwacehlal (TA) he makes him lonely
  stem 1:   -kiwacehl-
kiwacinaqot (II) it looks lonely
  stem 1:   kiwacinaqot(o) type A
  Neqt pemkiskahk, Koluskap peciyat oqimuwi utenek, komac kiwacinaqot. One day, Koluskap arrives at the loon village-- it looks very lonely.
kiwaciye (AI) he is lonely
  stem 1:   -kiwaciy(a)-

kiwhos (A) muskrat
  plural: kiwhosuwok
  poss: 'kiwhosumol
  loc: kiwhosuhsis
kiwhosuhke (AI) he hunts muskrats; he traps muskrats
  plural: kiwhosukhotuwok, kiwhosuhkahtuwok
  stem 1:   -kiwhosuhk(e)-
kiwonik (A) otter
kiyahq (A) seagull
  plural: kiyahqok, kiyahqiyik
  poss: 'kiyahqomol, 'kiyahkumol, 'kiyahqemol
  dim: kiyaqsis, kiyahqehsis
kiyahqiw (P) straight
'kocalokiqawon (I) (dep.) the edge of his eye
  (Compare kecalokiqat.)
'kocicihtun (TI) he knows it
  (See 'kosicihtun "he knows it.")
'kocicihtuwan (DOV) he knows something of his; he knows something about him
  (also: 'kosicihtuwan)
  Nit olu wen kcicihtuwat ewapolikok, nostuhmonc. Then if anyone knows anything wrong about him, he will make it known.
  Kotama 'kocicihtuwawoniya tan 'toli piluwitposilin. They did not know of his supernatural power.
'kociciyal (TA) he knows him; he knows (someone else) what he is like
  (See 'kosiciyal "he knows him.")
  'Kociciyal eli wasisol alatuwelit oposik. He knows that the child is climbing around in the tree.
kocokikilahs (A) chickadee
  plural: kocokikilahsuwok
  dim: kocokikilahsis
'kocoskehlal (TA) he lets him loose
  stem 1a: -kocoskehl-
  stem 1b: kcoskehl-
  stem 2:   kecoskehl-
'kocoskeksomon (TI) he nearly cuts it (a part of his body), but misses
  stem 1:   -kocoskeksom-: kocoskeksok if he nearly cuts it
  stem 2:   kecokeksom-: kecoskeksok when he nearly cut it
'kocoskuwalal (TA) he is jealous of him
  stem 1a: -kocoskuwal-
  stem 1b: kcoskuwal-: kcoskuwalat if he is jealous of him
  stem 2:   kecoskuwal-: kecoskuwalat when he was jealous of him
  'Kocoskuwalal eli piyemitposilit katop nekom. He is jealous of him because he has more power than he does.
kokepse (AI) he is deaf
  (See okepse.)
  Nehtaw psiw kokepsahtihtit, kat oc knutakuwihik. If they are all deaf, they won't hear you (sg.).

'kolahman (AI+OBJ) he keeps anyone from using it
  stem 1:   -kolahm(a)-
  stem 2:   kelahm(a)-
  'Kolahman 'kihtahkomikum. He keeps anyone from using his land.
'kolahmuwal (TA) he stops him (from doing something)
  stem 1:   -kolahmuw-: nkolahmaq he stops me
  stem 2:   kelahmuw-: kelahmaht when he (obv.) stopped him (prox.)
  Mihtaqsol eqeci kolahmaht, cikawessu. When his father tried to stop him, he went right ahead.
'kolamuksisol (A) (dep.) his uncle
  (also: 'tolamuksisol)
kolaptan (A) blacksmith
  plural: kolaptanok
  (Maliseet)
kolaqhikon (I) ankle
  plural: kolaqhikonol
  poss: 'kolaqhikon, 'qolaqhikon his ankle
kolhikon (I) trap
  plural: kolhikonol
  poss: 'kolhikonum
  loc: kolhikonok
  dim: kolhikonossis
  Kiwhos kolomu kolhikonok. The muskrat is caught in the trap.
koli (kol-) (PV)
  (variant of toli "is ...-ing")
  koliwtome (AI) he is smoking (=toliwtome)
'kolikatomon (TI) he hogs it (food)
  stem 1:   -kolikatom-
  stem 2:   kelikatom-
kolike (AI) he hogs food
  stem 1:   -kolik(e)-
  stem 2:   kelik(e)-
'kolikonatenal (TA) he holds him by the leg(s)
  stem 1:   -kolikonaten-
  stem 2:   kelikonaten-
'kolinskenal (TA) he takes his (someone else's) arm
  stem 1:   -kolinsken-
  stem 2:   kelinsken-
'koliptinenal (TA) he holds his (someone else's) hand(s)
  stem 1:   -koliptinen-
  stem 2:   keliptinen-
'kolocomulal (TA) he freezes it (an.)
  stem 1:   -kolocomul-
  stem 2:   kelocomul-
kolocomutikon (A) refrigerator; freezer
  plural: kolocomutikonok
  poss: 'kolocomutikonol
  loc: kolocomutikonok
  dim: kolocomutikonis
'kolocomutun (TI) he freezes it
  stem 1:   -kolocomut-
  stem 2:   kelocomut: kelocomutaq when he froze it

kolocoqe (AI) he is stuck
   plural: kolocoqahtuwok,
                kolocoqawolotuwok
   stem 1:   -kolocoq(e)-
   stem 2:   kelocoq(e)-
kolocu (AI) he, it (an.) freezes
   stem 1:   -koloc(i)-
   stem 2:   keloc(i)-
kolomu (AI, II) he, it sticks; he, it is stuck, caught
   stem 1:   -kolom(i)-
   stem 2:   kelom(i)-
'kolonal (TA) he holds onto him
   stem 1:   -kolon-
   stem 2:   kelon-
'kolonalokossenal, kolalokossenal (TA) he holds his (someone else's) ear(s)
   stem 1:   -kolonalokossen-
   stem 2:   kelonalokossen-
'kolonomahsin (AI, AI+OBJ) he goes on an errand to get it
   plural: 'kolonomahsinultiniya,
                'kolonomahsinuhtiniya
   stem 1:   -kolonomahs(i)-:
                kolonomahsin, kolonomahsu
                he goes on an errand
   stem 2:   kelonomahs(i)-: kelonomahsit
                when he went on an errand
   Nkolonomahsinol masqositol naka pocetesol. I went on an errand to get beans and potatoes.
'kolonomuwan (DOV) he holds onto something of his (someone else's); he holds onto it for him
   stem 1:   -kolonomuw-
   stem 2:   kelonomuw-
   'Kolonomuwan toqiw wonoski, naka 'poneqahkan eli psikapskiyak nisonul kci ponapskul. He holds onto him by both wings and throws him down into a crack between two big rocks.
'kolonomuwewal (TA) he gets something for him
   stem 1:   -kolonomuwew-
   stem 2:   kelonomuwew-
koloqehtamu (AI) he swallows
   plural: koloqehtamultuwok,
                koloqehtamuhtuwok
   stem 1:   -koloqehtam(i)-
   stem 2:   keloqehtam(i)-
koloqesson, koloqoskesson (II) it is twisted out of joint (of a bone)
   stem 1:   koloqesson(o)- type A
   stem 2:   keloqesson(o)-
koloqessu (II) it is twisted out of joint (of a bone)
   stem 1:   koloqess(i)-
   stem 2:   keloqess(i)
koloton (II) it freezes
   stem 1:   koloton(o)-
   stem 2:   keloton(o)-: kelotok when it
                was frozen

koluhtom (AI) he doubts
   stem 1:   -koluhtom(o)- type A
   stem 2:   keluhtom(o)-
'kolulal (TA) he argues with him: he scolds him
   stem 1:   -kolul-
   stem 2:   kelul-
   Kil te koluls! Argue with yourself!
   Kat cuwitpotu kolulin eci kotuhsomi. You (sg.) should not argue with me when I have been drinking.
'kolultiniyal (AI, AI+OBJ) he argues with him
   (from kolultuwok (AI) they (dual) argue (with each other), reciprocal form of 'kolulal "he argues with him")
   woli kolultiniyal (AI) he makes up with him after an argument
'koluluwewal (TA) he speaks for him
   stem 1:   -koluluwew-
   stem 2:   keluluwew-
'koluskakonimal (TA) he lies about him
   stem 1:   -koluskakonim-
   stem 2:   keluskakonim-
'koluskakonutomuwal (TA) he tells someone something false about him; he lies about him
   stem 1:   -koluskakonutomuw-
   stem 2:   keluskakonutomuw-
koluskapiw (AI) he exaggerates or lies a lot: he tells tall tales
   stem 1:   -koluskap(i)- type B
   stem 2:   keluskap(i)-
kolusku (AI) he lies
   plural: koluskultuwok, koluskuhtuwok
   stem 1:   -kolusk(i)-
   stem 2:   kelusk(i)-
   Weci mamselessit eli koluskit. He got into trouble because he lied.
koluwosu (AI) he is capable, useful for something; he is good for something; it (an.) is good for use
   plural: koluwosultuwok,
                koluwosuhtuwok
   stem 1:   -koluwos(i)-
   stem 2:   keluwos(i)-
komac (P) very much
   Komac Mali wisoki maleyu. Mary was very, very lazy.
   Nkocicihtun eleyiyin, kil komac mocahant. I know what you are like you terrible devil.
   Komac sikoluhke eqeci kisi kettuhusit. She worked very hard trying to cut herself loose.
'komaseyu (II) it is easy to do
   stem 1a: -nokomasey(i)-
   stem 1b: 'komasey(i)-
   stem 2:   nekomasey(i)-
   stem 3:   nkomasey(i)-
'komasi ('komas-) (PV) easy; easily
   prefixed form: -nokomasi (-nokomas-)
   neke form: nekomasi (nekomas-)
   combining form: nkomasi (nkomas-)
'komasopu (AI) he is accessible (physically); it (an.) is easy to get at

stem 1a: -nokomasop(i)-: nokomasopin it (an.) is easy to get at (Relative)
stem 1b: ˋkomasop(i)-
stem 2: nekomasop(i)-: nekomasopit when it (an.) was easy to get at
ˋkomaste, nkomaste (II) it is easy to get at
komiwon (II) it rains
stem 1: komiwon(o)- type A
stem 2: kemiwon(o)-: kemiwok when it rained
komiwonisiye (II) it sprinkles (rain)
stem 1: komiwonisiy(a)-
stem 2: kemiwonisiy(a)-
komoku (AI) he swims down under the water
plural: komokultuwok, komokuhtuwok
stem 1: -komoq(i)-
stem 2: kemoq(i)-
(Note: q changes to k before u.)
komoqiye (AI) he drowns
plural: komoqiyawolotuwok
stem 1: -komoqiy(a)-
stem 2: kemoqiy(a)-
Komoqiyahsu wasis qeci olhok monihkuk. The poor little child drowned when he tried to swim to the island.
komoqotkuhu (AI) he dives
plural: komoqotkuhultuwok
stem 1: -komoqotq_h(i)- type A
stem 2: kemoqotqih(i)-
(Note: q changes to k before u.)
Qeci kci ponapskuk ˋci komqotkuhultuwok. They (pl.) are trying to dive off of the big rock.
komotu, kamotu (P) all of a sudden
Kesq yaq etoli wolaqahqosultihtit, komotu yaq sakhi contomhak kukec utapakon. While they (pl.) were cooking supper, they say, all of a sudden the game warden's car pulled up and stopped.
komuci (komuc-, komut-) (PV) secretly
neke form: kemuci (kemuc-, kemut-)
ˋkomuci macephal (TA) he takes him away secretly
ˋkomuciphal (TA) he sneaks him away
stem 1: -komuciph-
stem 2: kemuciph-
ˋkomuciptun (TI) he sneaks it away
stem 1: -komucipt-
stem 2: kemucipt-
ˋkomutonalal (TA) he steals him, it (an.); he kidnaps him
stem 1: -komutonal-
stem 2: kemutonal-
Apaciyat, uhkomossol Muwinesqiyil naka Nimaqsuwehsuwol komutonalakk. When he returns, his grandmother She-bear and Sable have been kidnapped.
ˋkomutonan (AI, AI + OBJ) he steals it
plural: ˋkomutonahtiniya (AI + OBJ)
stem 1: -komuton(e)-: nkomutunepon we (nilun, dual) steal

stem 2: kemuton(e)-: kemutonet when he stole it; when he stole
Neke kemutonet atomupil, cuwi naci kpahasu. When he stole the car, he had to go to jail.
Komutonahtuwok piwsokul. They (pl.) are stealing pieces of firewood.
ˋkomutonatomon (TI) he steals it
stem 1: -komutonatom-
stem 2: kemutonatom-: kemutonatok when he stole it
ˋKomutonatomoniyal piwsokul. They are stealing pieces of firewood.
komutonesku (AI) he is a thief
plural: komutoneskultuwok
stem 1: -komutonesk(i)-
stem 2: kemutonesk(i)-
ˋkomutonomal (TA) he steals from him
stem 1: -komutonom-
stem 2: kemutonom-
komutse (AI) he steals wood
plural: komutsahtuwok
stem 1: -komuts(e)-
stem 2: kemuts(e)
konasis (A) nit
plural: konasisok
konasisuwatpe (AI) he has nits in his hair
konotiri (P) no (slang, Indian Township, Maine)
konusehs (A) willow
plural: konusehsuwok
ˋkophomon, ˋkoppahmon (TI) he shuts it
plural: ˋkoppahmuhtiniya
stem 1a: -kophom-, -koppahm-
stem 1b: kpahm-: kpahmun shut (sg.) it!; but: etuci kpam when I shut it
stem 2: keppahm-: keppahman when I shut it; but: keppohok, kephok when he shut it; kephom when I was shutting it
ˋkoppasokahmon (TI) he locks it
plural: ˋkoppasokahmuhtiniya
stem 1a: -koppasokahm-
stem 1b: kpasokahm-: kpasokahmun lock (sg.) it!
stem 2: keppasokahm-: keppasokahman when I locked it; but: keppasokohok when he locked it
ˋkoppektahal (TA) he shuts him in by hitting (something 2-dimensional: cloth, paper, etc.)
stem 1a: -koppekt_h-
stem 1b: kpekt_h-
stem 2: keppekt_h-
ˋkoppektehmon (TI) he covers it by hitting (something 2-dimensional: cloth, paper, etc.)
stem 1a: -koppektehm-
stem 1b: kpektehm-; but: kpektohok if he covers it
stem 2: keppekˋehm; but: keppektohok when he covers it

Neke keppektohok possiyantehsok, on miyawtehmon 'pihtin. When he covered the window, he accidentally hit his hand.

'koppihtonenal (TA) he holds his (someone else's) nose closed
- *stem 1a:* -koppihtonen-
- *stem 1b:* kpihtonen-
- *stem 2:* keppihtonen-

Nkoppihtonens eci cuwapotoqqi 'samaqanok. I hold my nose closed with my fingers whenever I jump into the water.

'koppotiyahkan (AI, AI + OBJ) he bangs it closed
- *stem 1a:* -koppotiyahk(e)-
- *stem 1b:* kpotiyahk(e)-
- *stem 2:* keppotiyahk(e)-

Qeni tehpu kpotiyahket khakon naka apc 'koppasokahmon. She just banged the door closed and then locked it.

'koptunahal (TA) he makes him shut up
- *stem 1a:* -koptun_h-
- *stem 1b:* kpotun_h-
- *stem 2:* keptun_h-

'koptunenal (TA) he covers his (someone else's) mouth with his hand
- *stem 1a:* -koptunen-
- *stem 1b:* kpotunen-
- *stem 2:* keptunen-

'kosehlal (TA) he hurts him (physically)
- *stem 1a:* -kosehl-: nkosehloq he hurts me
- *stem 1b:* ksehl-, kosehl-: ksehlat if he hurts him
- *stem 2:* kesehl-: kesehlat when he hurt him

'kosehtun (TI) he hurts it
- *stem 1a:* -koseht-
- *stem 1b:* kseht-, koseht-: kosehtaq if he hurts it
- *stem 2:* keseht-: kesehtaq when he hurt it

'kosehtuwan (DOV) he hurts something of his (someone else's) (physically)
- *stem 1a:* -kosehtuw-: nkosehtakun he hurts mine
- *stem 1b:* ksehtuw-, kosehtuw-: ksehtuwat if he hurts his
- *stem 2:* kesehtuw-: kesehtuwat when he hurt his

'koselomal (TA) he likes him; he loves him
- *stem 1a:* -koselom-
- *stem 1b:* kselom-
- *stem 2:* keselom-: keselomacil the one whom he likes

Neke Piyel skat keselomamuhk, etucitahasit. When Peter was not liked, he was very sad.

'koseltomon (TI) he likes it
- *stem 1a:* -koseltom-
- *stem 1b:* kseltom-: kseltok if he likes it
- *stem 2:* keseltom-:

'kosi ihin (TI) he likes it
- *stem 1a:* -kosi ih-
- *stem 1b:* ksi ih-, ksi iy-: ksi iyyan if I like it
- *stem 2:* kesi ih-, kesi iy-: kesi iyyek when we (nilun) like it

(See paradigms for forms.)

'kosi iywal (TA) he likes him
- *stem 1a:* -kosi iyw-
- *stem 1b:* ksi iyw-: ksi iywa he is liked
- *stem 2:* kesi iyw-

(Note: iyw- undergoes the same contractions with endings as stems ending in -uw-: kosi iyul "I like you (sg.)," nkosi iyaq "he likes me.")

Neke kesi iyask, kuli witapehkamoq. When he liked you, he was friendly to you (sg.).

'kosicihtun, 'kocicihtun (TI) he knows it
- *stem 1a:* -kosiciht-, -kociciht-
- *stem 1b:* ksiciht-, kciciht-
- *stem 2:* kesiciht-, keciciht-,

'kosiciyal, kociciyal (TA) he knows him
- *stem 1a:* -kosiciy-, -kociciy-
- *stem 1b:* ksiciy-, kciciy-
- *stem 2:* kesiciy-, keciciy-

Kosiciya yat wasis pemuhset awtik? Do you (sg.) know that child who is walking along the road?

'kosinuhkan (AI, AI + OBJ) he is sick; he has pain in it
- *plural:* (AI forms) ksinuhkahtuwok, ksinuhkawolotuwok, ksinukhotuwok: they are sick
- *stem 1a:* -kosinuhk(a)-, -kosinuhk(e)-
- *stem 1b:* ksinuhk(a), ksinuhk(e): ksinuhka, ksinuhke he is sick
- *stem 2:* kesinuhk(a)-, kesinuhk(e)-

Ksinuhkahc tokec mahat cikonesisol. He will get sick if he eats a green apple.

'kosinuhkuwal (TA) he makes him sick
- *stem 1a:* -kosinuhkuw-: nkosinuhkakun it made me sick
- *stem 1b:* ksinuhkuw-: ksinuhkaht if it made him sick
- *stem 2:* kesinuhkuw-: kesinuhkaht when it made him sick

'kositahamal (TA) he likes him
- *stem 1a:* -kositaham-
- *stem 1b:* ksitaham-
- *stem 2:* kesitaham

'koskahtan (AI, AI + OBJ) he loses it
- *stem 1a:* 'koskaht(a)-: nkoskahtapon we (nilun dual) lose it
- *stem 1b:* ksihkaht(a)-: ksihkahta he loses it
- *stem 2:* keskaht(a)-

'koskahtun (TI) he loses it
- *stem 1a:* -koskaht-
- *stem 1b:* ksihkaht-
- *stem 2:* keskaht-

Nkoskahtunekol ntapqasokihikonokol. I lost my keys (which were here just a little while ago).

koskimkasuwiw (II) it (a part of the body) goes to sleep; it feels like pins and needles (sensation in skin)

'kosomahkalal (TA) he pushes him
stem 1a: -kosomahkal-
stem 1b: ksomahkal-
stem 2:   kesomahkal-

'kosomahkan (AI, AI+OBJ) he pushes it
plural: 'kosomahkahtiniya
stem 1a: -kosomahk(e)-: kosomahkepon we (kilun, dual) push
stem 1b: ksomahk(e)-: ksomahke he pushes
stem 2:   kesomahk(e)-: kesomahket when he pushed; when he pushed him, it

'kosomonal (TA) he pushes him
stem 1a: -kosomon-
stem 1b: ksomon-
stem 2:   kesomon-

'kosomonomon (TI) he pushes it
stem 1a: -kosomonom-
stem 1b: ksomonom-: ksomonok if he pushes it
stem 2:   kesomonom-

-koson- shoe
(See -akson-.)

kosona (P) or
Piyel kosona Mali opu. Peter or Mary is sitting down.

'kosonal (TA) he hurts him
stem 1a: -koson-
stem 1b: kson-
stem 2:   keson-

kospahtahsu (AI) he washes the floor
plural: kospahtahsultuwok
stem 1:   -kospahtahs(i)-
stem 2:   kespahtahs(i)-

kospisun, kspisun (I) belt
plural: kospisunol, kspisunol
poss: 'kospisun, 'qospisun, 'kospisunom, 'qospisunom
loc: kospisunok, kspisunok
dim: kospisunsis, kspisunsis

'kossatpenal (TA) he washes his (someone else's) hair
stem 1:   -kossatpen-
stem 2:   kessatpen-
Kossatpensu. He washes his (own) hair.

'kossehlal (TA) he lets him in
stem 1a: -kossehl-
stem 1b: ksehl-: ksehlat if he lets him in
stem 2:   kessehl-: kessehlat when he let him in

'kossekimal (TA) he calls him into the house
stem 1a: -kossekim-
stem 1b: ksekim-
stem 2:   kessekim-

'kossewsolal (TA) he takes her in (for her wedding)
stem 1a: -kossewsol-
stem 1b: ksewsol-
stem 2:   kessewsol-

kossicuwenike (AI) he washes dishes
plural: kossicuwenikhotuwok
stem 1:   -kossicuwenik(e)-
stem 2:   kessicuwenik(e)-

kossicuwenikon (A, I) dish rag (I); basin to wash dishes in (A)
plural: kossicuwenikonol (dish rags); kossicuwenikonok (basins)

kossicuwenikonap, kossicuwenikonop (I) dish water
loc: kossicuwenikonapik

'kossiptinenal (TA) he washes his (someone else's) hand(s)
stem 1:   -kossiptinen-
stem 2:   kessiptinen-
Kossiptinensu. He washes his (own) hands.

'kossiqenal (TA) he washes his (someone else's) face
stem 1:   -kossiqen-
stem 2:   kessiqen-
Kossiqensu. He washes his (own) face.

kostokonike (AI) he washes clothes; he does laundry
plural: kostokonikhotuwok
stem 1:   -kostokonik(e)-
stem 2:   kestokonik(e)

kostokonikon (I) soap
plural: kostokonikonol

kotama, katama (P) no; not

'kotomakitahamal (TA) he pities him
stem 1a: -kotomakitaham-
stem 1b: ktomakitaham-, 'tomakitaham-
stem 2:   ketomakitaham-

kotqesit (I) toe
plural: kotqesitol
poss: 'kotqesit, 'kotqesitom, 'kotqesitum
loc: kotqesitok
dim: kotqesitsis
(See wotqesit "his toe.")

kotqesitsis (I) little toe
plural: kotqesitsisol

'kotqihtahal (TA) he knocks him over
stem 1a: -kotqiht_h-: nkotqihtohoq he knocks me over
stem 1b: ktoqiht_h-
stem 2:   ketqiht_h-

kotuhkayiw (P) alone
(variant of 'qotuhkayiw)

kotuhmahsinuwintuwakon (I) drum song
plural: kotuhmahsinuwintuwakonol

kotuhmahsu (AI) he plays the drum
plural: kotuhmahsultuwok
stem 1:   -kotuhmahs(i)-
stem 2:   ketuhmahs(i)-
Eci skehewahtqik 'kotuhmahsin. On Friday he plays the drum.

kotuhpu (AI) he is hungry
plural: kotuhpultuwok
stem 1:   -kotuhp(i)-
stem 2:   ketuhp(i)-
Kosiciyulpa kil naka Mali ketuhpiyeq. I know that you (sg.) and Mary are hungry.

kotuhsomu (AI) he drinks (an alcoholic beverage)
plural: kotuhsomultuwok
stem 1: -kotuhsom(i)-: nkotuhsom I drink
stem 2: ketuhsom(i)-: ketuhsomit when he was drinking

kotuhtamu (AI) he craves some kind of food
stem 1: -kotuhtam(i)-
stem 2: ketuhtam(i)-

kotunke (AI) he hunts
plural: kotunkahtuwok
stem 1: -kotunk(e)-
stem 2: ketunk(e)-

kotunkewin (A) hunter
plural: kotunkewinuwok
On yaq kotunkewinuwok 'takonutomuwaniya Motahkomiqewi elelomoqehtit kcihkuk. Then, they say, the hunters told the people at Peter Dana Point, Maine, what had happened to them (dual) in the woods.

'kotunolal (TA) he hunts him; he is out to get him
stem 1: -kotunol-
stem 2: ketunol-

kotuwapuwe (AI) he wants a drink (of anything); he wants to eat soup, stew, etc.
plural: kotuwapuwahtuwok
stem 1: -kotuwapuw(e)-: nkotuwapu I want a drink
stem 2: ketuwapuw(e)-: ketuwapuwet when he wanted a drink

kotuwihtasu (II) it is going to be made (indef. subject form of 'kotuwihtun (TI) he is going to make it)

kotuwossomu (AI) he is thirsty
plural: kotuwossomultuwok
stem 1: -kotuwossom(i)-: nkotuwossom I am thirsty
stem 2: ketuwossom(i)-: ketuwossomit when he was thirsty
Nwahkehsipon ketuwossomultiyek. Several of us (nilun) are thirsty.
Piyel 'kosiciyal eli kotuwossomilit ahahsuwol. Peter knows that the horse is thirsty.

kpahasu (AI) he is locked up
stem 1a: -kophas(i)-
stem 1b: kpahas(i)-
stem 2: kephas(i)-

kpahasu (II) it is locked
stem 1: kpahas(i)-
stem 2: kephas(i)-

-kpehtihik(e)- pound ash logs (to obtain basket splints)
(forms AI verb stems)
macekpehtihike (AI) he begins pounding ash

kpihikon (I) lid; cover; dam
plural: kpihikonol
poss: 'kophikon
loc: kpihikonok
dim: kpihikonossis

kpocale (AI) he is hoarse
plural: kpocalhotuwok, kpocalahtuwok, kpocalawolotuwok, kpocalawotuwok
stem 1a: -kopocal(a)-, -kopocal(e)-: nkopocal I am hoarse
stem 1b: kpocal(a)-, kpocal(e)-: kpocalat if he is hoarse
stem 2: kepocal(a)-, kepocal(e)-: kepocalet when he was hoarse

kpoton (II) it is frozen over; it is frozen shut (e.g., a faucet)
stem 1: kpoton(o)-
stem 2: keppoton(o)-: keppotok when it was frozen over

ksacessu (AI) he stays too long on a visit

ksakuwiye (II) the tide is at its highest (in its monthly cycle)

ksalokosse (AI) he has good hearing
plural: ksalokossahtuwok, ksalokossawolotuwok, ksalokossawotuwok
stem 1a: -kosalokoss(a)-, -kosalokoss(e)-: nkosalokoss I have good hearing
stem 1b: ksalokoss(a)-, ksalokoss(e)-: ksalokosset if he has good hearing
stem 2: kesalokoss(a)-, kesalokoss(e)-: kesalokossat when he had good hearing

ksalosuhke (AI) he sweats; he basks in the sun
stem 1a: -kosalosuhk(e)-
stem 1b: ksalosuhk(e)-
stem 2: kesalosuhk(e)-

ksamkole (II) it blazes up
stem 1: ksamkol(e)-
stem 2: kesamkol(e)-: kesamkolek when it blazed up

ksap (I) soup; stew
plural: ksapihil, ksapiyil

ksate (II) it is very hot
stem 1: ksat(e)-
stem 2: kesat(e)-

ksatke (AI) he likes the place so much that he stays longer
stem 1a: -kosatk(e)-
stem 1b: ksatk(e)-
stem 2: kesatk(e)-

ksatokihtehsin (AI) it (an., a string-like object) strikes sharply against something; it (an., a string-like object) pounds against something
stem 1a: -kosatokihtehsin(o)- type B
stem 1b: ksatokihtehsin(o)-
stem 2: kesatokihtehsin(o)-

ksatqin (II) the waves are big
stem 1: ksatqin(o)- type B
stem 2: kesatqin(o)-

kse (ksiy-) (PV) in; inward; into
prefixed form: -kosse (-kossiy-)
neke form: kesse (kessiy-)
'kosse kpasokahmon (TI) he locks it in

ksehe (AI) he comes in; he goes in
stem 1a: -kossah(a)-: nkossaha I come in
stem 1b: ks_h(a)-
stem 2: kessah(a)-: kessahat when he came in

ksehkawotuwok (AI) they (dual) come in; they (dual) go in
stem 1a: -kossehkawot(i)-: nkossehkawotipon we (nilun, dual) come in
stem 1b: ksehkawot(i)-
stem 2: kessehkawot(i)-: kessehkawotihtit when they (dual) came in
(dual forms only)

ksephuwe (AI) he runs in
plural: ksephuwolotuwok, ksephuwotuwok
stem 1a: -kossephuw(e)-: nkossephu I run in
stem 1b: ksephuw(e)-
stem 2: kessephuw(e)-

ksewse (AI) he walks in
plural: ksiyapasuwok
stem 1a: -kossews(e)-
stem 1b: ksews(e)-
stem 2: kessews(e)-

ksewulqe (AI) he is tight (with his money, his tools, etc.)
plural: ksewulqahtuwok
stem 1a: -kosewulq(e)-
stem 1b: ksewulq(e)-
stem 2: kesewulq(e)-

ksihkehe (AI) he is lost
plural: ksihkahahtuwok, ksihkahawolotuwok
stem 1a: -koskah(a)-
stem 1b: ksihk_h-
stem 2: keskah(a)-, kesihkah(a)-
Neke keskahawolotihtit wasisok kcihkuk, etutpayultihtit nikihkuwa. When the children were lost in the woods, their parents were very scared.

ksihkot (II) the tide is at its lowest (in its monthly cycle); it is neap tide

ksihposu (AI) he is hot
plural: ksihposultuwok
stem 1a: -kosihpos(i)-: nkosihpos I am hot
stem 1b: ksihpos(i)-: ksihposit if he is hot
stem 2: kesihpos(i)-: kesihposit when he was hot

ksihpote (II) it is hot
stem 1: ksihpot(e)-: ksihpotek if it is hot
stem 2: kesihpot(e)_, kespot(e)-
(See ksopote "it is hot.")

ksihtehsin (II) he is hurt in a fall (or crash)
stem 1a: -kostehsin(o)-: kostehsin are you (sg.) hurt in a fall?
stem 1b: ksihtehsin(o)-

stem 2: kestehsin(o)-: kestehsit when he was hurt in a fall

ksikihin (II) it is sharp
stem 1: ksikihin(o)- type B
stem 2: kesikihin(o)-

ksinuhka, ksinuhke (AI) he is sick
(See 'kosinuhkan "he is sick, has pain in it.")

ksinuhkawinaqsu, ksinuhkewinaqsu (AI) he looks sick
stem 1a: -kosinuhkewinaqs(i)-
stem 1b: ksinuhkewinaqs(i)-
stem 2: kesinuhkewinaqs(i)-

ksinuhkehkalsu (AI) he pretends to be sick
stem 1a: -kosinuhkehkals(i)-
stem 1b: ksinuhkehkals(i)-
stem 2: kesinuhkehkals(i)-

ksinuhkewakon (I) sickness; disease
plural: ksinuhkewakonol
poss: 'kosinuhkewakon, 'qosinuhkewakon

ksiwsk (A) hemlock (tree)
plural: ksiwskok
poss: 'kosiwskumol
loc: ksiwskok
dim: ksiwskis

ksiyapasuwok (AI) they (pl.) come in, they (pl.) go in
stem 1a: -kossiyapas(i)-
stem 1b: ksiyapas(i)-
stem 2: kessiyapas(i)-
(plural meanings only)

ksiyaptu (AI) he tracks in
stem 1a: -kossiyapt(u)-
stem 1b: ksiyapt(u)-
stem 2: kessiyapt(u)-

ksiyaqsu (AI) he loves children
plural: ksiyaqsultuwok
stem 1a: -kosiyaqs(i)-: nkosiyaqs I love children
stem 1b: ksiyaqs(i)-: ksiyaqsit if he loves children
stem 2: kesiyaqs(i)-: kesiyaqsit one who loves children

ksiyawqe (AI) he is very sick;
stem 1a: -kosiyawq(e)-
stem 1b: ksiyawq(e)-
stem 2: kesiyawq(e)

kskomihike (AI) he takes a shortcut
stem 1a: -koskomhik(e)-: nkoskomihik I take a shortcut
stem 1b: kskomihik(e)-
stem 2: keskomhik(e)-
Keskomhiket, on 'koskahan. When he took a short cut, he got lost.

kskotqe (II) it is wide (of a brook)
stem 1: -kskotq(e)-
stem 2: keskotq(e)-: keskotqek it is wide

ksoka (ksokay-) (PV) across
prefixed form: -kosoka (-kosokay-)
neke form: kesoka (kesokay-)
(also: qsoka)

Kesokawset awtik, miyawtehkakun atomupil. When he was walking across the road, he was hit by a car.

ksokawse (AI) he walks across
plural: ksokayapasuwok
stem 1a: -kosokaws(e)-
stem 1b: ksokaws(e)-
stem 2: kesokaws(e)-

ksokayaskutew (P) across a field

ksokayiw (P) across
(also: qsokayiw)

ksopote (II) it is hot
stem 1: ksopot(e)
stem 2: ksopot(e)-, kespot(e)-: ksopotek, kespotek when it was hot
(See ksihpote.)

ksossiyehsin (AI) she (a bird) sits on her eggs
plural: ksossiyehsinultuwok, ksossiyehsinuhtuwok
stem 1a: -kosossiyehsin(o)- type B: 'kosossiyehsinon she sits on her eggs (Relative)
stem 1b: ksossiyehsin(o)-
stem 2: kesossiyehsin(o)-: kesossiyehsit when she was sitting on her eggs

Elatqonokosit stahqon anqiposehehs etoli ksossiyehsit. Where the tree branches, the robin is sitting on her eggs.

ksossiyehsu (AI) it (an.) nests
plural: ksossiyehsultuwok, ksossiyehsuhtuwok
stem 1a: -kosossiyehs(i)-
stem 1b: ksossiyehs(i)-
stem 2: kesossiyehs(i)-

kspisun (I) belt
(See kospisun.)

ksqopehsan (II) it rains and snows at the same time
stem 1: ksqopehsan(o)- type A
stem 2: kesqopehsan(o)-: kesqopehsak when it was raining and snowing

ktahkomiq (I) land; ground; earth
plural: ktahkomikul
poss: 'kihtahkomikum, 'qihtahkomikum
loc: ktahkomikuk
dim: ktahkomiqsis

ktanaqsuwok, ktenaqsuwok (AI) there are many of them (an.)
stem 1a: -kihtanaqs(i)-
stem 1b: ktanaqs(i)-
stem 2: kehtanaqs(i)-
Ktanaqsu molaqs. There's a lot of milk.
Ktanaqsu skicin etoli peciyat mawkamok. A big group of Indians came to the dance.

ktapehe (AI, II) he, it sinks
stem 1a: -kihtap_h(a)-; -kottap_h(a)-
stem 1b: ktapah(a)-
stem 2: kehtapah(a)-, kettapah(a)-

ktaqhomuhs (A) old man
plural: ktaqhomuhsok

ktomakelke (AI) he helps out because he is sympathetic
stem 1a: -kotomakelk(e)-
stem 1b: ktokmakelk(e)-
stem 2: ketomakelk(e)-
Sakhi ktomakelkahticik kosqehsuhs naka 'qenoss. An old woman and her grandchildren have come to help (someone) out (because they pity him).

ktomakeyu (AI) he is poor
plural: ktomakeyultuwok
stem 1a: -kotomakey(i)-: nkotomakey I am poor
stem 1b: ktomakey(i)-
stem 2: ketomakey(i)-: ketomakeyit when he was poor

ktomaki (ktomak-) (PV, PN) poor; unfortunate
prefixed form: -kotomaki (-kotomak-)
neke form: ketomaki (ketomak-)
ktomaki wasis (A) poor child
(also: 'tomaki)

ktomakiku (AI) he is in bad shape; he is not well off
stem 1a: -kotomakik(i)-
stem 1b: ktomakik(i)-
stem 2: ketomakik(i)-

ktomakiqewu (AI) he looks down and out
stem 1a: -kotomakiqew(i)-
stem 1b: ktomakiqew(i)-
stem 2: ketomakiqew(i)-

ktonukot (II) something big happens
stem 1: ktonukot(o)-
stem 2: kehtonukot(o)-: kehtonukahk when something big happens
Etuci ktonukkopon, an nekom tqonan. When there was something big going on he got arrested.

ktopeqon (II) there is a spring of water
stem 1: ktopeqon(o)- type A
stem 2: kehtopeqon(o)-

ktoqonu (AI) he stays over (at someone's house)
plural: ktoqonultuwok, ktoqonuhtuwok
stem 1a: -kotqon(i)-, -kottoqon(i)-: nkotqon, nkottoqon I stay over
stem 1b: ktoqon(i)-: ktoqonit if he stays over
stem 2: ketqon(i)-, kettoqon(i)-: ketqonit, kettoqonit when he stayed over

ktoton (A) mountain
loc: ktotonuk

ktuwan (A) big log for a fire
plural: ktuwanok

ku (A) log
plural: kuwiyik, kuwihik, kuwhik
poss: 'kuwemol
loc: kuwek, kuwik, kuwhik
dim: kuwehsis

kuhk (A) buttocks
plural: kuhkok
poss.:   'tahkuhkol his buttocks
kuhkukhahs (A) owl species; moth
(diminutive only); block and tackle (Pleasant
Point, Maine)
plural: kuhkukhahsuwok
poss.:   'kuhkukhahsumol,
              'kuhkukhahsomol
dim: kuhkukhahsis: little owl; moth
kuhu (AI) he sleeps; he falls asleep
plural: kuhultuwok, kuhuhtuwok
stem 1:   -kuw(i)-: nkuwipon we (du.
              exc.) sleep; but: kuwwol,
              kuwiwol, kuwiyil he (obv.)
              sleeps; kuwwok, kuwiwok,
              kuwiyik they (du.) sleep;
              kuwwa he has gone to sleep
stem 2:   kew(i)-: kewit when he fell
              asleep
(Note: Stem w changes to h before u.)
Kuhultukk nil nicanok. My children have
fallen asleep.
Tokec kuwit, cu puwihtu. If he goes to
sleep, he will dream.
kuhus (A) cow
plural: kuhusuwok
poss.:   'kuhusumol, kuhusomol
dim: kuhusis, kuhusossis, kuhusuhsis
(from English, cow)
kuhusey (I) beef
plural: kuhuseyal: pieces of beef
poss.:   'kuhuseyam
loc: kuhuseyak
dim: kuhuseyahsis: a little piece of
              beef
kuhusisey (I) veal
kuhut (I) bed
plural: kuhutiyil, kuhutihil
poss.:   'kuhutim
loc: kuhutik
dim: kuhutossis
kukec (A) game warden
plural: kukecok
kukonasikon (A) skeleton
plural: kukonasikonok
poss.:   'kukonasikonol,
              'kukonasikonumol
loc: kukonasikonok
dim: kukonasikonis
'kuskahtehkuwal (TA) he capsizes him
stem 1:   -kuskahtehkuw-
kuspem (I) lake
(variant of qospem)
kutoput (I) chair
plural: kutoputiyil, kutoputihil
poss.:   'kutoputim, 'toqtoput
loc: kutoputik
dim: kutoputossis
(variant of qotoput)
kuwehkcwikuwam (I) log cabin
plural: kuwehkewikuwamol

kuwes (A) pine
plural: kuwesok
poss.:   'kuwesomol
kuwesihq (A) pine pitch
plural: kuwesihqiyik
poss.:   'kuwesihqemol
loc: kuwesihqek
dim: kuwesihqehsis
'kuwhal (TA) he chops it (an.) down
stem 1:   -kuwh-
stem 2:   kewh-
   Neke kisi kuwhek oposihik,
nkisankuwekhannuk. When we (nilun)
chopped the trees down, we sold them.
kuwimkewey (A,I) something that helps one
sleep

L

l-
   (See also entries in "ol-".)
lahkaluson (I) high fence; high wall
plural: lahkalusonol
lahkalusonihikon (I) fence
plural: lahkalusonihikonol
poss.:   'tolahkalusonihikon
loc: lahkalusonihikonok
dim: lahkalusonihikonossis
(also: wahkalusonihikon (I) fence)
lahkalusonohom (AI) it (an.) has a ring
around it
stem 1a: -olahkalusonahm(o)- type A:
              without ending -am
stem 1b: lahkalusonahm(o)-; but:
              lahkalusonohok if it has a ring
              around it
stem 2:   elahkalusonahm(o)-; but:
              elahkalusonohok when it has
              a ring around it
Kisuhs lahkalusonohom. There is a ring
around the moon.
lahkap (I) cellar
plural: lahkapol
poss.:   'tolahkapom
loc: lahkapok
(from French, la cave)
lahkesawakon (I) plow
plural: lahkesawakonol
poss.:   'tolahkesawakonom,
              'tolahkesawakonum
loc: lahkesawakonok
dim: lahkesawakonis,
              lahkesawakonossis
lahkihikon (I) hoe
plural: lahkihikonol
poss.:   'tolahkihikonom,
              'tolahkihikonum
loc: lahkihikonok
dim: lahkihikonis

lahkomiksu (AI) he is a sinner
   stem 1a: -olahkomiks(i)-, -olkomiks(i)-
   stem 1b: lahkomiks(i)-, olkomiks(i)-
   stem 2:   elahkomiks(i)-, elkomiks(i)-
   (See also: olkomiksu.)
lahkomiksuwakon (I) sin
   plural: lahkomiksuwakonol
lahqostikon (I) hoop
   plural: lahqostikonol
lahtoqehsonuk north (Locative)
   Waptoqihik 'ci pecituwiyawolotuwok
lahtoqehsonuk. Canada geese fly here from
the North.
lahtu (A) trump (in cards)
   plural: lahtuwok
   (from French, l'atout)
lakomakon (A) round-headed mallet
   plural: lakomakonok
   poss: 'tolakomakonol
lakomitehtikon (A) boiler
   plural: lakomitehtikonol
lakutuwakon (I) relationship; kinship
lakutuwok (AI) they (dual) are related
   plural: lakutultuwok
   stem 1a: -olakut(i)-: ktolakutipon you
             (sg.) and I are related
   stem 1b: lakut(i)-
   stem 2:   elakut(i)-: elakutimok a place
             where everyone is related
   Neqt te lakutuwok. They (dual) are first
cousins.
lalokihikon (I) bit (of a drill)
   plural: lalokihikonol
lamahqem (A) heart-wood of a tree
lamaqtun (I) inside of the mouth
   poss: 'tolamaqtun
lamatqoniw (AI) it (an.) is knotty inside
   stem 1a: -olamatqon(i)- type B
   stem 1b: lamatqon(i)-
   stem 2:   elamatqon(i)-
lamiptin (I) palm (of the hand)
   plural: lamiptinol
   poss: 'tolamiptin
   (also: lamilc)
lamiw (P) inside; underneath
lamk (I) hell
   loc: lamkik
lamkikapuwuwok (AI) they are standing in a
line
   stem 1a: olamkikapuw(i)-
   stem 1b: lamkikapuw(i)-
   stem 2:   elamkikapuw(i)-
   (dual and plural forms only)
lamokut (I) sheet (for a bed)
   plural: lamokutiyil, lamokutihil
   poss: 'tolamokut
   loc: lamokutik
   dim: lamokutossis
lampeq (P) underwater
lamsewey (I) pistol
   plural: lamseweyal
   poss: 'tolamsewey
   loc: lamseweyak

   dim: lamseweyahsis
   (literally, "something worn inside")
   Milin pilasq neqektek lamseweyak. Give
(sg.) me the paper that is under the pistol.
lamsitawon (I) sole of the foot
   poss: 'tolamsitawon
lapasuwok (AI) they (pl.) walk there; they
(pl.) walk thus
   stem 1a: -olapas(i)-
   stem 1b: lapas(i)-
   stem 2:   elapas(i)-
   (plural meanings only)
lapekhasu (AI) he (a horse) is harnessed
lapekhikon (I) harness; shoelace
   plural: lapekhikonol
   poss: 'tolapekhikonum
   loc: lapekhikonok
   dim: lapekhikonossis
lapektuhusu (AI) he plays a stringed
instrument
   stem 1a: -olapektuhus(i)-
   stem 1b: lapektuhus(i)-
   stem 2:   elapektuhus(i)-
lapektuwakon (I) snare
   plural: lapektuwakonol
   poss: 'tolapektuwakon
   loc: lapektuwakonok
   dim: lapektuwakonis
lapomal (TA) he looks at him
   (variant of 't-olapomal)
lapu (AI) he looks (there)
   plural: lapultuwok, lapuhtuwok
   stem 1a: -olap(i)-: ntolap I look
   stem 1b: lap(i)-
   stem 2:   elap(i)-: elapit the way he
             looks (at something)
laput (I) instrument for looking (telescope,
microscope, etc.; pl., binoculars)
   plural: laputiyil, laputihil
   poss: 'tolaput
   loc: laputik
   dim: laputossis
laputihike (AI) he looks with a telescope,
binoculars, etc.
   stem 1a: -olaputihik(e)-
   stem 1b: laputihik(e)-
   stem 2:   elaputihik(e)-
laputihikon (I) instrument for looking
(telescope, microscope, etc.); (pl.) binoculars
   plural: laputihikonol binoculars
   poss: 'tolaputihikon
   loc: laputihikonok
   dim: laputihikonis
laqe (II) it is piled up
   stem 1:   laq(e)-
   stem 2:   elaq(e)-
lasksawakon (I) scythe; sickle
   plural: lasksawakonol
   poss: 'tolasksawakon,
             'tolasksawakonom,
             'tolasksawakonum
   loc: lasksawakonok
   dim: lasksawakonossis

latuwakon (I) ladder
    plural: latuwakonol
    poss: 'tolatuwakon
latuwe (AI) he climbs
    plural: latuwahtuwok,
                latuwawolotuwok,
                latuwultuwok
    stem 1a: -olatuw(e)-
    stem 1b: latuw(e)-
    stem 2:   elatuw(e)-
    Neke elatuwawolotihtit tehsahqiw wikuwamok, komiwonuhpon. When they were climbing on the roof, it was raining.
latuwewakon (I) language
    plural: latuwewakonol
    poss: 'tolatuwewakon
lawsu (AI) he lives there; he eats there
    plural: lawsultuwok
    stem 1a: -olaws(i)-: ntolaws I live there
    stem 1b: laws(i)-
    stem 2:   elaws(i)-: elawsit where he eats
layektakon (I) toy
    plural: layektakonol
lehsuwis (A) Jew
    plural: lehsuwisok
    (from French, le juif)
lekhikon (A) sail
    plural: lekhikonok
lekopisuwon (I) apron
    plural: lekopisuwonol
    poss: 'tolekopisuwon
lelomoqe (AI) something happens to him
    stem 1a: -olelomoq(e)-
    stem 1b: lelomoq(e)-
    stem 2:   elelomoq(e)-
    Nita, keqsey nkoti lelomoq. Uh oh, something is going to happen to me.
lelomu (AI) he smiles (in some way)
    stem 1a: -olelom(i)-
    stem 1b: lelom(i)-
    stem 2:   elelom(i)-
leptanet (A) lieutenant governor
    (from English, lieutenant--British pronunciation)
leyu (II) it happens; it is true
    stem 1:   ley(i)
    stem 2:   eley(i)-
    Tan al leyu welokiskahk. It's about time there was a good day.
leyuwakon (I) personal belongings; gear
    poss: 'toleyuwakon
    dim: leyuwakonossis
lihkahkonikon (I) crooked knife (a wood-working tool)
    plural: lihkahkonikonol
lihkutolakon (I) draw knife (for shaving wood)
    plural: lihkutolakonol
    Qetuwehkihin lihkutolakon, knossawatomon kmiyawsomon ktolamhok. When you (sg.) try to use a draw knife, be careful not to cut your stomach.

likew (P) (expresses sympathy)
    Likew kipossisuwiwa pilsqehsis mehcinelit wikuwossol. The poor girl was left an orphan when her mother died.
likon (II) it looks thus; it is such and such a kind
    stem 1:   likon(o)-
    stem 2:   elikon(o)-: elikok it looks awful; the way it looks
    eliksok it is cute
likpehtihike (AI) he pounds ash (to obtain basket splints)
    stem 1a: -olikpehtihik(e)-
    stem 1b: likpehtihik(e)-
    stem 2:   elikpehtihik(e)-
likpesawakon (I) gauge for cutting ash splints
    plural: likpesawakonol
    poss: 'tolikpesawakon
    loc: likpesawakonok
    dim: likpesawakonossis
    Likpesawakon oluwehkasu eci wen olsat wikpihil weci tetpikskeyuhtihtit. The splint gauge is used when one cuts ash strips so that they will be uniform in width.
liksawakon (I) saw
    plural: liksawakonol
    poss: 'toliksawakonum
    loc: liksawakonok
    dim: liksawakonis
liksawe (AI) he saws
    plural: liksawhotuwok
    stem 1a: -oliksaw(e)-
    stem 1b: liksaw(e)-
    stem 2:   eliksaw(e)-
liku (AI) he looks thus; he is of such and such a kind or nature
    plural: likultuwok
    stem 1a: -olik(i)-: ntolik I look thus
    stem 1b: lik(i)-: likit if he looks thus
    stem 2:   elik(i)-: elikit he looks awful; the way he looks
    elikossit he is cute
lilomonhikon (I) paint
    plural: lilomonhikonol
    poss: 'tolilomonhikon
lintu (AI) he sings
    plural: lintultuwok, lintuhtuwok
    stem 1a: -olint(u)-: ntolint I sing
    stem 1b: lint(u)-
    stem 2:   elint(u)-: elintaq the way he sings; he is singing
    Nilunc ntolintultiponc possiyanteskik. We (nilun, pl.) will sing at the window.
    Ipa tpostuwan elintaq. Hey, listen to the way he sings.
lintuwakon (I) song
    plural: lintuwakonol
    poss: 'tolintuwakon
    loc: lintuwakonok (e.g., on a written song)
    dim: lintuwakonossis
lipkotenoma (AI) he lights a smudge
    stem 1a: -olipkotenom(a)-
    stem 1b: lipkotenom(a)-

stem 2:   elipkotenom(a)-

lipkotenomakon (I) smudge
    plural: lipkotenomakonol

liqehe (II) it rolls thus, there
    stem 1:   liq_h(a)-
    stem 2:   eliqah(a)-

litahasu (AI) he thinks that...
    plural: litahasultuwok
    stem 1a: -olitahas(i)-: ntolitahas I think that...
    stem 1b: litahas(i)-: litahasit if he thinks that...
    stem 2:   elitahas(i)-: elitahasit when he thought that...

Litahasit nil nkoti macaha, wisoki wonatomine. If he thinks that I'm going to leave, he's really crazy.

litposuwakon (I) office, position (in an organization, government, etc.)
    plural: litposuwakonol
    poss: 'tolitposuwakon

Tan kehson litposuwakonol? How many positions are there?

litposuwin (A) office holder; tribal council member
    plural: litposuwinuwok
    poss: 'tolitposuwinumol
    loc: litposuwinuhsis

liwehse (II) the wind is blowing from there
    stem 1:   liwehs(e)-
    stem 2:   eliwehs(e)-

liwihtasu (II) it is called, named
    stem 1:   liwihtas(i)-
    stem 2:   eliwihtas(i)-

liwisu (AI) he is named; he is called
    plural: liwisultuwok
    stem 1a: -oliwis(I)-: ntoliwis I am named, my name is
    stem 1b: liwis(i)-
    stem 2:   eliwis(i)-: eliwisit what he is called

Keq liwisu? What is his name?

Tan not 'toliwisin? What is he named?

Nonuwa nil eliwisit Can. I know a man named John.

Li macewisu Piyel. His first name is Peter.

lontoq (I) fresh water

lontoqiyehs (A) wood duck
    plural: lontoqiyehsuwok

loqtewakon (I) piece of clothing
    plural: loqtewakonol
    (See oloqotewakon.)

lossin (AI) he lies down; he is lying down
    plural: lossinuhtuwok
    stem 1a: -olossin(o)-
    stem 1b: lossin(o)-
    stem 2:   elossin(o)-: elossit when he was lying down; the way he lies

luhke (AI) he works; he does (something)
    plural: lukhotuwok
    stem 1a: -oluhk(e)-: ntoluhk I work
    stem 1b: luhk(e)-: luhket if he works
    stem 2:   eluhk(e)-: eluhket when he worked

    stem 3:   -oluhk(e)-
    kisoluhke (AI) he worked; he can work
    tolluhke (AI) he is working

luhkewakon (I) work; tool
    plural: luhkewakonol tools
    poss: 'toluhkewakon
    loc: 'luhkewakonok
    dim: luhkewakonossis

luhkewin (A) worker
    plural: luhkewinuwok

luhse (AI) he walks there, thus
    plural: lapasuwok
    stem 1a: -oluhs(e)-
    stem 1b: luhs(e)
    stem 2:   eluhs(e)-

luks (A) wolverine (?); a malicious character in old stories

M

ma (P) not; no

Ma te ihiw. He is not there.

Ma te sukolisol. There is no candy.

mace (maciy-) (PV) start, begin; go away or start off while doing go along while doing

mace ksinuhka, mace ksinuhke (AI) he begins to get sick

macehe (AI) he leaves
    plural: macahawolotuwok, macahahtuwok
    stem 1:   -mac_h(a)-; macehe he leaves; maceyya he has left; maceyyik, macehhik they (du.) leave etc. (see paradigms)

'Ci maceyyik Neqotkuk. They (du.) are leaving from Tobique.

Macahawolotuwok wasisok sepawonu Kelisk. The children (pl.) are leaving tomorrow for Calais.

macehkawotuwok (AI) they (dual) start out on foot; they (dual) start to walk (toddlers)
    stem 1:   -macehkawot(i)-
    (Note: Dual forms only.)

macehkot (II) the tide is starting to go out
    stem 1:   macehkot(o)-

macehkuwal (TA) he forces him to go home by following him; he chases him away
    stem 1:   -macehkuw-: macehkakul he (obv.) follows him (prox.)

Ipal mihtaqsol nekom macehkaht. I wish his father would make him go home.

macehlal (TA) he moves him
    stem 1:   -macehl-

Nil te na amsqahs macehlukpon nonoskiyik. I was the first to move my wings.

macehpayu (AI) he runs away because he is scared
    stem 1:   -macehpay(i)-

macehulal (TA) he carries him away by boat
    stem 1:   -macehul-

macehutun (TI) he carries it away by boat
    stem 1:   -macehut-
macekotok next year
maceku (AI) he grows up
    stem 1:   -macek(i)-: macekit when he
        grew up
macekuhuke (AI) he floats away
    stem 1:   -macekuhuk(e)-
macelan (II) it starts to rain
    stem 1:   macelan(o)- type A
macelanisiye (II) it starts to sprinkle (rain)
    stem 1:   macelanisiy(a)-
macemiye (AI) he starts to pray
    stem 1:   -macemiy(a)-
macephuwe (AI) he runs away
    stem 1:   -macephuw(e)-: nmacephu I
        run away
maceptasu (II) it is taken away
    stem 1:   maceptas(i)-
maceptuwan (DOV) he takes it to him
    stem 1:   -maceptuw-
macessu (AI, II) he, it moves
    stem 1:   -macess(i)-
macewse (AI) he starts out on foot; he leaves
on foot; he starts to walk (toddler)
    plural: maciyapasuwok
    stem 1:   -macews(e)-
maciyamkessu (II) it moves in a mass of
pieces
    stem 1:   maciyamkess(i)-
maciyapasuwok (AI) they (pl.) leave on foot;
they start to walk (toddlers)
    stem 1:   -maciyapas(i)-
    (plural only)
On yaq skicinuwok maciyapasiniya. Then,
they say, the Indians left.
maciyapenike (AI) he starts to scratch around
    stem 1:   -maciyapenik(e)-
maciyaphal (TA) he starts to track him
    stem 1:   -maciyaph-
maciyehloqe (AI) he drifts away
    stem 1:   -maciyehloq(e)-
maciyessu (II) it starts to move; it moves
along
    stem 1:   maciyess(i)-
mahal (TA) he eats it (an.)
    stem 1:   -m_h-: mohot if you eat it
        (an.); muhut when it (an.) was
        eaten
mahkut (I) dress
    plural: mahkutiyil, mahkutol
    poss: mahkut
    loc: mahkutik, mahkutok
    dim: mahkutsis
mahqan (I) sap of the sugar maple; maple
syrup (or sugar); anything sweet
    plural: mahqanol
    poss: mahqanom, mahqanum his
        sweet thing (e.g. candy)
    loc: mahqanok
    dim: mahqanis
    (Note: mahqanomol (A) his sweetheart.)

mahsus (I) fiddlehead (young fern)
    plural: mahsusiyil, mahsusihil
    poss: mahsusom, mahsusum
    loc: mahsusok
    dim: mahsusis
mahsuske (AI) he picks fiddleheads
    stem 1:   -mahsusk(e)-
mahtoqehs (A) rabbit
    plural: mahtoqehsuwok, mahtoqehsok
    poss: mahtoqehsumol,
        mahtoqehsomol
    dim: mahtoqehsis
Nkosiciyak eli nmihtaqs kisi peskhat newu
mahtoqehsu. I know that my father shot four
rabbits.
makasanikuwam (I) store (archaic)
    plural: makasanikuwamol
    loc: makasanikuwamok
    (from French, magasin, and -ikuwam,
house or building)
makasanke (AI) he goes to the store (archaic)
    stem 1:   -makasank(e)-
makotem (A) a man's brother-in-law
    nmakotem my brother-in-law (man
speaking)
makotemtuwok (AI) they are brothers-in-law
to each other
    stem 1:   -makotemt(i)-
    (i.e. they call each other nmakotem)
    (dual and plural forms only)
maksonol (A) his shoe
    (See pkoson "shoe".)
maleyu (AI) he is lazy
    plural: maleyultuwok
    stem 1:   -maley(i)-: nmaley I am lazy
malihkin (A) an American
    plural: malihkinok
    (from English, American)
malikikemosku (AI) he is someone who makes
fun of people
    stem 1:   -malikikemosk(i)-
malikikemu (AI) he makes fun of (someone)
    stem 1:   -malikikem(i)-
malikimal (TA) he makes fun of him
    stem 1:   -malikim-
Eci nomihit, nit te nmalikimkun. When he
sees me, he makes fun of me.
malom (P) finally; at last; eventually
    (usually used with "te" and contracted to
make "mamote")
    (See mamote.)
malsanhok (A) store-keeper
    malsanhom (AI) he keeps a store
    malsan (A) store-keeper
    (from French, marchand)
malsapsq (I) flint
    plural: malsapskul
    poss: malsapskum
    loc: malsapskuk
    dim: malsapsqis
malsom (A) wolf
    plural: malsomuwok, malsomok
    poss: malsomumol

loc: malsomuhsis, malsomsis, malsomis

malsonu (AI) he is weak
plural: malsonultuwok, malsonuhtuwok
stem 1: -malson(i)-

malsqosit, masqosit (I) bean
plural: malsqositol, masqositol

maltuhsis (A) hammer
plural: maltuhsisok
poss: maltuhsisomol
loc: maltuhsisok
dim: maltuhsossis
(from French, marteau)

mamam (A) mother
poss: mamamol

mamatuwiku (AI) he is crippled
stem 1: -mamatuwik(i)-

mamote (P) finally; at last; eventually
(See malom.)
Mamote moskuwawal. At last they found him.
Maceqahtuhukhotiniya eli pitpek 'samaqan, mamote supekuk etolitomek. They (pl.) floated off in the foaming water, and finally to the deep ocean.

mamselessu (AI, II) he, it has has many problems
stem 1: -mamseless(i)-

man (I) money
poss: manim
loc: manik, maniyik, manihik
dim: manis a little bit of money
(from English, money)
Ntihin nil kekesk manis. I have only a little money.

manimiw, manimu (AI) he has money
plural: manimultuwok, manimuhtuwok
stem 1a: -umanim(i)-: numanimipon we (nilun, dual) have money
stem 1b: manim(i)-: manimiwa, manimuwa he had money
stem 2: wemanim(i)-
(from English, money)
Skat wemanimihtihq, ma te 'kisonuhmuwoniya micuwakon. When they (dual) don't have money, they can't buy food.

maqe (maqiy-) (PV) coming together
(variant of mawe)

maqehe (II) it comes together
stem 1: maq_h(a)-

maqehhik, maqeyhik (AI) they (pl.) assemble
plural: maqahawolotuwok, maqahahtuwok
stem 1: -maq_h(a)-
(Dual and plural forms all have plural meanings.)

maqena (TA) he takes them into his home

maqenasu (II) it is collected
stem 1: maqenas(i)-

maqenike (AI) he takes people into his home; he gathers (food, clothing) for some worthy cause

stem 1: -maqenik(e)-

maskap (A) stud; over-sexed man

maskapiw (AI) he is over-sexed

maski (mask-) (PV) smelly
maskihtuwe (AI) he has smelly whiskers
maskotekone (AI) he has smelly skin
maskilqiye (AI) he has smelly armpits
maskosone, maskaksone (AI) he has smelly shoes
maskahqaluwe (AI) he has a smelly tail
maskaltoqe (AI) he has smelly hair

maskoqone (AI) she has sexy shoes; she has high heels
stem 1: -maskoqon(a)-

maskosit (I) smelly foot
plural: maskositol

maskosite (AI) his feet stink
stem 1: -maskosit(a)-

maspotekone (AI) he has thick skin
stem 1: -maspotekon(a)-

masq (I) birchbark
plural: masqiyil
dim: masqes

masqemus (A) birch tree
plural: masqemusiyik

masqewuloq (I) birchbark canoe
plural: masqewulokul
poss: masqewulokum
loc: masqewulokuk
dim: masqewulokuhsis

masqolamu (AI) he screams
plural: masqolamultuwok
stem 1: -masqolam(i)-
Wichuhketuwakon pawatomon, kmasqolamin. If you (sg.) need help, scream.

masqosit (I) bean
(See malsqosit.)

matayamkahte (II) a pile reaches its end
stem 1: matayamkaht(e)-
stem 2: matayamkaht(e)-, metayamkaht(e)-: matayamkahtek, metayamkahtek the end of the pile

matonal (TA) he fights him
stem 1: -maton-
'Cipiluwehsuwol matonokul. He is suffering from pleurisy. (Literally, pleurisy fights him.)
Mesq ote wen kiluwaw kmatonotihpa? Did you (sg.) ever fight with anybody? (Literally, did you (dual) ever fight each other?)

matsehkessu (AI) he has an infection
stem 1: -matsehkess(i)-

matsehkiye (AI) she is in heat; he is rutting
plural: matsehkiyawolotuwok, matsehkiyawolotuwok
stem 1: -matsehkiy(a)-

mattahal (TA) he beats him
stem 1: -matt_h-: kmattuhulc I'll beat you; mattehek when we (nilun) beat him
"Beats him" in the sense of punishing someone and of beating someone in a fight.

matuwehs (A) porcupine
plural: matuwehsuwok
poss: matuwehsumol
dim: matuwehsis

mawe (mawiy-) (PV) coming together (of more than two or of a mass)

mawe putuwosuwok (AI) they (pl.) come together and hold a council meeting
Kakehsukoniw mawe putuwosinya. For many days, they held a great council together.

mawehe (II) it comes together
stem 1:   -maw_h(a)-: mawahak when it comes together
(See maqehe.)
Tama toli mawehe samaqan eci komiwok? Where does the water come together when it rains?

mawehhik, maweyyik (AI) they (pl.) assemble
plural: mawahawolotuwok,
               mawahahtuwok
stem 1:   -maw_h(a)-

mawekak (AI) they (pl.) come together dancing
plural: mawekahtuwok,
               mawekawolotuwok
stem 1:   -mawek(a)-

mawi (maw-) (PV) together; in a group
mawihpuwok (AI) they (pl.) eat together

mawiw (P) together (of more than two or of a mass); in a group

mawona (TA) he gathers them (an.)
stem 1:   -mawon-
mawonal (TA) he gathers it (an.) together
Mawonal putawehtikonol ketuwocokonat. He gathers up the dough when he is going to knead it.

mawossominiyal (AI, AI+OBJ) they drink with him
plural: mawossomultiniyal,
               mawossomuhtuniyal
stem 1:   -mawossom(i)-

mawwenal (TA) he holds back (someone else's) hair
stem 1:   -mawwen-

mec (P) still; yet; keep(s) on
Cel mec tolapitehtehsin. And it keeps on snapping its teeth.
Mec ote yut wiku. He still lives here.

mecimi (P) always
Mecimi te mahqalsin. He always borrows it.

mecimihponoltuwok (AI) they (dual) are always fighting (each other)
plural: mecimihponoltultuwok
stem 1:   -mecimihponolt(i)-
(dual and plural forms only)

mecimihponosu (AI) he is always fighting
plural: mecimihponosultuwok they (pl.) are always fighting (separately, not with each other)
stem 1:   -mecimihponos(i)-

mecimiw (P) formerly; used to; in the past
Mecimiw wikuhpon Motahkomikuk. He used to live at Peter Dana Point, Maine.

mecimolamiye (AI) he has whooping cough
stem 1:   -mecimolamiy(a)-

mecimtehsinon (AI, AI+OBJ) he gets stuck in it
stem 1:   -mecimtehsin(o)- type B

mecopal (P) please; would it be possible? (=mec + op + al)
Mecopal op olu kisi acihtuwan 'tolamhok pomawsuwin? Is it possible for you to change a person's stomach?
Mecopal nuci utenek? May I go to town?

mehcikonahsin (AI) he is wasting away
stem 1:   -mehcikonahsin(o)- type B

mehcikoton (II) the year ends
mehcikotok the end of the year

mehcine (AI) he dies; he is dead
plural: mehcinhotuwok,
               mehcinahtuwok,
               mehcinawolotuwok
stem 1:   -mehcin(e)-
Psi te coqolsok mehcinhotukk. All the frogs are dead.

mehcintu (AI) he stops singing
stem 1:   -mehcint(u)-

mehciqqiye (AI, II) he, it stops bleeding
plural: mehciqqiyawolotuwok (AI)
stem 1:   -mehciqqiy(a)-

Mehqamkesk Red Beach, Maine (Locative)

mehqeyik, mehqeyit
(See pqeyu.)
Niktok nehtaw cikonihik skat mehqeyuhtihtihq, musa mahahkoc. If those apples aren't red, don't (sg.) eat them.

mehsi (PV) why; (what) for
(Note: Mehsi is always used with unchanged conjunct verb forms.)

mehsihpit (AI) why is he eating?
plural: mehsihpultihtit
(Conjunct forms only)

mehsikapuwit (AI) why is he standing?
plural: mehsikapuwultihtit
(Conjunct forms only)

mehtamkole (AI, II) it stops burning; it burns out
stem 1:   -mehtamkol(e)-

mehtapeksu (AI) that is the end of him
plural: mehtapeksultuwok
stem 1:   -mehtapeks(i)-

mehtatom (AI) he dies of old age
stem 1:   -mehtatom(o)- type A

mehtatomi naksq (A) old maid
plural: mehtatomi naksqiyik

mehtewestu (AI) he finishes speaking
plural: mehtewestuhtuwok
stem 1:   -mehtewest(u)-

mehtoluhke (AI) he gets off work; he stops working
plural: mehtolukhotuwok
stem 1:   -mehtoluhk(e)-

mehtonaskiye (II) it is all over; it is all finished
stem 1: mehtonaskiy(a)-
mehtuwehe (AI) his hair is falling out
plural: mehtuwahawolotuwok, mehtuwahahtuwok
stem 1: -mehtuw_h(a)-
Mekikatewik St. George, New Brunswick (Locative)
memhuwi (memhuw-) (PV) as much as possible
memhuwi kakaluwamal (TA) he calls out to him as loud as he can
memhuwi wihqahkan (AI, AI+OBJ) he pulls on it as hard as he can
memhuwi sehtayiw (P) as far back as possible; way back
memihpu (AI) he has eaten enough; he is full
plural: memihpultuwok, memihpuhtuwok
stem 1: -memihp(i)-
memonal (TA) he can and does reach him, it (an.) with his hand
stem 1: -memon-
Ma te memonawiyil skitap maltuhsisol. The man cannot reach the hammer.
memonomon (TI) he can and does reach it with his hand
stem 1: -memonom-
Menahqesk St. John, New Brunswick (Locative)
menakaciw (P) quietly; slowly
Nitap menakaciwoss pomi suku. My friend quietly paddled along.
Ksaha menakaciw weci skat tuhkimawot wasis. Go in quietly so that you (sg.) won't wake the baby.
menakaciye (AI) he goes slowly
plural: menakaciyahtuwok, menakaciyawolotuwok
stem 1: -menakaciy(a)-
menakacuhse (AI) he walks slowly
plural: menakatapasuwok
stem 1: -menakacuhs(e)-
menakatapasuwok (AI) they (pl.) walk slowly
stem 1: -menakatapas(i)-
(plural meanings only)
menakatkawotuwok (AI) they (dual) walk slowly
stem 1: -menakatkawot(i)-
(Note: Dual forms only.)
meqehsis (A) pimple
plural: meqehsisok
meqiyik, meqihik (A) Mohawks
mesotemit (AI) why is he crying?
(Conjunct forms only)
mesq (P) not yet; before
(used with negative verb forms)
Mesq piskiyanuhk, mottokhomoniya. Before it is dark, they (dual) swim to the other shore.
Mesq nokotomuwan yut uten, ntolluhkanc nit. Before I leave this town, I'll do that.
Mesq nomihtuwon. I haven't seen it yet.

messunal (TA) he shows him (to someone)
stem 1: -messun-
messunom (AI) he shows (something)
stem 1: -messunom(o)- type A
Mecimi te yali messunom eleyit. He is always going around showing his ways.
messunomon (TI) he shows it
plural: messunomultiniya, messunomuhtiniya
stem 1: -messunom-
messunomuwan (DOV) he shows it to him
stem 1: -messunomuw-
Neke messunomask epeskomakonol, wihqehtuwotsopon. When he showed you (sg.) the ball, you should have taken it away from him.
Neke messunomuwit yut qotoput, pileyawiwuhpon. When he showed me this chair, it was new.
messuwessu (AI) he appears
stem 1: -messuwess(i)-
messuwiw (AI) he is visible
stem 1: -messuw(i)- type B
metka (AI) he stops dancing
stem 1: -metk(a)-
metsoqsu (AI) he sleeps late
stem 1: -metsoqs(i)-
mettaqot (II) it stops playing (radio, record, etc.); it is over; the sound stops
stem 1: mettaqot(o)-: mettaqahk when it stops playing
mettehsin (AI) he is tired
stem 1: -mettehsin(o)- type B (Maliseet)
mettemu (AI) he finishes crying
stem 1: -mettem(i)-
mettokot (II) it is over; it comes to an end
stem 1: mettokot(o)-: mettokahk when it is over
(Said of something string-like or of a movie, story, etc.)
mewiyawiw (AI) he is feeling better
stem 1: -mewiyaw(i)- type B
micin (TI) he eats it
plural: micultiniya
stem 1: -mic(i)-: nmicin I eat it; micit when he ate it
micuwakon (I) food
plural: micuwakonol
poss: micuwakonum
loc: micuwakonok
dim: micuwakonis
Amucalu alatuwe micuwakonok. The fly is climbing around on the food.
mihkom (A) Micmac Indian
plural: mihkomak
abs: mihkomahsis
Mihkomahkik Micmac territory (Locative)
mihkomasqehs (A) Micmac woman
plural: mihkomasqehsuwok, mihkomasqehsok
abs: mihkomasqehsis Micmac girl

mihku (A) squirrel
  plural: mihkuwiyik, mihkuwok
  poss: mihkuwemol, mihkumol
  dim: mihkuwehsis, mihkuhsis
mihkumal (TA) he preaches to him; he
lectures to him; he counsels him
mihkutan (I) knife
  plural: mihkutanol
  poss: mihkutanom, mihkutanum
  loc: mihkutanok
  dim: mihkutanis small knife; table
                knife
mihqaphal (TA) he comes to his tracks
  stem 1:   -mihqaph-: kmihqaphul I
                come to your (sg.) tracks
mihqitahamal (TA) he recalls him; he thinks
of him
  stem 1:   -mihqitaham-
  Tokec mihqitahamiyin, ktimiyewin. If you
(sg.) happen to think of me, pray for me.
mihqitahatomon (TI) he remembers it
(suddenly)
  stem 1:   -mihqitahatom-
  Sesolahki te nmihqitahatomon neke
weciyayek Sitank. All of a sudden, I
remembered when we (nilun, dual) went to
St. Anne.
mihqotakon (I) knife
  (See mihkutakon.)
mihtaqs (A) father; priest
  plural: mihtaqsok
  poss: mihtaqsol
  dim: mihtaqsis
mikahke (AI) he fights
  stem 1:   -mikahk(e)-
mikikon (I) chest (body part)
  poss: mikikon
mikut (A) thorn
  plural: mikutiyik
mikutimus (A) thorn tree
  plural: mikutimusiyik
milahkomike (II) it is hilly land
  stem 1:   milahkomik(e)-
milan (DOV) he gives it to him
  stem 1:   -mil-
  Piyel nkisehtakun kmillon olomuss. Peter
made me give you (sg.) a dog.
  Kisi milin Mali 'temisol. You (sg.) gave
me Mary's dog.
  Mali 'kisi milanol wasis posonutiyil. Mary
gave the children baskets.
milapske (AI, II) it comes in many shapes; it
sticks out in one or more places
  stem 1:   -milapsk(e)-
milapskihke (II) it is bumpy
  stem 1:   -milapskihk(e)-
milapskosu (AI) it (an.) comes in many
shapes; it (an.) sticks out in one or more
places
  stem 1:   milapskos(i)-
milatqihton (II) the water is choppy
  stem 1:   milatqihton(o)- type A

milawiw (P) out in the water; out on the ice
milehtakesku (AI) he is a joker; he is always
getting into mischief
  stem 1:   -milehtakesk(i)-
mili (mil-) (PV) many; various; in a variety
of ways
  militposu (AI) he has many jobs, many
talents
  milicpikon (II) there are many kinds of it
militahasu (AI) he thinks of many different
things
milkomon (TI) he moves it every which way;
he drives it (e.g., a car) erratically
  Musa milkomuhkoc ktoqtoput! Don't
keep moving your chair around!
milluhke (AI) he does many things; he causes
many kinds of trouble
milomahtu (AI) he is mischievous
miltehkasu (II) it is danced in various ways
miluwan (AI, AI+OBJ) he gives it away
  plural: miluwahtiniya
  stem 1:   -miluw(e)-: miluwe he gives;
                miluwet when he gave it away;
                nmilu I give
  Mesq al ote miluwew, tehpu wikuwaci
wihqonom. He never gives; he just takes.
  Mali 'kisi miluwanol 'temisol. Mary gave
her dog away.
  Nkisehtaq nmihtaqs nmiluwan ntemis. My
father made me give my dog away.
mimey (I) grease; oil
mimuwipon (II) the water is perfectly calm
  stem 1:   mimuwipon(o)- type A
minkasu (AI) it (an.) bears fruit
  stem 1:   -minkas(i)-
minsoss (A) raspberry
  plural: minsossok
  poss: minsossumol
  loc: minsossok
  dim: minsossis
minsossimus (A) raspberry bush
  plural: minsossimusiyik
  poss: minsossimusemol
  loc: minsossimusek
  dim: minsossimusis
mip (I) leaf
  plural: mipiyil, mipihil
  poss: mipim
  loc: mipik
  dim: mipsis, mipisis
miskot (II) there is enough to go around
  stem 1:   miskot(o)-
  Miskot luhkewakon. There is enough work
to go around.
misuwes (I) flake of dry skin
  plural: misuwesol
mit (I) poplar
  plural: mitiyik
  poss: mitemol, mitimol
  loc: mitek, mitik
  dim: mitehsis, mitis
mitacaskekapuhu, mitacaskekapuwu (AI) he
stands with his legs spread apart
  stem 1:   -mitacaskekapuw(i)-

(Note: Stem w may be changed to h before u.)

Mitacaskekapuhultuwok eci tolewestultihtit. They (pl.) stand with their legs spread apart when they talk.

mitsu (AI) he eats
plural: mitsultuwok
stem 1: -mits(i)-

mitsut (I) fork (utensil)
plural: mitsutiyil
poss: mitsutim
loc: mitsutik
dim: mitsutossis

miyaw (P) exactly; just the one

Wen miyaw? Which one is which? Which is the right one?

Nikt nisicik kotama wewinuwawiyik wen miyaw. The two of them cannot be told apart.

Kotama wewinuwawiyil wenil miyaw. They do not know which is which.

Nit te miyaw nil eli pawatom. That is exactly the way I want it.

Not te miyaw kemutoneskit. He is the thief.

miyawiluweyuwal (TA) he makes him very happy
stem 1: -miyawiluweyuw-

miyawtahal (TA) he hits him with a well-aimed blow
stem 1: -miyawt_h-
stem 2: meyawt_h-

miyawtehmon (TI) he hits it with a well-aimed blow
stem 1: -miyawtehm-; but: miyawtohok if he hits it
stem 2: meyawtehm-; but: meyawtohok when he hit it; meyawtem when I hit it

miyawtelasu (AI) he wounds himself (by shooting)
plural: miyawtelasultuwok
stem 1: -miyawtelas(i)-

miyawteluwal (TA) he shoots him accurately; he shoots him and hits him; he wounds him
stem 1: -miyawteluw-: nmiyawtelaq he shoots me
stem 2: meyawteluw-: meyawteluwat when he shot him

mkihkon (I) fish hook
(See pkihkon.)

mocacomuwakon (I) false statement; libel; dirty story
plural: mocacomuwakonol

mocahant (A) devil
plural: mocahantuwok

mocalokotune (AI) he has a dirty mouth (uses dirty language)
stem 1: -mocalokotun(a)-
stem 2: mecalokotun(a)-

mocatuwe (AI) he talks dirty
stem 1: -mocatuw(e)-
stem 2: mecatuw(e)

mocawtosson (II) it is a bad road
stem 1: mocawtosson(o)-
stem 2: mecawtosson(o)-: mecawtossok when it was a bad road

moccoke (II) it is dirty
stem 1: moccok(e)-
stem 2: meccok(e)-

Nehtaw possiyantehsok moccokek, kospahtun. If the window is dirty, wash (sg.) it.

moccokiptinehlal (TA) he gets his (someone else's) hand dirty
stem 1: -moccokiptinehl-
stem 2: meccokiptinehl-

mocehs (I) article of clothing
plural: mocehsuwol
poss: mocehsum

moci (moc-) (PV, PN) bad, evil; "dirty"; sexy
neke form: meci (mec-)
mocelomoqe (AI) he has bad luck

mocihpukot (II) it tastes bad

mocihpuksu (AI) it (an.) tastes bad

mocihtaqot (II) it sounds bad

mocikon (II) it is spoiled, no good

mociku (AI) he is bad (bad at what he does, evil, etc.)

mocimahsu (AI) he, it (an.) smells bad
plural: mocimahsultuwok
stem 1: -mocimahs(i)-
stem 2: mecimahs(i)-: mecimahsit when he smelled bad

mocimahte (II) it smells bad
stem 1: mocimaht(e)-
stem 2: mecimaht(e)-

mocinaqot (II) it looks bad
stem 1: mocinaqot(o)-
stem 2: mecinaqot(o)-

Nehtaw mocinaqahk nit wikuwam, musa monuhmuhkoc. If that house is ugly, don't (sg.) buy it.

mocinaqsu (AI) he looks bad
plural: mocinaqsultuwok, mocinaqsuhtuwok

mocitahamal (TA) he thinks badly of him

mocitahamtuwok (AI) they (dual) think badly of each other
plural: mocitahamtultuwok, mocitahamtuhtuwok

mocitahasuwamal (TA) he thinks evil thoughts about him

mociyehs (A) partridge

mociyehsuhke (AI) he hunts partridges
plural: mociyehsukhotuwok, mociyehsuhkahtuwok
stem 1: -mociyehsuhk(e)-: nmociyehsuhk I hunt partridges; mociyehsuhket if he hunts partridges
stem 2: mociyehsuhk(e)-: mociyehsuhket when he hunted partridges

Mecimiw mociyehsuhket, nwiciyema.
When he used to hunt partridges, I went with
him.

mocokiskot (II) it is a bad day (bad weather,
bad events, etc.)
stem 1: mocokiskot(o)-
stem 2: mecokiskot(o)-: mecokiskahk
when the weather was bad

mocolamson (II) the wind is blowing from a
bad direction, in bad weather, etc.

mocomolsu (AI) he feels ill
plural: mocomolsultuwok

mocomomqosu (AI) it (an.) is uncomfortable
(of clothing: too tight, scratches the skin,
etc.)
plural: mocomomqosuhtuwok

mocomomqot (II) it is uncomfortable (of
clothing: too tight, scratches the skin, etc.)

moconome (AI) he is sloppy

mocuwe (AI) he has messy hair

mok (I) scab
plural: mokiyil
poss: mokim
loc: mokik
(See mokis "scab".)

mokahk (A) striped bass; sea bass
plural: mokahkiyik
poss: mokahkemol
dim: mokahkehsis

mokahkehke (AI) he spears striped bass
plural: mokahkehkahtuwok
stem 1: -mokahkehk(e)-
stem 2: mokahkehk(e)-

mokalip (A) caribou (Maliseet)
plural: mokalipuwok
poss: mokalipumol
dim: mokalipuhsis, mokalipuwis
Mokalip 'tahcuwi muskaliyikhomon
elihpit. The caribou has to move the snow
aside where he eats.

mokis (I) scab
plural: mokisol
poss: mokisom
loc: mokisok
dim: mokisis
(See mok "scab".)

mokonal (TA) he picks him out
stem 1a: -mokon-
stem 1b: pkon-: pkonat if he picks him
out
stem 2: mekon-: mekonat when he
picked him out
stem 3: -mkon-: 'totolimkonat he is
picking him out

mokos (I) soot; dead coal
plural: mokosiyil
poss: mokosem
loc: mokosek
dim: mokosesis

mokosewalokiqe (AI) he has a black eye
stem 1: -mokosewalokiq(a)-
stem 2: mekosewalokiq(a)-

mokosewaluhkiye (II) there are black clouds

mokosewatpe (AI) he has black hair
stem 1: -mokosewatp(a)-
stem 2: mekosewatp(a)-

mokoseweyu (AI, II) he,it is black

mokosewi (mokosew-) (PV) dark; black
neke form: mekosewi (mekosew-)
mokosewinaqot (II) it looks black
mokosewaqosu (AI) it (an.) is cooked
black

mokosewiye (AI) he turns black

mokosewocossu (AI) he, it (an.) is colored
black; he is black and blue

molaqs (A) milk
plural: molaqsok
poss: molaqsumol
loc: molaqsok

molaqsinut (A) milk container
plural: molaqsinutiyik

molaqsipom (I) butter
plural: molaqsipomiyil, molaqsipomol
poss: molaqsipomum
loc: molaqsipomok
dim: molaqsipomis piece of butter

molihkapocu (AI) he has a strong grip
stem 1: -molihkapoc(i)-
stem 2: melihkapoc(i)-

molihkikone (AI) he is strong
stem 1: -molihkikon(a)-
stem 2: melihkikon(a)-

molihkiptine (AI) he has strong arms (or
hands)
stem 1: -molihkiptin(a)-
stem 2: melihkiptin(a)-

molihkiw (P) frequently

moliksonu (AI) he is strong
poss: -molikson(i)-
dim: melikson(i)-

molomahkonoma (AI) his gun goes off by
accident
plural: molomahkonomahtuwok
stem 1: -molomahkonom(a)-
stem 2: melomahkonom(a)-

molomeqalal, monomeqalal (TA) it (lightning)
strikes him
stem 1: -molomeqal-, -monomeqal-
stem 2: melomeqal-, menomeqal-
(Used at Pleasant Point, Maine.)
Neke melomeqalat petak oposiyil, psikessu.
When the lightning hit the tree, it split open.

molomeqatomon, monomeqatomon (TI) it
(lightning) strikes it
stem 1: -molomeqatom-,
-monomeqatom-
stem 2: melomeqatom-,
-menomeqatom-
(Used at Pleasant Point, Maine.)
Mecimi te molomeqatomon petak etoli
spahkomikek. Lightning always strikes
where the ground is high.

Monahnuk Grand Manan Island, New
Brunswick (Locative)

monapitehtahal (TA) he knocks his (someone else's) teeth out
  stem 1:   -monapiteht_h-
  stem 2:   menapiteht_h-
monessu (AI) it (an.) peels off; he gets off, gets out of a trap
monhiqe (AI) he peels off bark
  (See pqonhike.)
monhomon (TI) he skims it off
monihq (I) island
  plural: monihkul
  poss: monihkum
  loc: monihkuk
  dim: monihkuhsis
  Ntolhom monihkuhsisok. I'm going to swim out to the little island.
monipqotatomon (TI) he takes the ashes out of it
  stem 1:   -monipqotatom(o)-
  stem 2:   menipqotatom(o)-
  Monipqotatomon papskot. He takes the ashes out of the stove.
moniptinephal (TA) he pulls his (someone else's) hand quickly off (something)
  stem 1:   -moniptineph-
  stem 2:   meniptineph-
monkehtun (TI) he digs it out with its roots
monnomon (TI) he peels it off
monolamson (II) the wind blows something off
monomeqalal (TA) he storms at him
  stem 1:   -monomeqal-
  stem 2:   menomeqal-
  (Maliseet)
  monomeqalawal it (literally, they) (lightning) strikes him
  (See molomeqalal.)
  Neke petakiyik menomeqalahtit oposiyil, wpossikteluwawal. When lightning struck the tree, it split it open.
  Npeci monomeqaloq. He came and stormed at me.
monomeqatomon (TI) he storms at it
  stem 1:   -monomeqatom-
  stem 2:   menomeqatom-
  (Maliseet)
  monomeqatomoniya it (literally, they) (lightning) strikes it
  (See molomeqatomon.)
monomeqe (AI) lightning strikes
  monomeqiyik lightning strikes
monoqan (A) rainbow
  plural: monoqanok
monossapsq (I) rock island
  plural: monossapskul
montelomuwan (DOV) he shoots off something of his (someone else's) (e.g. he shoots his hand off)
monuhmon (TI) he buys it
  plural: monuhmuhtiniya
  stem 1:   -monuhm-
  stem 2:   menuhm-: menuhman when I bought it; but: menuwok when he bought it

stem 3:   -onuhm-: 'kisonuhmon he bought it
monuhmuwan (DOV) he buys it from him; he buys something of someone else's
monuhmuwewan (DOV) he buys it for him
  stem 1:   -monuhmuwew-
  stem 2:   menuhmuwew-: menuhmuwewot when you (sg.) bought it for him
  stem 3:   -onuhmuwew-: 'kisonuhmuwewan he bought it for him
  Mehsi al monuhmuwewolans nahsqehtakon? Why did I buy you (sg.) a ring?
monuhsehkasu (AI) he fasts
monuwal (TA) he buys it (an.)
  stem 1:   -monuw-
  stem 2:   menuw-: menuwat when he bought it (an.)
  stem 3:   -onuw-: 'kisonuwal he bought it (an.)
  (Note: These stems do not contract with endings beginning with o or i. See -onuw-.)
moqin (II) it swells; it is swollen
  stem 1a: moqin(o)- type B
  stem 1b: meqin(o)-
moqisu (AI) he swells; he is swollen
  stem 1:   -moqis(i)-
  stem 2:   meqis(i)-
moqqeyin
  (See pqeyu.)
moscehtun (TI) he swallows it whole; he swallows it without chewing it
  stem 1a: -mosceht-
  stem 1b: psoceht-
  stem 2:   mesceht-
moshunine
  (See psuhunine.)
mosiyal (TA) he gives him a disease; he infects him
  stem 1:   -mosiy-
  stem 2:   mesiy-
moskeyin (AI, AI + OBJ) he is sorry about it
  stem 1a: -moskey(i)-
  stem 1b: psahkey(i)-: psahkeyu he is sorry about something
  stem 2:   meskey(i)-: meskeyit when he was sorry about it
  stem 3:   msahkey(i)-: kisi msahkeyu he was sorry about something
moskomon (TI) he finds it
  stem 1a: -moskom-
  stem 1b: pskom-
  stem 2:   meskom-
  stem 3:   mskom-
moskuwal (TA) he finds him
  stem 1a: -moskuw-
  stem 1b: pskuw
  stem 2:   meskuw-
  stem 3:   mskuw-
moskuwecinon (AI, AI + OBJ) he gets a splinter from it
  stem 1a: -moskuwecin(o)- type B

stem 1b: pskuwecin(o)-
stem 2:   meskuwecin(o)-

mosonal (TA) he catches him; he gets it (an.)
stem 1a: -moson-: nmosona I catch him
stem 1b: pson-: psonat if he catches him
stem 2:   meson-: mesonat when he caught him
stem 3:   mson-

Neqt welaqiwik ali kotunki, on nmosonoken. Once when I was out hunting at night, I got caught.

Mosonahsal esponsisol. He caught a little raccoon.

Mosonal elomipuwelit. He caught him running away.

mosonomon (TI) he gets it
stem 1a: -mosomon-
stem 1b: psonom-
stem 2:   mesonom-: mesonok when he got it
stem 3:   msonom-: eli msonokopon, eli msonokpon what he got

mosop (I) region across the back at the waist
plural: mosopihil
loc: mosopik

mosopine (AI) he has hip pain
stem 1:   -mosopin(e)-
stem 2:   mesopin(e)-

mosqon (I) chest (body part) (Maliseet)
(See mikikon "chest.")

mossis (A) older sister
plural: mossisok
poss: mossisol

mosson (I) muck
loc: mossonok

Motahkokmikuk Peter Dana Point, Maine (Locative)

motahkomiqew (A) a person from Peter Dana Point, Maine
plural: motahkomiqewiyik

motape (motapiy-) (PV) downhill
neke form: metape (metapiy-)
motapewse (AI) he walks downhill
motapiyapasuwok (AI) they (pl.) walk downhill

motapekuloq (I) ship; warship
plural: motapekulokul
poss: motapekulokum
loc: motapekulokuk

motapekuwin (A) warrior (archaic)
plural: motapekuwinuwok

motapeqehe (AI, II) it rolls downhill

motapetomehe (AI, II) he, it goes downhill on wheels
stem 1:   -motapetom_h(a)-
stem 2:   metapetomah(a)-

motapetomhe (AI, II) he, it goes downhill with a gliding motion

motapew (P) downhill

motapiyahkiw (P) downhill

motaqs (A) lady; older woman (primarily a term of address)

mote (motiy-) (PV) be heard ...ing
neke form: mete (metiy-)
mote kakaluwe (AI) he is heard calling out
mote suku (AI) he is heard paddling:
Nutaq weckuwi mote suki. He heard me coming toward him paddling.
motewehtu, motiyewehtu (AI) he (a dog) is heard howling
motiyaphal (TA) he is heard tracking him
motiyayye (AI) he is heard playing
motiyewestu (AI) he is heard speaking

motehehsim (A) duck (especially black duck)
plural: motehehsimok
poss: motehehsimmol
dim: motehehsimsis

motehsan (A) youngest child
plural: motehsanok
poss: motehsanol

motehtehsin (AI) he is heard falling with a crash

motekon (I) skin
plural: motekonol

motekoniyehs (A) bat (animal)
plural: motekoniyehsuwok

motepehs (A) catfish
plural: motepehsuwok
poss: motepehsumol

moteqsu (AI) he is heard sleeping; he snores

motetemu (AI) he is heard crying
Solahki te nutuwawal wasisol metetemilit. Suddenly they heard a child crying.

motewahqem (A) flag pole
plural: motewahqemok
poss: motewahqemomol,
               motewahqemmol,
               motewahqemol
loc: motewahqemok

motewekon (I) flag
plural: motewekonol
poss: motewekonum
loc: motewekonok
dim: motewekonossis

motewekonahasu (II) it has a flag on it
stem 1:   motewekonahas(i)-
stem 2:   motewekonahas(i)-,
               metewekonahas(i)-:
               motewekonahasik,
               metewekonahasik when it had a flag on it

Nit te nomihtuhtit mihkomak weckuwyak oqiton motewekonahasik, 'kisi nsotuhmoniya keq itomuwiw. If the Micmacs see a canoe coming bearing a flag, they can tell what it means.

motewolon, ptewolon (A) person with extraordinary power; witch (contemporary usage)
plural: motewolonuwok,
               ptewolonuwok

motewolonuwintuwakon (I) song of great magical power

'Tolintuwatomon
motewolonuwintuwakon, wihqintuwama
putepiyi. He sings a song of great magical
power, luring the whales with his song.

motiyaqasokonike (AI) he is heard walking in
high bushes

motiyewestu (AI) he is heard speaking
stem 1: -motiyewest(u)-
stem 2: metiyewest(u)-
Yat nit metiyewestaq ntutemisq. My
girlfriend is the one that you hear speaking
over there. (Literally, ...the one who is heard
speaking.)

motkapkotete (II) smoke rises straight up;

motkayakhom (AI) he aims (a gun) straight
up
stem 1a: -motkayakhom(o)- type B
stem 1b: ptokayakhom(o)-
stem 2: metkayakhom(o)-

motkayiw (P) straight up; directly overhead
Nipawset pomuhse motkayiw. The moon
is moving directly overhead in the sky.

motutomesku (AI) he bums
stem 1a: -motutomesk(i)-
stem 1b: motutomesk(i)-, 'tutomesk(i)-
stem 2: metutomesk(i)-

motutomuwan (DOV) he bums it from him

motutuwalal (TA) he starts it (an.) burning;
he kindles it (an.)
stem 1: -motutuwal-
stem 2: metutuwal-

motutuwatomon (TI) he starts it burning; he
kindles it
stem 1: -motutuwatom-
stem 2: metutuwatom-

motutuwe (AI) he builds a fire
stem 1: -motutuw(e)-
stem 2: metutuw(e)-

motuweyu (II) it is difficult, hard to deal with
'sami motuweyu that's too bad

mqeyu (AI, II) he,it is red
(See pqeyu.)

msi, msiw (P) all; every
(See psi, psiw.)

muck (P) (not) even
Muck ote pesq ma 'tasqessiwon. Not even
one is left behind.
Kotama tehc muck pesq sqihtahawon tan
wot pomawsuwinuwihpit. Not even one shall
be spared who eats people.

muhsacin (AI, AI + OBJ) he is fond of it
stem 1: -muhsac(i)-
Komac muhsacinol. He is very fond of
her.

muhsalal (TA) he likes him very much
stem 1: -muhsal-

muhsaltomon (TI) he likes it very much
stem 1: -muhsaltom-

muhsilepehk (A) bishop
(from French, monsieur l'évêque)

muhsums (A) grandfather
plural: muhsumsok
poss: muhsumsol

muhsumi, muhmumi, muhmum grampa
(term of address)

mulatomuwehe (II) it (a boat) sets deep in the
water
stem 1: mulatomuw_h(a)-

mulcess (A) mitten
plural: mulcessok

munimqehs (A) woodchuck; groundhog
plural: munimqehsuwok

munsayuwal (TA) he does things to gain his
favor
stem 1: -munsayuw-
munsayawotuwok (AI) they do things to
gain each other's favor

mus (A) moose
plural: musuwok, musok
poss: musumol
dim: musuhsis, musossis
Kotunkewin musuwol 'peskhan pahq. The
hunter shot the moose with an arrow.

mus, musa, musahk (P) not; don't
Musa milihtic sahtiyil, npawatomonol
sunol. Don't have them give me blueberries;
I want cranberries.
Musahk komutonehkoc. Thou shalt not
steal.

musahkuhs (A) sea urchin
plural: musahkuhsok
poss: musahkuhsomol
dim: musahkuhsis

musal (TA) he cuts his (someone else's) hair
stem 1: -mus-
Ma te nmusukuwinnuk wolaku. They
didn't cut our (nilun) hair yesterday.
Mecimi te wmusal 'qossol. He always cuts
his son's hair.

musawe (AI) he cuts hair; he barbers

mushawapun, moshawapun (A) eyelash
plural: mushawapunok
(Pleasant Point, Maine)

muskessu (AI, II) he, it comes out; he breaks
out in a rash
Apiqsehs 'ci muskessu elomalokahsok.
The rat emerged from a little hole.

muskiye (AI, II) he, it comes out
stem 1: -muskiy(a)-
Kis muskiye nipawset. The moon has
already come out.

musqelomal (TA) he reprimands him
stem 1: -musqelom-

musqitahamal (TA) he hates him
stem 1: -musqitaham-

musqiye (II) it (weather) clears off
stem 1: musqiy(a)-

musuhke (AI) he hunts moose
plural: musukhotuwok,
musuhkahtuwok
stem 1: -musuhk(e)-

muwikasu (AI) he has a swollen gland
stem 1: -muwikas(i)-

muwin (A) bear
plural: muwiniyik, muwinuwok
poss: muwinemol, muwinumol

dim: muwinesis, muwinehsis, muwinuhsis

obv: muwiniyil, muwinuwol

Ktaqhomuhs nehpahal muwinihil. The old man killed a bear.

Nomiyal muwinuwol ihtoli sukayewotasultimok. He saw a bear at the dump.

muwinesq (A) she-bear

plural: muwinesqihik

muwinewey (I) bear meat

muwinuhke, muwinehke (AI) he hunts bear

stem 1: -muwinuhk(e)-, -muwinehk(e)-

N

na, ona (P) also, besides; for his part; here (when handing something to someone)

Piyel na cipokihtaqsu. Peter, too, yells.

Kil na kotuhp? How about you (sg.), are you hungry?

naci (nac-, nat-) (PV) change location; go (or come) to...

nataphal (TA) he goes (or comes) to track him

natsoqe (AI) he goes (or comes) to check traps

natawone (AI), he goes (or comes) to gather eggs

naciksomon (TI) he goes (or comes) to cut it

nacitahamal (TA) he hates him

nacitahamtuwok they (du.) hate each other 'Keskuhtehkuwal elomi pusilicil Mociyehsuwol, kci nacitahamtihticil, naka Koluskap 'siwiyi. He comes upon Partridge, his great enemy, pushing off in a boat with Koluskap's relatives.

nacossin (AI) he goes (or comes) and lies down

nahaht, nahahtew, nahahtiw (P) a little while ago

nahahtiwoss, nahahtiwossis (P) a little while ago

nahsahqehtakon (I) ring

plural: nahsahqehtakonol

poss: nahsahqehtakonum

loc: nahsahqehtakonok

dim: nahsahqehtakonossis

nahsehtun (TI) he puts it (clothing) on

nahsiye (AI, II) it goes onto (something)

stem 1: -nahsiy(a)-

Keq pileyawik, nitte nahsiye. Whenever something (e.g. clothing, jewelry) is new, it goes right on.

naka (P) and; with

Opin naka kutoman. Sit down (sg.) and smoke.

Mali macehhik naka Piyel. Mary and Peter are leaving.

Wen macahat naka Piyel? Who is leaving with Peter?

naksq (A) young woman

plural: naksqiyik

dim: naksqehsis

nama (P) no

(used mainly at Indian Township, Maine) (Compare kotama, ne, cu.)

nan (P) five (in counting)

nominal forms: animate nanuwok; obviative nanu; inanimate nanonul

nanakiw (P) suddenly; all of a sudden; immediately

On apc yaq nanakiwoss 'tiyal yaq, "Ma te mahtoqehs yut tuciyew?" And then again, he suddenly said to him, "Hasn't a rabbit gone by here?"

nanuhsalqot (II) it is five miles

stem 1: nanuhsalqot(o)-

napaha (A) rooster

plural: napahak

poss: napahamol

dim: napahahsis

napehsom (A) male animal

plural: napehsomok, napehsomuk

poss: napehsomumol, napehsehsumol

dim: napehsomis

Ntemis nil napehsom. My dog is a male.

napisqahman (AI, AI+OBJ) he trips over it

plural: napisqahmahtiniya

stem 1: -napisqahm(a)-: napisqahma he trips; but: napisqam I trip; knapisqam you (sg.) trip

napolup (I) one of the reins for a horse

plural: napolupiyil

poss: napolupim

loc: napolupiyik, napolupik

dim: napolupossis

nashutasu (AI) it (an.) is threaded

stem 1: -nashutas(i)-

Nashutasu sahkat. The needle is threaded.

naskahtaqsu (AI) he is loud and angry, obnoxious

stem 1: -naskahtaqs(i)-

naskahtaqsuwamal (TA) he hollers at him discouragingly

stem 1: -naskahtaqsuwam-

naskaluwemal (TA) he discourages him

stem 1: -naskaluwem-

Musa naskaluwemahkoc. Don't (sg.) discourage him.

naskatahamal (TA) he is discouraged about him

stem 1: -naskataham-

naskatahasu (AI) he feels discouraged

stem 1: -naskatahas(i)-

naskuwal (TA) he shares a bed with him

stem 1: -naskuw-

naskuwamal (TA) he sleeps in the same house with him

stem 1: -naskuwam-

naskuwaniyal (AI, AI+OBJ) he sleeps with him (in the same bed or in the same house)

stem 1: -naskuw(a)-: naskuwa someone sleeps with him

nasqahal (TA) he combs his (someone else's) hair

stem 1: -nasq_h-

(Note: The vowel before the h of the stem always matches the vowel which begins the ending. When the vowel before h is u, the q before it changes to k.)

Mecimi te naskuhusu spasuwiw. He always combs his (own) hair in the morning.

nassewe (AI) he gets dressed

plural: nassewhotuwok, nassewahtuwok

stem 1: -nassew(e)-: nassewet when he was getting dressed

nassewhutolal (TA) he dresses him

stem 1: -nassewhutol-

nassewhutolosu (AI) he dresses himself

nastahal (TA) he hits it (an.) to make it go on (e.g. a ring over a post)

stem 1: -nast_h-

naste (II) it (clothing) is on; it (clothing) is being worn

nastehmon (TI) he hits it to make it go on

stem 1: -nastehm-; but: nastohok when he hits it on

natassihkuwal (TA) he goes to meet him

stem 1: -natassihkuw-

On yaq ehpit nuteqasqin naka natassihkuwan. And then, they say, the woman ran out and went to meet him.

natewotuwan (DOV) he comes (or goes) and gets it for him

stem 1: -natewotuw-

natkuwal (TA) he goes right to him

stem 1: -natkuw-

natolasihkuwal (TA) he goes (or comes) to greet him

stem 1: -natolasihkuw-

natomaskute (II) it is quite a big field

stem 1: natomaskut(e)-

natomokihqon (II) it is fairly big

stem 1: natomokihqon(o): natomokihqahk a fairly big one (inan.)

natomokil (AI) he is fairly big

stem 1: -natomokil(o)-: natomokilok a fairly big one (an.)

natonihiqe (AI) he goes (or comes) to get birchbark

natqahsu (AI) he goes somewhere to sleep

stem 1: -natqahs(i)-

nattokaphuwe (AI) he gets out and runs away

plural: nattokaphuwawotuwok, nattokaphuwolotuwok

stem 1: -nattokaphuw(e)-: nattokaphu I get out and run away

nattomimal (TA) he goes (or comes) to hire him

stem 1: -nattomim-

nattutuwe (AI) he goes (or comes) to build a fire

stem 1: -nattutuw(e)-

Nattutu pahkak weci kisahqosuhtihiq. Go (sg.) build a fire out back so that we (kilun. pl.) can cook.

nawiw (P) among

Nawiw te sehke. He is standing in a group of people (among objects, etc.)

nawtaqsu (AI) he sounds far away

stem 1: -nawtaqs(i)-

ne (P) no (sassy)

(Compare nama, kotama, cu.)

nehkayiw, nehkayi (P) all the time

nehm (A) turkey

(variant of nem)

nehpahal (TA) he kills him

stem 1: -nehp_h-: knehpihi you (sg.) kill me

nehpahtun (TI) he kills it

stem 1: -nehpaht-

nehse (AI) he breathes

stem 1: -nehs(e)-

Wahkehs eli nehsemok muskamqehtun. After but a few breaths, he pulls it from the coals.

nehsewon (I) breath

neke, neket (P) then, at that time (past); long ago

Koluskap neke wikuss monihkuk. Long ago, Koluskap lived on an island.

neke, neket, nekew (I) (PRO) that (inan., absent or dead, near person spoken to)

(Absentative form of nit "that (inan.)": see not "that (an.)".)

nekom (A) (PRO) he, she

plural: nekomaw they

(Note: There are no obviative or absentative forms of nekom.)

(Nekom is used only for people or animals.)

Nekom nit 'toposim. That's his stick.

Nekomaw opiyahtuwok. They (more than two) are sitting.

nekosantuphat (A) short stop (in baseball)

plural: nekosantuphacik

(literally, "one who catches quickly")

nekosun (A, I) sleeping mat (blanket, animal skin, etc.)

plural: nekosunok, nekosunol

poss: 'tonekosunol, 'tonekosun

nem, nehm (A) turkey

plural: nemiyik

poss: nemimol

dim: nemsis

Nwikahpa nem. I like to eat turkey.

nemaht (P) to, at my home

nemq (P) barely

Kci monossapskuk nemq ote sakpe, nit elossit. On a great rock island, barely showing above the water, there he lay.

Nemq ote kisiwtome, on mace neqhomon. He had barely started to smoke when he began to cough.

nenehsawte (II) it could go either way; it could be changed, knocked off, etc., easily; it is precarious *stem 1:*   nenehsawt(e)-

nenehson (II) it flips over easily
   stem 1:   nenehson(o)- type A

nepskihkamq (I) red willow; squaw bush
   plural: nepskihkamkul
   poss: nepskihkamkum
   loc: nepskihkamkuk
   dim: nepskihkamqis
   Mecimiw skicinuwok utomektuniya nepskihkamq wawikiw 'tomawey. The Indians used to smoke red willow mixed with tobacco.

neqasuke (AI) he wades under (something, e.g., a bridge)
   stem 1:   -neqasuk(e)-

neqhom (AI) he coughs
   plural: neqhomultuwok,
           neqhomuhtuwok
   stem 1:   -neqhom(o)- type A

neqiw (P) underneath

neqiye (AI) he goes under
   stem 1:   -neqiy(a)-

neqoloqessu (AI) he goes under the ice
   stem 1:   -neqoloqess(i)-

Neqotkuk Tobique, New Brunswick (Locative)

neqotom (AI) he chokes (on liquid)
   stem 1:   -neqotom(o)- type A

neqskihqessuhke (AI) he hunts woodcock
   stem 1:   -neqskihqessuhk(e)-

neqskiqessoss (A) woodcock
   plural: neqskiqessossok

neqt (P) one (in counting); once
   Neqt ewasisuwi, natsakiya kincemossusq. Once when I was little, I went to see the queen.
   Neqt te wiqsonepal, psi te 'kihkayaqotete 'tomeway. He puffs once and all the tobacco is burned away.

neqtuwikhikon (A) ace (in cards)
   plural: neqtuwikhikonok

new (P) four (in counting)
   nominal forms: animate newwok; obviative newu; inanimate newonul

newuhsalqot (II) it is four miles
   stem 1:   newuhsalqot(o)-

newukoniw (P) for four days; after four days
   newukonohok (P) on the fourth day

nicalkul (A) (dep.) his (or her) uncle (father's brother)
   nicaloq my uncle

nicaniw (AI) she has a child
   plural: nicanultuwok, nicanuhtuwok
   stem 1a: -unican(i)-: nunican I have a
           child
   stem 1b: nican(i)- type B
   stem 2:   wenican(i)-: wenicanit one
           who has a child
   stem 3:   wnican(i)-: 'sami wnicaniw she
           has too many children
   Can nicaniwok naka En. John and Ann are having a child.

nicanol (A) (dep.) his child
   plural: nican his children
   dim: nicansisol
   'Kihkanhotossultukk knicankokk. Your (sg.) poor little children are all dead.

nihi (P) three (in counting)
   nominal form: animate nuhuwok; obviative nuhu; inanimate nohonul (also, in counting: 'sis three)

nihkanatpe (AI) he heads (an organization)
   plural: nihkanatpahtuwok,
           nihkanatpawolotuwok,
           nihkanatpawotuwok
   stem 1:   -nihkanatp(a)-: nihkanatpat
           head (of an organization)

nihkaniw (P) ahead; in front

nihkanke (AI) he paddles in the front of a canoe
   stem 1:   -nihkank(e)-

nihkaskuwal (TA) he encourages him
   stem 1:   -nihkaskuw-

nihkoskawe (AI) he has a nightmare (of being unable to move)

nihluwacomin (AI, AI+OBJ) he stirs up trouble by talking about it
   plural: nihluwacomultiniya
   stem 1:   -nihluwacom(i)-: nihluwacomu
           he stirs up trouble by talking
   Nospi nihluwacominok ehpicik weci cocepiyahtit. I fouled things up by talking about the women, with the result that the couple split up.

nihluwehtun (TI) he fouled it up by tinkering with it
   stem 1:   -nihluweht-

nihluweyuwal (TA) he makes trouble for him
   stem 1:   -nihluweyuw-

nihluwinaw, nihluwinaq (P) to make matters worse; on top of that
   Kis eci milelomoqi, apc nihluwinaq nokothuken. On top of everything that had already happened to me, I got left behind.

nihtakihtomuwal (TA) he is in mourning for him
   stem 1:   -nihtakihtomuw-

nihtakihtuwal, 'takihtuwal (TA) he mourns for him
   stem 1a: -nihtakihtuw-, -takihtuw-
   stem 1b: nihtakihtuw-, 'takihtuw-
   stem 2:   nehtakihtuw-, 'takihtuw-:
           nehtakihtuwat when he was
           mourning for him
   stem 3:   ntakihtuw-
   (See 'taku "he is in mourning".)

nihtaphal (TA) he nets it (an., a fish)
   stem 1a: -nihtaph-
   stem 1b: 'taph-
   stem 2:   nehtaph-
   stem 3:   ntaph-, 'taph-

nihtuphal (TA) he catches him, it (an.)
   stem 1a: -nihtuph-: nihtuphukun (and
           then) he caught me
   stem 1b: 'tuph-: 'tuphat if he catches
           him

stem 2: nehtuph-: nehtuphat when he caught him
stem 3: ntuph-
(Note: refers only to catching something (an.) or someone thrown or falling.)
nihtuptun (TI) he catches it
(Note: refers only to catching something thrown or falling.)
nika mother (term of address)
Cu te olu nika, nomiya nhesis. Yes, really, mother, I do see my older brother.
nikcahke (AI) it (an., an animal) digs up the ground noisily and angrily
stem 1: -nikcahk(e)-
nikcahkehtun (TI) he (e.g. a rutting animal) tears it (e.g. the ground) up noisily and angrily
stem 1: -nikcahkeht-
niktuhkomon (TI) he holds it between his legs
stem 1: -niktuhkom-
niktuwahqonehc (A) spike-horn deer
plural: niktuwahqonehcuwok
niktuwikonehe (AI) it (an.) forks out into a V; it (an.) branches out into a V
stem 1: -niktuwikon_h(a)-
niktuwiku (AI) it (an.) has two prongs, branches, extensions, etc.
stem 1: -niktuwik(i)-
nil (A) (PRO) I, me; my; mine
plural: nilun we (not including you); kilun we (including you)
nila it's me; I'm the one; me myself
nilun (A) (PRO) we, us (not including you); our, ours (not including you)
(Compare kilun.)
nima, nime (AI) he takes his lunch with him
stem 1: -nim(a)-
nimaqsuwehs (A) sable (animal)
plural: nimaqsuwehsuwok
poss: nimaqsuwehsumol
dim: nimaqsuwehsis
nimawonikhal (TA) he packs a lunch for him
stem 1: -nimawonikh-
nimcokonike (AI) he eats with his fingers; he eats with his (own) hand
stem 1: -nimcokonik(e)-
nimskehe (AI) he drops by to visit
stem 1: -nimsk_h(e)-
nipawse (AI) he goes out at night; he walks at night
nipawset (A) the moon
obv: nipawselicil
nipayapon (II) the northern lights are shining
stem 1: nipayapon(o)-: nipayapok when the northern lights were shining
nipayimiye (AI) he goes to midnight mass
stem 1: -nipayimiy(a)-
nipayimiyamk midnight mass; Christmas
nipehe (AI) he goes out at night
stem 1: -nip_h(a)-
niponahkik region where it is always like summer (Locative)

niponiw (P) in the summer
nipskatuwe (AI) he swears; he blasphemes
stem 1: -nipskatuw(e)-
nipskatuwesku (AI) he swears all the time
stem 1: -nipskatuwesk(i)-
nipuwamal (TA) he marries her (or she... him)
stem 1: -nipuwam-
nipuwikhal (TA) he marries him (performs the wedding ceremony)
stem 1: -nipuwikh-
nipuwilcuhun (I) wedding ring
plural: nipuwilcuhunol
poss: nipuwilcuhunom
loc: nipuwilcuhunok
dim: nipuwilcuhunsis
nis (P) two (in counting)
nominal forms: animate nisuwok; obviative nisu; inanimate nisonul
(also: in counting, tapu two)
nisayye, nisahye (AI) he plays with someone
nisahhihik they (dual) play together
nisekopisit (A) ghost
plural: nisekopisicik
(literally, one that is wrapped twice)
nisekopisu (AI) it (an.) is folded twice; it (an.) is wrapped twice
stem 1: -nisekopis(i)-
nisekopu (AI) it (an.) has two layers
stem 1: -nisekop(i)-
nisekte (II) it has two layers
stem 1: nisekt(e)-
nisewey (A, I) second (in number)
plural: niseweyak, niseweyal
niseyiniyal (AI, AI+OBJ) he is living as married with her (or she... with him)
stem 1: -nisey(i)-
niseyuwok they (dual) are living as married
nisihtuniyal (TI) they (two) make it together
stem 1: -nisiht-
nisikotone (AI) he is two years old
stem 1: -nisikoton(e)-
nisininiyal (AI, AI+OBJ) he lives with him
plural: (none)
stem 1: -nisin(i)-: nisinuwok they (dual) live together
nisinsk (P) twenty
nisiw (P) together; with (of two things, people, etc.)
niskawotuwok (AI) they (two) are walking together
plural: (none)
stem 1: -niskawot(i)-
nisokehs (P) twice
nisoluhkamal (TA) he works with him
stem 1: -nisoluhkam-
nisoluhke (AI) he works with someone; he does two jobs
stem 1: -nisoluhk(e)-
nisossominiyal (AI, AI+OBJ) he drinks with him
plural: (none)
stem 1: -nisossom(i)-

nisuhsalqot (II) it is two miles
stem 1:	nisuhsalqot(o)-
nisukoniw (P) for two days; after two days
nisukonohok (P) on the second day
nisukonokkiwiw (II) it is two days
nisuwikhikon (A) deuce
plural:	nisuwikhikonok
nisuwiniyal (AI, AI + OBJ) he is married to her (or she... to him)
stem 1:	-nisuw(i)-: nisuwuwok, nisuwiwok they (dual) are married
nisuwiyek (A) my spouse
nisuwihticil (A) his or her spouse
nit (I) (PRO) that (inanimate, near person spoken to); that (location unspecified); it
plural:	nihtol those (inan.); they (inan.)
(See not "that (an.)".)
nit (P) then; there; thus, so
(See nit "that (inan.).")
Nit etolimskuwat sakomal. There he finds the chief.
Nit nahsonan 'takom. Then he puts on his snowshoes.
Nit na elomahtuhtihtit. Thus also they acted.
nita (P) well, then; uh-oh!
Nita, kotama kpawalluhpa! Uh-oh, I don't want you (pl.)!
Nita, tan 'toli kisi qsokahsin? Well, then, how can he get across?
nita (I) (PRO) that one (inan.)
plural:	(none)
(See not "that (an.)".)
nituwin (AI, AI + OBJ) he needs it
stem 1:	-nituw(i)- type B
nokalal (TA) he fears him
stem 1:	-nokal-
stem 2:	nekal-
nokasu (AI) he is afraid
plural:	nokasultuwok, nokasuhutuwok
stem 1:	-nokas(i)-: nokasipon we (nilun, dual) are afraid
stem 2:	nekas(i)-: nekasit when he was afraid
nokatomon (TI) he fears it
plural:	nokatomuhtiniya
stem 1:	-nokatom-
stem 2:	nekatom-
nokhoma, nokhome (AI) he stutters
plural:	nokhomahtuwok, nokhomawolotuwok, nokhomhotuwok
stem 1:	-nokhom(a)-
stem 2:	nekhom(a)-
-nokka (-nokkay-) (PV) completely; entirely; to completion
unprefixed form: 'kihka ('kihkay-)
neke form: nekka (nekkay-)
nokkayapomal (TA) he watches him until he is out of sight
'kihkaka (AI) he dances until the end (of the number)

nokkahlal (TA) he eats it (an.) all
stem 1a:	-nokkahl-
stem 1b:	'kihkahl-
stem 2:	nekkahl-
nokkahsuwehtun (TI) he puts it (fire, light) out
stem 1a:	-nokkahsuwehtuw-
stem 1b:	'kahsuwehtuw-: 'kahsuweht put (sg.) it out!
stem 2:	nekkahsuwehtuw-: nekkahsuwehtaq when he is putting it out
nokkahsuwiyapawotun (TI) he douses it
nokkahteluwa (TA) he shot them (an.) all
stem 1a:	-nokkahteluw-
stem 1b:	'kihkahteluw-
stem 2:	nekkahteluw-
Nokkahteluwa te musu. He shot all the moose.
nokkahtun (TI) he eats it all
stem 1a:	-nokkaht-
stem 1b:	'kihkaht-
stem 2:	nekkaht-
nokkalahtomon (TI) he licked it all
nokkanal (TA) he takes it (an.) all
nokkapkiksomon (TI) he burns it up
nokkayahpal (TA) he licked it (an.) all
nokkayaqosal (TA) he burns it (an.) completely in cooking it
nokkayaqosomon (TI) he burns it completely in cooking it
nokolal (TA) he leaves him
stem 1:	-nokol-
stem 2:	nekol-
-nokomasi (-nokomas-) (PV) easily
unprefixed form: 'komasi ('komas-)
neke form: nekomasi (nekomas-)
nokomasiw, 'komasiw (P) easily
Nokomasiw tehc sakomawkan Neqotkuk. They can easily have a governor's ball in Tobique, New Brunswick.
nokosa (nokosay-) (PV) quickly; without delay
neke form: nekosa (nekosay-)
nokosanome (AI) he is quick
plural:	nokosanomahtuwok, nokosanomawolotuwok
stem 1:	-nokosanom(a)-, -nokosanom(e)-: nokosanomapon, nokosanomepon we (nilun, dual) are quick
stem 2:	nekosanom(a)-, nekosanom(e)-: nekosanomat, nekosanomet a quick person
nokosantuphal, nokosahtuphal (TA) he catches it (an.) quickly
stem 1:	-nokosantuph-
stem 2:	nekosantuph-
nokosayiw (P) soon
nokothal (TA) he leaves him behind (by leaving in a vehicle, a boat; in a race, etc.)
stem 1:	-nokoth-
stem 2:	nekoth-

nokothomon (TI) he leaves it behind (by leaving in a vehicle, a boat, etc.)
  stem 1:   -nokothom-
  stem 2:   nekothom-
nokotomon (TI) he leaves it
Nolomok Princeton, Maine. (Locative)
  (term used at Pleasant Point, Maine: the literal meaning is "upriver")
noluwiw (P) everywhere
nomehs (A) fish
  plural: nomehsuwok, nomehsok
  poss: nomehsumol
  dim: nomehsis
  Olomi ktapehe olomuss nomehsuwihkuk. The dog is sinking down to where the fish are.
nomestuns (A) whirlpool
  plural: nomestunsok
  dim: nomestunsis
nomihqosu (AI) he is born
  plural: nomihqosultuwok, nomihqosuhtuwok
  (also, Maliseet: monihqosu)
  Nmihtaqs toli nomihqosu Qonasqamkuk. My father was born in St. Andrews, New Brunswick.
nomihtu (AI) he sees
  stem 1:   -nomiht(u)-
  stem 2:   nemiht(u)-
nomihtun (TI) he sees it
  stem 1:   -nomiht-
  stem 2:   nemiht-
nomiyal (TA) he sees him
  stem 1:   -nomiy-
  stem 2:   nemiy-: nemiyat when he saw him
nomocini (nomocin-) (PV) sideways; to the side
  neke form: nemocini (nemocin-)
  nomocini nutehkawotuwok (AI) they (dual) walk out sideways
nomociniw (P) on the side
nomocinuhse (AI) he walks sideways
  stem 1:   -nomocinuhs(e)-
  stem 2:   nemocinuhs(e)-
nomocinuhsehs, nomocinuhsehsit (A) crab
  plural: nomocinuhsehsuwok, nomocinuhsehsicik
nonuwal (TA) he knows him; he recognizes him
  stem 1:   -nonuw-: nonaq he knows me
  stem 2:   nenuw-
  Nit te nonuwan nemiyuk. I recognized him when I saw him.
nopakotuwal (TA) he lies to him
  stem 1a: -nopakotuw-: nopakotaq he lies to me
  stem 1b: 'pakotuw-: 'pakotuwat if he lies to him
  stem 2:   nepakotuw-: nepakotuwat when he lied to him
  stem 3:   npakotuw-
  Eli kisi npakotask, musa apc wolamsotuwahkoc. Since he lied to you (sg.), don't believe him anymore.

nopal (P) I wish; if only
  (= on + op + al)
  Nopal iywuk cikon. I wish I had an apple.
  Nopal oliyayan Sitank. I wish I could go to St. Ann's.
  Nopal macahat. If only she would leave.
nopim (I) (dep.) his liquid; his drink (water, etc.)
nopuwakon (I) death rattle
  plural: nopuwakonol
noskiqetutom (AI) he has a sour look on his face
  stem 1:   -noskiqetutom(o)- type A
  stem 2:   neskiqetutom(o)-
noskomakon (A) metal disk worn as an ornament
  plural: noskomakonok
  poss: noskomakonol
  loc: noskomakonok
  dim: noskomakonossis
noskonoma (AI) he is sloppy
  stem 1:   -noskonom(a)-
  stem 2:   neskonom(a)-
nospiptun (TI) he takes it by accident; he takes it along
  stem 1a: -nospipt-
  stem 1b: spipt-, nspipt-
  stem 2:   nespipt-
nospopin (AI, AI+OBJ) he sits down with something he should have taken off or put down (e.g. knapsack, coat, pocketbook)
  plural: nospopultiniyal they sit down with them (inan.)
  stem 1a: -nospop(i)-
  stem 1b: nspop(i)-, spop(i)-
  stem 2:   nespop(i)-: nespopit when he sat down with it
  Nospopinol wasisol. He sat down with the child (but he should have put him down first).
nossamaqan (I) his (or my) water
  (See 'samaqan "water".)
nossawalal (TA) he is careful with him; he watches out for him
  stem 1a: -nossawal-
  stem 1b: 'sawal-
  stem 2:   nessawal-
nossawapun, moshawapun (A) eyelash
  plural: nossawapunok
  poss: nossawapunol
  loc: nossawapunok
  (See moshawapun.)
nossawatomon (TI) he is careful with (or about) it; he watches out for it
  stem 1a: -nossawatom-
  stem 1b: 'sawatom-: 'sawatomun! watch (sg.) out for it!
  stem 2:   nessawatom-
nostomon (TI) he understands it
  plural: nostomultiniya, nostomuhtiniya
  stem 1a: -nostom-
  stem 1b: 'sotom-: 'sotok if he understood it

stem 2:   nestom-: nestok when he understood it

stem 3:   nsotom-

Tokec op 'sotok keq etoli skuhutomuhtit, cu op wisokiluwehe. If he understood what they were talking about, he would be angry.

nostuhmon (TI) he reveals it by saying it; he mentions it

stem 1a: -nostuhm-

stem 1b: 'sotuhm-

stem 2:   nestuhm-; but: nestuwok when he mentions it

stem 3:   nsotuhm-

nostuhmuwan (DOV) he tells him about it

stem 1a: -nostuhmuw-

stem 1b: 'sotuhmuw-

stem 2:   nestuhmuw-

stem 3:   nsotuhmuw-

'Sotuhmuwin, tan wot oc kecoskehluk? Tell (sg.) me, which of these (an.) shall I let go?

nostuwal (TA) he understands him; he mentions him

stem 1a: -nostuw-: nostaq he understands me; but: nostuwoq he mentions me

stem 1b: 'sotuw-: 'sotuwat if he understands him

stem 2:   nestuw-: nestuwat when he understood him

stem 3:   nsotuw-: 'totoli nsotuwal he is mentioning him

(The final -uw in the stem of nostuwal, meaning "he mentions him," does not contract with endings that begin with o or i; the -uw in nostuwal, "he understands him," does contract. See paradigms.)

'sotuwiht if they mentioned him

Tokec op nihiht skitapiyi 'sotaht, cu op wolitahasu nekom. If those men understood him, he would be happy.

not (A) (PRO) that ((an.) near person spoken to); that (location unspecified); he, him, it (an.)

plural: niktok, nikt, nikk those, they

obv: nihtol (sg.); nihiht (pl.)

(See nit "that (inan.).")

notuwot (II) it is scarce

'Tomawey notuwot. Tobacco is scarce.

npisun (I) medicine

(See 'pisun.)

nsawatom

(See 'sawatom.)

-nt(u)- sing

(forms AI verb stems)

olomintu (AI) he sings as he goes away

ksentu (AI) he sings as he enters

nucahkomasut (I) mirror

plural: nucahkomasutiyil

(also: pinucahkomasut, pinucahkomat, penucahkomat)

nuci (nuc-, nut-) (PV) do something on a regular basis or as an occupation

(Note: Forms verbs of occupation which usually occur in nominalized form, indicating the agent who carries out the regular activity or occupation.)

nuci emenahket (A) wrestler

nuci nehtahsit (A) tearer

nuci pipiqet (A) musician who plays a wind instrument

nuci pokuhulet (A) drummer

nuci tokotok (A) batter (in baseball)

nuci wisuwoniket (A) maid

nuci tqonket (A) policeman

plural: nuci tqonkecik (two); nuci tqonkahticik (more than two)

poss: nuci tqonketomol

dim: nuci tqonkehsit

(literally, "one who arrests")

Nuci tqonket peciye Sipayik. The policeman arrived at Pleasant Point, Maine.

Nuci tqonketomuwa psqolehlak. Their policemen were fired.

Sakom kisi psqolehlacihi nuci tqonkelicihi, wisokiluwehhik. When the chief fired the policemen, they got mad.

nucihponosit (A) fighter

nucinseqehmat (A) boxer

nucintaq (A) singer

nuciqqiyat (A) hemophiliac bleeder

nucituwiye (AI) he flies (a plane) on a regular basis; he pilots

nucomuwiw (AI) he has tuberculosis

nuhkahkomike (II) the ground is soft

stem 1:   nuhkahkomik(e)-

nuhkaqosu (AI) it (an.) is cooked tender

stem 1:   -nuhkaqos(i)-

nuhkaqote (II) it is cooked tender

stem 1:   nuhkaqot(e)-

nuhkeyu (AI, II) it is soft, tender

stem 1:   -nuhkey(i)-

nuhkomeq (A) cod

plural: nuhkomeqok

dim: nuhkomeqis

nuhkomeqotekon (I) codfish skin

nuhsuhkuwal (TA) he chases him

stem 1:   -nuhsuhkuw-: nuhsuhkaq he chases me

nuhsuphoqalal (TA) he chases him

stem 1:   -nuhsuphoqal-

nuhuwewey (A, I) third; third one

plural: nuhuweneyak, nuhuweweyal

(also: nuwwewey)

nuhuwok, nuhuwiwok (AI) there are three of them (an.)

plural: nuhuhultuwok, nuhuhuhtuwok

stem 1:   -n__h(i)- type A

(See nuwwiwok "there are three of them (an.)".)

nukcokhal (TA) he crushes him up

stem 1:   -nukcokh-

nukcokonomon (TI) he crushes it by hand

stem 1:   -nukcokonom-

nukcokotamu (AI) he chews

plural: nukcokotamultuwok, nukcokotamuhtuwok

stem 1: -nukcokotam(i)-

nukcoktahal (TA) he smashes it (an.) into small pieces; he smashes it (an.) (something soft)

stem 1: -nukcokt_h-

nukcoktehmon (TI) he smashes it into small pieces; he smashes it (something soft)

stem 1: -nukcoktehm-; but: nukcoktohok, nukcokotohok when he smashes it

Neke nukcoktohok ponapsq, eci milocihtek lamiw. When he smashed the rock, it was all different colors inside.

nukcoktihikon (A) a maul; pounding tool

plural:	nukcoktihikonok
poss:	nukcoktihikonol
loc:	nukcoktihikonok
dim:	nukcoktihikonis, nukcoktihikonossis

Wahka te nkisi wolehlannuk nikk nukcoktihikonok. We (nilun) can hardly repair those mauls.

nukhomon (I) flour

plural:	nukhomonol
poss:	nukhomonum
loc:	nukhomonok in the flour

nukhomoniw (II) it has flour on it

stem 1: -nukhomon(i)- type B

nukhomonumiw (AI) he has flour

stem 1a:	-unukhomonum(i)-
stem 1b:	nukhomonum(i)-
stem 2:	wenukhomonum(i)-

nulomolamson (II) there is a slight breeze

stem 1: nulomolamson(o)- type A

nunuwal (TA) she breast-feeds him

stem 1: -nunuw-

(Note: The final -uw of this stem does not contract with endings beginning in o or i.)

Neke nunuwiht wikuwossol eci wolokamit, tokec kcoci te skonis. When her mother was breast feeding her, she was nice and fat, but now she is nothing but bones.

nusakon (A) breast

plural:	nusakonok
poss:	nusakonol

nutahket (A) pitcher (in baseball)

nutahkuhket (A) blacksmith

plural:	nutahkuhkecik

nutahqet (A) cook

nutapektuhusit (A) musician who plays a stringed instrument; fiddler

nutaqsawet (A) carver

nutaqsu (AI) he is heard

stem 1: -nutaqs(i)-

Pihce kiskul, mesq wen etolewestuhk, nil te amsqahs nutaqsiyanpon. In distant days, before anyone spoke, I was the first to be heard.

nutaqsu (AI) he has not slept enough

stem 1: -nutaqs(i)-

nutaqtihiket (A) wood-cutter

nutasksawet (A) grass-cutter (person)

nutatahamal (TA) he thinks poorly of him

stem 1: -nutataham-

nute (nutiy-) (PV) out; going out; coming out

nutehlal, nutelal (TA) he gets him out, he lets him out; he puts him out

stem 1: -nutehl-

nutew (P) coming out; going out

Keka te yut nutew awtik ntoli nomiya otuhk. I see a deer almost to the point where the road comes out.

nutewestaq (A) talker

nuthutahsit (A) guide (e.g. for a hunting trip)

nutiyahkatom (AI) he is married out of his group

stem 1: -nutiyahkatom(o)-

nutiyalkatomon (TI) he digs it out

stem 1: -nutiyalkatom(o)-

nutiyamu (AI, II) he, it falls out (of a window, basket, etc.)

plural:	nutiyamultuwok, nutiyamuhtuwok
stem 1:	-nutiyam(i)-

nutiyapeku (AI) he crawls out

plural:	nutiyapekultuwok
stem 1:	-nutiyapek(i)-

nutiyaphal (TA) he tracks him out

stem 1: -nutiyaph-

Nutiyaphal kcihkuk. He tracked him out of the woods.

nutkat (A) dancer

nutokehkikemit (A) teacher

nutomon (TI) he hears it

stem 1: -nutom-

nutonahket (A) altar boy; one who tends (something)

nutuwal (TA) he hears him

stem 1: -nutuw-: nutaq he hears me

Kilun knutuwannuk metiyayyawoloticik okamok sipuhsisok. We (kilun) hear them playing across the river.

Knutulpon mete kakaluwihin. We (nilun) hear you (sg.) hollering.

nuwwiwok (AI) there are three of them (an.)

stem 1: -nuww(i)-: nuwwihtit when there were three of them (an.)

(See nuhuwok "there are three of them (an.)".)

O

oc (P) will; shall (indicates future)

(Note: Also occurs suffixed to other words as -hc (after vowels) or -c (after consonants): knomiyulc I will see you.)

Tan oc olu ktolehlanen? What shall we (kilun) do to him?

okalhike (AI) he shovels snow

plural:	okalhikhotuwok
stem 1:	-okalhik(e)-
stem 2:	ekalhik(e)-: neke ekalhiket when he shovelled snow

(See also akalhike.)

't-okalhomon (TI) he shovels snow off it
stem 1:	-okalhom-
stem 2:	ekalhom-

okamok (P) across (i.e., on the other side)
Nomiya okamok etoli epeskomhotilicihi.
He sees them playing ball across (the water).

't-okehkimal (TA) he teaches him
stem 1a:	-okehkim-
stem 1b:	kehkim-
stem 2:	ekehkim-
stem 3:	-okehkim-

't-okelhal (TA) he asks him to stay
stem 1a:	-okelh-
stem 1b:	okelh-, kelh-: kelhak they are asked to stay
stem 2:	ekelh-: ekelhat when he asked him to stay
stem 3:	-okelh-: 'kisokelhukul he (obv.) asked him (prox.) to stay

okepse (AI) he is deaf
plural:	okepsahtuwok, okepsawolotuwok
stem 1:	-okeps(a)-, -okeps(e)-
stem 2:	ekeps(a)-, ekeps(e)-: ekepsat one who is deaf

(Note: Forms of this verb are sometimes made from the stems okeps(i)-, ekeps(i)-, but i-stem forms are not usually possible for the third person (nekom, nekomaw).)
(also: kokepse, kekepsat)

okeya (P) ouch!
(variant of okiya)

't-okihkan (AI+OBJ) he plants with it
(See kihke "he plants.")
'Tokihkanol pocetesol. He plants with seed potatoes.

't-okihkatomon (TI) he plants it
stem 1a:	-okihkatom-
stem 1b:	kihkatom-
stem 2:	ekihkatom-
stem 3:	-okihkatom-

okitomakon (I) counter; counting stick

't-okitomuwan (DOV) he reads it to him
stem 1:	-okitomuw-
stem 2:	ekitomuw-

't-okitomuwewan (DOV) he reads it for him
stem 1:	-okitomuwew-
stem 2:	ekitomuwew-

okiya (P) ouch!

okocu, akocu (P) (interjection)
(used when one comes into contact with something cold or hot: going into cold water, getting splashed, etc.)

ol-
(See oli; also, see entries in l-.)

't-olahkalusonahal (TA) he fences him out (or in)
stem 1a:	-olahkaluson_h-
stem 1b:	lahkaluson_h-
stem 2:	elahkaluson_h-
stem 3:	-olahkaluson_h-

't-olahkan (AI, AI+OBJ) he throws it; he lets go of it; he drops it
plural:	'tolakhotiniya, 'tolahkahtiniya, 'tolahkawolotiniya
stem 1a:	-olahk(e)-: ntolahk I throw
stem 1b:	lahk(e)-: lahke he throws
stem 2:	elahk(e)-: elahket when he threw; when he threw it

't-olahkewan (DOV) he throws it to him

't-olahsenomuwal (TA) he shines a light there for him
stem 1a:	-olahsenomuw-
stem 1b:	lahsenomuw-
stem 2:	elahsenomuw-

't-olahsewhutolal (TA) he dresses him
stem 1a:	-olahsewhutol-
stem 1b:	lahsewhutol-
stem 2:	elahsewhutol-

't-olakomitehlal (TA) he boils it (an.)
stem 1a:	-olakomitehl-
stem 1b:	lakomitehl-
stem 2:	elakomitehl-

't-olakomitehtun (TI) he boils it
stem 1a:	-olakomiteht-
stem 1b:	lakomiteht-
stem 2:	elakomiteht-

't-olaksuhutun, 't-oliqsuhutun (TI) he aims at it (second form used at Pleasant Point, Maine)

't-olaksuhutuwal, 't-oliqsuhutuwal (TA) he aims at him

't-olamhok (I) (dep.) his stomach
loc:	'tolamhokek

(also: 'tolamohok)
(See lamhok, stomach.)

't-olamhokewine (AI) he has a stomach ache

't-olamilc (I) (dep.) his palm (of the hand)
plural:	'tolamilciyil

't-olamsitawon (I) his sole (of the foot)
plural:	'tolamsitawonol
loc:	'tolamsitawonok

't-olapomal (TA) he looks at him
stem 1a:	-olapom-
stem 1b:	lapom-
stem 2:	elapom-

(See lapomal "he looks at him.")
Skat lapominomohq, kmacephuweponc.
If they don't look at us, we (kilun, dual) will run away.
Mesq wenihi elapomokulihtihq, 'kisi wihqonawa cikoni. They took apples before any people saw them.

't-olapotomon (TI) he looks at it
stem 1a:	-olapotom-
stem 1b:	lapotom-
stem 2:	elapotom-

't-olapotomuwan (DOV) he looks at it for him; he looks at something of his (someone else's)

't-olapuhkewal (TA) he makes soup (stew, etc.) for him

't-olaqosal (TA) he cooks it (an.); he burns it (an.)
stem 1a:	-olaqos-
stem 1b:	laqos-
stem 2:	elaqos-

Wen yut elaqosok lamokut? Who burned this sheet?

't-olaqosomon (TI) he cooks it

-olatom- breathe
(See tollatom "he is breathing.")

't-olawsikhal (TA) he boards him

't-olehlal (TA) he does something to him
poss: -olehl-
loc: lehl-
dim: elehl-
'tolehtuwan (DOV) he does it for him
Mesq ote nit kil wen ktoqeci lehlokuwon?
Did anyone ever try to do that to you (sg.)?

't-olekisomon (TI) he cuts it (sheet-like object)
stem 1a: -olekisom-
stem 1b: lekisom-
stem 2: elekisom-
'Tolekisomon pilasq ewehket tomosponhunol. He cut the paper with scissors.

't-oleksal (TA) he slices it (an.)
stem 1a: -oleks-
stem 1b: leks-
stem 2: eleks-

't-oleksomon (TI) he slices it

't-olelomal (TA) he bestows a gift, a talent on him
stem 1a: -olelom-
stem 1b: lelom-
stem 2: elelom-
Nit te not elelomut 'kikehtahsin. He is gifted with the ability to heal.

't-olelomuhtuwal (TA) he smiles at him

't-olewotun (TI) he arranges it
stem 1a: -olewot-
stem 1b: lewot-
stem 2: elewot-

olhom (AI) he swims to that place
stem 1: -olhom-
stem 2: elhom-: elhok when he swims there
Ntolhom monihkuhsisok. I'm going to swim out to the little island.
Skat kilun elhomuwohq monihkuk, Susehp 'kosicihtun eli cuwi nit olhok. When we (kilun, dual) didn't swim to the island, Joseph knew that he had to swim there.

oli (ol-) (PV) in that way; to that place, there; at that time
neke form: eli (el-)
(Note: The o of oli and ol- is dropped in some combinations when no prefix precedes it.)
lewestu (AI) he speaks
li suku (AI) he paddles there
oliye (AI) he goes there

't-olintuwatomon (TI) he sings it
stem 1a: -olintuwatom-
stem 1b: lintuwatom-
stem 2: elintuwatom-

't-oliphoqalal (TA) he follows him there
stem 1a: -oliphoqal-
stem 1b: liphoqal-
stem 2: eliphoqal-

't-oliphoqatomon (TI) he follows it there
stem 1a: -oliphoqatom-
stem 1b: liphoqatom-
stem 2: eliphoqatom

't-oliwihtomon (TI) he calls it (by a name); he names it
stem 1a: -oliwihtom-
stem 1b: liwihtom-
stem 2: eliwihtom-

't-oliwiyal (TA) he calls him (by a name); he names him
stem 1a: -oliwiy-
stem 1b: liwiy-: liwiyat if he calls him
stem 2: eliwiy-: eliwiyat the name he called him
'Toliwiyawal Wocawson, nuci putuwet. They call him Wocawson, the wind-maker.

oliye (AI) he goes there
plural: oliyawolotuwok
stem 1: -oliy(a)-
stem 2: eliy(a)-: eliyat when he is going there
Nil nit eliyay Kelisk. I'm the one who is going to Calais.

olkawotuwok, lihkawotuwok (AI) they (du.) walk there
(Note: Dual forms only. See -hkawot(i)-.)

olkihqon (II) it is big (by so much); it is of a (certain) size
stem 1: olkihqon(o)-
stem 2: elkihqon(o)-; elkihqahk it is big
Oposiyil olkihqonul tahalu nkat. The sticks are the same size as my leg.
Eci assokitahasi elkihqahk qotoput. I'm surprised that the chair is so big.

olkil (AI) he is big (by so much); he is of a (certain) size
stem 1: -olkil(o)-
stem 2: elkil(o)-: elkilok he is big
Tan 'tolkilon? How big is he?

olkomiksu (AI) he sins thus
stem 1a: -olkomiks(i)-, -olahkomiks(i)-
stem 1b: olkomiks(i)-, lahkomiks(i)-
stem 2: elkomiks(i)-, elahkomiks(i)-
(See also: lahkomiksu.)

't-olkomon (TI) he drives it there
stem 1: -olkom-
stem 2: elkom-

't-olokimal (TA) he tells him to do thus
stem 1: -olokim-
stem 2: elokim-
Kisehtuness elokimolok? Did you (sg.) do what you were told?

't-olokinehkomon (TI) he rips it (clothing) by wearing it when it is too small for him

't-olokinehkomuwan (DOV) he rips something (clothing) of his (someone else's) by wearing it when it is too small for him
stem 1: -olokinehkomuw-
stem 2: elokinehkomuw-
Ntolokinehkomakun nmahkut. She tore my dress by wearing it when it was too small for her.

't-olokinehkuwal (TA) he rips it (an., clothing) by wearing it when it is too small for him

stem 1a: -olokinehkuw-
stem 1b: elokinehkuw-

't-olokinehlal (TA) he splits it, rips it (e.g., ripping a jacket by catching it on something)

stem 1:   -olokinehl-
stem 2:   elokinehl-

't-olokinehtun (TI) he tears it

stem 1:   -olokineht-
stem 2:   elokineht-

olomahkuhucin (AI) he is bent over (rear end facing away)

olomahtu (AI) he acts thus; he has such and such a nature

plural: olomahtuhtuwok
stem 1:   -olomaht(u)-
stem 2:   elomaht(u)-

olomamu (AI, II) he, it falls away; he, it flies by

plural: olomamultuwok,
          olomamuhtuwok
stem 1:   -olomam(i)-
stem 2:   elomam(i)-: elomamik when
          it flew by

Nitap ntolahkewkun posonut, yet te olomamuwe. My friend threw a basket to me, but it fell right over there.

olomaskute (II) there is a long field

stem 1:   olomaskut(e)-
stem 2:   elomaskut(e)-: elomaskutek
          long field

olomatqin (II) the waves are heading away (i.e. the wind is blowing from behind on the water)

Elomatqik 'tolapin. He gazes out over the waves.

olomelku (AI) he paces off so much

Tepaskutaq wik, cuwi olomelku nananku elomelkimok. When he measures his house, he should pace off fifteen paces (i.e. fifteen yards).

olomeske (AI) he says mass

olomi (olom-) (PV) away (direction of motion or extension or orientation)

neke form: elomi (elom-)
olomapasuwok (AI) they (pl.) walk away
olomatuwe (AI) he climbs away
olomessu (II) it goes away quickly
olomi qasku (AI) he runs away
olomihkawotuwok (AI) they (dual) walk away (dual forms only)
olomuhse (AI) he walks away

olomihkot (II) the tide goes out

olomiye (AI, II) he, it goes away

plural: olomiyawolotuwok

olomolsu (AI) he feels thus

stem 1:   -olomols(i)-
stem 2:   elomols(i)-

Tan ktolomolsin? How do you (sg.) feel?

olomomomqot (II) it feels as if it is going along (something)

(e.g. a pain shooting up or down one's leg)

olomomqot (II) it feels thus

stem 1:   olomomqot(o)-
stem 2:   elomomqot(o)-

olomuss (A) dog

plural: olomussok
poss: 'tolomussomol (usually
          'temisol)
dim: olomussis

(See 'temisol.)

olonahkuloq (I) iron ship

plural: olonahkulokul

olonahq (I) iron

olonahqakom (A) ice skate

plural: olonahqakomok
(literally, "iron snowshoe")

olonahqap (I) chain; wire

plural: olonahqapiyil
poss: 'tolonahqapim
loc: olonahqapik, olonahqapiyik,
          olonahqapihik

Akiyan yat sipsis epit olonahqapihik. Look at that bird sitting on the chain.

olonahqey ahpap (A) cable

olonakson (A) moccasin

plural: olonaksonok

olonomtehsin (AI) he strikes head first (making a dent)

stem 1:   -olonomtehsin(o)- type B
stem 2:   elonomtehsin(o)-

't-olonomuwan (DOV) he hands it to him

stem 1:   -olonomuw-
stem 2:   elonomuw-

Nokosa olonomuwan. He hands it to him quickly.

Tehpu pilsqehsossis qeni olonomuwat. The little girl just handed it to him.

olonukot (II) it happens thus

stem 1:   olonukot(o)-: skat
          olonukotunuhk if it does not
          happen; olonukaksopon if it
          had happened
stem 2:   elonukot(o)-: elonukahk what
          is going on; skat
          elonukotunuhk what does not
          happen

Mecimiw olonuktopon. It used to happen that way.

Pihce elonukkopon. What happened a long time ago.

Pihce nit olonukotuhpon. That happened a long time ago.

't-oloqaphal (TA) he tracks him in that direction

stem 1:   -oloqaph-
stem 2:   eloqaph-

'Toloqaphal oloqiw qospemok. He tracked him toward the lake.

oloqekte (II) it is folded back thus

oloqi (oloq-) (PV) in that direction; over that way

oloqiye (AI) he goes in that direction
olokuhse (AI) he walks in that direction
(Note: q changes to k when followed by u.)

oloqiw (P) in that direction; over that way

Weci macahayin Sipayik, ktahcuwi tuci oloqiw Wehqapiqek. When you (sg.) leave Pleasant Point, Maine, you have to go by Perry.

oloqoqotehe (AI) he swims in that direction under the water

oloqotewakon (I) article of clothing
(See loqtewakon "article of clothing.")

't-olosal (TA) he cuts it (an.) with a knife
(See 't-olsal.)

olotokku (AI) he jumps there
stem 1: -olotoqq(i)-: ntolotoqq I jump
stem 2: elotoqq(i)-: elotoqqit when he jumps

't-olpekehtun (TI) he sprinkles (something) with it

Pahtoliyas 'tolpekehtun imiyewp keti macemiyamok. The priest sprinkles holy water when church is going to start.

olqehsin, luhkehsin (AI) he lays his head down
stem 1a: -olqehsin(o)- type B
stem 1b: olqehsin(o)-, luhkehsin-
stem 2: elqehsin(o)-: elqehsit the way he lays his head

olqepu (AI) he sits thus
plural: olqepultuwok, olqepiyyik, olqepiyahtuwok
stem 1: olqep(i)-
stem 2: elqep(i)-: elqepit the way he sits

Olqepu cess tehp psi keq kesicihtaq. He sits as if he knew everything.

't-olsal, 't-olosal (TA) he cuts it (an.) with a knife
stem 1: -ols-, -olos-
stem 2: els-, -elos-

't-olsomon, 't-olosomon (TI) he cuts it with a knife
stem 1: -olsom-, -olosom-
stem 2: elsom-, elosom-

't-oltahal (TA) he hurts him thus by hitting
stem 1: -olt__h-
stem 2: elt__h-

Ma te nkocicyaw wen eltahat. I don't know who hurt him.

Temonuk keq oltuhutuwok. Soon they will hurt each other in some way (by hitting each other).

Tan olu oltahan? How was he hurt?

oltaqot (II) it sounds thus
stem 1: oltaqot(o)-
stem 2: eltaqot(o)-

oltokopu (AI) it (an.) is set (in a direction) (e.g., rope)
stem 1a: -oltokop(i)-
stem 1b: latokop(i)-, oltokop(i)-
stem 2: eltokop(i)-

oltokte, latokahte (II) it is set (in a direction) (e.g., wire)
stem 1: oltokt(e)-, latokaht(e)-
stem 2: eltokt(e)-, elatokaht(e)-

olu, lu (P) but; however; as for (focuses on preceding word)

Kil lu 'ven? And who are you?

Wikuwossol olu itom... Her mother, she says...

Qaqsoss olu 'tiyal elihc qsokahulat. But Fox tells him that he will ferry him across.

Mec ote olu 'toqecimulal nicalkul witayalin. But still, he asked his uncle to take part in the games.

Komac oc mocessu, kenoq olu cuwi leyu. It will go badly, but that is the way it has to be.

't-oluhkamal (TA) he works with him
stem 1a: -oluhkam-
stem 1b: luhkam-
stem 2: eluhkam-
stem 3: -oluhkam-: 'tolluhkamal, witoluhkamal he is working with him

't-oluhkatomon (TI) he works on it

't-oluhkatomuwan (DOV) he works on it for him

't-oluhkekhal (TA) he makes him work; he puts him to work
stem 1a: -oluhkekh-
stem 1b: luhkekh-: luhkekhat if he makes him work
stem 2: eluhkekh-: eluhkekhat when he made him work
stem 3: -oluhkekh-

Tokec luhkekhat, manimiwol oc. If she makes him work, he'll have money.

't-oluhkewal (TA) he works for him
Natoluhkewal. He goes to work for him.

oluwikonok (P) seven (in counting)

-omaht(u)- act; be of a nature; behave
(forms AI verb stems)
assokomahtu he is odd

-omols(i)- feel
(forms AI verb stems)
mocomolsu (AI) he feels unwell

on, an (P) and; and then
On skinuhsisok 'pokkikalaniya wasisol. And then the boys grabbed the child.

Kotama pihcetu oliyew, on 'qastehsinon. He does not go far, and then he stumbles.

't-onekosunol, 't-onekosun (A, I) his sleeping mat
(See nekosun "sleeping mat.")

onote (P) only (sense of disappointment)
Onote nisuwok peciyahtit. Only two arrived.

Onote nisuwok peciyacik. Only two arrived. (more recent)

-onuhm- buy
1) Stems ending in -onuhm- are TI stems. They form plurals in -ult(i)- and -uht(i)-: 'kisonuhmultiniya, 'kisonuhmuhtiniya "they (pl.) bought it."
2) Before the third person (nekom) ending -ok of Conjunct forms, -onuhm- appears as -onuw-: kisonuwok "when he was buying it."
3) When -onuhm- ends a word, the h is dropped: kisonum "when I bought it."
4) See monuhmon "he buys it,": onuw- "buy."

'kisonuhmon (TI) he bought it; he can buy it

natonuhmon (TI) he goes to buy it
'totolonuhmon (TI) he is buying it
-onukot(o)- happen
(forms II verb stems)
mehtonukot (II) it's over (an event)
-onuw- buy
(Stems ending in -onuw- are TA stems.)
(Stems ending in -onuw- do not undergo
contraction of uw-vowel to a when endings
beginning with o or i are added: nkisonuwoq
"he bought me.")
(See monuwal "he buys it (an.)" ; -onuhm-
"buy.")
'kisonuwal (TA) he bought it (an.)
op (P) would (indicates possibility)
Note: Also occurs suffixed to other words
as -hp (after vowels) or -p (after consonants).
Wen op apc wen piluwey skitap, cu op
'tomotomakun 'sit. If he were any other
man, it would surely bite off his foot.
Mecopal op olu kisihtun? Would you (sg.)
be able to make that?
opan (A) bread; piece of bread; loaf of bread
plural: opanok
poss: 'topanomol
loc: opanok
dim: opanis
Miliq yat opanis. Give (pl.) me that little
piece of bread.
Ehpit 'kisaqosa newu opan. The woman
baked four loaves of bread.
opanke (AI) he mixes bread dough
stem 1:   -opank(e)-
stem 2:   opank(e)-
(Note: the o of the stem is not changed to
e in neke forms.)
opokekon (II) it is flat
stem 1:   opokekon(o)-
stem 2:   epokekon(o)-: epokekahk
             when it was flat
Opokekonuss nuspehpol mesq eqtopihq
nitap. The newspaper was flat before my
friend sat on it.
opokeku (AI) it (an.) is flat
stem 1:   -opokek(i)-
stem 2:   epokek(i)-
opos (I) stick; pole
plural: oposiyil, oposihil
poss: 'toposim, 'topos
loc: oposik
dim: oposis
opos (A) tree
plural: oposiyik, oposihik
poss: 'toposimol, 'toposiyil, 'toposihil
loc: oposik
dim: oposis
(Note: Stahqon ("fir" at Peter Dana Point,
Maine,) is used in place of opos at Pleasant
Point, Maine, in the meaning "tree.")
Mihku spiqatuwe oposik. The squirrel is
climbing up the tree.
'Tomtahal oposihil. He chopped down the
tree.

oposenta (A) sun dog
plural: oposentawok
Tinahkatuwey oposenta tomk
nekkahsuwet. The right-hand sun dog went
out first.
't-oposonut (I) his basket
(See posonut "basket".)
oposuloq (I) wooden boat
't-opqehsimuhtuwal (TA) he lays his head on him
stem 1a: -opqehsimuhtuw-
stem 1b: puhkehsimuhtuw-,
             opqehsimuhtuw-
stem 2:   epqehsimuhtuw-
Npawatomuwan ntopqehsimuhtakun naka
'kuwin. I want him to lay his head on me and
go to sleep.
opqehsimut (I) pillow
(See puhkehsimut.)
opqehsimutiyey (I) pillow case
plural: opqehsimutiyeyal
poss: 'topqehsimutiyey
loc: opqehsimutiyeyak
dim: opqehsimutiyeyahsis
't-opqehsinon (AI, AI+OBJ) he lays his head on
it
stem 1a: -opqehsin(o)- type B
stem 1b: puhkehsin(o)-, opqehsin(o)-:
             puhkehsin, opqehsin he lays
             his head on something
stem 2:   epqehsin(o)-
'Topqehsinon puhkehsimut. He lays his
head on a pillow.
opsqons (I) man's coat
plural: opsqonsihil
poss: 'topsqons
optan (A) woman's coat
plural: optanok
poss: 'toptanol
opu (AI) he sits; it (an.) is in position
plural: opultuwok, opiyahtuwok,
             opiyyik
stem 1:   -op(i)-: opin you (sg.) sit
             down!
stem 2:   ep(i)-: epit when he was sitting
Mali 'tiyal 'qossol 'topilin. Mary told her
son to sit down.
Opin naka kutoman. Sit down (sg.) and
smoke.
Wasisok opiyahtuwok pemsokhasik. The
children (pl.) are sitting on the floor.
opun (I) bed
plural: opunol
poss: 'topun
(See 'topun "his spot.")
't-oqecimal (TA) he asks him
't-oqecimulal, 'qecimulal (TA) he asks him
stem 1a: -oqecimul-
stem 1b: qecimul-
stem 2:   eqecimul-
oqehe (AI) he runs his canoe up on shore
plural: oqahawolotuwok
stem 1:   oq_h(a)-: oqayyik, oqahhik
             they (dual) run their canoe up
             on shore

stem 2:   eqah(a)-: eqahat when he ran
his canoe up on shore

't-oqehtuwal (TA) he sets him up for a jump (in
checkers)

't-oqetokelhal (TA) he tries to get him to stay
Malom te Koluskap keti macahat, on apc
aqamok 'toqetokelhaniya. At last, when
Koluskap gets ready to leave, they try to get
him to stay over for a longer time.

't-oqetomal, 'qetomal (TA) he tests the taste of it
(an.)
stem 1a: -oqetom-
stem 1b: qetom-
stem 2:   eqetom-

oqim (A) loon
plural: oqimuwok
poss: 'toqimumol
dim: oqimuhsis

't-oqithal (TA) he soaks it (an.)
stem 1:   -oqith-
stem 2:   eqith-

oqiton (I) canoe
plural: oqitonul
poss: 'toqitonum
loc: oqitonuk
dim: oqitonuhsis

oqom (A) louse
plural: oqomok
poss: 'tahqomol

oqomolcin
(See ukomolcin.)

oqons (A) shag, cormorant
plural: oqonsok

-os- cut
(See -s-.)

't-osakihtun (TI) he looks at it
stem 1a: -osakiht-
stem 1b: sakiht-
stem 2:   esakiht-

't-osakiyal (TA) he looks at him
stem 1a: -osakiy-
stem 1b: sakiy-
stem 2:   esakiy-

't-osemahal, 't-osemhal (TA) he whips him
stem 1a: -osem_h-
stem 1b: sem_h-, osem_h-: semahan
whip (sg.) him!
stem 2:   esem_h-: esemahat when he
whipped him
(Note: The vowel indicated by the
underlined space in the stems agrees with the
vowel following the h. This vowel before h
may be omitted.)

't-osihmuwal (TA) he gives him a drink
stem 1a: osihmuw-: ntosihmaq he gives
me a drink
stem 1b: sihmuw-: sihmuwat if he gives
him a drink
stem 2:   esihmuw-: esihmuwat when
he was giving him a drink
Kissihmuwat, on tqonan. When he gave
him a drink, he got arrested.
Esihmuwat, on 'sukahtehmon. When he
was giving him a drink, he spilled it.

-osom- cut
(see -som-.)

ososq
(See sosq.)

-ossin(o)- lie down; be lying down
(changes to -hsin(o)- after preverbs ending
in a or e)
wolossin (AI) he lies comfortably
qsokahsin (AI) he lies across (something)

ote (II) it is in position
stem 1:   ot(e)-
stem 2:   eht(e)-: ehtek where it is
Tuwihput wikuwamok ote. The table is in
the house.
Neke ponapskul sitomok ehtek, kotama te
wen nit 'kotuwi toli tkahsomiwon. When the
rocks were on the shore, no one wanted to
swim there.
Posonutekol otesoponil wikuwamok, nit
weci skat pskomuwans. The baskets were in
the house in a different place, so I couldn't
find them.

ote (P) (emphatic)
(See te.)

-otekon- skin
(See motekon "skin".)
maskotekone (AI) he has smelly skin
maspotekone (AI) he has thick skin
pipuwotekone (AI) he has thin skin
sakolotekone (AI) he has tough skin
nuhkomeqotekon (I) cod-fish skin

-otem(i)- cry
1) Stems ending in -otem(i)- are AI or
AI+OBJ stems. They form plurals in -ult(i)-
or -uht(i)-.
2) The initial o of -otem(i)- drops out in
some combinations: 'toteminol, utteminol
"he cries about them (inan.)"
tolotemu, totolotemu (AI) he is crying
'totemin, uttemin (AI, AI+OBJ) he cries
about it

't-otkumol, 'totuhkomol (A) (dep.) his buck
(deer)

't-otolahkesal (TA) he is plowing it (an.)
stem 1a: -otolahkes-
stem 1b: tolahkes-, totolahkes-
stem 2:   etolahkes-

't-otolahkesomon (TI) he is plowing it
'Totolahkesomon etoli kotuwahkihket. He
is plowing the area where he wants to plant.

't-otolapehlal (TA) he is scratching him

't-otolapuwewan (DOV) he drinks something of
his (someone else's)

't-otolapuwhal, 't-otolapuhkewal (TA) he is
making soup (stew, etc.) for him

't-otolaskuwyal (TA) he is waiting for him
(Stem-final -y may change to -h before i:
etolaskuwhit when he waits for me.)

't-otolatokonomewal (TA) he braids someone
else's hair; he ties someone else's hair with a
ribbon, string, etc.

-otoli (-otol-) (PV)
(See toli "is ...ing".)

unprefixed form: toli (tol-) or totoli (totol-)

neke form: etoli (etol-)

't-otolihtehmon (TI) he is hitting it
- *stem 1a:*   -otolihtehm-
- *stem 1b:*   tolihtehm-: tolihtehmon if you (sg.) are hitting it; but: tolihtohok if he is hitting it
- *stem 2:*   etolihtehm-: etolihtehman when I was hitting it; but: etolihtohok when he is hitting it; etolihtem when I am hitting it

't-otoliksomon (TI) he is cutting it
't-otolomal (TA) he is eating it (an.)
't-otolonuhmon (TI) he is buying it
- *stem 1a:*   -otolonuhm-
- *stem 1b:*   tolonuhm-: tolonuhman if I am buying it; but: tolonuwok if he is buying it
- *stem 2:*   etolonuhm-: etolonuhman when I was buying it; but: etolonuwok when he was buying it

(See -onuhm- "buy".)

Etolonum sukolisol, on nutomeyakenen. When I was buying candy, we (nilun) were bothered.

-otoqq(i)-, -otq_h(i)- jump

(forms AI verb stems)

(Certain preverbs require one form of this or the other; many can be used with either form.)

(Note: q changes to k (and qq changes to kk) when followed by u.)

macetokku, macetkuhu (AI) he starts to jump

sakhotkuhu (AI) he jumps into view
akuwotokku (AI) he jumps behind (something)

otuhk (A) deer
- *plural:*   otuhkok
- *poss:*   'totuhkomol
- *dim:*   otuksis

otuhkatop (I) deer head
- *plural:*   otuhkatpiyil, otuhkatpihil, otuhkatpol
- *poss:*   'totuhkatpem, 'totuhkatpum
- *loc:*   otuhkatpek, otuhkatpuk
- *dim:*   otuhkatpossis

otuhkew (A) deer skin
- *plural:*   otuhkewiyik
- *poss:*   'totuhkewemol

otuhkewahsom (A) deer-hunting dog
otuhkey (I) deer meat
- *plural:*   otuhkeyal
- *poss:*   'totuhkeyam
- *loc:*   otuhkeyak
- *dim:*   otuhkeyis

otuhki, (otuhk-) (PN) deer; deer's

Tan lessu otuhki 'qat? What happened to the deer leg?

otuhkomeq (A) tuna
otukke (AI) he hunts deer
- *plural:*   otukkahtuwok
- *stem 1:*   -otukk(e)-
- *stem 2:*   otukk(e)-

(Note: The o of the stem is not changed to e in neke forms.)

Kis kisi maqehhik otukkahticik? Have the deer hunters assembled yet?

P

'pahkam (I) his back
- *loc:*   'pahkamok

pahkamilc (I) back of hand
- *plural:*   pahkamilciyil
- *poss:*   'pahkamilc

'pahkamine (AI) he has a back ache
- *stem 1:*   -pahkamin(e)-: neke pahkaminet when he had a backache; but: 'pahkamine his back aches

(Note: All third-person and obviative Independent forms take a personal prefix.)

pahkuwon (II) the fog lifts
'pahpiyal (TA) he plays with him
- *stem 1:*   -pahpiy-

pahpu (AI) he plays
- *stem 1:*   -pahp(i)-

pahq (I) arrow
- *plural:*   pahqiyil, pahqihil
- *poss:*   'pahqem
- *loc:*   pahqek
- *dim:*   pahqesis

pahqonuwiye (II) the fog is lifting
- *stem 1:*   pahqonuwiy(a)-: pahqonuwiyak when the fog was lifting

pahseyu (AI, II) he, it is thick
- *stem 1:*   -pahsey(i)-

pahsi (pahs-, pas-) (PV) thick
'pahseksal (TA) he slices it (an.) thick
'pahseksomon (TI) he slices it thick
pahsikpeksu (AI) it (an.) is thick-grained

paht (A) blood clot
- *plural:*   pahtuwok

pahtanom (AI) he is left-handed
- *stem 1:*   -pahtanom(o)- type A

'pahtat (I) (dep.) his left hand
- *loc:*   'pahtatok, 'pahtatuk

pahtawe (AI) his plans are not to work out
- *plural:*   pahtawhotuwok
- *stem 1:*   -pahtaw(e)-

Pahtawe neke keti nicanit koti miluwaneponil. When she was going to have her baby she wanted to give it away, but her plans were not to work out.

pahtoliyas (A) priest
- *plural:*   pahtoliyasok
- *poss:*   'pahtoliyasumol
- *dim:*   pahtoliyasis

(from French, patriarche)
pahtoliyasuwiw (AI) he is a priest
  stem 1:   -pahtoliyasuw(i)- type B
  Cel ehta uhsimisol pahtoliyasuwiwol.
Moreover her younger brother was a priest.
'pak (I) fib
  Tehpu nit 'pak. That's just a fib.
'pakikpenomon (TI) he folds over the standers
(vertical splints) of it (a basket)
  stem 1:   -pakikpenom-
'pakolapsqehlal (TA) he boils it (an.)
  stem 1:   -pakolapsqehl-
'pakolapsqesal (TA) he boils it (an.); he broils
it (an.)
  stem 1:   -pakolapsqes-
  (refers specifically to cooking)
pakolapsqesu (AI) it (an.) is boiled
  stem 1:   -pakolapsqes(i)-
  (refers specifically to cooking)
'pakotahsu (AI) he tells a lie
  plural: 'pakotahsultuwok,
          pakotahsuhtuwok
  stem 1a: -nopakotahs(i)-
  stem 1b: 'pakotahs(i)-
  stem 2:   nepakotahs(i)-
  stem 3:   npakotahs(i)-
  'Pakotahsu neke itok eli kinhokat. She lied
when she said she was pregnant.
  Mecimi te nilun nopakotahsultipon eci
tama oliyawolotiyek. We (nilun pl.) always
lie when we go someplace.
'pakotahsuwakon (I) lie
  plural: 'pakotahsuwakonol
  poss: nopakotahsuwakon,
          'pakotahsuwakon
  Mecimi te not 'tuwehkan
'pakotahsuwakon. He always uses a lie.
'pakotuwal (TA) he lies to him
  (variant of nopakotuwal)
  Neke 'pakotask, kat cuwitpotuhk
kulamsotuwanehpon. When he lied to you
(sg.), you shouldn't have believed him.
paksis (I) box
  plural: paksisol
  (from English, box)
pal (P) (indicates possibility and uncertainty;
= op + al)
  Tan pal ktoli nomiyanennuss? How could
we (nilun) have seen him?
  Keq pal apc? What else?
palapiw, palapihiw, palapiyiw (AI) he is proud
  stem 1:   -palap(i)- type B
palapuwitahasu (AI) he thinks proudly
  stem 1:   -palapuwitahas(i)-
paliqewu (AI) he looks proud; he looks stuck
up
  stem 1:   -paliqew(i)-
'palitahamal (TA) he thinks he (someone else)
is stuck up
  stem 1:   -palitaham-
palitahamsu (AI) he is stuck up; he thinks
highly of himself
  stem 1:   -palitahams(i)-

'palitahasikhal (TA) he pleases him
  stem 1:   -palitahasikh-
palitahasu (AI) he is pleased; he is proud
  stem 1:   -palitahas-
  Komac palitahasu ktaqhomuhs, 'sami kisi
ksinuhka, on ma te keq kisi olluhkawon. The
old man was very pleased, for he had gotten
sick and then he could not do anything.
'panahkalal (TA) he uncovers him quickly
  stem 1:   -panahkal-
'panahkewan (DOV) he uncovers something
on him (i.e. against his wishes)
  stem 1:   -panahkew-
'panehtun (TI) he uncovers it
  stem 1:   -paneht-
'panekonal (TA) he uncovers it (an.) by
moving something sheet-like aside with his
hand
  stem 1:   -panekon-
panekopu (AI) it (an.) is open
  stem 1:   -panekop(i)-
panekte (II) it is folded open
  stem 1:   panekt(e)-
pankomike (II) there is a clearing
  stem 1:   pankomik(e)-
panskute (II) there is a clearing
  stem 1:   panskut(e)-
Panuwapskek Indian Island, Maine
(Locative)
panuwapskew (A) a Penobscot
Panuwapskewtoq (I) Penobscot River
  loc: Panuwapskewtokuk
panuwosite (AI) his feet point out (when he
walks)
  stem 1:   -panuwosit(e)-
papahtok (A) a Christian; a religious person
  plural: papahtokik, papahtomucik,
          papahtomuhticik
papahtom (AI) he is religious
  plural: papahtomuhtuwok
  stem 1:   -papahtom(o)- type A
papahtomuwakon (I) religion; prayer
'papahtomuwewal (TA) he says prayers for
him
  stem 1:   -papahtomuwew-
papehcikesu (AI) he inquires
  stem 1:   -papehcikes(i)-
'papehcimal (TA) he finds out the truth from
him
  stem 1:   -papehcim-
'papehcimanol (AI, AI+OBJ) he finds out the
truth from him
  stem 1:   -papehcim(a)-: papehcima he
          finds out the truth
  Naci papehciman sakom kehtol te koti
putuwosin wolakuk. I'm going to find out
for sure from the governor if there is going to
be a council meeting tonight.
papehk (P) exactly the same
papkehloqe (AI) he floats downstream
papkiw (P) downriver
papkiye (AI) he goes downriver
  stem 1:   -papkiy(a)-

papskot (I) stove
plural: papskotihil
poss: 'papskotem
loc: papskotek
dim: papskotehsis
ksapskot: stove (Maliseet)
paqahqaha (A) woodpecker
plural: paqahqahawok
paqahson (II) the moon is shining
stem 1:   paqahson(o)- type A
Eci woli paqahsok. The moon is shining
beautifully.
paqolus (A) medicinal plant species (ginseng?)
pashaqe (AI) he collects wood for craft work
plural: pashaqhotuwok,
pashaqawolotuwok
stem 1:   -pashaq(e)-
Api pashaqet, pcituhusu. When he went
out and collected wood for craft work, he
accidentally cut himself (with an axe).
pasici (pasic-, pasit-) (PV) over; on (or to) the
other side; passing over
pasicossin (AI) he lies across (an edge)
pasicuhse (AI) he walks over (a boundary)
pasitapeku (AI) he crawls over
pasitkawotuwok (AI) they (dual) walk
over
pasittokku (AI) he jumps over
pasituhucin (AI) he leans over (something)
pasiciw (P) over; on the other side; passing
over
Pasiciw lahkalusonihikonok pokossin
epeskomakon. The ball landed on the other
side of the fence.
'paskatpehtahal (TA) he hits him on the head,
breaking it open (literally or figuratively)
stem 1:   -paskatpeht_h-:
paskatpehtahat when he hit
him on the head
Mec ote pomawsu kiwhos kolhikonok,
ntahcuwi te paskatpehtaha weci kisi
nehpuhuk. When a muskrat is still alive in a
trap, I have to hit him on the head so that I
can kill him.
paskesson (II) it bursts
stem 1:   paskesson(o)- type A
paskessu (AI) he, it (an.) bursts
stem 1:   -paskess(i)-
paskeyu (AI, II) it is broken
stem 1:   -paskey(i)-
'paskinehtun (TI) he tears it apart
stem 1:   -paskineht-
'paskocokonal (TA) he breaks it (an.,
something soft) by hand
'paskocokonomon (TI) he breaks it (something
soft) by hand
paskoloqessu (AI) he is moving across the ice
as it cracks
plural: paskoloqessultuwok
stem 1:   -paskoloqess(i)-
Ali paskoloqessi aluhsi pqomik, kenoq ma
te ncuwahpiyaw. I was walking on the ice as
it was cracking, but I didn't fall into the
water.

Ali paskoloqessuwok wasisok 'sami pqom
ma te tepi sakolociw. The ice is cracking as
the children (dual) move around on it because
the ice hasn't frozen hard enough.
'paskonal (TA) he breaks it (an.) by hand
'paskonomon (TI) he breaks it by hand
pasokos (A) sturgeon
plural: pasokosuwok
dim: pasokosuhsis
pasqe (II) it is noon
stem 1:   pasq(e)-
koti pasqe (II) it is almost noon
kisi pasqe (II) it is afternoon: kisi pasqek
in the afternoon
pasqihihpu (AI) he eats dinner (noon meal)
pasqiyahqe (AI) he cooks dinner (noon meal)
'patosikhal (TA) he makes him choke on
smoke
stem 1:   -patosikh-
patosu (AI) he chokes on smoke
stem 1:   -patos(i)-
'pawalal (TA) he wants him
stem 1:   -pawal-
(See 'puwalal.)
Yahan kuhsimis eli mihtaqsol pawaliht.
Tell (sg.) your younger brother (or sister) that
his father wants him.
Kpawalol kmacahan. I want you (sg.) to
leave.
pawalqot (II) it is needed
stem 1:   -pawalqot(o)-: pawalqahk
what is needed
'pawatomon (TI) he wants it
stem 1:   -pawatom-
(See 'puwatomon.)
Npawatomon micuwakon. I want food.
'pawatomuwan (DOV) he wants him to...; he
wants something of his (someone else's)
stem 1:   -pawatomuw-
Kpawatomulon kmacahan. I want you
(sg.) to leave.
pciliw (P) especially
Nuhu wisoki woliku 'tus, pciliw ewasisuwit.
His three daughters are very beautiful,
especially the youngest.
Psi te skicinuwi micuwakon
'tokihkatomoniya, pciliw piyeskomonol.
They planted all the Indian foods, especially
corn.
pcossolewey (A, I) last one
plural: pcossoleweyak, pcossoleweyal
Tayuwek pcossolewey kil kisi
ktomakelkihin? When was the last time that
you (sg.) helped someone out of sympathy?
pecessu (AI) he comes and then leaves again
immediately
peci (pec-, pet-) (PV) come; become
'peci kiluwahal (TA) he comes looking for
him
peci kolusku (AI) he comes to lie
peci komiwon (AI) the rain approaches
'peci nomiyal (TA) he comes to see him
'peci pcitahkan (AI + OBJ) he sends it here
'peciphal (TA) he brings him

peciphuwe (AI) he flees to here

peci suku (AI) he comes paddling

'peci 'tomeyuwal (TA) he comes and bothers him

'peci tqonal (TA) he comes and arrests him

peci wiciye (AI) he comes with others

'peci wikuwamkomal (TA) he comes to visit him

peci wolaqihpu (AI) he comes and eats supper

'peci yahal (TA) he comes and tells him

pecihpun (II) winter is coming
stem 1: pecihpun(o)- type A: pecihpuk when winter came

peciluwehe (AI) he becomes angry

'pecimal (TA) he makes him come by talking or calling to him

'peciptun (TI) he brings it
stem 1: -pecipt-

'peciptuwan (DOV) he brings it to, for him

pecitihkessu (II) the shock of it (impact, explosion, etc.) comes to here

peciw, peci (P) even
Waht peciyay etoli mawiyamok, peciw te toli wiciye puktewick. When I got over to the gathering, even liquor was included.

peciwehse (II) a gust of wind comes

'peciyamal (TA) he comes to him

peciye (AI, II) he, it arrives
plural: peciyawolotuwok, peciyahtuwok
stem 1: -peciy(a)-

pecuhse (AI) he comes walking

'pehenomumol (A) (dep.) his sister (archaic)
npehenomum my sister (man speaking)

pehke (I) shed (behind a house)
loc: pehkewok

pehkehkihtone (AI) he has a nosebleed

'pehkehkihtonehtahal (TA) he bloodies his (someone else's) nose

pehki (pehk-, pek-) (PV) all; completely
'pehkakonutomuwan (DOV) he tells him all about it
pehkine (AI) he is completely dead
'pehki wihqehtun (TI) he takes it all
'pehkonal (TA) he takes it (an.) all; he takes everything from him
'pehkonomon (TI) he takes it all
'pektahal (TA) he hits all of it (an.); he wins everything from him (e.g. in a poker game)

'pehkihtun (TI) he cleans it
plural: 'pehkihtuhtiniya
stem 1: -pehkiht-

pehkikon (II) it is clean

pehkiw, pehki (P) for sure
Pehkiw te 'tiywal wikpihil weci kisihtaq posonutihil temonu kisi pasqek. She has brown ash for sure so that she can make baskets later during the afternoon.

'pehkiyal (TA) he cleans him

'pehkonomuwan (DOV) he takes all of it from him; he takes all of something of his

Ktomaki skitap npehkonomuwan utomawey. Poor man, I took all of his tobacco.

pehkuwoske (AI) he bends
stem 1: -pehkuwosk(a)-
pehkuwoskat joint (of the body)
pehkuwoskamok joint (of the body); pehkuwoskamkil joints

pehkuwoskot (II) it bends
stem 1: -pehkuwoskot(o)-

pehqey (I) meat obtained by hunting; wild meat
Qettomun pehqey. Taste (sg.) the wild meat.

pehqitahasu (AI) he reminisces
stem 1: -pehqitahas(i)-

pehqiye (AI) he comes back (to friends or family) after a long absence
stem 1: -pehqiy(a)-

pehsuwahsuwehsok, pesqahsuwehsok (I) flower
plural: pehsuwahsuweskil, pesqahsuweskil
(See psqahsuwe.)

pekkiktehsok (I) potato slice cooked on stove top
plural: pekkikteskil
(See pkikte.)

'pektahal (TA) he hits all of it (an.)
stem 1: -pekt_h-
'pektaha he cleaned them all out (e.g. in poker); he hit them all

pektahasu (II) everything is taken away

'pektehmon (TI) he gets it all; he hits it all
stem 1: -pektehm-; but: pektohok when he got it all
Nokka pektehmon te man elaqekpon tuwihputik. He won all the money that had been piled up on the table.
Nokka pektehmon te etoli wolahqemihkekpon. He cut all the wood in the good wood stand.

pemskutek (I) field
plural: pemskutekil

pemsokhas (I) floor
loc: pemsokhasik, pemsokhasuk

peqositahasu (AI) he feels discouraged; he feels disappointed; he feels unconvinced

'peskhal (TA) he shoots him
stem 1: -peskh-
Nehtaw peskhukuhtit nihtol skitapiyil, cu tqona. If that man (obv.) shoots them (prox.), he'll get arrested.

'peskhikosamal (TA) he flicks him
(He hits him with his finger, snapping it with his thumb.)

peskote (II) it shoots off; it blows up
stem 1: -peskot(e)-

peskotehsok (I) firecracker; bean (slang)
plural: peskoteskil

peskotom (A) pollock
plural: peskotomuk
poss: 'peskotomumol
dim: peskotomuhsis

peskotomuhkat (A) a Passamaquoddy
(literally, "one who spears pollock")
(See pestomuhkat.)
peskuhs (A) one; one of them; one of them in
particular
plural: (none)
obv: (none)
peskuwat (I) rifle
plural: peskuwatiyil
poss: 'peskuwatim
loc: peskuwatik
dim: peskuwatossis
peskuwotasu (II) it is fired (of a gun, a
cannon, etc.)
pesq (P) one (in counting)
(See neqt "one".)
pesq (A) one
plural: peskuwok several, some
obv: peskuwol (sg.); pesku, peskuhu
(pl.)
Not ehpit peskuwol te wnicanol. That
woman has only one child.
pesqahsuwehsok (I) flower
(variant of pehsuwahsuwehsok)
Pessikapskiyak Split Rock (place on the shore
near Pleasant Point, Maine)
(See psikapskiye.)
pessoni (pesson-) (PV) full; fully
(See psoni.)
pestomuhkat (A) a Passamaquoddy
plural: pestomuhkatiyik,
pestomuhkatihik
older form: peskotomuhkat
pestomuhkati (PN) Passamaquoddy
Pestomuhkatik Passamaquoddy territory
(Locative)
petahkemolsu (AI) he has a sharp pain (from
pleurisy)
petakiw (II) it thunders
petakiyik (A) (pl.) thunder
(sometimes used with the meaning
"lightning")
petakolan (II) there is a thunder shower
petamoqessu (II) a storm comes
petapasuwok (AI) they (pl.) come walking
stem 1: -petapas(i)-
petapeku (AI) he comes crawling
petkawotuwok (AI) they (dual) come walking
(Note: Dual forms only.)
petkil (AI) he reaches a size (in growth)
stem 1: -petkil(o)-
Etusonit, petkil ote aluhkihkuk. He is so
powerful, he grows to the height of the
clouds.
Kis cel petkiluwa tokkiw tuwihputik. He
has already grown as tall as the table.
petkupu (AI) he kneels
petolamsuke (II) the wind blows toward here
petonike (AI) he carries firewood
petonom (AI) he gets there
stem 1: -petonom(o)- type A
Wahka te npetonomupon. We (nilun,
dual) barely got there.

petonome (AI) he gets there
stem 1: -petonom(a)-
Mamote petonome wikuwak. He finally
got to his (literally, their) house.
'pettomimal (TA) he comes to hire him
petute (AI) he moves (his household) into...
plural: petuthotuwok
stem 1: -petut(e)-
Peskuwok pomawsuwinuwok
petuthotuwok pilikuwamihkuk. Some people
are moving into new houses.
Neke nisuwiyek nikihku nekka petutehtit,
nit te nil nuci maciyutan. When my spouse's
parents moved in, I moved out.
-phoqal- follow
(Stems ending in -phoqal- are TA stems.)
'peciphoqalal (TA) he follows him here
'taliphoqalal (TA) he follows him around
-phoqatom- follow
1) Stems ending in -phoqatom- are AI or
TI stems.
2) They form plurals in -ult(i)- or -uht(i)-:
'taliphoqatomultiniya, 'taliphoqatomuhtiniya
"they (pl.) follow it around."
't-aliphoqatomon (TI) he follows it around
't-iyaliphoqatomon (TI) he follows it
around
't-oliphoqatomon (TI) he follows it there
'peciphoqatomon (TI) he follows it here
pihce (P) long ago
pihcehe (AI, II) he, it goes far
stem 1: -pihc_h(a)-
'pihcehtahal (TA) he hits it (an.) far
'Pihcehtahal tekotok, nit te wewciyan. He
hit it (the ball) a long way when he batted,
then made a home run!
pihceqehe (II) rolls far
pihcetu (P) far away
Kotama pihcetu luhsew. He doesn't walk
far.
Qaqsoss nutuwal, apeq pihcetu. Fox hears
him, although it is far.
pihceyu (AI) it (an.) is long and inflexible
plural: pihceyultuwok
stem 1: -pihcey(i)-
Pihceyultuwok stahqonuk wetonukik
kcihkuk. The trees that I got from the woods
are long.
pihcintu, pihcentu (AI) he sings far
stem 1: -pihcent(u)-
(That is, his voice carries far when he sings;
he sings in the distance.)
pihciqehe (AI) he goes against the wind
stem 1: -pihciq_h(a)-
pihtahqot (II) it is long and stick-like
stem 1: pihtahqot(o)-
Eci pihtahqahk nit opos. That stick is very
long.
pihtakome (II) it is a long lake
stem 1: pihtakom(e)-
pihtal (A) lion
plural: pihtaluwok

pihtaqsu (AI) it (an.) is long and stick-like; it (an.) is tall and stick-like
  plural: pihtaqsultuwok,
                 pihtaqsuhtuwok
  stem 1:   -pihtaqs(i)-
  Eci pihtaqsultihtit nikt oposihik. Those trees are tall.

pihtatokosu (AI) he is long (horizontally); he, it (an.) is long (said of something string-like)
  plural: pihtatokosultuwok,
                 pihtatokosuhtuwok
  stem 1:   -pihtatokos(i)-

pihtenskosu (AI) he is tall (said of people only)
  plural: pihtenskosultuwok
  stem 1:   -pihtenskos(i)-
  Eci pihtenskosit qoss, tanehk nuci macahanehk yut 'qocikoton. Your (sg.) son has gotten very tall since I left here a year ago.

'pihtin (I) (dep.) his hand; his forearm (including the hand)
  plural: 'pihtinol
  loc: 'pihtinok

'pihtinahqem (I) (dep.) his arm (excluding the hand)
  plural: 'pihtinahqemol

pik (A) rib
  plural: pikiyik
  dim: pikehsis

pikews (I) vest
  plural: pikewsiyil

piks (A) spade (in cards)
  plural: piksok
  (from French, pique)

piks (A) pig
  plural: piksok
  (from English, pig)

piksey (I) pork
  plural: pikseyal
  poss: 'tahpikseyam
  loc: pikseyak
  dim: pikseyis

pilasq (I) paper
  plural: pilaskul, pilasqiyil
  poss: 'pilaskum, 'pilasqem
  loc: pilaskuk, pilasqek
  dim: pilasqis
  (literally, new bark, i.e., new birchbark)

pilasqhike (AI) he papers (a wall)
  plural: pilasqhikhotuwok
  stem 1:   -pilasqhik(e)-

pilasqhikon (I) wallpaper
  plural: pilasqikonol
  poss: 'pilasqikonum
  loc: pilasqikonok

pileyahsis (A) new baby
  plural: pileyahsisok
  poss: 'pileyahsisomol
  dim: pileyahsossis

pili (pil-) (PV, PN) new
  pili kisuhs (A) new moon
  pilikuwam (I) new house
  piley (A, I) new one

pilkatom (AI) he is newly married
  stem 1:   -pilkatom(o)-

pilsqehsis (A) girl
  plural: pilsqehsisok
  poss: 'pilsqehsisomol
  dim: pilsqehsossis

piltal (I) lead (metal)
  plural: piltalol

piluhse (AI) he gets out of the way (variant of poli luhse)

piluwapiyuwakon (I) extraordinary power
  Nit milan 'kospisun Nimaqsuwehsuwol--nit wici milan na piluwapiyuwakon. There he gives his belt to Sable--with it he gives him extraordinary power.

piluwatuwe (AI) he speaks a different language
  stem 1:   -piluwatuw(e)-

piluwessu (AI) he is going to die
  stem 1:   -piluwess(i)-

piluwi (piluw-) (PV, PN) different
  piluwey (A, I) different one

piluwikemosku (AI) he spreads false stories a lot; he is a jealous person
  stem 1:   -piluwikemosk(i)-

piluwikemu (AI) he is jealous
  stem 1:   -piluwikem(i)-

'piluwimal (TA) he is jealous of him
  stem 1:   -piluwim-

piluwitposu (AI) he has a different position or office; he has extraordinary power
  plural: piluwitposuhtuwok
  stem 1:   -piluwitpos(i)-

piluwitposuwakon (I) extraordinary power
  Eluwe te msiw 'tihiniya piluwitposuwakon. Almost all had extraordinary power.

pimolehsun (I) pus
  plural: pimolehsunol

pimolehsuniw (AI) he has pus on him
  stem 1:   -pimolehsun(i)- type B

pimonikon (I) brace (of a drill)
  plural: pimonikonol

pinucahkomasut (I) mirror
  (also: nucahkomasut)

pinucahkomat (I) mirror
  plural: pinucahkomatiyil
  poss: 'pinucahkomatim
  loc: pinucahkomatik
  dim: pinucahkomatossis

pipuwi (pipuw-) (PV) thin (said of a layer)
  'pipuweksal (TA) he slices it (an.) thin
  'pipuweksomon (TI) he slices it thin
  'pipuwiksomon (TI) he cuts it thin (with a saw)
  pipuwotekone (AI) he has thin skin
  pipuwapitehe (II) it is thin grained

piqeku (AI) it (an.) is hollow
  stem 1:   -piqek(i)-
  Espons olu nit te macephuwan, 'pistehshinon piqekit opos. But Raccoon immediately starts running away and dives into a hollow tree.

piqonewatpe (AI) he has bushy hair
'pisacqehtun (AI) he puts it into the oven; he slides, pushes it into something
'pisamin (AI, AI + OBJ) he falls into it
    stem 1:   -pisam(i)-
pisessu (AI) he goes in
    stem 1:   -pisess(i)-
pisi (pis-) (PV) into, out (through a boundary in either direction)
pisiw (P) into, out (through a boundary in either direction)
    Yut pisiw awtik skicinuwok wikihtit. This is where the road goes into where the Indians live.
piski psan (II) it is snowing so hard that it's dark or it's hard to see
    stem 1:   piski psan(o)- type A
piskiqehpusu (AI) he blinks repeatedly
    stem 1:   -piskiqehpus(i)-
piskiqewu (AI) he closes his eyes
    plural: piskiqewultuwok, piskiqewuhtuwok
    stem 1:   -piskiqew(i)-
piskolan (II) it is raining so hard that it's dark or it's hard to see
    Tanehk mace piskolanunuhk ma te tama nkisiliyaw. Ever since it began to rain so hard, I haven't been able to go anywhere.
piskuwon (I) fog
    plural: piskuwonol patches of fog
    loc: piskuwonok
    Ali ksihkehe lamiw piskuwonok. He is lost in the fog.
piskuwon (II) it is foggy
    stem 1:   piskuwon(o)- type A
pisokonike (AI) he walks into high grass, brush, etc.
    stem 1:   -pisokonik(e)-
pistehsin (AI) he falls in
    stem 1:   -pistehsin(o)- type B
    Pistehsin elomalokahk. He fell into a hole.
'pisun, npisun (I) medicine
    plural: 'pisunol
    poss: nopisun
    loc: 'pisunok
    dim: 'pisunsis
    Kiwhosuwasq nit skicinuwi npisun. Flag root is an Indian medicine.
'pisuwahqimal (TA) he tells false information about him
    stem 1:   -pisuwahqim-
pithasu (II) it is stuffed; it is loaded
pithawiw (P) upriver
pithawiye (AI) he goes upriver
    stem 1:   -pithawiy(a)-
pithawopu (AI) he is upriver
    stem 1:   -pithawop(i)-
'pithotuhkatomon (TI) he stuffs it
    stem 1:   -pithotuhkatom-
'pitkatomon (TI) he packs it (puts it in a pack, a bag, etc.)
    stem 1:   -pitkatom-

'pitkatomuwan (DOV) he loads his (someone else's) gun
    stem 1:   -pitkatomuw-
'pitkomalal (TA) he stuffs it (an., e.g. pipe, chicken)
    stem 1:   -pitkomal-
'pitkoman (AI, AI + OBJ) he packs it; he makes preparations with it
    stem 1:   -pitkom(a)-: pitkoma, pitkome he packs, he makes preparations
    'Keki te pitkoma keti macahat. He made preparations all day when he was going to leave.
    Puktewick na wici pitkoman wiciw 'toloqotewakonol. He packed liquor along with his clothes.
'pitkomewal (TA) he packs for him; he makes preparations for him
    stem 1:   -pikomew-
'pitkosewan (AI, AI + OBJ) he loads it (a gun)
    stem 1:   -pitkosew(e)-: pitkosewe he loads a gun
    On pol 'pitkosewan, keti peskhat otuhkol. Before he could shoot the deer, he had to load his gun.
    'Totoli pitkosewan 'peskuwat. He is loading his gun.
'pitkotomon (TI) he packs it (a pack, a bag, etc.)
    stem 1:   -pitkotom-
'pitkotomuwan (DOV) he packs it for him
'pitkotomuwewal (TA) he packs for him; he makes preparations (e.g. winterizing a house) for him
'pitkotomuwewan (DOV) he gets it ready for him
'pitkotuwatomon (TI) he gets it ready
    Npitkotuwatomon wiki. I'm winterizing my house.
pitsonakon (I) pocket
    plural: pitsonakonol
    poss: 'pitsonakon
    loc: pitsonakonok
    dim: pitsonakonossis
pitsone (AI) he fills his (own) pipe
    stem 1:   -pitson(e)-
'pitsonewal (TA) he fills his pipe for him
    stem 1:   -pitsonew-
pitsonosu (AI) he stuffs his (own) pipe
    stem 1:   -pitsonos(i)-
pittokot (II) it is long (said of something string-like, or a film, story, etc.)
    stem 1:   pittokot(o)-: pittokahk when it was long; skat pittokotunuhk if they are not long
pittoksu (AI) it (an.) is long (said of something string-like)
piwsokuhke (AI) he gathers firewood
    stem 1:   -piwsokuhk(e)-
piwsoq (I) firewood
    plural: piwsokul pieces of firewood
    poss: 'piwsokum
    loc: piwsokuk

dim: piwsoqis
piyaqtihikon (I) wood chip
   plural: piyaqtihikonol
   dim: piyaqtihikonossis
piyaqtihikonihke (AI) he gathers wood chips
   plural: piyaqtihikonikhotuwok
   stem 1:   -piyaqtihikonihk(e)-
   stem 2:   peyaqtihikonihk(e)-
   (also: piyaqtihikonuhke)
Peyaqtihikonihket, mecimi te mskuwecin.
When he gathers wood chips, he always finds something to cut himself on.
piyehs (I) (single) hair
   plural: piyehsuwol
   poss: 'piyehsum: 'piyehsumol his hair (the hair on his head)
   loc: piyehsuwok
   dim: piyehsuwis
piyemi (piyem-) (PV) the most
   neke form: peyemi (peyem-)
   piyemi wasisuwiw (AI) he is the youngest
piyemitposu (AI) he has more power than anyone else; he is in a higher office than anyone else
   plural: piyemitposultuwok
   stem 1:   -piyemitpos(i)-
   stem 2:   peyemitpos(i)-: peyemitposit the most powerful person
piyeskomon (I) ear of corn; grain of corn
   plural: piyeskomonol
   poss: 'piyeskomonum
   loc: piyeskomonok
   dim: piyeskomonis
Wetossis lamiw iyu piyeskomonok. There is a worm in the ear of corn.
pkahkonikon (I) crooked knife (woodworking tool)
   plural: pkahkonikonol
   poss: 'pihkahkonikon
pkihkon (I) fish hook
   plural: pkihkonol
   poss: 'pokkihkon, mokkihkon
   loc: pkihkonok
   dim: pkihkonossis
pkihkonahtoq (I) fishing pole
   plural: pkihkonatkul
   poss: mokkihkonahtoq
pkiksu (AI) it (an.) is burned; it (an.) is scorched
   plural: pkiksultuwok
   stem 1a: -pokkiks(i)-
   stem 1b: pkiks(i)-
   stem 2:   pekkiks(i)-
Pkiksuwol maksonol. His shoe is burned.
pkikte (II) it is burned; it is scorched
   stem 1:   pkikt(e)-
   stem 2:   pekkikt(e)-
pkoson (A) shoe
   plural: pkosonok
   poss: maksonol
   loc: pkosonok
   dim: pkosonossis
'Totoliyal pkosonol. He is making a shoe.

Ponapskul pistehsonul pkosonihkuk.
Rocks fell into the shoes.
Kcuwihc monuhmuwewoloniyak kmaksonuwak. I will have to buy shoes for you (pl.).
pkosonap (I) shoelace
   plural: pkosonapihil, pkosonapiyil
pkot (I) smoke
   loc: pkotek
pkotesawe (AI) he smokes (meat, fish, etc.)
   stem 1a: -pokkotesaw(e)-
   stem 1b: pkotesaw(e)-
   stem 2:   pekkotesaw(e)-
pkotete (II) it is smoky, misty
   stem 1:   pkotet(e)
   stem 2:   pekkotet(e)-
pkotewpiw (II) there is mist over the water
pkotewqiw (II) it is hazy
Woli sepawiw sepay, cel kekesk pkotewqiw. This morning was nice, but a little hazy.
pkuwahq (I) heath (open, boggy land)
   plural: pkuwahkul
   loc: pkuwahkuk
   dim: pkuwaqsis
Sesokatokiyehs pkuwahkuk skuweyu. The spruce partridge hangs around in the heath.
pkuwakiye (II) it is curved
   stem 1:   pkuwakiy(a)-
   stem 2:   pekkuwakiy(a)-
'poccipilal (TA) he hooks him by accident
   stem 1a: -poccipil-
   stem 1b: pcipil-: pcipilat if he hooks him by accident; but note: pcipilolan if I hook you (sg.) by accident
   stem 2:   peccipil-: peccipilat when he hooked him by accident
pocetes (I) potato
   plural: pocetesol
   poss: 'topcetesom, 'pocetesom
   loc: pocetesok
   dim: pocetesis
   (from (?) English, potato)
'pocitahkan (AI, AI + OBJ) he sends it
   stem 1a: -pocitahk(e)-
   stem 1b: pcitahk(e)-
   stem 2:   pecitahk(e)-
'pocitahkewan (DOV) he sends it to him
pokahkon (I) blood
   plural: pokahkonol
   poss: 'pokkonum, 'pokahkonum
   loc: pokahkonok
pokahkonaptu (AI) he leaves bloody tracks
   stem 1:   -pokahkonapt(u)-
   stem 2:   pekahkonapt(u)-
pokahkonekon (II) it (e.g. cloth, garment) is bloody
   stem 1:   pokahkonekon(o)-: pokahkonekonul they are bloody
   stem 2:   pekahkonekon(o)-: pekahkonekok something bloody

'pokahkonihtahal (TA) he bloodies him; he hits him, drawing blood
stem 1: -pokahkoniht_h-
stem 2: pekahkoniht_h-
pokahkoniptine (AI) he has bloody hands
pokahkoniw (II) it is bloody, bleeding
pokehloqe (AI) he has a toothache
stem 1: -pokehloq(e)-
stem 2: pekehloq(e)-
pokhu, pokhuwe (AI) it (an.) hatches
plural: pokhuwolotuwok,
pokhuwholotuwok;
pokhultuwok
stem 1: -pokhuw(e)-, -pokh(i)-
stem 2: pekhuw(e)-, pekh(i)-
(Note: The stems -pokh(i)- and pekh(i)- are used in third person and obviative forms only.)
pokhutike (AI) she hatches her eggs
plural: pokhutikhotuwok
stem 1a: -pokhutik(e)-
stem 1b: pekhutik(e)-
'pokkikalal (TA) he grabs him
stem 1a: -pokkikal-
stem 1b: pkikal-: pkikalat if he grabs him
stem 2: pekkikal-: pekkikalat when he grabbed him
'Pokkikalaponil nomehsol. He grabbed the fish.
'pokkikatomon (TI) he grabs it
'pokkiksal (TA) he burns it (an.)
stem 1a: -pokkiks-
stem 1b: pkiks-
stem 2: pekkiks-
'Pokkiksomon lamokut. He burned the sheet.
pokomakon (I) club (used in splitting wood into strips)
plural: pokomakonol
pokomk (A) fisher (animal)
plural: pokomkiyik, pokomkihik
poss: 'pokomkemol
dim: pokomkehsis
pokossin (AI) he falls down; it (an.) falls; he, it (an.) lands
stem 1: -pokossin(o)- type B
stem 2: pekossin(o)-
pokossuhunol (I) (pl.) necklace
pokotahqewiye (II) it echoes
stem 1: pokotahqewiy(a)-
stem 2: pekotahqewiy(a)-: pekotahqewiyak when it was echoing
Nekatoman kukec nutomon npeskuwat elomi pokotahqewiyak. I was afraid that the game warden would hear the echo from my rifle.
pokotahsu (AI) he casts a shadow
plural: pokotahsultuwok,
pokotahsuhtuwok
stem 1: -pokotahs(i)-
stem 2: pekotahs(i)-

Cel not pekotahsit nomociniw wikuwamok. And he is casting a shadow on the side of the house.
Skat pekotahsihq, ma tehc kisuhsuwiw. If he doesn't cast a shadow, there won't be any sun.
pokuhulakon (I) drum
plural: pokuhulakonol
poss: 'pokuhulakon
loc: pokohulakonok
dim: pokuhulakonossis
pokuwoss (A) sailor
plural: pokuwossok
poss: 'pokuwossomol
(translation of the English, "tar")
pol (P) first (indicating priority of action)
Pol wiciyemin. First come (sg.) with me.
Pol nacihpin. First I have to go eat.
polam (A) Atlantic salmon
plural: polamuwok
poss: 'polamumol
dim: polamuhsis
'polaphal (TA) he misses his tracks
stem 1: -polaph-
stem 2: pelaph-
polecomon (A) Frenchman
(from English, Frenchman)
polecomonatuwe (AI) he speaks French
stem 1: polecomonatuw(e)-
stem 2: polecomonatuw(e)-
(The first o does not change to e in Stem 2.)
poles (A) pigeon; dove
plural: polesok
dim: polesis
'polhal (TA) he misses him (with a shot)
stem 1: -polh-
stem 2: pelh-
polhike (AI) he misses his target (with a shot)
plural: polhikhotuwok, polhikahtuwok
stem 1: -polhik(e)-
stem 2: pelhik(e)-
polhikesku (AI) he is a bad shot
plural: polhikeskultuwok
stem 1: -polhikesk(i)-: npolhikeskipon we (nilun, dual) are bad shots
stem 2: pelhikesk(i)-: pelhikeskit a bad shot
poli (pol-) (PV) moving away; moving out of the way
poli liptinewu (AI) he moves his hand out of the way
poli liptinessu (AI) he moves his hand out of the way quickly
poli luhse (AI) he walks away; he gets out of the way
polosehta (AI) he (a nursing baby) misses the nipple when nursing
plural: polosehtahtuwok
stem 1: -poloseht(a)-
stem 2: peloseht(a)-: pelosehtat
'polsotuwal (TA) he misunderstands him; he disobeys him
stem 1: -polsotuw-

stem 2:   pelsotuw-
'poltahal (TA) he misses him (with a blow)
  stem 1:   -polt_h-: kpoltihi you (sg.)
          miss me
  stem 2:   pelt_h-: peltahat when he
          missed him; peltuhuk when I
          missed him
pomalukte (II) there is a stretch of cloud
  stem 1:   pomalukt(e)-
  stem 2:   pemalukt(e)-
pomapotuhusu (AI) he walks with a cane
pomaptahsu (AI) he tracks (a person, animal, etc.)
pomaptu (AI) he goes along leaving tracks
  stem 1:   -pomapt(u)-
  stem 2:   pemapt(u)-
pomaqte (II) it (something stick-like) lies there
  stem 1:   pomaqt(e)-
  stem 2:   pemaqt(e)-
pomasuke (AI) he wades along
pomawsu (AI) he lives; he is alive
  plural: pomawsultuwok
  stem 1:   -pomaws(i)-: pomawsit if he
          is alive
  stem 2:   pemaws(i)-: pemawsit when
          he was alive
Tokec op pomawsitsopon, cu op kcikotone. If he were alive, he would be old.
pomawsuwakon (I) life
  poss: 'pomawsuwakonum
pomehloqe (AI) he floats along
  stem 1:   -pomehloq(e)
  stem 2:   pemehloq(e)
pomessu (AI) he goes along fast
pomi (pom-) (PV) along in space or time
  neke form: pemi (pem-)
  pomacqessu (II) it slides along
  pomacqiye (AI) he holds on to something (e.g. a car) and is dragged along.
  pomahqossin (AI) he lies straight; he lies along (something)
  pomamkiye (II) it is sandy along (a beach)
  pomamkuhusu (AI) he poles himself along (in a boat)
  'pomaphal (TA) he goes along tracking him
pomi suku (AI) he paddles (or rows) along
pomicuwon (II) it flows along
  stem 1:   -pomicuwon(o)- type A
  stem 2:   pemicuwon(o)-
pomikoton (II) the year is not over yet; the year is going on
  pemikotok this year
'pomiphal (TA) he carries him; he gives him a ride in a vehicle
  stem 1:   -pomiph-
  stem 2:   pemiph-
'Pomiphawal skinuhsisol naci cuwahpahkaniyal sitomok. They are carrying the boy in order to go throw him into the water down at the shore.
pomiqehe (AI, II) it rolls along
  stem 1:   -pomiq_h(a)-
  stem 2:   pemiqah(a)-

pomituwiye (AI) he flies along
  plural: pomituwiyahtuwok
  stem 1:   -pomituwiy(a)-
  stem 2:   pemituwiy(a)-
Pomituwiye cihpolakon aluhkok. The eagle is flying in the cloud.
Pomituwiyahtuwok sipsisok. The birds are flying along.
pomkawotuwok (AI) they (dual) walk along
  (Note: Dual forms only.)
  (See -hkawot(i)-.)
'pomkomon (TI) he drives it
pomoka, pomoke, pomka, pomke (AI) he dances (along)
  plural: pomokawolotowok, pomokahtuwok
  stem 1:   -pomok(a)-, -pomk(a)-
  stem 2:   pemok(a)-, pemk(a)-
Nekomawc pomkak sepawonu. They (dual) will dance tomorrow.
Neke pemokahtit skicinuwok, wolinaqsuponik. When the Indians were dancing, they looked good.
pomolamson (II) the wind blows along
pomoloqihton (II) the ice is breaking up and floating downstream
  stem 1:   pomoloqihton(o)- type A
  stem 2:   pemoloqihton(o)-: pemoloqihtok when the ice was breaking up etc.
Pemoloqihtok skicinuwok 'toli wolamsotomuhtiniya 'tahsihpilsultiniya naka naci cuhpahkan wen amalekok weci maciyeloqek 'qosinuhkewakon.
The Indians believed that they could cure themselves when the ice was breaking up and floating downstream, and one would go throw a piece of cloth into the water so that his sickness would float away (with it).
pomoqotehe (AI) he goes along underwater
  stem 1:   -pomoqot_h(a)-
  stem 2:   pemoqotah(a)-
pomossin (AI) he is lying down
  stem 1:   -pomossin(o)- type B
  stem 2:   pemossin(o)-
pomotomhe (AI) he slides along
pomotone (II) a ridge runs along
pomskute (II) there is a field
pomsokhasu (II) the floor is on (stage in building a house); it is on another part of the same floor
'Totolihtun wikuwam. Kis cel te pomsokhasu. He is building a house. The floor is already on.
pomuhse (AI) he walks along
pomuhse imiyan Corpus Christi
  (literally, walking along praying)
'pomumqamal (TA) he carries him on his back
  stem 1:   -pomumqam-
  stem 2:   pemumqam-
Pemumqamit, npoliphukun. When he was carrying me, he dropped me.

pomumqe (AI) he rides a horse
pomutewey (I) pack basket
  plural: pomuteweyal
ponapsq (I) rock
  plural: ponapskul
  poss: 'ponapskum
  loc: ponapskuk
  dim: ponapsqis
ponapsqahson (A) stone pipe
  Nqenoss, kotama ktiywaw ponapsqahson naka 'tomawey? My grandson, don't you have a stone pipe and some tobacco?
ponapsqehs (A) chub (fish)
  dim: ponapsqehsis
ponapsqisamq (I) gravel
  plural: ponapsqisamkul little pebbles
ponatom (AI) she lays an egg (or eggs)
  plural: ponatomuhtuwok
  stem 1:   -ponatom(o)-
  stem 2:   penatom(o)-: penatok when she laid an egg
'poneqahkan (AI, AI + OBJ) he throws it down
  stem 1:   -poneqahk(e)-
  stem 2:   peneqahk(e)-
'poneqehlal (TA) he gets him down; he puts him down
  stem 1:   -poneqehl-
  stem 2:   peneqehl-
poneqi (poneq-) (PV) down, downward
  neke form: peneqi (peneq-)
poneqiw (P) down; below; downward
poneqotokku (AI) he jumps down
popu (AI) he (a child) has a rash on his tongue and inside his mouth
  stem 1:   -pop(i)-
  stem 2:   pep(i)-
'poqanal (TA) he can lift and carry him
  stem 1:   -poqan-
  stem 2:   peqan-
  Yet eqeci wesuwe punat, wahka te 'poqanal. When she tried to put him back there, she could barely lift and carry him.
'poqqenal (TA) he breaks a piece off of it (an.) with his hand
  stem 1a: -poqqen-
  stem 1b: pqen-
  stem 2:   peqqen-
'poqqesal (TA) he slices a piece off of it
  stem 1a: -poqqes-
  stem 1b: pqes-
  stem 2:   -peqqes-
'poqqonahqehlal (TA) he peels it (an., something stick-like)
  stem 1a: -poqqonahqehl-
  stem 1b: pqonahqehl-
  stem 2:   peqqonahqehl-
'poqqonahqehtun (TI) he peels it (something stick-like)
'poqqonaskehtun (TI) he peels it
'poqqonhal (TA) he peels it (an.)
'poqqonomon (TI) he peels it

'poskomon (TI) he wears it
  plural: 'poskomuhtiniyal they (pl.) wear them (inan.)
  stem 1a: -poskom-
  stem 1b: psihkom-: psihkok if he wears it
  stem 2:   peskom-: peskok when he wore it
'poskuwal (TA) he wears it (an.)
'posokapecin (AI, AI + OBJ) he scratches himself on it
  stem 1a: -posokapec(i)-
  stem 1b: posokopec(i)-
  stem 2:   pesokapec(i)-
  Nekomaw 'posokapeciniyal posonutihil. They (dual) scratched themselves on the baskets.
posokiyan (I) mole (on skin)
  plural: posokiyanol
posonut (I) basket
  plural: posonutiyil, posonutihil
  poss: 'toposonut
  loc: posonutek (pl. loc. posonutihkuk)
  dim: posonutehsis
  Mali 'kisi punomonol pehsuwahsuweskil posonutehsisihkuk. Mary put the flowers into the little baskets.
posonutehke (AI) he makes baskets
  plural: posonutekhotuwok
  stem 1a: -oposonutehk(e)-
  stem 1b: posonutehk(e)-
  stem 2:   eposonutehk(e)-, posonutehk(e)-
  Neke eposonutehket, eci wolinaqahk 'toposonutihil. When he made baskets, his baskets were very beautiful.
'posqihtuwahal (TA) he shaves him
  stem 1a: -posqihtuw_h-
  stem 1b: psqihtuw_h-
  stem 2:   pesqihtuw_h-: pesqihtuwahat when he shaved him
'posqolehlal (TA) he ignites it (an.); he fires him (from a job)
  stem 1a: -posqolehl-
  stem 1b: psqolehl-
  stem 2:   pesqolehl-
'posqolehtomon (TI) he lights it (something to smoke)
'posqolehtun (TI) he ignites it
  stem 1a: -posqoleht-
  stem 1b: psqoleht-, psqoleht-: psqolehtaq if he ignites it
  stem 2:   pesqoleht-; pesqolehtaq when he ignited it
'posqolenomon (TI) he kindles it
'posqolepal (TA) he lights it (an., something to smoke)
possa (P) too
  Possa 'kihtomatomon. He is too tired to want to do it.
  Possa ktahkiqol. You (sg.) are too heavy.

'possahal (TA) he smells him
stem 1a: -poss-h-
stem 1b: ps_h-
stem 2: pess_h-

possahtuwe (II) it shines
stem 1: possahtuw(e)
stem 2: pessahtuw(e)

'possahtuwehtun (TI) he puts it (a light) on

possaqal (P) must be
(The speaker is interpreting a situation.)
Possaqal kotuhp. You must be hungry.
Possaqal nkotuhpips. I must have been hungry.

possaqhe (AI, II) it is lit up

possaqhessoss (A) firefly
plural: possaqhessossok

'possehlal (TA) he skins him
stem 1a: -possehl-
stem 1b: psehl-, possehl-: psehlat if he skins him
stem 2: pessehl-: pessehlat when he skinned him
Pessehlat otuhkol, psi te pokahkoniptine. When he skinned the deer, his hands got all bloody.

'possehtun (TI) he smells it
stem 1a: -posseht-
stem 1b: pseht-: psehtaq if he smells it
stem 2: pesseht-: pessehtaq when he smelled it

possesom (A) star
plural: possesomuk
poss: 'possessomumol
dim: possesomuhsis

possetokahmuwal (AI) he parts his (someone else's) hair
stem 1a: -possetokahmuw-
stem 1b: psetokahmuw-
stem 2: pessetokahmuw-

'possetokahmuwan (DOV) he parts it (his hair) for him

possetoqahal (TA) he parts his (someone else's) hair
npossetoqohoq he parts my hair

possiyantehsok (I) window
plural: possiyanteskil
loc: possiyanteskik

posson (A) reef of ice
plural: possonok

-possoni (-posson-) (PV) full; fully
(See psoni.)

'possulin (AI, AI+OBJ) he has it lodged in his throat
plural: psuluhtuwok they have something lodged in their throats
stem 1a: -possul(i)-: npossul I have something lodged in my throat
stem 1b: psul(i)-: psulu he has something lodged in his throat
stem 2: pessul(i)-: pessulit when he had something lodged in his throat

posu (A) bobcat
plural: posuwok
poss: 'posumol
dim: posuhsis
Yet messuwessit Koluskap, nomiya eli seksultilit, tahalu tehp mahtoqehsuwok eli siktehpawolokuhtit posuwol. When Koluskap appears, he sees how frightened they are, like rabbits scared by a bobcat.

'pothal (TA) he hooks him
stem 1a: -poth-
stem 1b: pt_h-: ptahat if he hooks him; ptihihin, ptihhin if you (sg.) hook me
stem 2: peth-: pethat when he hooked him

'pothomon (TI) he hooks it
plural: 'pothomultiniya, 'pothomuhtiniya
stem 1a: -pothom-
stem 1b: ptahm-: ptahman if I hook it; but: ptohok if he hooks it
stem 2: pethom-: pethoman when I hooked it; but: pethok when he hooked it
stem 3: ptahm-: 'kisi ptahmon he hooked it; but: 1) without ending: etoli ptam where I hooked it (all such forms are neke forms with nil as subject); 2) with nekom: etoli ptohok where he hooked it (neke form).

potsusu (AI) he cuts himself accidentally (variant of ptosusu)

'pottahal (TA) he hits him accidentally
stem 1a: -pott_h-
stem 1b: pciht_h-
stem 2: pett_h-

'pottaqosal (TA) he burns him accidentally

'pottaqosomon (TI) he burns it accidentally

'pottehmon (TI) he hits it accidentally
stem 1a: -pottehm-
stem 1b: pcihtehm-; but: pcihtohok if he hits it accidentally
stem 2: pettehm-; but: pettohok when he hits it accidentally

'potteluwal (TA) he shoots him accidentally
stem 1a: -potteluw-: npottelaq he shoots me accidentally
stem 1b: pcihteluw-: pcihteluwat if he shoots him accidentally
stem 2: petteluw-: when he accidentally shot him

pqalokiqe (AI) he has red eyes
stem 1a: -moqqalokiq(a)-, -mihqalokiq(a)-
stem 1b: pqalokiq(a)-
stem 2: mehqalokiq(a)-
Kisossomit, nit te mihqalokiqan. When he had been drinking, his eyes were red.

pqapit, qapit (A) beaver
plural: pqapitihik
poss: pqapitemol, 'poqqapitemol

dim: pqapitehsis, pqapitsis
(See qapit "beaver".)

pqatpe (AI) he has red hair
stem 1a: -moqqatp(a)-, -mihqatp(a)-
stem 1b: pqatp(a)-
stem 2:   mehqatp(a)-

pqeku (AI) he is dressed in red
stem 1a: -moqqek(i)-, -mihqek(i)-
stem 1b: pqek(i)-
stem 2:   mehqek(i)-

pqesikon (A) loaf of unsliced bread
plural: pqesikonok
poss: 'poqqesikonumol

pqeyu (AI, II) he, it is red
plural: pqeyultuwok, pqeyuhtuwok
stem 1a: -mihqey(i)-, -moqqey(i)-:
               nmihqey, nmoqqey I am red
stem 1b: pqey(i)-
stem 2:   mehqey(i)-
stem 3:   -mqey(i)-, -pqey(i)-
    Eci pqeyit 'sak, on oc 'kisaqosin. When the
lobster is red, it will be cooked.
    Pqeyuwol mipihil eci toqakuwik. The
leaves are red when it is fall.

pqom (A) ice
plural: pqomiyik, pqomihik pieces of
               ice
poss: 'poqqomumol
loc: pqomik
    Nil not npoqqomum. That's my ice.
    Wasisok ali pokomultuwok pqomik. The
children are skating around on the ice.

pqomuwessu (II) it is turning into ice
stem 1:   pqomuwess(i)-: pqomuwessik
               when it was turning into ice

pqonahqehtasu (AI, II) it (something
stick-like) is peeled
(See 'poqqonahqehtun "he peels it
(something stick-like)".)

pqonhike (AI) he peels bark off
stem 1a: -poqqonhik(e)-
stem 1b: pqonhik(e)-
stem 2:   peqqonhik(e)-

psahkeyuwinaqot (II) it looks regrettable; it
looks tragic
(See moskeyin "he is sorry about it".)

psan (II) it snows
stem 1:   psan(o)- type A: psak if it
               snows
stem 2:   pessan(o)-: pessak when it
               snows

psehpon (A) onion
plural: psehponok
poss: 'possehponumol
loc: psehponok
dim: psehponis

psekon (II) it is like a sheet
stem 1:   psekon(o)- type A
stem 2:   pessekon(o)-
(e.g. it looks like a sheet because it moves
by very fast; e.g., fence posts, "sheets" of
rain)

pseku (AI) it (an.) is like a sheet
stem 1a: -possek(i)-
stem 1b: psek(i)-
stem 2:   pessek(i)-
(e.g. it looks like a sheet because it moves
by very fast)

psew (I) gunpowder
plural: psewihil

psi, psiw (P) all, every
older form: msi, msiw
Psi tehc 'tiyultiniya naksqiyik. All the
young girls will be there.
Nit te msiw. (or, nit te psiw.) That's all.

psihkuwosuwon, psikusuwon (I) necklace
plural: psihkuwosuwonol

psikapskiye (II) there is a crack in the rock
stem 1:   psikapskiy(a)-
stem 2:   pessikapskiy(a)-:
               pessikapskiyak where there is
               a crack in the rock

psikessu (AI) it (an.) splits
stem 1a: -possikess(i)-
stem 1b: psikess(i)-
stem 2:   pessikess(i)-

psikipahsu (AI) it (an.) cracks because it is
dry

psikiye (AI, II) it breaks up
stem 1a: -possikiy(a)-
stem 1b: psikiy(a)-
stem 2:   pessikiy(a)-

psiksoq (I) piece of wood; board
plural: psiksokul
dim: psiksokuhsis wooden shingle,
               wood scrap

pskelute (II) smoke is coming out (of it)
because it cannot escape through a flue,
stovepipe, etc.
stem 1:   pskelut(e)-
stem 2:   peskelut(e)-
    Nisuwiyek psi te nokka pkiksomonol
pocetesol, etuci pskelutek papskot
lamikuwam. My wife burned the potatoes
and a lot of smoke was coming out of the
stove in the house.

psketqon (I) knot (in wood)
plural: psketqonul

psketqonhike (AI) he chops limbs off a tree
stem 1a: -posketqonhik(e)-
stem 1b: psketqonhik(e)-
stem 2:   pesketqonhik(e)-

pskihq (I) blade of grass
plural: pskihqol, pskihqihil blades of
               grass; grass (collectively)
poss: 'poskihkum
loc: pskihkuk; pskihqihkuk (pl.) in
               the grass
dim: pskihqis

pskihqimins (A) strawberry
plural: pskihqiminsok
poss: 'poskihqiminsumol,
               'taspihqiminsumol,
               uskihqiminsumol
loc: pskihqiminsok
dim: pskihqiminsis

pskotemu (AI) he cries himself to sleep
  stem 1a: -poskotem(i)-
  stem 1b: pskotem(i)-
  stem 2:   peskotem(i)-
pskuwhe (AI) he sheds (his hair)
  plural: pskuwhawolotuwok,
     pskuwhahtuwok,
     pskuwhawotuwok
  stem 1a: -poskuwh(a)-: nposkuwha I
     lose hair; pskuwhihik they
     (dual) shed their hair
  stem 1b: pskuwh(a)-: pskuweyya he has
     lost his hair; but: kehsi
     pskuwhat he lost so much hair
  stem 2:   peskuwh(a)-: peskuwhat when
     he shed
(Note: The forms of pskuwhe are made in basically the same way as forms of stems ending in _h(a)-, but a before h is dropped and i is retained before -hik, -hil, etc.)
pskuwhetul (II) hairs fall out (when a person is losing hair or an animal is shedding)
(Note: Plural forms only.)
psonekte (II) it (something sheet-like) covers
  stem 1:   psonekt(e)-
  stem 2:   pessonekt(e)-
Yut tahk psi te psonekte motewekon tuwihputik. Here a flag completely covered the table.
psoni (pson-) (PV) full; fully
  prefixed form: -possoni (-posson-)
  neke form: pessoni (pesson-)
  psoni pkotete (II) it is full of smoke
psonopulce (AI) he has a handful
  plural: psonopulcahtuwok
  stem 1a: -possonopulc(a)- (type B):
     npossonopulc I have a handful
  stem 1b: psonopulc(a)-: eli psonopulcay
     I have a handful
  stem 2:   pessonopulc(a)-: pessonopulcat
     one who has a handful
(also, with stem-vowel e: pessonopulcet one who has a handful)
psonpe (AI) it (an.) is full of liquid
  plural: psonpawolotuwok,
     psonpahtuwok
  stem 1a: -possonp(e)-: 'possonpan it
     (an.) is full of liquid (Relative)
  stem 1b: psonp(e)-
  stem 2:   pessonp(e)-: pessonpet when
     it was full of liquid
Psi te niktok psonpihik. They are all full.
psonpehe (II) it is high tide
  stem 1:   psonp_h(a)-
  stem 2:   pessonpah(a)-
psonpewse (AI) it (an.) fills up
psonte (II) it is full
Ehemuwikuwam psonte ehemuwok. The chicken coop is full of chickens.
psosahq (A) horsefly
  plural: psosahqok
psqahsuwe (II) it blooms
  stem 1:   psqahsuw(e)-

  stem 2:   pesqahsuw(e)-: pesqahsuwek
     when it bloomed
Psqahsuweksopon pesqahsuweskil, wolinaqotuponil op. If the flowers had bloomed, they would have been beautiful.
psqahsuwe (AI) she blooms
  poss: -posqahsuw(e)-
  loc: psqahsuw(e)-
  dim: pesqahsuw(e)-
psqentu (AI) he bursts into song
  plural: psqentuhtuwok
  stem 1a: -posqent(u)-: 'posqentun he
     bursts into song (Relative)
  stem 1b: psqent(u)-
  stem 2:   pesqent(u)-: pesqentaq when
     he burst into song
psqihtuhusu (AI) he shaves (himself)
(See 'posqihtuwahal "he shaves him".)
psqihtuhusut (I) razor
  plural: psqihtuhusutiyil
psqihtuwewakon (I) razor
  plural: psqihtuwewakonol
  poss: 'posqihtuwewakon
psqocis (I) war club
  plural: psqocisol
psqolehtoma, psqolehtome (AI) he lights up (a cigarette)
  plural: psqolehtomahtuwok
  stem 1a: -posqolehtom(a)-
  stem 1b: psqolehtom(a)-
  stem 2:   pesqolehtom(a)-
psqolessu (AI) it (an.) bursts into flames
  plural: psqolessultuwok
  stem 1a: -posqoless(i)-
  stem 1b: psqoless(i)-
  stem 2:   pesqoless(i)-
psqotemu (AI) he bursts into tears
  stem 1a: -posqotem(i)-
  stem 1b: psqotem(i)-
  stem 2:   pesqotem(i)-: pesqotemit when
     he bursts into tears
psuhun (I) heart
  plural: psuhunol
  poss: moshun
  loc: psuhunok
  dim: psuhunsis
psuhun, psuhunsis (A) heart (in cards)
  plural: psuhunok
psuhunine, moshunine (AI) he has heart trouble
  plural: psuhuninhotuwok
  stem 1a: -moshunin(e)-
  stem 1b: psuhunin(e)-
  stem 2:   meshunin(e)-
psuhunsis
(See psuhun.)
psuhutolosu (AI) he has something in his eye
  stem 1a: -poshutolos(i)-
  stem 1b: psuhutolos(i)-
  stem 2:   peshutolos(i)-
psuwis (A) cat
  plural: psuwisok
  poss: 'posumol
  dim: psuhsis, psuwossis

(See posu "bobcat.")

ptahma, ptahme (AI) he hooks a fish; he "hooks" a girl
plural: ptahmahtuwok, ptahmawolotuwok, ptahmawotuwok
stem 1a: -pothom(a)-: npothomapon we (nilun, dual) hook fish
stem 1b: ptahm(a)-: ptahmak they (dual) hook fish
stem 2: pethom(a)-: pethomat when he hooked a fish
stem 3: (See ptohom.)

ptewolon
(See motewolon.)

ptihike (AI) he catches fish
plural: ptihikhotuwok. ptihikahtuwok, ptihikawolotuwok, ptihikawotuwok
stem 1a: -pothik(e)-: npothik I catch fish
stem 1b: ptihik(e)-
stem 2: pethik(e)-: pethiket when he caught fish

-ptine- hand
poli liptinewu (AI) he moves his hand out of the way
kossiptinensu (AI) he washes his (own) hands

ptohom (AI) he hooks a fish
plural: ptahmultuwok, ptahmuhtuwok
stem 1a: -pothom(o)-: npothomupon we (nilun, dual) hook fish
stem 1b: ptahm(o)-: ptahmuk they (dual) hook fish; but: ptohok if he hooks a fish
stem 2: pethom(o)-: pethoman when I hooked a fish; pethok when he hooked a fish
stem 3: ptahm-: weli ptahman when I hooked a lot of fish; without ending: kisi ptohom he hooked a fish; but: 1) ptohom in Independent forms with no ending; 2) ptam in neke forms with no ending
Op al apc nit tuci woli ptahman. I wish I could hook as many fish again as I did then.

ptoqakin (II) it is round
stem 1: ptoqakin(o)- type B
stem 2: petqakin(o)-: petqakik something round
Wot nutapektuhusit pesqon ptoqakin 'qat. This fiddler had one round foot (i.e., a hoof).

ptoqakisu (AI) it (an.) is round (e.g., a coin)
stem 1a: -potqakis(i)-
stem 1b: ptoqakis(i)-
stem 2: petqakis(i)-

ptoqap (I) bag
plural: ptoqapiyil
poss: motqapim. motqap
loc: ptoqapik
dim: ptoqapossis

ptoqcokpe (AI) he is soaked to the skin
stem 1a: -potqocokp(e)-: npotqocokp I am soaked to the skin
stem 1b: ptoqcokp(e)-
stem 2: petqocokp(e)-: petqocokpet one who is soaked to the skin

ptoqilc (I) fist
plural: ptoqilciyil
poss: 'potqilc

ptosusu, potsusu (AI) he cuts himself accidentally
stem 1a: -potsus(i)-
stem 1b: ptosus(i)-, potsus(i)-
stem 2: petsus(i)-

puccokpe (AI) he is wet (variant of puscokpe)

pucokossu, pucoqossu (AI) he drowns
stem 1: -pucoqoss(i)-

puhkakon (A) white perch
plural: puhkakoniyik
poss: 'puhkakonemol
dim: puhkakonehsis

puhkalokiqewu (AI) he squints
stem 1: -puhkalokiqew(i)-

puhkehsimut, opqehsimut (I) pillow
plural: puhkehsimutiyil, opqehsimutiyil
poss: 'topqehsimut
loc: puhkehsimutik, opqehsimutik
dim: puhkehsimutossis, opqehsimutossis

puhkes (A) maggot
plural: puhkesok

puhkiluwan (A) kidney
plural: puhkiluwanok

puhkonikciyepu (AI) only the bottom of it (an.) is covered (e.g. a cup with only a few berries inside)
stem 1: -puhkonikcyep(i)-

puhpuhkomiqe (AI) he has freckles
stem 1: -puhpuhkomiq(e)-

puhtay (A) bottle
plural: puhtayak
poss: 'puhtayamol
loc: puhtayak
dim: puhtayahsis
(from French, bouteille)
Ma te ihiw molaqs puhtayawihkuk. There is no milk in the bottles.

pukcinsqehs (A) jug; name of a malicious character in legends
plural: pukcinsqehsuwok

pukocalahs (A) periwinkle
plural: pukocalahsuwok
dim: pukocalahsis

pukset (I) live coal
plural: puksetol

puktewick (I) liquor
(from the Micmac word, meaning "fire water")

pun (I) winter; last winter
Mehciniya pun nhesis. My older brother died last winter.
Toke pun. It's winter now.

Nkomuttehkakun pun. Winter sneaked up on me.

'punal (TA) he puts him, it (an.) (somewhere)
  stem 1: -pun-
punam (A) whitefish
  plural: punamuwok
punamuhke (AI) he fishes for whitefish
  stem 1: -punamuhk(e)-
punawe (AI) he sets traps
  plural: punawhotuwok
  stem 1: -punaw(e)-
puniw (P) in the winter
punkik region where it is always winter (Locative)
'punomon (TI) he puts it (somewhere)
  stem 1: -punom-
pupukhawihq (A) balsam fir blister (with pitch inside)
  plural: pupukhawihqiyik
pupukhawihqe (AI) he gathers balsam fir pitch
  stem 1: -pupukhawihq(e)-
pus- wet
  puskosone (AI) he has wet shoes
puscokpe, puccokpe (AI) he is wet
  plural: puscokpahtuwok,
    puscokpawolotuwok,
    puscokphotuwok
  stem 1: -puscokp(e)-, -puccokp(e)-

Neke cuwahpiyayan, psi te npuccokp, tehpu ma nkatol. When I fell into the water I got all wet except for my feet.

Kisi ksihkahawolotiyek, psi te npuccokphotipon, 'sami komiwon. When we (nilun, pl.) got lost, we got all wet, because it rained.

puskiw (P) sometimes; often

Neket Koluskap mec yali wiciyemat skitapiyi, puskiw na nekom mace suku 'tulok, sipsuhke. At that time, when Koluskap still went around among men, often he too would go paddling in his canoe, hunting birds.

puskiyelcan (I) finger
  plural: puskiyelcanol
  poss: 'puskiyelcan
puskolahqe (AI) he par-boils something
  stem 1: -puskolahq(e)-
'puskolaqosal (TA) he par-boils it (an.)
  stem 1: -puskolaqos-
'puskolaqosomon (TI) he par-boils it
  stem 1: -puskolaqosom-
'puskonal (TA) he buries him
  stem 1: -puskon-
puskonasu (II) it is buried
  stem 1: -puskonas(i)-
puskonike (AI) he goes to a funeral
  stem 1: -puskonik(e)-
puskonikon (I) casket
  plural: puskonikonol
  poss: 'puskonikonum
  loc: puskonikonok;
    puskonikonihkuk (pl.) graveyard
  dim: puskonikonossis

'puskonomon (TI) he buries it
  stem 1: -puskonom-
puspekihke (II) the grass is wet
  stem 1: puspekihk(e)-: puspekihkek when the grass was wet
pusu (AI) he leaves by boat
  plural: pusultuwok
  stem 1: -pus(i)-: pusit when he left by boat
putawehe (AI) it rises (e.g. bread)
  stem 1: -putaw_h(a)-
putawehtikon (A) raised bread
  plural: putawehtikonok
putawiyapskessu (AI) he is bloated
  stem 1: -putawiyapskess(i)-
putep (A) whale
  plural: putepiyik
  dim: putepehsis
putoma (AI) she has a miscarriage
  stem 1: -putom(a)-
'putoman (AI+OBJ) he loses it
  plural: 'putomahtiniya
  stem 1: -putom(a)-
(Note: AI forms made from this stem have only the special sense "have a miscarriage." See putoma "she has a miscarriage")

'Kisi putomahtiniyal 'qolhikonuwal. They (pl.) lost their traps.

putuwakon (I) whistle; moose-call (or anything one makes noise with by blowing)
  plural: putuwakonol
  poss: 'putuwakon
  loc: putuwakonok
  dim: putuwakonossis
putuwe (AI) he blows
  plural: putuwahtuwok
  stem 1: -putuw(e)-: nputu I blow; putuwet when he was blowing
'puwalal (TA) he wants him (See 'pawalal.)
'puwatomon (TI) he wants it (See 'pawatomon "he wants it.")
'puwehlal (TA) he shakes him
  stem 1: -puwehl-
puwihta (AI) he dreams
  stem 1: -puwiht(a)-
(See puwihtu "he dreams.")
puwihtu (AI) he dreams
  plural: puwihtultuwok, puwihtuhtuwok
  stem 1: -puwiht(u)-
  stem 2: pewiht(u)-
Tokec kuwiyin, cu kpuwiht. If you go to sleep, you will dream.
'puwihtun (TI) he dreams about it
  stem 1: -puwiht-
  stem 2: pewiht-
puwin (A) corpse
  plural: puwinuwok
  poss: 'puwinumol
  dim: puwinuhsis
(also: 'puwin, a corpse)

'**puwiyal** (TA) he dreams about him
   stem 1:   -puwiy-

Q

-**q_h(a)**- roll
   (forms AI and II verb stems)
   kakawiqehe (II) it rolls fast
   motapeqehe (II) it rolls downhill
qanotuwan (I) (?) dance hall (archaic)
   loc: qanotuwanok
qanusq (I) piece of driftwood
   plural: qanuskul
qapit (A) beaver
   (See pqapit "beaver.")
qaqeyu (AI) he is dirty
   stem 1:   -qaqey(i)-
qaqopos (A) soot
   plural: qaqoposiyik
qaqsoss (A) fox
   plural: qaqsossok
   poss: 'qaqsossomol, 'qaqsossumol
   dim: qaqsossis
   Akiyan not aliyat qaqsoss ehemuwihkuk. Look at that fox who is going around among the chickens.
   Nkisi komutonala qaqsossom. I stole your (sg.) fox.
'**qasahkan** (AI, AI+OBJ) he throws it away
   plural: 'qasakhotiniya, 'qasahkahtiniya
   stem 1:   -qasahk(e)-: qasahke he throws something away
qasi (PV) quite
   qasi piluwocossu (AI) he is quite a different color
qaskewoton (II)_ ice is forming
   stem 1:   qaskewoton(o)- type A
qasku (AI) he runs (on foot)
   stem 1:   -qasq(i)-
qasqomehe (AI) it (an.) melts by degree
   stem 1:   -qasqom_h(a)-
'**qasqomesomon** (TI) he melts it
   stem 1:   -qasqomesom-
qasqomessu (AI) it (an.) melts
   stem 1:   -qasqomess(i)-
qasqomete (II) it thaws
   stem 1:   qasqomet(e)-
qasqomiye (AI) it (an.) melts
   stem 1:   -qasqomiy(a)-
'**qayihtawotuwok** (AI) they (du.) are mad at each other
   (See 'qayu "he is angry," uhkayihtuwal "he is mad at him.")
'**qayu** (AI) he is angry
   plural: 'qayultuwok
   stem 1a: -uhkay(i)-: nuhkay I am angry
   stem 1b: 'qay(i)-
   stem 2:   wehkay(i)-: wehkayit when he was angry
   'Qayossuwa Sakom. Little Sakom has gotten angry.

   Itomuk psite wen 'qayuwa. They say everyone got angry.
'**qecihtun, 't-oqecihtun** (TI) he tries to make it
   stem 1a: -oqeciht-, -qeciht-
   stem 1b: qeciht
   stem 2:   eqeciht-, qeciht-
'**qecimulal** (TA) he asks him
   (variant of 't-oqecimulal)
qecuhse (AI) he tries to walk
   stem 1a: -oqecihs(e)-
   stem 1b: qecuhs(e)-
   stem 2:   eqecuhs(e)-
qenoq, kenoq, kenuk (P) but; however
   (See kenoq "but; however".)
   Tokec, qenoq kat oc sipkiw. For now, but not for long.
qenoss (A) grandchild
   plural: qenossok
   poss: 'qenossol
   dim: qenossis
-**qep(i)-. -uhkep(i)-** sit, be sitting
   (forms AI verb stems)
   ckuhqepu (AI) he sits facing toward here
   olomuhkepu (AI) he sits facing away
'**qetomal** (TA) he tests the taste of it (an.)
   (variant of 't-oqetomal)
qihiw (P) near; by
   Tokec ntahcuwi wiwisa natsakiyak kotokik npomawsuwinumok, supekuk qihiw wikulticik. Now I must hurry away to visit others of my people, who live by the sea.
'**qiluwahal, 'kiluwahal** (TA) he looks for him
   stem 1:   -qiluw_h-, -kiluw_h-
'**qiluwahtun, 'kiluwahtun** (TI) he looks for it
   stem 1:   -qiluwaht-, -kiluwaht-
'**qiluwapomal, 'kiluwapomal** (TA) he looks for him (specifically by vision)
   stem 1:   -qiluwapom-, -kiluwapom-
qin (P) really
   Qin te? Really?
qinuskeyu, qonusqeyu (AI, II) it is sharp; it is pointed
   stem 1:   -qinuskey(i)-, -qonusqey(i)-
   stem 2:   qenuskey(i)-, qenusqey(i)-
qiwosun (I) bundle
   plural: qiwosunol
'**qoci ('qoc-, 'qot-)** (PV) one; alone
   prefixed form: -noqci (-noqc-, -noqt-)
   neke form: neqci (neqc-, neqt-)
   older unprefixed form (sometimes heard after vowels): nqoci (nqoc-,.nqot-).
   'qocikotone (AI) he is one year old
   'qocuhse (AI) he walks right to it without stopping
   'qotuhkanu (AI) he lives by himself
'**qocikoton** (II) it is one year
   ehtahsi nqocikotok every year, once a year
qocom (I) the outdoors
   loc: qocomok outdoors; outside
   Eci wolimahtek qocom. The outdoors smells very nice.
'**qolapomal** (TA) he won't look at him (because he is angry with him)
   stem 1:   -qolapom-

stem 2:   qelapom-

Tanek nqolapomokunennuhk, nit te na ma te ntolewestuwamawinnuk. Ever since they began refusing to look at us (nilun), we haven't talked to them.

qolopapehkikonoss (A) silver hake

qolopapessu (AI) he looks back quickly over his shoulder
stem 1:   -qolopapess(i)-
stem 2:   qelopapess(i)-

'qolopehlal (TA) he turns him over; he makes him change his mind
stem 1:   -qolopehl-
stem 2:   qelopehl-

qolopessu (AI) he turns around
stem 1:   -qolopess(i)-
stem 2:   qelopess(i)-

'qolopihtahal (TA) he turns or flips him around by hitting him, knocking against him, etc.

qolopihtahasu (II) it is flipped or turned a little by accident

'qolopihtehmon (TI) he turns or flips it by striking it
stem 1:   -qolopihtehm-
stem 2:   qelopihtehm-; but qelopihtohok when he turned it

'qolopitahamal (TA) he changes his mind about him
stem 1:   -qolopitaham-
stem 2:   qelopitaham-

qolopitahasu (AI) he changes his mind
stem 1:   -qolopitahas(i)-
stem 2:   qelopitahas(i)-

'qolopitahatomon (TI) he changes his mind about it

qolopiye (AI) he changes the direction he is facing; he goes in the wrong direction (as a result of not following directions); he changes his mind

qonakome (II) the lake is long by so much

'qonaskuwyal (TA) he waits for him (through some period of time)
stem 1:   -qonaskuwy-
stem 2:   qenaskuwy-
(Stem final y may change to -h before i.)

Qonasqamkuk St. Andrews, New Brunswick (Locative)
(literally, "at the sandy point")

qonasqihtone, qinusqihtone (AI) he has a pointed nose
stem 1:   -qonasqihton(a)-, -qinusqihton(a)-
stem 2:   qenasqihton(a)-, qenusqihton(a),

qonatokosu, qontoksu (AI) he, it (an.) is long by so much
plural: qonatokosultuwok, qonatokosuhtuwok
stem 1:   -qonatokos(i)-, qontoks(i)-
stem 2:   qenatokos(i)-, qentoks(i)-
Tan 'qonatokosin wasossis? How big (in length) is the little lady?

Qenatokosit ahpap. The rope is long.

qonatokot, qontokot (II) it is long by so much
stem 1:   qonatokot(o)-, qontokot(o)-
stem 2:   qenatokot(o)-, qentokot(o)-
Opos qonatokot talu tuwihput 'qat. The stick is as long as the leg of the table.
Opos qentokahk. The stick is long.
Qonatokotoc opos talu tuwihput 'qat. Have the stick be as long as the leg of the table.

qonenskosu (AI) he is tall by so much

qoni (qon-) (PV) through or during a length of space or time
neke form: qeni (qen-) long; while
Qoni cikopultuwok ote pemoluhkemkil. They sat silently for one week.
Qeni alonawonat Pokomk, Pukcinsqehs tuci nokothat. While Fisher goes around gathering eggs Pukcinsqehs leaves him (leaving by vehicle, here a boat.)
Kat cu skat ktahkahsomihpon qeni tkeyik 'samaqan. Let's (du.) not swim while the water is cold.

qontokot (II) it is long by so much
(See qonatokot.)

qonus (A) pickerel
plural: qonusiyik
poss: 'qonusimol
dim: qonusis

'qosokahsinon (AI, AI+OBJ) he lies across it
stem 1a: -qosokahsin(o)- type B
stem 1b: qsokahsin(o)-: qsokahsin he lies across
stem 2:   -qesokahsin(o)-
'Qosokahsinon kuhut. He is lying across the bed.

qospem (I) lake
plural: qospemol
poss: 'qospem
loc: qospemok
dim: qospemsis: pond, small lake
(Note: Also kuspem.)

'qossihtun (TI) he pays reverence to it; he follows the proper observances with respect to it he cherishes it
stem 1a: -qossiht-
stem 1b: qsiht-
stem 2:   qessiht-

'qossiyal (TA) he follows the proper observances with respect to him
stem 1a: -qossiy-
stem 1b: qsiy-
stem 2:   qessiy-

'qossol (A) (dep.) his son
nqoss my son
qoss son! (a term of address or endearment, said to a boy or to any man younger than the speaker)

'qotakisu (A) one dollar
plural: 'qotakisuwok dollars

'qotakon (I) (dep.) his throat

'qotakonap (I) windpipe
plural: 'qotakonapiyil

'qotakonine (AI) he has a sore throat; he has throat trouble
stem 1a:	-kutakonin(e)-
stem 1b:	'qotakonin(e)-
stem 2:	'qotakonin(e)-

'qotalokamqahk (P) one million

'qotalokiqessu (AI) he winks
plural:	'qotalokiqessultuwok
stem 1a:	-noqtalokiqess(i)-: notqtalokiqess I wink
stem 1b:	'qotalokiqess(i)-
stem 2:	neqtalokiqess(i)-

Ntus op li pawatom skat skinuhsisok 'kisi 'qotalokiqessultiwoniya. My daughter would like the boys not to be able to wink.

qotasq (I) pool of water; pond
plural:	qotaskul
poss:	'qotaskum
loc:	qotaskuk
dim:	qotasqis

'qotatokiye (II) it is one string (e.g. of beads); it has one strand
stem 1:	'qotatokiy(a)-
stem 2:	neqtatokiy(a)-: neqtatokiyak one string

'qotatokot (II) it is one continuous length (in space or time)

'Qotatokot te elewestaq. He spoke without stopping, continuously.

'qotinsk (P) ten

qotoput (I) chair
plural:	qotoputiyil, qotoputihil
poss:	'toqtoput
loc:	qotoputik
dim:	qotoputossis

(Note: also kutoput.)

'qotuhkanu (AI) he lives alone
plural:	'qotuhkanultuwok, 'qotuhkanuhtuwok, 'qotuhkanihtuwok
stem 1a:	-noqtuhkan(i)-: noqtuhkan I live alone
stem 1b:	'qotuhkan(i)-
stem 2:	neqtuhkan(i)-: neqtuhkanit when he lived alone
stem 3:	nqotuhkan(i)-

'Qotuhkanuhpon pesqolek wik. He was living alone when his house caught on fire.

'qotuhkayiw, 'qotuhkayi (P) alone

(Note: Also kotuhkayiw.)

'Qotuhkayi te 'qisihtun. He built it alone.

'qotuhsalqot (II) it is one mile

'qotulom (AI) he is in a canoe alone; he has one point (in the traditional dice game, altestakon)
stem 1a:	-noqtulom(o)- type A: noqtulom I am in a canoe alone
stem 1b:	'qotulom(o)-
stem 2:	neqtulom(o)-

S

-s-, -os- cut
(forms TA verb stems)
'kissal he cut it (an.)
monosal he cuts it (an.) off

sahkat (A) needle
plural:	sahkatiyik
poss:	'sahkatemol
loc:	sahkatek
dim:	sahkatossis

'sahsaksitehe (AI) he is barefoot
(See ahsaksitehe.)

sahsap (A) jellyfish
plural:	sahsapiyik
poss:	'sahsapimol

sahsapu (AI) he glances quickly
stem 1:	-sahsap(i)-

sahsessu (AI, II) it goes back and forth quickly
stem 1:	-sahsess(i)-

sahsewestu (AI) he talks fast
stem 1:	-sahsewest(u)-

sahseyu (II) it is slippery
stem 1:	-sahsey(i)-

sahsimiye (AI) he prays fast
stem 1:	-sahsimiy(a)-

sahsomahtu (AI) he does everything fast
stem 1:	-sahsomaht(u)-

saht (I) blueberry
plural:	sahtiyil, sahtihil, sahthil
poss:	'sahtemol
loc:	sahtek
dim:	sahtesis

sahtewi (PN) blueberry
sahtewi skonimin blueberry seed

'sak, sak (A) lobster
plural:	(')sakiyik, (')sakihik
poss:	'sakemol, nossakemol, 'tahsakemol
dim:	(')sakehsis

Pqeyuwok 'sakiyik eci kisaqosihtit. Lobsters are red when they are cooked.

sakhahte (II) it sticks out into view

sakhalokittiyhe (AI) (intensive or angry form of sakhiye "he comes into view")

sakhi (sakh-, sak-) (PV) into view; unexpectedly
sakhamkole (AI) it (an.) bursts into flames
sakhohom (AI) he swims into view
sakhuhqepu (AI) he sits, protruding into view
'sakhuhulal (TA) he ferries him into view
'sakhotomimal (TA) he appears, calls on the phone, etc. to hire him

Wot iya sakhiksahat. Gracious! Here he is! (Literally, he is walking in unexpectedly.

sakhiye (AI) he comes into view
stem 1:	-sakhiy(a)-

sakholiqehe (AI) (intensive or angry form of sakhiye "he comes into view")

sakhotkuhu (AI) he jumps into view
(See -otoqq(i)- "jump".)

sakoleyu (AI, II) it is hard to the touch; it is difficult
stem 1: -sakoley(i)-

sakoli opos (A) hardwood tree; witch hazel

sakoli (sakol-) (PV, PN) hard (to the touch); difficult; tough
sakolahkepolasu (II) a path is packed down in the snow
sakoliksasu (II) it is hard to saw
'sakoliksomon (TI) he saws it with difficulty
sakolotekone (AI) he has tough skin

sakolitehe (AI) he is strong-willed
plural: sakolitahawolotuwok, sakolitahahtuwok
stem 1: -sakolit_h(a)-

sakolomtu (AI) he is healthy
stem 1: -sakolomt(u)-

'sakolonomon (TI) he holds it tight
stem 1: -sakolonom-

sakom (A) chief; tribal governor
plural: sakomak
poss: 'sakomamol
dim: sakomahsis
Sakom kisi psqolehlacihi nuci tqonkelicihi, wisokiluwehhik. When the chief fired the policemen, they got mad.

Sakomawi Mali (A) the Virgin Mary

sakomawikuwam (I) governor's house
loc: sakomawikuwamok

sakomawka (AI) he does a governor's dance
sakomawkan there is a governor's ball

sakpe, sakhope (II) water is coming into view
Kis mace sakpe kuspem. The lake is already beginning to show through (the ice).
Mus 'sami punomuhkoc 'samaqan. Tehpu kekesk sakpec. Don't (sg.) put in too much water. Just let a little show.

saku (P) so; therefore
Nit eli nomihtaq 'kihkahan, on saku mace nuhsuhkuwan. He saw that they had all gone, and so he began to follow them.
Kis ma kciksotuwiw, saku tan te kil. You (sg.) are already not listening, so it's up to you.

salawehpukot (II) it tastes salty
stem 1: salawehpukot(o)-
Tokec piksey salawehpukahk, kat cipotuk kosqehsuhs micin. If the pork tastes salty, the old woman should not eat it.
Musey salawehpukotoc. Have the moose meat be salty.

salawehpuksu (AI) it (an.) tastes salty
plural: salawehpuksultuwok
stem 1: -salawehpuks(i)-
Eci salawehpuksihtit nomehsok, nwikahpak. When the fish taste salty, I like them.

salawehtasu (II) it is pickled in salt; it is salted

salawey (I) salt
plural: salaweyal
poss: 'salaweyam
loc: salaweyak
dim: salaweyis, salaweyahsis

'samamkole (II) it burns too much

'samaqan, samaqan (I) water
plural: 'samaqanol
poss: 'samaqanum, nossamaqanum
loc: 'samaqanok
older form: nsamaqan
Nomehsuwok wikultuwok 'samaqanihkuk. Fish live in bodies of water.

'samcuwe (AI) she has too many children
stem 1a: -usamcuw(e)-
stem 1b: 'samcuw(e)-
stem 2: wesamcuw(e)-

'sami (P) because
Ntapi tkahsom 'sami ksihpote. I went swimming because it's hot.
Nhesis ktapi macephoqaloq 'sami kisi wihqehtuwan 'tahsukolisom. My older brother chased you because you took his candy.

'sami (sam-) (PV) too much; excessively
prefixed form: -usami (-usam-)-
neke form: wesami (wesam-)

'samitposu (AI) he has awesome power

'samitpot (II) it has awesome power

'sanaqot (II) it is dangerous
stem 1: 'sanaqot(o)-
stem 2: nessanaqot(o)-: nessanaqahk it is dangerous

sankewikapuwu, sankewikapuhu (AI) he stands still
stem 1: -sankewikapuw(i)-
(Stem final -w may change to h before u.)

sankewimiye (AI) he prays quietly; he prays calmly

sankewiw (P) slow and easy; calmly

sankewopu (AI) he sits still
sankewop sit (sg.) still!

'sanku (P) thirteen

sapessu (AI) he has diarrhea
stem 1: -sapess(i)-

saphome, saphoma (AI) he gets by; he does all right
plural: saphomahtuwok, saphomhotuwok
stem 1: -saphom(a)- (also, in Independent forms only: saphom(e)-): nsaphom I get by, ksaphomapa you (dual) are doing all right
stem 2: saphom(a)-: saphomat when he got by
Mate saphomaw. He's not all there.

'saphomuwan (DOV) he pokes, injects something of his (someone else's)

saphutin (AI) there are injections being given
stem 1: saphut(i)-
(Note: Forms for unspecified (indefinite) subject only.)

Wasisok oliyawolotuwok etoli saphutimok.
The children (pl.) are going to the place where
shots are being given.

sapi (sap-) (PV) through
  sapiye (AI, II) he, it goes through
  sapuhse (AI) he walks through

sapitimeq (A) killer whale

sapiw (P) through
  Keskomihiket sapiw kcihkuk, on
'koskahan. When he took a short cut
through the woods he got lost.

sapol (I) shovel
  plural: sapolol
  (from English, shovel)

'sapolahal (TA) he shovels it (an.)
  'Totoli sapolahal wastiyil etutaqahtek.
There was so much snow that he was
shoveling it.

'sapolahtomon (TI) he licks through it
  'Sapolahtomom tekcokek. He licked
through his ice cream.

'sapolatomon, 'sapolahmon (TI) he shovels it
  'Sapolatomon eluhset. He shoveled a path
(for himself).

sapossomu (AI) he takes a physic

sapute (saputiy-) (PV) through
  saputehe (AI) he goes through
  saputehtehsin (AI) he falls through
  saputiyapu (AI) he looks through
  saputiyamu (AI) he falls through

'saputchtun (TI) he puts it through

saputessu (AI, II) he, it goes through

'saputiyalokotomon (TI) he eats through it

saqtemin (A) blackberry
  plural: saqteminok
  poss: 'saqteminomol
  loc: saqteminok
  dim: saqteminsis
  Nit elomiyat, 'pecuhsan saqteminihkuk.
Going along, he comes to a blackberry patch.

saqteminimus (A) blackberry bush
  plural: saqteminimusiyik
  poss: 'saqteminimusemol
  loc: saqteminimusek
  dim: saqteminimusis
  Psi te sukskicin wen weci sapiyat
saqteminimusihkuk. One is all ripped up
when one comes out of a blackberry patch.

sashoma (AI) he slips on something
  stem 1:   -sashom(a)-

sasokamu (AI) it (an.) flies straight
  stem 1:   -sasokam(i)-
  Sasokamit kakawessu. A straight ball goes
fast.

'sasokatokehlal (TA) he stretches it (an.) out

sasokatokot (II) it is a long straight length

sasokiye (AI) he moves in a straight line

sasokuhqepu (AI) he half stands; he half sits;
he is leaning against something

sasotemu (AI) he cries
  stem 1:   -sasotem(i)-

sasotokku (AI) he jumps up and down quickly

'satq (P) three hundred

'sawatom, nsawatom (AI) he is careful
  stem 1a: -nossawatom(o)- type A
  stem 1b: 'sawatom(o)-, nsawatom(o)-
  stem 2:   nessawatom(o)-
  stem 3:   nsawatom(o)-
  Komac woli nsawatom elomelkit ahahs.
A horse is very careful about where he steps.

sawe (sawiy-) PV often; many times
  sawe wtome (AI) he smokes often
  sawe pitkoma (AI) he packs often
  sawe pitsone (AI) he fills his pipe often
  sawiyaphal (TA) he tracks him many times

sawecuwe (AI) she has children often

sawew (P) often

sawonehson (II) the wind is blowing from the
south
  (also: sawonosson)

sawonehsonuk south (Locative)
  Tet te 'ci nusolamson sawonehsonuk. The
breeze is just starting up from the south.

sehkahapiye (AI) he paddles standing up
  (variant of sehkehepiye)

sehke (AI) he stands
  plural: sehkotuwok, sehkahtuwok,
               sehkawolotuwok,
               sehkawotuwok, sehkolotuwok,
               sehkolotiyawolotuwok
  stem 1:   -sehk(e)-: sehket when he was
               standing
  (Note: Stand up! (sg.) may be either
sehken or sehk.)
  Sehke ketsokek. He is standing at the
corner.

sehkehepiye, sehkahapiye (AI) he paddles
standing up

'sehkehlal (TA) he stands him up
  stem 1:   -sehkehl-

sehkomu (AI, II) it stands
  stem 1:   -sehkom(i)-

'sehkomutun (TI) he stands it up
  stem 1:   -sehkomut-

sehpal
  (See stehpal.)

sehsoluhke (AI) he works so hard he is ready
to cry
  stem 1:   -sehsoluhk(e)-

sehta (sehtay-) (PV) backwards
  sehtawse (AI) he walks backwards
  sehtahkawotuwok (AI) they (dual) walk
backwards (dual forms only)
  Sehta pisessiyin weciyay, on yakahc
kmosonin, nit tehc nmehcinan. If you (sg.)
back in where I came in, then you will get
me and I will die.

sehtapasuwok (AI) they (pl.) walk backwards
  (See -apas(i)- "walk (pl.)," sehtayapasuwok
"they (pl.) walk backwards.")

sehtatkuhu (AI) he jumps backwards

sehtawse (AI) he walks backwards
  plural: sehtayapasuwok,
               sehtawsahtuwok,
               sehtawsawolotuwok

sehtawtahapiye (AI) he paddles backwards
sehtayapasuwok, sehtapasuwok (AI) they (pl.) walk backwards
    plural: sehtayapasultuwok,
                sehtayapasuhtuwok,
                sehtapasultuwok,
                sehtapasuhtuwok
    stem 1:   -sehtayapas(i)-
    (Note: plural meanings only.)
sehtehe (AI) he goes backwards
    stem 1:   -seht_h(a)-
sekonoss (A) porpoise fin
    plural: sekonossok
'sekopu (AI) it (an.) has three layers
    stem 1a: -nossekop(i)-
    stem 1b: 'sekop(i)-
    stem 2:   nessekop(i)-
sekotepokahtek (I) plaintain leaf
    plural: sekotepokahtekil
seksu (AI) he is scared
    plural: seksultuwok
    stem 1:   -seks(i)-
    Eci wasossis seksit, nit te macetemin. When the baby is scared, he starts crying.
    Musa seksultihkeq eci petakik. Don't (pl.) be scared when it thunders.
sepawonu (P) tomorrow
    Macahawolotuwok wasisok sepawonu Kelisk. The children are leaving tomorrow for Calais, Maine.
sepay (P) this morning (past only)
    Sepay nit kisi leyik. It happened this morning.
    (Compare: Naci utenehk pemispasahkiwik. I'm going shopping this morning.)
seqqe (II) there is an eclipse
    stem 1:   seqq(e)-: seqqek when there is an eclipse
seskoqone (AI) he has a fancy heel (on his shoe)
sesolahkiw, sesolahki (P) suddenly; all at once
    (also: 'solahkiw, 'solahki)
    'Solahki te nutuwal wikuwossol. Suddenly he heard his mother.
sesomi, (sesom-) (PV) completely
    Sesomi mehtonu micuwakon. The food is completely gone.
    Nsesomi te wonitahasin keti itomanpon. I completely forgot what I was going to say.
    Sesomessu nmoshun. I'm speechless. (idiomatic expression)
'sesomitahamal (TA) he does not know about him; he cannot imagine about him
    stem 1:   -sesomitaham-
    Ksesomitahamol mehsi Susehp tokomosk. I can't imagine why Joseph hit you (sg.)
'sesomitahatomon (TI) he does not know about it; he cannot imagine about it
    stem 1:   -sesomitahatom-
    Nsesomitahatomon tan oc cel ntoli kisi liyan utenek. I can't imagine how I'll be able to go downtown.

sespayu (AI) he cries out of fear
    stem 1:   -sespay(i)-
'sestahal (TA) he makes him cry
    stem 1:   -sest_h-
Sesuhs (A) Jesus
    (from French, Jésus)
'sicihqehmon (TI) he pastes it on
    stem 1:   -sicihqehm-; but: sicihqohok when he pastes it on
sihku (A) sheldrake
    plural: sihkuwiyik
    dim: sihkuwehsis
sihpac (A) pail
    plural: sihpacuwok
sihtomuhkakon (I) weir
    plural: sihtomuhkakonol
    loc: sihtomuhkakonok
sihtomuhke (AI) he fishes in a weir
    stem 1:   -sihtomuhk(e)-
sikeyu (II) it is hard to do
    stem 1:   sikey(i)-
sikiliyem (A) cricket
    plural: sikiliyemok
    poss: 'sikiliyemol
sikinaqsu (AI) he is stingy
    stem 1:   -sikinaqs(i)-
'sikine (AI) he dies horribly
    stem 1:   -sikin(e)-
sikolat (A) shark
    plural: sikolatiyik
    poss: 'sikolatemol, 'sikolatimol
    dim: sikolatehsis
sikonoss (A) sunfish
    plural: sikonossok
    poss: 'sikonossomol
    dim: sikonossis
sikopu (AI) he, it (an.) is hard to get at
    stem 1:   -sikop(i)-
sikte (II) it is hard to get to; it is hard to get at
    stem 1:   -sikt(e)-
'siktehkomon (TI) he makes it (a part of the body) go to sleep (e.g. he makes his leg go to sleep by the way he is sitting)
    stem 1:   -siktehkom-
'siktehkomuwan (DOV) he makes it (a part of the body) go to sleep on him (e.g. a child making his mother's leg go to sleep by the way he is sitting on her lap)
    'siktehkomuwanol he kills something (an.) of his by running into (or over) it with a vehicle.
    Etucitahasit pilsqehsis siktehkomuwut 'temisol. The girl was very sad when her dog was killed by a car.
'siktehkuwal (TA) he kills him by running into (or over) him with a vehicle
    stem 1:   -siktehkuw-
'siktehpawolal (TA) he scares him to death (literally or figuratively)
    stem 1:   -siktehpawol-
siktehpayu (AI) he is very scared
    stem 1:   -siktehpay(i)-

siktehsin (AI) he dies from a fall; he dies from a crash
> *stem 1:*   -siktehsin(o)- type B

siktehsonu (AI) he is tired
> *stem 1:*   -siktehson(i)-: nsiktehsonipon we (nilun, dual) are tired

'siktehtaqsuwamal (TA) he talks about him annoyingly often

siktelamu (AI) he starves; he is starving (literally or figuratively)
> *plural:*   siktelamultuwok, siktelamuhtuwok
> *stem 1:*   -siktelam(i)-: nsiktelam I am starving; siktelamit one who is starving

Skat somahq, siktelamuwol 'temisol. If he does not feed him, his dog will starve.

siktelomu (AI) he smiles

siktelomuwiqewu (AI) he smiles a small smile

siktepskelusu (AI) he smothers in smoke

siktihikon (I) club (for killing)
> *plural:*   siktihikonol

siktiyaqosu (AI) he is very hot; he burns to death

siktiyelomu (AI) he laughs very hard

sikusas (A) fried sliced salt pork
> *plural:*   sikusasok

sikusq (A) widow; pear; beetle species
> *plural:*   sikusqiyik
> *poss:*   'sikusqemol
> *dim:*   sikusqehsis young widow

sikuwan (I) arrowhead
> *plural:*   sikuwanol

sikuwit (A) widower
> *plural:*   sikuwicik

'silom (AI) he is paddling alone
> *stem 1a:*   -nossilom-: nossilom I paddle alone
> *stem 1b:*   'silom-
> *stem 2:*   nessilom-: nessilok when he was paddling alone

simis (A) slip (garment)
> *poss:*   'simisomol
> (from French, chemise)

sincokkot (II) the tide is at its lowest in its monthly cycle it is neap tide

sinpisiye (AI) he turns blue
> *stem 1:*   -sinpisiy(a)-

'sinsk (P) thirty

sip (I) river
> *plural:*   sipul
> *poss:*   'tosipum, 'sipum
> *loc:*   sipuk
> *dim:*   sipuhsis

Sipayik Pleasant Point, Maine (Locative)

sipayikew (A) person from Pleasant Point, Maine
> *plural:*   sipayikewiyik

sipine (AI) he dies hard
> *stem 1:*   -sipin(e)-

sipitahasu (AI) he remembers very well

'sipkaskuwyal (TA) he waits for him for a long time
> *stem 1:*   -sipkaskuwy-; stem-final -y may change to -h before i: sipkaskuwhit when he waited a long time for me

Kenoq 'sipkaskuwyal uhsimisol eli wisokamoqessik. But she waited for her younger brother for a long time because there was a bad storm.

sipki (sipk-) (PV) for a long time
> sipkiye (AI) he is gone for a long time
> sipki peciye (AI) it takes him a long time to arrive, to get home

'sipkihkomon (AI, AI+OBJ) it takes him a long time to get to it

'Sipkihkomoniyal wikuwawihkuwal 'samamoqesson. It took them a long time to get to their (respective) houses because the storm was so bad.

'Sipkihkomon eliyat 'sami mocihkasu. It took a long time to where he was going because the going was rough.

sipkiw (P) for a long time

Sipkiw pomiye, malom te peicye Oktokomq. He journeys for a long time; finally he arrives in Newfoundland.

sipkiye (AI) he is gone for a long time
> *plural:*   sipkiyawolotuwok
> *stem 1:*   -sipkiy(a)-

sips (A) bird (esp. duck)
> *plural:*   sipsok
> *poss:*   'sipsumol, 'tahsipsumol
> *dim:*   sipsis small bird, bird; sipsossis

Cihpolakon na yat sips. That bird is an eagle.

Can 'sipsum kinkilu. John's birds are big.

sipsuhke (AI) he hunts birds (esp. ducks)
> *plural:*   sipsukhotuwok, sipsuhkahtuwok
> *stem 1:*   -sipsuhk(e)-

siptoku (AI) he stretches
> *plural:*   siptokultuwok, siptokuhtuwok
> *stem 1:*   -siptok(i)-

sipun (A) black fly
> *plural:*   sipunok

sipunis (A) midge, no-see-um
> *plural:*   sipunisok

siqehe (AI, II) it is emptying
> *stem 1:*   -siq_h(a)-

siqepu (AI, II) it (an.) is empty
> *stem 1:*   -siqep(i)-

siqeyawiw (AI, II) it is empty
> *stem 1:*   -siqeyaw(i)- type B

siqeyu (AI, II) it is empty
> *stem 1:*   -siqey(i)-

siqon (II) it is spring

siqoniw (P) in the spring

siqonomeq (A) alewife, gaspereau (Maliseet)
> *plural:*   siqonomeqok

'sis, (P) three (in counting) (no nominal forms)

(Note: The word 'sis is used in verbs to show three-ness. Unprefixed form: 's-; prefixed form: -noss-; neke form: ness-.)

'sulomuk (AI) they are three in a canoe

'suhkak (AI) they are three on a team
'supisuwok (AI) they are tied in threes
'sanokahte (II) it has three pages, sheets, etc.
'sisolapsqehlal (TA) he fries it (an.)
  stem 1:   -sisolapsqehl-
sisolapsqehtikon (A) frying pan
  plural: sisolapsqehtikonok
'sisolapsqehtun (TI) he fries it
  stem 1:   -sisolapsqeht-
sisolastike (AI) he fries pork
  stem 1:   -sisolastik(e)-
sisoq (I) face; eye
  plural: siskul
  poss: 'sisoq
  loc: siskuk
  dim: siskuhsis
sisqeyal (I) (pl.) eyeglasses
  poss: 'sisqeyal
  loc: sisqeyawihkuk
  dim: sisqeyahsisol
'sisqine (AI) his eye (or eyes) hurts (hurt)
  stem 1:   -sisqin(e)-
(Note: a personal prefix is used in all third-person and obviative Independent forms.)
sisse (sissiy-) (PV) in all directions; scattering
  'sisse pcitahkan (AI, AI+OBJ) he sends it out in all directions
sissessu (II) it spreads out; it disperses; it scatters
sistoss (A) nun, religious sister
  plural: sistossok
(from English, sister)
(Compare 'sistalomol "his sister (sibling)," which is also from English, sister.)
'sit (I) (dep.) his foot
  plural: 'sitol
Sitank Ste.-Anne-de-Beaupré, Québec (Locative)
Sitansisk Fredericton, New Brunswick (Locative)
(literally, at little St. Ann's)
sitom (I) shore
  plural: sitomol
  loc: sitomok
Skinuhsisok kisi acihhik sitomok tokkiw elomocokek. The boys moved from the shore to the mud flats.
'siwehsol (A) (dep.) his brother
  nsiwehs my brother (man speaking)
(See 'siwiyil "his relative.")
'siwestuwok (AI) they (dual) are brothers
  plural: 'siwestultuwok
  stem 1:   -siwest(i)-: dual and plural forms only
siwi (siw-) (PV) be tired of...
siwi tpitahasu (AI) he is tired of thinking
'siwiyil (A) (dep.) his relative
  plural: 'siwiyi, 'siwihi, 'siwi his relatives
  nsiw my relative
  ksiwennuk our (kilun) relatives

siwoluhke (AI) he is tired of working
siwskuwasu (AI) he is tired waiting
'siwskuwyal (TA) he is tired of waiting for him
  stem 1:   -siwskuwiy-, -siwskuwy-
(Note: The stem-final y may be changed to h before i: ksiwskuwihi, ksiwskuwhi "you (sg.) are tired of waiting for me.")
-sk(i)- urinate
(See soku "he urinates.")
ska, skat (P) not; if not
Skat nemiyawanik, otuhkok, nikt kisiphuwoloticik. Those deer that I didn't see were the ones that got away.
Skat luhkehq, cu nposqolehla. If he doesn't work, I'll fire him.
Mali mihtaqsol wisokiluwehe skat Piyelol akonutomalihq. Mary's father was mad because Peter didn't tell a story.
Skat pekotahsihq, ma tehc kisuhsuwiw. If he doesn't cast a shadow, there won't be any sun.
skawewintuwakon (I) greeting song
  plural: skawewintuwakonol
  older form: nskawewintuwakon
skawey, skawey opan (A) bread cooked in the oven
(also: skawsisey)
skehewahtoq (I) Friday
  plural: skehewatkul
  skehewatqik on Friday (also: eskehewatqik, weskehewatqik)
skicin (A) Indian
  plural: skicinuwok
  poss: uskicinumol
  dim: skicinuhsis
skicinuwatuwe (AI) he speaks an Indian lanuage; he speaks Maliseet-Passamaquoddy
  stem 1a: -uskicinuwatuw(e)-
  stem 1b: skicinuwatuw(e)-
  stem 2:   weskicinuwatuw(e)-
skicinuwi (skicinuw-) (PN, PV) Indian
  prefixed form: -uskicinuwi (-uskicinuw-)
  neke form: weskicinuwi (weskicinuw-)
  skicinuwehtasu (II) it is done in the Indian way
skicinuwoka, skicinuwoke (AI) he does an Indian dance
  stem 1a: -uskicinuwok(a)-
  stem 1b: skicinuwok(a)-
  stem 2:   weskicinuwok(a)-
skihkipolasu (AI) it (an.) is packed down by tramping
  stem 1:   skihkipolas(i)-
  stem 2:   eskihkipolas(i)-
skinuhs (A) young man (archaic)
  plural: skinuhsuwok, skinuhsok
  poss: uskinuhsumol, uskinuhsomol
  dim: skinuhsis small young man; boy
skinuhsis (A) boy
  plural: skinuhsisok
  poss: uskinuhsisomol
  dim: skinuhsossis

skitahqem (A) outer wood (of a tree)
skitap (A) man
    plural: skitapiyik, skitapihik
    poss: uskitapemol
    dim: skitapehsis
skitapewehlosu (AI) he (e.g., an animal) turns himself into a man; she turns herself into a man
    plural: skitapewehlosultuwok
    stem 1a: -uskitapewehlos(i)-
    stem 1b: skitapewehlos(i)-
    stem 2:   weskitapewehlos(i)-
    Kisi yaq na skitapewehlosultuwok tan te etuci wolitahatomuhtit. They could, it is said, change themselves into men whenever they pleased.
skitoqotehe (AI) he swims underwater near the surface
    stem 1a: -uskitoqotah(a)-
    stem 1b: skitoqot_h(a)-
    stem 2:   weskitoqotah(a)-
skitpeq (P) on the water
skiwon (I) urine
    poss: 'sokiwon
skolunsq (I) bullet lead
    plural: skolunskul: bird shot
skonahq (I) piece of steel
    plural: skonahqol
skonahq (A) magnet
    plural: skonahqok
skonimin (I) seed
    plural: skoniminol
    poss: uskonimin
    loc: skoniminok
    dim: skoniminsis
skonis (I) bone
    plural: skonisol
    poss: 'taskonisom, uskonisom
    loc: skonisok
    dim: skonisossis
skonoqoss (A) corbie
    plural: skonoqossok
skuweyu (AI) he often spends a lot of time (there)
    plural: skuweyultuwok
    stem 1a: -uskuwey(i)-: nuskuwey I often spend a lot of time there
    stem 1b: skuwey(i)-: skuweyit if he often spends a lot of time there
    stem 2:   weskuwey(i)-: weskuweyit when he used to spend a lot of time there.
'sokiptinenal (TA) he shakes hands with him
    stem 1:   -sokiptinen-
    stem 2:   sekiptinen-
sokku (AI) he vomits
    plural: sokkultuwok, sokkuhtuwok
    stem 1:   -soqq(i)-: nsoqqipon we (nilun, dual) vomit; but: nsokoq, nsoqq I vomit; ksokoq, ksoqq you (sg.) vomit
    stem 2:   seqq(i)-: seqqiyan when I vomited
    (Note: qq changes to kk before u.)

sokossuhun (I) earring
    plural: sokossuhunol
sokotiyapske (II) it is a flat rock
    stem 1:   sokotiyapsk(e)-
    stem 2:   sekotiyapsk(e)-: sekotiyapskek where there is a flat rock
soku (AI) he urinates
    plural: sokultuwok, sokuhtuwok
    stem 1:   sok(i)-: nsok I urinate
    stem 2:   sek(i)-: sekit when he urinated
    stem 3:   -sk(i)-: nacisk I am going somewhere to urinate
    Ntotoliskultipon. Musa yut oloqiw ckuwyahkoc. We (nilun, pl.) are urinating. Don't (sg.) come over this way.
solanimus (A) sumac
    plural: solanimusiyik
-som-, -osom- cut (forms TI verb stems)
    'kissomon (TI) he cuts it
    monosomon (TI) he cuts it off
'somakonoss (A) soldier
    plural: 'somakonossok
    poss: usomakonossomol
    dim: 'somakonossis
'somal (TA) he feeds him (variant of 't-ahsomal)
soni piskuwon (II) there is a thick fog
    Elomiphukiyek Sipayik, yet al ote peciphukiyek Mehqamkesk, soni piskuwon. When we were going to Pleasant Point, Maine, by the time we (nilun) got to Red Beach, Maine, it was very foggy.
soni kpoputon (II) the view is blocked (by fallen snow) through the trees
soniku (AI) he blows his nose
    plural: sonikultuwok, sonikuhtuwok
    stem 1:   -soniq(i)-
    (Note: The q of the stem changes to k before u.)
sonuciw (P) on (or along) the edge
    Koluskap sipkiw sankewikapuwu sonuciw, 'tapotukonapinol 'tahtapiyil. Koluskap stands still for a long time at the edge of the water leaning on his bow.
    Maciyaphan sitomok sonuciw. He begins trailing them along the shore at the edge of the water.
sonucuhse (AI) he walks along the edge
sonutaskutew (P) along the edge of a field
sonutasokiw (P) along the edge of a floor
sonutasuke (AI) he wades along the edge
sonutsekotonuk southwest (Locative)
    'Ci peciwehse sonutsekotonuk. A sudden heavy wind came up out of the southwest.
sopayahkiw (P) along a hill
sopayakom (P) along a lake
sopayakomiw (P) along a lake
sopayawtiw (P) along (or by) the edge of a road
sopayiw (P) by way of; along the edge
    Nit te mace menakatkeniniya elomi sonuceyik sopayiw Unamakik. Then slowly

they make their way along the coast by way of Cape Breton.

Sopayiw awtik tuciye. He went along the side of the road.

sopiqon (I) tear
plural: sopiqonol
dim: sopiqonis teardrop

soqasuwakon (I) bridge, trestle
plural: soqasuwakonol
poss: 'soqasuwakonum
loc: soqasuwakonok
dim: soqasuwakonossis
(originally (?) qsokawsuwakon or qsokassuwakon)

soqehs (A) weasel
plural: soqehsuwok
poss: 'soqehsumol, 'soqehsomol
dim: soqehsis

'soqskosal (TA) he cuts him up into pieces
stem 1: -soqskos-
stem 2: -seqskos-
(also: 'sosqosal)

sosq, ososq (I) stove ashes mixed with water; mud
loc: soskuk

'sosqihtahal (TA) he cuts him, it (an.) up (with a knife, fist, etc.)
stem 1: -sosqiht_h-
stem 2: sesqiht_h-
(also: 'soqskihtahal)

sossoq (I) saliva
poss: 'sossoq

'sotom, nostom (AI) he understands (what is said)
plural: 'sotomuhtuwok, nostomuhtuwok
stem 1a: -nostom(o)-: nostom I understand
stem 1b: 'sotom(o)-, nostom(o)-
stem 2: nestom(o)-: nestok one who understands

'sotuwa (TA) he is understood, mentioned
(See nostuwal "he understands, mentions him.")

spaqahte (II) the snow is deep
stem 1: spaqaht(e)-
stem 2: espaqaht(e)-

spasu (AI) he is awake
plural: spasultuwok, spasuhtuwok
stem 1a: -uspas(i): nuspas I am awake
stem 1b: spas(i)-
stem 2: wespas(i)-
spasultin wake (before a funeral)

spasuwiw (P) in the morning

spekopu (AI) he, it (an., a sheet-like object) is high up (officially or physically)
stem 1a: -aspekop(i)-: ntaspekop I am high up
stem 1b: spekop(i)-
stem 2: espekop(i)-: espekopit when he was high up

Woli spekopu sipelekhikon. The canvas tent is nice and high.

Piyel yaq woli spekopu. Peter has quite a good position.

spemuk sky (Locative)
Possesomuk iyuwok spemuk. There are stars in the sky.

spiqi (spiq-) (PV) upward
prefixed form: -aspiqi (-aspiq-)
neke form: espiqi (espiq-)
spiqamu (AI) he moves rapidly upward involuntarily
spiqatuwe (AI) he climbs up
spiqiye (AI, II) he, it moves upward
spiqi kikimskahsu (AI) he moves upward without making any noise
spiqi kikimuhse (AI) he walks upward without making any noise

spomk (I) heaven
loc: spomkik

spomok (P) up; above

spopu (AI) he sits up high
plural: spopultuwok, spopiyyik, spopiyahtuwok
stem 1a: -aspop(i)-: ntaspop I sit up high
stem 1b: spop(i)-
stem 2: espop(i)-: espopit when he sat up high

Spopitsopon, pihce nomihtu op. If he were sitting up high, he would see far.

spote, (spotiy-) (PV) during the day
prefixed form: -uspote (-uspotiy-), -aspote (-aspotiy-)
neke form: wespote (wespotiy-), espote (espotiy-)
spoteqsu (AI) he sleeps during the day

spotew (P) in the daytime; during the day
spotewi (PN) of the daytime
spotewse (AI) he walks during the day

sqasuntoq (A) thread (for sewing)
plural: sqasuntokuk

sqehkiqs (A) female animal
plural: sqehkiqsok
poss: sqehkiqsomol
dim: sqehkiqsis

Nutuwhemin espons, ma tahk nkosiciyaw napehsom kosona al sqehkiqs. I have a raccoon as a pet, but I don't know whether it is male or female.

sqehsomuhs (A) bitch
plural: sqehsomuhsok
poss: 'tasqehsomuhsomol
dim: sqehsomuhsis

sqewtomuhs (A) spirit woman
plural: sqewtomuhsok

Mecimiw sqewtomuhs alotemuhpon eci wen koti mehcinet. It used to be that a spirit woman would wander around crying when someone was going to die.

sqon (I) liver
plural: sqoniyil, sqonihil
poss: 'tasqonum

sqot (I) fire
plural: sqotiyil, sqotihil
poss: 'tahsqotem, usqotem

loc: sqotek
dim: sqotesis, sqotehsis
Knomihtuness sqot welaqik kci wikuwamok? Did you see the fire in the big house last night?

sqotes (I) spark; ember; glowing coal
plural: sqotesol

sqotewahkosu (AI) it (an.) is red hot
stem 1a: -asqotewahkos(i)-
stem 1b: sqotewahkos(i)-
stem 2:   esqotewahkos(i)-

sqotewahkote (II) it is red hot

sqotewāmq (I) ashes
loc: sqotewamkuk,
                sqotewamqihkuk

stahqon (A) fir (Peter Dana Point, Maine); tree (Pleasant Point, Maine)
plural: stahqonuk
poss: stahqonul, 'tastahqonumol,
                'tastahqonemol
loc: stahqonuk
dim: stahqonossis, stahqonis

stahqoney (I) something made of fir (Peter Dana Point, Maine)
plural: stahqoneyal
poss: 'tastahqoneyam

stehpal, sehpal (P) as if
(= cess + te + op + al)
Mahtoqehs stehpal qaqeyik 'qatol. A rabbit's feet look as if they were dirty.

stiti (P) constantly
(from English, steady)
Stiti te wasisok yaliwtutomahtuwok. Kids are constantly going around begging.

suhkacu (AI) he breaks camp

suhkessu (II) it collapses
Nit tehc suhkessu keti nipuwultimkopon. Then the marriage which was to have taken place is broken off ("collapses").

'suhsalqot (II) it is three miles
stem 1:   'suhsalqot(o)-
stem 2:   nesuhsalqot(o)-

'sukahtehmon (TI) he spills it (by hitting it)
plural: 'sukahtehmuhtiniya
stem 1:   -sukahtehm-; but: sukahtohok
                when he spills it

'sukahtestun (TI) he pours it out; he empties it; he spills it (because it's too full or because he's not paying attention to it)
stem 1:   -sukahtest-

sukayewotahsu (AI) he dumps (liquid)
plural: sukayewotahsultuwok
stem 1:   -sukayewotahs(i)-

sukol (I) sugar
plural: sukolol
poss: 'sukolum, 'tahsukolum
loc: sukolok
dim: sukolis a little sugar; piece of
                candy
(from French, sucre, or English, sugar)

sukolan (II) it pours (rain)
stem 1:   sukolan(o)- type A

sukolis (I) piece of candy
plural: sukolisol
poss: 'sukolisom, 'tahsukolisom
loc: sukolisok
dim: sukolossis
(diminutive of "sukol")

sukolopan (A) cake (pastry)
plural: sukolopanok
poss: 'sukolopanomol
loc: sukolopanok
dim: sukolopanis
(literally, "sugar bread")

sukonalokiqe (AI) he puts drops in his eyes
stem 1:   -sukonalokiq(a)-

'sukoniqewal (TA) he puts drops in his (someone else's) eyes
stem 1:   -sukoniqew-

suksahqe (AI) he cooks
plural: suksaqhotuwok,
                suksahqahtuwok,
                suksahqawolotuwok
stem 1:   -suksahq(e)-

sumsqe (AI) he spits
plural: sumsqhotuwok,
                sumsqahtuwok,
                sumsqawolotuwok
stem 1:   -sumsq(e)-

sun (I) cranberry
plural: sunul, sunol
poss: 'sunum
loc: sunuk, sunok
dim: sunis

supeq (I) salt water; ocean
plural: supeqol
loc: supekuk
Skitap neke kuskawet 'tulok, nit te supekuk etoli komoqiyat. When the man capsized his canoe, he drowned in the ocean.

supeqatoq (A) white spruce
plural: supeqatoqihik
Supeqatoqi lami wolokasq wolikon wen 'qotakoninet. The inner bark of the white spruce is good when one has a sore throat.

supeyu (II) it is smooth
stem 1:   supey(i)-: supeyik when it was
                smooth
Eci supeyik yut tuwihput. This table is very smooth.

'susqihtahal (TA) he knocks him flat on his back
stem 1:   -susqiht_h-

suwahqihikon (I) bell
plural: suwahqihikonol
poss: 'suwahqihikonum
loc: suwahqihikonok
dim: suwahqihikonossis

suwaskutew (P) out in the middle of a field
suwasokiw (P) out in the middle of the floor
suwawtiw, suwawtihiw (P) out in the middle of the road
Suwawtiw pemi ksokayapasicik espons naka nicans. A raccoon and her young are out in the middle of the road as they walk across.

suwhewik (I) moose sled; bob sled; pack sled
plural: suwhewikil, suwhewikol
poss: 'suwhewikom
loc: suwhewikok
dim: suwhewiksis
'suwikhikon (A) three (in cards)
plural: 'suwikhikonok
suwonap (I) jam; jelly
plural: suwonapiyil, suwonapuwol
poss: 'suwonapim, 'suwonapum
loc: suwonapuk
suwonhuke (AI) he puckers up from eating something sour
stem 1:   -suwonhuk(e)-
stem 2:   sewonhuk(e)-

T

't- ('ci, 'c-) (PV) from; because
(See 'ci.)
prefixed form: -ut- (-uci, -uc-)
neke form: wet- (weci, wec-)
'tahakon (I) paddle
plural: 'tahakonol
poss: uthakon, wothakon
loc: 'tahakonok
dim: 'tahakonossis
'Koskahtun 'tahakon neke kisi ktoqessit. He lost the paddle when he capsized.
tahalu, talu (P) as; like
Nit te etuci macephoqalat, tahalu tehp malsom pemi nuhsuhkuwat mahtoqehsuwol. Then he chased her, as a wolf would run after a rabbit.
Ksikultuwok tahalu te moci weyossisok. They were very ugly, like evil beasts.
-tahas(i)- think
(forms AI verb stems)
macetahasu (AI) he starts to think
sipkitahasu (AI) he thinks for a long time
tahkahsomu (AI) he swims (to cool off)
(variant of tkahsomu)
'tahkinuwehtuwal (TA) he informs him
stem 1:   -tahkinuwehtuw-
tahkitom (A) wild potato
plural: tahkitomuk
poss: 'tahkitomumol
tahkomons (I) seed
plural: tahkomonsol
'tahqomiw (AI) he has lice
(See oqom, "louse.")
tahqonahke (AI) he arrests
plural: tahqonahkahtuwok
stem 1:   -tahqonahk(e)-: ntahkqonahkepon we (du. exc.) arrest
stem 2:   tehqonahk(e)-
(variant of tqonke)
Nuci tqonket kisi tahqonahke wolakn. The policeman was arresting yesterday.

'tahqonal (TA) he arrests him
stem 1a: -tahqon-
stem 1b: tqon-
stem 2:   tehqon-
Ma te ntahqonokehpon: tehpu tehqonomuhtit peskuwat. We (nilun) were not arrested; they just impounded the gun.
'tahqonomon (TI) he impounds it
stem 1a: -tahqonom-
stem 1b: tqonom-
stem 2:   tehqonom-
Ma te 'tahqonomuwon peskuwat. He didn't impound the gun.
'tahqonomuwan (DOV) he impounds something of his
stem 1a: -tahqonomuw-
stem 1b: tqonomuw-
stem 2:   tehqonomuw-
Ntahqonomakun npeskuwat 'sami nucanomuwan man. He impounded my gun because I owed him money.
'tahsihpulal (TA) he "chases" her (or she... him)
(Slang for "he tries to gain her affection.")
'tahsomeluk in his lap (Locative)
ntahsomeluk in my lap, (etc.)
'takomiw (AI) he has snowshoes
stem 1a: -utakom(i)- type B
stem 1b: 'takom(i)-
stem 2:   wetakom(i)-
'taku (AI) he is in mourning
plural: 'takultuwok, 'takuhtuwok
stem 1a: -nihtak(i)-: nihtak I am in mourning
stem 1b: 'tak(i)-
stem 2:   nehtak(i)-: nehtakit one who is in mourning
stem 3:   ntak(i)-
talu (P) as; like
(See tahalu.)
tama (P) where; somewhere
Tama nti? Where am I?
Ma te tama nmoskuwaw. I didn't find him anywhere.
'tamihkessu (AI) he gets up from there
stem 1a: -utamihkess(i)-
stem 1b: 'tamihkess(i)-
stem 2:   wetamihkess(i)-
'tamoqesson (II) the storm is coming from there
'tamoqessu (II) the storm is coming from there
'tamuteluwal (TA) he wounds him
poss: -tamuteluw-: ntamutelaq he wounds me; tamuteluwat when he wounded him
tan (P) how; where; thus
(See tan etuci.)
Tan? Well?
Tan ktolihtun posonut? How do you make a basket?
Tan eloqiyat? Which way did he go?
Tan tuceyu? What time is it?

'Toqecimulaniya tan ehtek nehpahtaq.
They ask him where his kill is.

tan + Pronoun -ever: the one who, the one
which; which one of... (these, those, them)?
    (See tan tehpu.)

    Nuhsuhkakulc tan wen putuwatok. He will
follow whoever blows on it (flute).

    Nehpahal tan wot mesonat. He will kill
whoever gets her.

    Tan yut milimok, nit nil. What is given to
me, that is mine.

    Tan wot nit ktoptan? Which one of these
is your (sg.) coat?

tan etuci when; as soon as
    (See tan.)

    Tan etuci peciyayin, knomihtun wikuwam.
When you (sg.) arrive, you will see the house.

tan ote, tan te however; in whatever way; as...
as
    (See tan.)

    Ehpit, kisi kenoq skitapewehlosu, tan ote
welitahatok. A woman, she could, however,
change herself into a man whenever she
pleased.

    Naka kuckuwiphuwamin tan te kisi
tuciyayin. And then run to me as fast as you
(sg.) can go.

    Tan te kil. It's up to you (sg.). (It's your
choice.)

tan tehpu (P) -ever; however
    (See tan + Pronoun.)

    Kat te keq oleyiw tan tehpu wen. It
doesn't matter who it is.

tanehk, tanek, tane (P) from the first time;
ever since

    Tanehk nomihtunehk 'samaqan, etuci
wolinom. Ever since I saw the water, I have
liked the looks of it very much.

tap (A) bow (for shooting arrows)
plural:	tapiyik, tapihik
poss:	'tahtapiyil, 'tapiyil,'tahtapimol
loc:	tapiyik, tapihik, tapik
dim:	tapossis

    Skinuhsisok 'puwatomoniya 'tapiyi. The
boys want bows (literally, their bows).

    Sipsis tehsaqopu tapihik. The bird is
sitting on the bow.

'tapakon (I) sled; car; wagon
plural:	'tapakonol
poss:	utapakon
loc:	'tapakonok
dim:	'tapakonossis

    Etutapskosultihtit nicanuwa, 'cuwi
monuhmoniya piley utapakonuwa. Their
children (pl.) were so fat that they had to buy
a new car (literally, their new car).

tapehkikon (I) chin
poss:	'tapehkikon

'taptu (AI) he leaves tracks from there
plural:	'taptuhtuwok, 'taptultuwok
stem 1a:	-utapt(u)-: nutapt I leave tracks there
stem 1b:	'tapt(u)-: 'taptaq if he leaves tracks there

stem 2:	wetapt(u)-: wetaptaq where he left a track

tapu (P) two (in counting)
    (Note: no nominal forms)

taqanan (A) land-locked salmon
plural:	taqananok
poss:	'taqananomol
dim:	taqanansis

tatat (A) father (but not priest)
poss:	'tatatol

tat dad!
(from English, dad or dada)

'tawatkuwe (II) it rides the waves well
stem 1:	'tawatkuw(e)-
stem 2:	nehtawatkuw(e)-

'Tawatkuwe wtul. His boat rides the waves
well.

'tawe (II) he knows how to talk
plural:	'tawhotuwok
stem 1a:	-nihtaw(e)-: nihtaw I know how to talk
stem 1b:	'taw(e)-
stem 2:	nehtaw(e)-: nehtawet when he knew how to talk
stem 3:	ntaw(e)-

Kis ote ntawehpon ('tawehpon). He
already knew how to talk.

'tawi ('taw-) (PV) know how; be good at
    prefixed form: -nihtawi (-nihtaw-)
    neke form: nehtawi (nehtaw-)
    combining form: ntawi (ntaw-)
    'tawi kotunke (AI) he knows how to hunt
    'tawhike (AI) he is a good shot
    'tawoluhke (AI) he is good at doing (some
kind of) work
    'tawwikhike (AI) he knows how to write

'tawokisu (AI) he knows how to read
plural:	'tawokisultuwok
stem 1a:	-nihtawokis(i)-: nihtawokis I know how to read
stem 1b:	'tawokis(i)-: 'tawokisit if he knows how to read
stem 2:	nehtawokis(i)-
stem 3:	ntawokis(i)-: woli ntawokisit he knows how to read well

'tawtutuwe (AI) he knows how to build a fire
stem 1a:	-nihtawtutuw(e)-: nihtawtutu I know how to build a fire
stem 1b:	'tawtutuw(e)-
stem 2:	nehtawtutuw(e)-: nehtawtutuwet good fire-builder

te, ote (P) (emphatic)
    tehc (future) = te + oc
    tehp (conditional) = te + op
    Utapakonuwal etutonahsultihtit tehc
wiyuhs. Their sleds will be loaded up with
meat.

    Assokitahasultuwok ote ehpicik. The
women (pl.) are surprised indeed.

tehpisewey (I) pepper (ground black pepper,
green pepper, etc.)
plural:	tehpiseweyal
loc:	tehpiseweyak

Tehpiseweyal nkisehtakunol nteksqin. The pepper made me sneeze.

tehpu, tehpukt (P) only (restrictive); just; all; the only thing

tehpu qeni suddenly and without reason, without being asked, etc.

Nit kahk na tehpu oli pawalqahk, musa 'tomitahatomuhkoc. If that's all that is wanted, don't (sg.) worry about it.

Tehpu sankewopu. He just sits quietly.

Nil tehpukt. Only me.

Tehpu qeni tokomat skinuhsisol. She just up and hit the boy.

'tehsahqaphal (TA) he tracks him on high ground
stem 1: -tehsahqaph-

'tehsahqehlal (TA) he lifts him up and puts him on top
stem 1: -tehsahqehl-

tehsahqi (tehsahq-, tehsaq-) (PV) on top of
tehsahqoluhke (AI) he works on a table, desk, etc.

'tehsahqikapuwin (AI, AI+OBJ) he stands on top of it
plural: 'tehsahqikapuwultiniya, 'tehsahqikapuwuhtiniya, 'tehsahqikapuwiyaniya, 'tehsahqikapuwiyahtiniya
stem 1: -tehsahqikapuw(i)-: tehsahqikapuwu, tehsahqikapuhu he stands on top
(See -kapuw(i)- "stand.")

tehsahqiw (P) above; on top

'tehsahqossinon (AI, AI+OBJ) he lies on top of it
plural: 'tehsahqossinultiniya, 'tehsahqossinuhtiniya
stem 1: -tehsahqossin(o)-: tehsahqossin he is lying on top; tehsahqossit when he was lying on top
(See -hsin- "lie; come to rest.")

tehsaqhom (AI) he swims on top of something which is under the water

'tehsaqopin (AI, AI+OBJ) he sits on top of it
stem 1: -tehsaqop(i)-: tehsaqopu he sits on top
(Note: Some speakers use ntehsahqop instead of ntehsaqop "I am sitting on top.")
(See opu "he sits.")

tehsaqotokku (AI) he jumps on top

'tehsaqtehsinon (AI, AI+OBJ) he falls on it
plural: 'tehsaqtehsinultiniya, 'tehsaqtehsinuhtiniya
(See -hsin- "lie; come to rest.")

tehsaqtihikon (I) shelf
plural: tehsaqtihikonol
loc: tehsaqtihikonok

'teksal
(See uteksal.)

telihpum (I) telephone
plural: telihpumol
loc: telihpumok

(from English, telephone)

temonu, temonuk (P) later; just a minute
Temonuk npeci. I will come later.
Temonuk musa pol! Just a minute--not yet!

tepahkalusoniw (P) within the fence, the enclosure

'tepahkan (AI, AI+OBJ) he throws it in; he pushes it in; he drops it in
stem 1: -tepahk(e)-

tepessu (AI) he gets into a vehicle or boat
stem 1: -tepess(i)-

'tephomuwal (TA) he dishes out food to him
stem 1: -tephomuw-

tepi (tep-) (PV) enough
tepkil (AI) he is big enough
'tepihtun (TI) he makes enough of it, he has enough of it

tepi (tep-) (PV) in, within
teppu (AI) he sits in it

'tepitahatomon (TI) he thinks enough of it (to do such and such); he thinks well of it
stem 1: -tepitahatom-

tepiw (P) inside
Naci punomun opqehsimutiyil tepiw oqitonok. Go put the pillows inside the canoe.

tepot (P) nevertheless; however
Tepot olu 'tolitahasin Pokomk, Espons nit wilitpan psi te nutehtehmuwan. However, Fisher thought that it was Raccoon's brain that he had smashed out.

tepuloq (I) the inside of a canoe
plural: tepulokul

tetomaskuwikotone, teponaskuwikotone (AI) his birthday falls on the day of the week on which he was born
plural: tetomaskuwikotonhotuwok, tetomaskuwikotonahtuwok, tetomaskuwikotonawolotuwok
stem 1: -tetomaskuwikoton(e)-

'tetomihkuwal (TA) he catches up with him (on foot)
stem 1: -tetomihkuw-

tetpahkomike (II) it is flat land

'tetpekisomon (TI) he cuts it (sheet-like object) straight; he trims it to the same length

tetpi (tetp-) (PV) to the same extent as (something else); evenly

tett, tetta (P) in that direction
Yat te nekom pesq, apc kotok tetta. Each one went his own way, some this way, others that.
Tett te olomamuwe woniyakon. His head rolled away that way. . .

ti (I) tea
plural: tiwol
poss: 'tahtim
loc: tiwok
dim: tiwossis
(from English, tea)

tihtiyas (A) bluejay
plural: tihtiyasok

tihtokol (A) owl species (great horned owl?)
plural: tihtokolok
'tinahkat (I) (dep.) his right hand
tinahkatuwey (A, I) the one on the right
plural: tinahkatuweyak,
             tinahkatuweyal
tkahsomu, tahkahsomu (AI) he swims (to cool off)
plural: tkahsomultuwok
stem 1a: -tahkahsom(i)-: ntahkahsom I
             swim
stem 1b: tkahsom(i)-, tahkahsom(i)-
stem 2:   tehkahsom(i)-, tahkahsom(i)-:
             tehkahsomit, tahkahsomit
             when he was swimming

Kat cu skat ktahkahsomihpon qeni tkeyik
'samaqan. Let's (dual) not swim while the
water is cold.

Naci tkahsomine sipuhsisok. Let's (dual)
go swim in the brook.

tkeyu (AI) he is cold (to the touch)
plural: tkeyultuwok, tkeyuhtuwok
stem 1a: -tahkey(i)-: ktahkey you (sg.)
             are cold
stem 1b: tkey(i)-
stem 2:   tehkey(i)-: tehkeyit when he
             was cold
tkeyu (II) it is cold (to the touch); it (weather)
is cold
stem 1:   tkey(i)-
stem 2:   tehkey(i)-: tehkey(i)-: tehkeyik
             when it was cold
tki (tk-) (PV, PN) cold
prefixed form: -tahki (-tahk-)
neke form: tehki (tehk-, tek-)
tki sepawiw (II) it is a cold morning
tkolamson (II) there is a cold wind
tkiqol (AI) he is heavy
stem 1a: -tahkiqol(o)-: ntahkiqol I am
             heavy
stem 1b: tkiqol(o)-
stem 2:   tehkiqol(o)-: tehkiqolok when
             he was heavy
tkiqon (II) it is heavy
stem 1:   tkiqon(o)- type A
stem 2:   tehkiqon(o)-; but: tehkiqahk
             (some speakers also say
             tehkiqok) it is heavy
tkiqtehsin (AI) he falls and hits heavily
(See -hsin- "lie; come to rest.")
tkokiskot (II) it is a cold day
tkolamson (II) there is a cold wind
stem 1:   tkolamson(o)- type A
stem 2:   tehkolamson(o)-: tehkolamsok
             when there was a cold wind
tkopeq (I) cold water
'tokan (AI, AI + OBJ) he hits him, it
plural: 'tokhotiniya, 'tokahtiniya
stem 1:   -tok(e)-: toke he hits
stem 2:   tek(e)-: teket when he hits
toke (P) now
  Toke kisi macaha. Now you (sg.) can
leave.

tokec (P) now; if
  Tokec kisi leyik, wihqehtuwin keti
lelomoqi. If it is possible, take this fate from
me.
tokkiw, tokki (P) until; up to; to
  Nuspas tokkiw nihi aciyak. I was awake
until three o'clock.
tokkopu (AI) he sits up to some point; he sits
at some distance, he sits until some time
plural: (See opu "he sits.")
stem 1:   -tokkop(i)-
stem 2:   tekkop(i)-: tekkopit
  Tokkopu wastek tokkiw 'tolomakonihkuk.
He is sitting in the snow, with snow up to his
shoulders.
  Msi te tekkopit skicin kinuwehtuwa nit kci
lakutuwakon kotuwihtasu. Every Indian, no
matter now far away, was informed that the
great alliance was going to be formed.
'tokomal (TA) he hits him (usually implies
intention)
stem 1:   -tokom-: tokomat if he hits
             him
stem 2:   tekom-: tekomuk when I hit
             him
  Peciyayan, on oc ntokoman. When I
arrive, I will hit him.
tokotikon (I) something to hit with; bat
(baseball)
plural: tokotikonol
poss: 'tokotikon
dim: tokotikonossis
tokotom (AI) he hits; he bats (baseball)
stem 1:   -tokotom(o)-
stem 2:   tekotom(o)-: tekotok when he
             batted
'tokotomon (TI) he hits it (usually implies
intention); he strikes at it
toku (A) wave
plural: tokuwok, tokuwiyik
loc: tokuk
'tokuhteluwal (TA) he wounds him (with a
shot)
stem 1:   -tokuhteluw-: ntokuhtelaq he
             wounds me
stem 2:   tekuhteluw-: tekuhteluwat
             when he wounded him
tol-
  (See also entries in -otol-.)
tolahkesawe (AI) he plows
  Utapakon ewehket etolahkesawet. He
plowed with his car.
tolahqe (AI) he is cooking
tolahsu (II) it is shining
tolahtuwessu (AI) it is twinkling
tolahye
  (See tolayye.)
tolakomitehe (AI) it (an.) is boiling
tolalke (AI) he is digging
tolamkole (II) it is burning
'tolamuksisol, 'kolamuksisol (A) (dep.) his
uncle (esp. his mother's brother)

tolapilom (AI) he is fetching water
  stem 1a: -otolapilom(o)- type A: ntotolapilom I am fetching water
  stem 1b: tolapilom(o)-
  stem 2: etolapilom(o)-
tolaptahsu (AI) he is tracking
tolapuwe (AI) he is drinking (anything); he is eating liquid food (soup, stew, etc.)
  plural: tolapuwultuwok, tolapuwahtuwok
  stem 1a: -otolapuw(e)-: ntotolapu I am drinking
  stem 1b: tolapuw(e)-
  stem 2: etolapuw(e)-: etolapuwet one who drinks
tolaqosu (AI) it (an.) is cooking
tolaqote (II) it is burning, cooking
tolasksawe (AI) he is cutting grass with a scythe or sickle
'tolasol (I) (pl.) his underwear
  loc: 'tolasihkuk
  dim: 'tolasossisol, 'tolasisomol
  (from English, drawers)
tolasuke (AI) he is wading
tolatokihtehson (II) it is pounding, throbbing (e.g., a pulse)
tolatokihtesta (AI) he is casting (a fishing line)
  plural: tolatokihtestawolotuwok
  stem 1a: -otolatokihtest(a)-
  stem 1b: tolatokihtest(a)-
  stem 2: etolatokihtest(a)-
tolayye, tolahye (AI) he is playing
  plural: tolayyahtuwok, tolayyawolotuwok, tolayyawotuwok
  stem 1a: -otolayy(a)-, -otolahy(a)-: ntotolayyapon, ntotolahyapon we (nilun, dual) are playing
  stem 1b: tolayy(a)-, tolahy(a)-; but: tolahhik, tolahhihik they (dual) are playing
  stem 2: etolayy(a)-, etolahy(a)-: etolayyat, etolahyat when he was playing
tolehp (A) playing card
  plural: tolehpok
  dim: tolepsis club (in cards)
  (from French, trèfle, club)
tolekihpute (II) it (sheet-like object) is flapping, waving, etc.
  stem 1: tolekihput(e)-
  stem 2: etolekihput(e)-
toleksawe (AI) he is slicing
tolewehtu (AI) he (a dog) is howling
  Koluskap 'kisokehkiman wihqintuwewakon, ansa oltaqot tahaluhp olomuss etolewehtaq. Koluskap taught them a calling song that sounds like the howling of a dog.
tolewestu (AI) he is speaking
  plural: tolewestultuwok, tolewestuhtuwok
  stem 1a: -otolewest(u)-
  stem 1b: tolewest(u)-
  stem 2: etolewest(u)-: etolewestaq when he was speaking
  Neke etolewestaq, nit te etoli wihqiyat. When he was speaking, he fainted.
toli (tol-) (PV) is... -ing
  prefixed form: -otoli (-otol-)
  neke form: etoli (etol-)
  tolahkihke, tolkihke (AI) he is planting
  tolamke (AI) he is running (for office); he is playing (a game)
  toli nehse (AI) he is breathing
  't-otolonuhmon (TI) he is buying it
tolicuwon (II) it is flowing
tolihponoltuwok (AI) they (dual) are fighting each other
  plural: tolihponoltultuwok
tolihponosu (AI) he is fighting
tolikonahtehsin (AI) he is tapping his foot
  plural: tolikonahtehsinultuwok, tolikinahtehsinuhtuwok
  stem 1a: -otolikonahtehsin(o)-
  stem 1b: tolikonahtehsin(o)-
  stem 2: etolikonahtehsin(o)-: etolikonahtehsit when he is tapping his foot
toliksawe (AI) he is sawing
toline (AI) he is dying
  plural: tolinhotuwok
  stem 1a: -otolin(e)-: 'totolinan he is dying (Relative)
  stem 1b: tolin(e)-
  stem 2: etolin(e)-: etolinet where he died
  Nit te wtotolinan. He is dying right there.
tolintu (AI) he is singing
  plural: tolintultuwok, tolintuhtuwok
  stem 1a: -otolint(u)-
  stem 1b: tolint(u)-
  stem 2: etolint(u)-: etolintaq he is singing
  Anqiposehehsuwok tolintultuwok. The robins are singing.
tolipkotesu (AI) it (an.) is smoking
toliqahsu (AI) he is sewing
  plural: toliqahsultuwok, toliqahsuhtuwok
tolisuku (AI) he is paddling
tolitahasu (AI) he is worrying; he is thinking
tolituwiye (AI) he is flying
  plural: tolituwiyahtuwok, tolituwiyawolotuwok, tolituwiyawotuwok
  stem 1a: -otolituwiy(a)-
  stem 1b: tolituwiy(a)-
  stem 2: etolituwiy(a)-
toliye (II) it is going; it is running
  stem 1: toliy(a)-
  stem 2: etoliy(a)-
  Eci toliyak liksawakonol, cuwi wen 'sawatomonol. When the saws were going, one had to watch out for them.

Neke etoliyak liksawakon, nit te etoli wekinewik. When the saw was running, it broke down.

tollan (AI) it is raining
    stem 1:   tollan(o)- type A
    stem 2:   etololan(o)-: etololak when it is raining

tollatom (AI) he is breathing
    plural: tollatomuhtuwok
    stem 1a: -otololatom-: ntotololatom I am breathing
    stem 1b: tollatom-
    stem 2:   etololatom-: etololatok one who is breathing

tolluhke (AI) he is working
    plural: tollukhotuwok, tolluhkahtuwok
    stem 1a: -otololuhk(e)-: ktotololuhkepon we (kilun, dual) are working
    stem 1b: tolluhk(e)-
    stem 2:   etololuhk(e)-: etololuhket when he was working

tolokuhuke (AI) he is floating

tolomakon (I) shoulder
    plural: tolomakonol
    poss: 'tolomakon
    loc: tolomakonok

tolomomtihike (AI) he is driving something (e.g. stakes) into the ground

'tolonapemol (A) (dep.) his relative

tolonesse (AI) he is digging clams

tolonukot (II) it is happening, going on

toloqahsu (AI) he is sleeping

toloqotehe (AI) he is swimming underwater

toloqsu (AI) he is sleeping

tolotemu (AI) he is crying
    plural: tolotemultuwok, tolotemuhtuwok

tolotomhe (AI, II) he, it is moving (sliding, rolling, etc.) with a smooth, gliding motion

tolotutuwe (AI) he is building a fire
    plural: tolotutuwahtuwok, tolotutuwultuwok

tolpektihike (AI) he is splashing

tolsoqe (AI) he is checking traps
    stem 1a: -otolosq(e)-: ntotolosqepon we (nilun, dual) are checking traps
    stem 1b: tolsoq(e)-
    stem 2:   etolosq(e)-: etolosqet he is checking traps

tolsusu, tolosusu (AI) he is cutting himself (deliberately)
    stem 1a: -otolosus(i)-
    stem 1b: tolsus(i)-, tolosus(i)-
    stem 2:   etolosus(i)-

tolute (AI) he is moving (changing residence)
    stem 1a: -otolut(e)-
    stem 1b: tolut(e)-
    stem 2:   etolut(e)-

'tomaki ('tomak-) (PV, PN) (See ktomaki.)

'tomakiku (AI) he is in bad shape
    plural: 'tomakikultuwok, 'tomakikuhtuwok
    stem 1a: -kotomakik(i)-
    stem 1b: 'tomakik(i)-, ktomak(i)-
    stem 2:   ketomakik(i)-

Neke ketomakikit, wehqanomehpon. When he was in bad shape, he had a hard time.

'tomakon (A) pipe (for smoking)
    plural: 'tomakonol
    poss: utomakon
    loc: 'tomakonok
    dim: tomakonossis

'tomakonahtoq (A) pipe stem; stove pipe
    poss: utomakonatqemol

'tomapskihtahal (TA) he chops it (an.) into sections

'tomapskihtehmon (TI) he chops it into sections

'tomawey (I) tobacco
    poss: utomawey
    abs: 'tomaweyaw (sg.)

'tome, 'toma (AI) he smokes (cigarettes etc.)
    plural: 'tomahtuwok, 'tomhotuwok, 'tomawolotuwok
    stem 1a: -utom(a)-: nutom I smoke
    stem 1b: 'tom(a)-
    stem 2:   wetom(a)-: wetomat one who smokes
    stem 3:   wtom(a)-: kisi wtome he smoked

Nilunc nutomawolotipon qeniyayin. We (nilun, pl.) will smoke while you (sg.) are gone.

'tomehtuwan (DOV) he breaks something of his (someone else's) in two

'tomeksomon (TI) he cuts a slice off of it (with a knife)

tomesson (II) it breaks

tomessu (AI, II) it breaks

tomhikon (I) axe
    plural: tomhikonol
    poss: 'tomhikon
    loc: tomhikonok
    dim: tomhikonossis

Ksikihinul nihtol 'tomhikonuwal. Their axes are sharp.

tomhikonahtoq (I) axe handle
    plural: tomhikonatkul
    poss: 'tomhikonahtoq
    loc: tomhikonatkuk
    dim: tomhikonatkuhsis

Tomhikonatkul wecihtasik welikit akomahq weli pahsikpeksit, kat kahk kahkakomahq. Axe handles are made of good wide-grained white ash, not of brittle white ash.

tomhuwe (AI) he wins
    plural: tomhuwhotuwok, tomhuwolotuwok

Tomhuwiyin, cu kuttihik, If you (sg.) win, you will get a prize.

tomi (tom-) (PV) cut, break into two separate pieces
   neke form: temi (tem-)
  'tomalokossenal (TA) he takes his ear off by hand
  'tomalokossepal (TA) he bites (or chews) his ear off
  'tomiskipenal (TA) he twists his neck off
  tomiye (II) it breaks
  'tomonal (TA) he breaks it (an.) in two by hand
  'tomonomon (TI) he breaks it in two by hand
'tomihkesku (AI) he is always in the way
  stem 1a: -utomihkesk(i)-
  stem 1b: 'tomihkesk(i)-
  stem 2:   wetomihkesk(i)-
'tomihkuwal (TA) he breaks it (an.) by stepping on it
  'Tomihkuwal cihkihikonol. He broke the broom by stepping on it.
tomikonatessu (AI) he breaks his (own) leg
'tomikosiyesal (TA) he cuts his (someone else's) fingernails
'tomiye (AI) he is always on the go
  stem 1a: -utomiy(a)-
  stem 1b: 'tomiy(a)-
  stem 2:   wetomiy(a)-
tomk (P) first (before others)
'tommal (TA) he bites him in two
  stem 1:   -tomm-: tomma he was bitten in two
  stem 2:   temm-: temmat when he had bitten him in two
  Espons neqt te pekehlat athusossuwol, 'tommal. The raccoon, biting the snake once, bit him in two.
tomoliqawon (I) hardened eye secretion
  plural: tomoliqawonol
'tomosal (TA) he cuts it (an.) in two
'tomosomon (TI) he cuts it in two
  (See 'tomsomon "he cuts it into two pieces.")
'tomosponhunol (I) (pl.) scissors
  tomihponuhunol (Maliseet)
'tomotomon (TI) he bites it in two
  plural: 'tomotomultiniyal, 'tomotomuhtiniyal they (pl.) bite them (inan.) in two
  stem 1:   -tomotom-
  stem 2:   temotom-: temotok when he bit it in two
tomsokhasu (II) it is divided by a partition (e.g., a room)
'tomsomon, 'tomosomon (TI) he cuts it in two
  Nehtaw opos 'samkihqahk, tomosomun epahsiw. If the stick is too long, cut it in half.
'tomtahal (TA) he chops it down (of a tree); he hits it (an.) and makes it break into two pieces
  'Tomtahal oposihil. He chopped down the tree.

'tomtehmon, 'tomihtehmon (TI) he hits it and breaks it apart
  stem 1:   -tomtehm-, tomihtehm-
  stem 2:   temtehm-, temihtehm-; but: temtohok, temihtohok when he hits it...
tomtehson (II) it strikes something and breaks
tomtihike (AI) he chops
tomtihikon (I) chopping tool
  plural: tomktihikonol
  poss: 'tomtihikon, 'tomtihikonum
  loc: tomtihikonok
  dim: tomtihikonossis
  (See also: tomhikon.)
'topelomal (TA) he owns it (an.)
  stem 1a: -topelom-
  stem 1b: tpelom-
  stem 2:   tepelom-
'topeltomon (TI) he owns it
  stem 1a: -topeltom-
  stem 1b: tpeltom-
  stem 2:   tepeltom-
'topitahatomon (TI) he thinks about it
  stem 1a: -topitahatom-
  stem 1b: tpitahatom-
  stem 2:   tepitahatom-
'topolumal (TA) he talks about him
  stem 1a: -topolum-
  stem 1b: tpolum-
  stem 2:   tepolum-
topskuhk (A) neck
  plural: topskuhkiyik
  poss: 'topskuhkiyil his neck
'topun (I) (dep.) his spot (where he usually hides or rests, where he stays when not doing something); his bed
  plural: 'topunuwal their hiding places
  loc: 'topunok
  dim: 'topunsis
  Malom te wahkac nmoskomonen mahtoqehs 'topun. Finally after much difficulty we found the rabbit's hiding place.
'toputoss (I) (dep.) his (an animal's) hiding place
  plural: 'toputossuwal their hiding places
  loc: 'toputossok
  Eci woli kattek mahtoqehs 'toputoss. A rabbit's hiding place is very well hidden.
topuwepu (AI) he has curly hair
  stem 1:   -topuwep(i)-
  stem 2:   tepuwep(i)-
toqakiw (II) it is fall
  Tanehk toqakinuhk etuci wolokiskahk. Ever since it has been fall, the days have been very nice.
toqakuwiw (P) in the fall
  Mecimi te mokonomoniyal toqakuwiw pocetesol. They always pick potatoes in the fall.
toqakuwiw (II) it is fall
  stem 1:   toqakuw(i)-
  stem 2:   teqakuw(i)-: teqakuwik when it was fall

Nehtaw skat nomihtuwan mipihil wisaweyikil nkosicihtun oc eli skat toqakuwinuhk. If I don't see yellow leaves, I'll know it isn't fall.

toqc, toqca (P) without further delay

Toqc sankewop! Sit still already!

Toqc cikihtuwin! Leave me alone!

Akonutomuwin toqca! Tell me a story without further delay!

toqci (toqc-, toqt-) (PV) on

neke form: teqci (teqc-, teqt-), eqci (eqc-, eqt-)

'toqcikapuwin (AI, AI+OBJ) he stands on it

toqehs (A) twin

plural: toqehsuwok
poss: 'toqehsumol
dim: toqehsis

toqehsiscuwe (AI) she has twins

stem 1: -toqehsiscuw(e)-, -toqehsiscuw(a)-
stem 2: teqehsiscuw(e)-, teqehsiscuw(a)-

'toqesiktun (TI) he is ashamed of it

stem 1a: -toqesikt-
stem 1b: tqesikt-
stem 2: teqesikt-

toqiw, toqi (P) both

Nit toqi te 'kisi nisuwiniya. So they both were married.

Etutsonit toqi te 'pihtinol, tehpu kekesk wakcuwakehtun. With the strength of both his hands, he bends it just a little.

toqolukheku (AI) he is knock-kneed

stem 1: -toqolukhek(i)-
stem 2: teqolukhek(i)-

toqonastoq (A) ground hemlock

plural: toqonastokuk
poss: 'toqonastokumol
loc: toqonastokuk
dim: toqonastoqis

Toqonastoq nehpahal misuwesol. Ground hemlock kills dandruff.

toqoss (A) marker (in a game)

plural: toqossok

'toqtopin (AI, AI+OBJ) he sits on it

plural: 'toqtopultiniya,
'toqtopuhtiniya,
'toqtopiyaniya,
'toqtopiyahtiniya
stem 1: -toqtop(i)-: toqtopu he sits on something
stem 2: teqtop(i)-, eqtop(i): teqtopit, eqtopit what he is sitting on

Ma te keq eqtopiyahtit pomawsuwinuwok wahsiw. There is nothing for the people in the other room to sit on.

tosikon (I) foot wrap (worn under stockings)

plural: tosikonol

totoli (totol-) (PV) is... -ing

(Note: alternate form of toli; not used in neke forms. See -otoli.)

totolaqtihike (AI) he is cutting wood

totolasksawe (AI) he is cutting grass

totolewestu (AI) he is speaking

totoline (AI) he is dying

totolotemu (AI) he is crying

tpahqonikon (I) ruler; yardstick

plural: tpahqonikonol

tpahqonoqce (AI) he is constipated

stem 1a: -topahqonoqc(e)-
stem 1b: tpahqonoqc(e)-
stem 2: tepahqonoqc(e)-

tpapekhikon (I) scale (for weighing)

plural: tpapekhikonol
poss: 'topapekhikon
loc: tpapekhikonok
dim: tpapekhikonossis

tpaskutike (AI) he measures

stem 1a: -topskutik(e)-, -topaskutik(e)-: ntopskutik, ntopaskutik I measure
stem 1b: tpaskutik(e)-
stem 2: tepskutik(e)-, tepaskutik(e)-: tepskutiket, tepaskutiket (wood-)scaler

tpaskutikon (I) measuring stick

plural: tpaskutikonol marks on a measuring stick

tpaskutikon (A) letter (of the alphabet); numeral

plural: tpaskutikonok

tpeltom (AI) he owns

stem 1a: -topeltom(o)- type A
stem 1b: tpeltom(o)-
stem 2: tepeltom(o)-

tpitahasu (AI) he thinks

stem 1a: -topitahas(i)-
stem 1b: tpitahas(i)-
stem 2: tepitahas(i)-

Tepitahasiyin cu 'kisehtuwan 'tapenkatomolin? Do you (sg.) think that he can make him pay?

tpitahatasu (II) it is thought about (by a lot of people)

stem 1: -tpitahas(i)-
stem 2: tepitahas(i)-

tpitahatom (AI) he thinks

stem 1a: -topitahatom(o)- type A
stem 1b: tpitahatom(o)-
stem 2: tepitahatom(o)-

-tpiy(a)- happen

kisitpiye (II) it happened; it can happen

tpolukemosku (AI) he gossips a lot

tpolukemu (AI) he gossips

stem 1a: -topolukem(i)-
stem 1b: tpolukem(i)-
stem 2: tepolukem(i)-

tqesusqihiw, tqesusqiw (AI) she is a shy woman

stem 1a: -toqesusqih(i)- type B
stem 1b: tqesusqih(i)-
stem 2: teqesusqih(i)-

tqesuwapiw, tqesuwapihiw (AI) he is a shy man

tqonke (AI) he arrests

plural: tqonkahtuwok

stem 1a: -tahqonahk(e)-:
ntahqonahkepon we (nilun, dual) arrest

stem 1b: tqonk(e)-: nuci tqonket policeman

stem 2: tehqonahk(e)-: tehqonahket when he arrested

(See tahqonahke "he arrests.")

Tqonkec nuci tqonket. Let the policeman do the arresting.

tuccossu (AI) he is dark
stem 1: -tuccoss(i)-
stem 2: etuccoss(i)-

tuci (tuc-, tut-) (PV) (going) past, by; very, extremely; at a certain point
prefixed form: tuci (tuc-, tut-)
neke form: etuci (etuc-, etut-)
(See etuci "very; to an extreme; at that point.")
tuci qasku (AI) he runs by
tucuhse (AI) he walks past
tutte (II) it is located (at a certain point)

tucicuwon (II) it flows by
etucicuwok it flows by; it flows fast

tucitahasu (AI) he is sad
Etucitahasit pilsqehsis siktehkomuwut 'temisol. The girl was very sad when her dog was killed by a car.

tuciw (P) moreover; besides; right away
Tuciw elintaq. Moreover, he sang.
Milan ti naka tuciw opanol. He gave him tea, and bread besides.

tuciye (AI, II) he, it goes by; he, it goes fast
plural: tuciyawolotuwok, tuciyawotuwok, tuciyahtuwok
stem 1: -tuciy(a)-: ntuci I go by; I go fast
stem 2: etuciy(a)-: etuciyat he is going by; he is going fast

tuhkikuwocu (AI) he wakes up cold
stem 1: -tuhkikuwoc(i)-
(also: tukocu)

'tuhkimal (TA) he wakes him up
stem 1: -tuhkim-

tuhkis (A) mouse (Maliseet)

tuhkiye (AI) he wakes up
plural: tuhkiyawolotuwok, tuhkiyahtuwok, tuhkiyawotuwok
stem 1: -tuhkiy(a)-

tuhp (I) (Maliseet A) alder
plural: tuhpihil, tuhpiyil (tuhpiyik)

tuhpe (AI) it (an.) contains liquid
plural: tuphotuwok, tuhpahtuwok, tuhpawolotuwok
stem 1a: -ahtuhp(e)-, tuhp(e)-: 'tahtuhpan, 'tuhpan it contains liquid (Relative)
stem 1b: tuhp(e)-
stem 2: ehtuhp(e)-: ehtuhpet when it was full

Npawatomon ntahtuwossomut 'tahtuhpan. I want some liquid in my cup.

tuhpiyahtoq (I) alder pole
plural: tuhpiyatkul

'tuhpolal (TA) he fills it (an.)
stem 1: -tuhpol-

tuhsan (I) shed
plural: tuhsanol
poss: 'tahtuhsan
loc: tuhsanok

tukocu (AI) he wakes up cold
stem 1: -tukoc(i)-
(also: tuhkikuwocu)

'tul (I) (dep.) his canoe; his boat
plural: 'tulol

'tuliw (AI) he has a boat or canoe
stem 1a: -utul(i)- type B
stem 1b: 'tul(i)-
stem 2: wetul(i)-

'tuloq (I) (dep.) his boat
poss: 'tulokul
loc: 'tulokuk

tumahsis (A) Tom Francis (fry bread)
plural: tumahsisok

tumahsisey (A) fry bread
plural: tumahsiseyak

'tun (I) (dep.) his mouth
plural: 'tunol
loc: 'tunok

Mokim 'tunok kelomik. He has a scab on his mouth.

tupankakon (A) mold for making bread
plural: tupankakonok

tupqan (I) soil; dirt
loc: tupqanok

'tuptahsu (AI) he catches (esp. in baseball)
plural: 'tuptahsultuwok, 'tuptahsuhtuwok
stem 1a: -nihtuptahs(i)-: nihtuptahs I catch
stem 1b: 'tuptahs(i)-: 'tuptahsit if he catches
stem 2: nehtuptahs(i)-: nehtuptahsit when he was a catcher
stem 3: ntuptahs(i)-: nuci ntuptahsit catcher (also nuci 'tuptahsit)

tupu (AI) she is pregnant (said of animals)
plural: tupultuwok, tupuhtuwok
stem 1: -tup(i)-

'tusal (TA) he operates on him
stem 1: -tus-

'tusol (A) (dep.) his daughter
ntus my daughter
'tus his daughters
tus daughter! (friendly term of address for a girl or any woman younger than the speaker)

tutahtuwessu (AI, II) he, it goes by flashing a light
stem 1: -tutahtuwess(i)-
stem 2: etutahtuwess(i)-: etutahtuwessik when it goes by flashing light; it flashes very brightly or frequently

tutamoqesson (II) there has been a severe storm

tutamoqessu (II) there is a severe storm

tutatqin (II) there is a heavy sea; the waves are very high
- *stem 1:*   tutatqin(o)- type B
- *stem 2:*   etutatqin(o)-: etutatqik there is a heavy sea

'tutemisqiyil (A) (dep.) his white (female) friend

'tutemol (A) (dep.) his white (male) friend

tuthom (AI) he swims by
- *stem 1:*   -tuthom(o)- type B
- *stem 2:*   etuthom(o)-

Tuthom nahaht kiwhos. A muskrat swam by a while ago.

tutkihqon (II) it is big to such an extent
- *stem 1:*   tutkihqon(o)-
- *stem 2:*   etutkihqon(o)-: etutkihqahk it is very big

tutkil (AI) he is big to such an extent
- *stem 1:*   -tutkil(o)-
- *stem 2:*   etutkil(o)-

'tutomesku (AI) he begs, he bums
(See motutomesku.)

tutopu (AI) he is far along (in rank, etc.; of a woman, in pregnancy); he is sitting a long way off

Tan 'tutopin? What grade is he in (in school)?

tutsonu (AI) he is very strong; he is very powerful

Etutsonit. petkil ote aluhkihkuk. He is so powerful, he grows to the height of the clouds.

'tuwalokihkomon (TI) he puts a hole through it by stepping on it

'tuwalokihkuwal (TA) he puts a hole through it (an.) by stepping on it

'tuwalokihtahal (TA) he puts a hole through it (an.) by hitting it

'tuwalokihtehmon (TI) he puts a hole through it by hitting it

'tuwalokotomon (TI) he "eats" into it (makes a hole into it by gnawing, dissolving away material, etc.)
- *stem 1:*   -tuwalokotom-
- *stem 2:*   tewalokotom-: tewalokotok when he "ate" into it

On mace tuwalokotomon khakon. Then he started to eat into the door.

tuwapuwakon (A) cup
- *plural:*   tuwapuwakonok
- *poss:*   'tuwapuwakonol
- *loc:*   tuwapuwakonok
- *dim:*   tuwapuwakonossis

tuwihput (I) table
- *plural:*   tuwihputiyil
- *poss:*   'tahtuwihputim
- *loc:*   tuwihputik

tuwiskut (A) chamber pot; toilet
- *plural:*   tuwiskutiyik
- *poss:*   'tahtuwiskutiyil
- *loc:*   tuwiskutik

tuwossomut (A) cup
- *plural:*   tuwossomutiyik
- *poss:*   'tahtuwossomutiyil
- *loc:*   tuwossomutik
- *dim:*   tuwossomutossis

U

u-
(See also: entries in wo-.)

ucanomuwan (DOV) he owes it to him
- *stem 1a:*   -ucanomuw-
- *stem 1b:*   wocanomuw-
- *stem 2:*   wecanomuw-

ucemal, wocemal (TA) he kisses him
- *stem 1a:*   -ucem-, -wocem-
- *stem 1b:*   wocem-
- *stem 2:*   wecem-

Nit te eli ksahalit moshunol, nit te wecemat. When her sweetheart came in, she kissed him.

-uci (-uc-, -ut-) (PV) from; out of (e.g. made out of); on account of
- unprefixed form: 'ci ('c-, 't-)
- neke form: weci (wec-, wet-)
- (Compare weci (PV) so that; because.)

'Cimilin. Give me some of it.

ucihponoltiniya (AI, AI+OBJ) they fight (each other) over (or about) it
- *plural:*   ucihponoltultiniya they fight over it
- (See tolihponoltuwok.)

Ucihponoltiniya layektakon. They fought over a toy.

ucihtun (TI) he makes it (of something)

Ucihtuniyal akomahqey 'tahakonol. They are making paddles out of white ash.

ucikpenal (TA) he breaks a piece off of it (an.) by hand
- *stem 1a:*   -ucikpen-: nucikpena I break a piece off of it by hand
- *stem 1b:*   'cikpen-: 'cikpenat if he breaks a piece off of it by hand
- *stem 2:*   wecikpen-: wecikpenat when he broke a piece off of it by hand

uckuhnomuwan, uckuwonomuwan (DOV) he hands it to him

uckuwahkan (AI, AI+OBJ) he throws it toward here

uhc
(See 'ciw.)

uhkayihtuwal (TA) he is mad at him
- *stem 1a:*   -uhkayihtuw-: nuhkayihtaq he is mad at me
- *stem 1b:*   'qayihtuw-: 'qayihtuwat if he is mad at him
- *stem 2:*   wehkayihtuw-: wehkayihtuwat when he was mad at him
- (See 'qayu "he is angry," 'qayihtawotuwok "they (dual) are mad at each other.")

-uhkep(i)- sit, be sitting
(See -qep(i)-.)

uhkomossol (A) (dep.) his grandmother
plural: uhkomoss
dim: uhkomossisol
uhkomossok at his grandmother's
uhkomi grandmother! (term of address)
nuhkomi my grandmother! (term of address)

-uhs(e)- walk
(forms AI verb stems; changes to -ws(e)- after preverbs ending in a or e)
pomuhse (AI) he walks along
sehtawse (AI) he walks backward
wesuwewse (AI) he walks back there
apacuhse (AI) he walks back here

uhsimisol (A) (dep.) his (or her) younger brother (or sister)
dim: uhsimossisol

ukomolcin, oqomolcin (P) eight

ulamsotomon (AI, AI + OBJ) he believes in it
(See wolamsotomon.)

ulankeyuwal (TA) he takes good care of him
stem 1a: -ulankeyuw-
stem 1b: wolankeyuw-
stem 2: welankeyuw-

ulasuwiyal (TA) he pleases him

ulewolal (TA) he arranges him; he puts it (an.) away
(also: wolewolal)

ulewotun (TI) he arranges it he puts it away
(also: wolewotun)

-uli (-ul-)
(See woli-.)

ulimal (TA) he talks to him pleasantly

ulinomon, wolinomon (TI) he likes the way it looks
Eci wolinok nahsahqehtakon. He likes the looks of the ring very much.

ulitahasuwehlal (TA) he makes him happy

unitahasin (AI, AI + OBJ) he forgets it
plural: unitahasultiniya, unitahasuhtiniya
stem 1a: -unitahas(i)-
stem 1b: wonitahas(i)-: wonitahasit if he forgets
stem 2: wenitahas(i)-: wenitahasit when he forgot it

untemal, wontemal (TA) he distracts him while he is talking
stem 1a: -untem-
stem 1b: wontem-
stem 2: wentem-
wontemsu (AI) he forgets what he is talking about (e.g., because his mind wanders)

upiye (AI) he comes in over and over
stem 1: -upiy(a)-

usikiyal (TA) he makes him suffer; he punishes him
stem 1a: -usikiy-
stem 1b: 'sikiy-: 'sikiyat if he punishes him

stem 2: wesikiy-: wesikiyat when he punished him
stem 3: wsikiy-: 'koti wsikiyal he is going to punish him

uskicinuhsisomol (A) (dep.) his pupil (of the eye)
(literally, "his little Indian")

uskitewolal (TA) he puts it (an.) on top
stem 1a: -uskitewol-
stem 1b: skitewol-
stem 2: weskitewol-
Uskitewolal wikpihil tehsahqiw ihik 'tahtuwikcihikonok. He puts the brown ash on top of his work board (for basket making).

uskuhutomon (TI) he talks about it
stem 1a: -uskuhutom-
stem 1b: skuhutom-
stem 2: weskuhutom-
Weskuhutok ehta eleyik welaqik. He is discussing what happened last night.

uskuhutomuwan (DOV) he talks about it for him; he talks to him about it

uskuwimal (TA) he talks about him

ustiwin, hustiwin (A) host (altar bread)
(from French, hostie)

utawsin (AI, AI + OBJ) he survives it; he lives by means of it
stem 1a: -utaws(i)-
stem 1b: 'taws(i)-
stem 2: wetaws(i)-
Etuttehsitpon, kenoq utawsin. He got into a bad accident, but he survived.
Nutawsinen nilun elonessiyek. We (nilun, dual) live by digging clams.

uteksal, 'teksal (TA) he cuts a slice from it (an.)
stem 1a: -uteks-
stem 1b: 'teks-
stem 2: weteks-
Naci 'teksahpon sukolopan, kenoq peciyay kis wakat 'kihka 'teksass. I went to cut a piece of the cake, but when I got there it had all been cut up and taken.

uteksomon, 'teksomon (TI) he cuts a slice from it
stem 1a: -uteksom-
stem 1b: 'teksom-
stem 2: weteksom-

uten (I) town
plural: uteniyil
poss: 'tutenem
loc: utenek
dim: utenehsis
Ma te psi te wen wikiw utenewihkuk. Not everyone lives in towns.

utenehke (AI) he goes shopping in town
plural: utenekhotuwok, utenehkahtuwok
stem 1: -utenehk(e)-: ntutenehk I go shopping in town

utomektun (TI) he smokes it (tobacco, etc.)
stem 1a: -utomkekt-
stem 1b: 'tomekt-
stem 2: wetomekt-

utomeyuwal (TA) he bothers him
> *stem 1a:*   -utomeyuw-
> *stem 1b:*   'tomeyuw-
> *stem 2:*   wetomeyuw-

utomitahamal (TA) he thinks about him
> *stem 1a:*   -utomitaham-
> *stem 1b:*   'tomitaham-: 'tomitahamsu he thinks about himself
> *stem 2:*   wetomitaham-

Etuci kci 'tomitahamsit skitap, ma te nossawalawi amewinu. The man thinks so highly of himself that he does not watch out for the fishermen.

Utoqehkakom (I) West Grand Lake, Maine
> *loc:*   Utoqehkakomuk, Utoqehkakomek

utsal (TA) he cuts a piece from it
> *stem 1a:*   -uts-
> *stem 1b:*   'tos-
> *stem 2:*   wets-

utsomal (TA) he feeds him with something
> *stem 1a:*   -utsom-
> *stem 1b:*   'tahsom-
> *stem 2:*   wetsom-

Utsomal nicanol emqansisok. He fed his child with a little spoon.

utsomon (TI) he cuts a piece from it
> *stem 1a:*   -utsom-
> *stem 1b:*   'tosom-: 'tosok if he cuts a piece from it
> *stem 2:*   wetsom-: wetsok when he is cutting a piece from it

utsomuwan (DOV) he cuts a piece from something of his (someone else's); he cuts a piece of it for him

'Tosomuwin wiyuhs. Cut (sg.) me some meat.

'Kisi 'tosomuwan wiyuhs nisuwihticil. He cut a piece of meat for his wife.

utuwheminol (AI, AI+OBJ) he has it (an.) as a pet
> *plural:*   utuwhemultiniyal, utuwhemuhtiniyal
> *stem 1a:*   -utuwhem(i)-: nutuwhem I have a pet
> *stem 1b:*   'tuwhem(i)-: 'tuwhemiw he has a pet
> *stem 2:*   wetuwhem(i)-: wetuwhemit one who has a pet.

Nqoss utuwheminol esponsol kis 'qocikoton. My son has had a pet raccoon for a year.

't-uwapolehtun (TI) he messes it up; he does it wrong

't-uwapolitahamal (TA) he thinks about him improperly; he thinks there is something wrong with him
> *stem 1a:*   -uwapolitaham-
> *stem 1b:*   wapolitaham-
> *stem 2:*   ewapolitaham-

't-uwawikehtun (TI) he mixes it
> (See wawikehtun.)

't-uwehkahal (TA) he uses him, it (an.)
> *stem 1a:*   -uwehk_h-: ntuwehkohoq he uses me
> *stem 1b:*   wehk_h-: wehkahan use (sg.) him!
> *stem 2:*   ewehk_h-: ewehahat when he used him; using him, it (an.)
> *stem 3:*   -uwehk_h-: 'kisuwehkahal he used him

't-uwehkan (TI) he uses it
> *stem 1a:*   -uwehk(e)-
> *stem 1b:*   wehk(e)-
> *stem 2:*   ewehk(e)-: ewehket when he uses it; using it
> *stem 3:*   -uwehk(e)-

'Tomahkan, tehpu 'cihcinol ewehkecil. He breaks it in two, using only his thumbs.

uwhem (A) pet
> *plural:*   uwhemok
> *poss:*   'tuwhemol
> *dim:*   uwhemsis

uwon (II) it is foggy; it is misty
> *stem 1:*   uwon(o)- type A
> *stem 2:*   ewon(o)-: neket ewok when it was foggy

W

wahant (A) devil
> *plural:*   wahantuwok
> *poss:*   wahantumol
> *dim:*   wahantuhsis little devil; bug

mocahant (A) evil devil

wahk, wahka, wahkac (P) barely; hardly
> Wahkac ote npetonomupon. We (nilun, dual) barely got there.

wahkaliqs (A) wheel
> *plural:*   wahkaliqsok

wahkaluson (I) fort
> *plural:*   wahkalusonol

wahkathoma, wahkathome (AI) he has little sense
> *stem 1:*   -wahkathom(a)-

wahsiw, wahsi (P) in (or into) the other room; on the other side (of a hill or other barrier)
> Wahsi oliye. He goes into the other room.

waht (P) far away; over there; far off
> Waht elomiyat. He went far off. (or: There he goes.)
> Waht ote pemskutek tolayyik. They are playing far away in the field.
> Waht weckuwyamok eci wolinaqahk. The route here from there is very beautiful.

wakon (I) bait
> *plural:*   wakonol

walcopekuhs (I) puddle
> *plural:*   walcopekuhsol
> *loc:*   walcopekuhsok
> *dim:*   walcopekuhsis

walineyu (II) there is a cove
  stem 1:   waliney(i)-: walineyik where a
                cove is
walke (AI) he digs
  stem 1:   -walk(e)-
  stem 3:   -alk(e)-: tolalke he is digging
walkomike (II) the ground is uneven (hills and
valleys)
waloq, aloq (I) hole
  plural: walokul, alokul
  loc: walokuk, alokuk
walot (A) plate; dish; bowl
  plural: walotiyik
  poss: 'tahtuwalotemol
  loc: walotek
  dim: walotehsis
waltestakon (A) wooden dish used in a
traditional dice game
  (See altestakon.)
wapahkuhs (A) pail; bucket
  dim: wapahkuhsis
wapalokiqe (AI) he has blue (or white) eyes
  stem 1:   -wapalokiq(a)-
wapap (I) wampum
  plural: wapapiyil, wapapihil
  loc: wapapik
wapaqosal (TA) he cooks it (an.) until it is
white
wapaqosu (AI) it (an.) cooks until it is white;
it (an.) fades; it (an.) is bleached
wapaqsit (A) cigarette
  plural: wapaqsicik
wapatpe (AI) he has white hair
  stem 1:   -wapatp(a)-
wapeyit (A) white man
  plural: wapeyicik
wapeyu (AI, II) he, it is white
  stem 1:   -wapey(i)-
wapi latuwan (A) fungus species
  plural: wapi latuwanok
wapi (wap-) (PV, PN) white
Wapikonok Campobello, New Brunswick
(Locative)
wapinaqot (II) it looks white
wapoli (wapol-) (PV) wrong; improperly
  prefixed form: -uwapoli (-uwapol-)
  neke form: ewapoli (ewapol-)
  'tuwapoliwihtomuwal (TA) he was
speaking for him and said something wrong
  wapololuhke (AI) he does wrong
Waponahkik Wabanaki territory (Locative)
wapqe (AI) he has gray hair
  stem 1:   -wapq(a)-
wapsq (A) polar bear
  plural: wapsqiyik
waptoq (A) Canada goose
  plural: waptoqihik
wás (A) child (archaic except as a term used
in addressing a child)
wasis (A) child
  plural: wasisok
  poss: 'tuwasisomol
  dim: wasossis
  wasistuk! children! (term of address)

wasisuwiw (AI) he is young
  plural: wasisuwultuwok
  stem 1a: -uwasisuw(i)- type B:
             ntuwasisu I am young
  stem 1b: wasisuw(i)-
  stem 2:   ewasisuw(i)-: ewasisuwit when
             he was young
wast (A) snow (on the ground; fallen snow)
  loc: wastek
Ncuwi iywannuk akomok 'sami ktanaqsu
wast. We (nilun) had to have snowshoes
because there was so much snow.
wawapiw (AI) he is smart
  stem 1:   -wawap(i)- type B
wawikehtun, 't-uwawikehtun (TI) he mixes it
  stem 1a: wawikehtuw-, -uwawikehtuw-
  stem 1b: wawikehtuw-: wawikehtaq if
             he mixes it
  stem 2:   wawikehtuw-, ewawikehtuw-:
             wawikehtaq, ewawikehtaq
             when he mixed it
wawikiw (P) mixed together with
wawikon (I) backbone
  plural: wawikonol
wawon (I) egg
  plural: wawonol
we-
  (See also: entries in u-, wo-.)
weci (PV) in order that; so that; because
  (See also: 'ci "from; out of; on account
of.")
  weci skat in order that... not; so that... not
  keq weci skat why... not
  'Toqecimulan keq weci skat
cpahkatomuhk. He asks him why he does
not marry.
  Kisi kalsuwok skinuhsisok weci skat
mihtaqsuwal nomiyukulihtihq. The boys hid
so that their father would not see them.
wecuwawkomon (TI) he gets closer to it; he
nears it
  stem 1:   -wecuwawkom-
Ahaci te 'tolomi wecuwawkomon khakon
not 'puwin. That corpse was gradually
getting closer to the door.
wecuwawsu (AI) he is near
  plural: wecuwawsultuwok
  stem 1:   -wecuwaws(i)-
wecuwawtaqot (II) it sounds close
wecuwawtaqsu (AI) he sounds close (talking,
etc.)
wehkewakon (I) implement
  plural: wehkewakonol
  poss: 'tuwehkewakon
  loc: wehkewakonok
  dim: wehkewakonossis
Sipekhikon skitewekopu wehkewakonok.
Canvas is draped over the implement.
wehqalamuhsuhke (AI) he cannot breathe; he
smothers, suffocates
  stem 1:   -wehqalamuhsuhk(e)-
Wehqapiqek Perry, Maine (Locative)
  (literally, "where there is a narrow cove")

Wehqayik Welshpool, New Brunswick
(Locative)
   (on Deer Island)
-wehs(e)- wind blows
   (forms II verb stems)
   peciwehse (II) the wind blows toward (a place)
   ckuwwehse (II) the wind blows toward here
wekehtun (TI) he breaks it
   stem 1:   -wekeht-
wekihtun (TI) he breaks it
   stem 1:   -wekiht-
wekihtuwan (DOV) he breaks something of his (someone else's)
   stem 1:   -wekihtuw-
   Nitap nwekihtakunol ntahtuwossomutiyil. My friend broke my cup.
   Tehpu qeni wekihtuwat skitapiyil 'possiyanteskum naka macephuwan. He just broke the man's window (for no reason) and ran away.
wekiyal (TA) he breaks it (an.)
   stem 1:   -wekiy-
wekoluhke (AI) he breaks something
wekososs (A) horseshoe
   plural: wekosossok
   poss: wekosossomol
   loc: wekosossok
   dim: wekosossis
welaqik (P) last night
wen (A) (PRO) who, what (an.); someone, something (an.)
   plural: wenik
   dim: wenossis: Wenossis wot? Who is this little one?
   obv: wenil (sg.), wenihi, weni (pl.)
wenhuket (A) silver fox
   plural: wenhukecik
   (See wonhuke.)
wenucqapsis (I) bead
   plural: wenucqapsisol
wenuhc (A) white man
   plural: wenuhcok
   (Compare Micmac wenuj, "Frenchman".)
wenuhcisqehs (A) white woman
   plural: wenuhcisqehsuwok
wenuhcuwihpon (A) turnip
   plural: wenuhcuwihiponok
wesqotewit (A) ball of fire
wesuwe (wesuwiy-) (PV) back; going back
   (Compare apaci, "back towards, coming back.")
   Ma te wesuwe milawoniya 'tahsusuwon wihqehtuwahtit. They didn't give him back the hat that they had taken from him.
wesuwessu (AI) he goes back
   stem 1:   -wesuwess(i)-
wet (A) intestinal worm
   plural: wetiyik
   dim: wetehsis, wetossis
wetihke (AI) he has worms
   plural: wetikhotuwok
   stem 1:   -wetihk(e)-

wewciye (AI) he goes somewhere and returns without stopping over; he makes a home run (in baseball)
wewcoskuwimal (TA) he finds out the truth from him
   stem 1:   -wewcoskuwim-
wewcoskuwimanol (AI, AI + OBJ) he finds out the truth from him
   stem 1:   -wewcoskuwim(a)-: wewcoskuwima he finds out the truth
wewehsimal (TA) he expresses sorrow about a death to him
   stem 1:   -wewehsim-
wewehsinaqot (II) it looks sorrowful (after a death)
wewehsitahamal (TA) he thinks about him (someone who has died) sorrowfully, with sympathy for his family, etc.
wewehsitahasu (AI) he thinks sympathetically, longingly, etc. about someone who has died
   (e.g. thinks about his family, his good qualities)
wewewestu (AI) he knows what he is talking about
   stem 1:   -wewest(u)-
wewi (wew-) (PV) correctly; knowledgeably; perceivably
   wewinaqot (II) it shows, it is visible
   wewwikhike (AI) he writes knowledgeably
wewisu (AI) he inquires
   plural: wewisultuwok
   stem 1:   -wewis(i)-
   Naci ali wewisultine. Let's (pl.) go nose around.
   Motahkomikuk ihtoli wewisimok. Peter Dana Point, Maine, is where they are always asking questions.
wewitahamal (TA) he remembers him
   stem 1:   -wewitaham-
   Nwewitahama not kaltolu kisi punuk. I remember where I put that quarter.
wewitahasu (AI) he remembers
wewitahatomon (TI) he remembers it
   stem 1:   -wewitahatom-
   Ma te nwewitahatomuwon mehsi Susehp tokomosk. I don't remember why Joseph hit you.
wewoluhke (AI) he knows what to do
wewtuhkesite (AI) his feet point in when he walks
   stem 1:   -wewtuhkesit(a)-
weyossis (A) animal
   plural: weyossisok
weyossisuwiwisu (AI) he has an animal name
   plural: weyossisuwiwisultuwok
   stem 1:   -weyossisuwiwis(i)-
   Koluskap neke wikuss monihkuk wiciw ktanaquswok skicinuwok, weyossisuwiwisultuwok-- nit te na elomahtuhtihtit-- naka wiciw mociyehsuwok.
   Long ago, Koluskap lived on an island with many Indians, who had animal names--

and that is the way they behaved-- and with some partridges.

wiccickep (I) bandage
plural: wiccickepiyil

wicikitihticil (A) his (or her) brother or sister; his family member
wicikitiyek my brother or sister

wicimiye (AI) he prays with others
(also: wiciw imiye)
(Compare witimiye.)

wiciw (P) together with
Koluskap atolahsimu oluwikonok kisuhsok wiciw 'temis. Koluskap rests for seven days, together with his dogs.

wiciye (AI) he receives communion; he goes along
stem 1:   -wiciy(a)-

wiciye (II) it is included
stem 1:   -wiciy(a)-

wiciyemal (TA) he goes around with him; he goes out with her (or she... with him); he accompanies him
stem 1:   -wiciyem-

wicuhkekemu (AI) he helps out
stem 1:   -wicuhkekem(i)-
'Tiyan 'pomawsuwinum nit nekom ulitahatomon naci wicuhkekemin, wicuhkeman 'siwehsol 'kipomol. He tells his people then that he is happy to go and help out, to help his brother's orphan.

wicuhkemal (TA) he helps him
stem 1:   -wicuhkem-

wihke (AI) he builds a house
stem 1:   -wihk(e)-
stem 2:   wihk(e)-, ewihk(e)-

wihkosu (AI) he builds a house for himself
stem 1:   -wihkos(i)-

wihkukelkesku (AI) he is unfeeling, heartless, uncharitable, etc.
stem 1:   -wihkukelkesk(i)-

wihkukelomal (TA) he is unfeeling, heartless, uncharitable, etc. toward him
stem 1:   -wihkukelom-

wihkukeltomon (TI) he is heartless, unfeeling, uncharitable, etc. toward it
stem 1:   -wihkukeltom-
Wihkukeltomon imiyewikuwam. He is uncharitable toward the church.

wihpulakson (A) lady's slipper (?)
plural: wihpulaksonok
Wihpulakson wolikon 'cipiluwehsuwi npisun. Lady's slipper is good as a medicine for pleurisy.

wihq (I) thigh
plural: wihqiyil, wihqihil
poss: wihq
loc: wihqek
dim: wihqehsis

wihqahkan (AI, AI+OBJ) he pulls it (sharply)
plural: wihqakhotiniya, wihqahkahtiniya
stem 1: -wihqahk(e)-
Tetpi te kiluwaw kwihqakhotiniya. All of you pull at the same time!

wihqaqhal (TA) he pulls it (an.) with a hook
stem 1:   -wihqaqh-
Wihqaqhal cuspesol nehpahacil. He pulled the porpoise in with a hook when he had killed it.

wihqaqhomon (TI) he pulls it with a hook
stem 1:   -wihqaqhom-
Wihqaqhomun oqiton tan te eci nokosayiw. Pull in the canoe (with a hook) as soon as possible.

wihqehtun (TI) he takes it
stem 1:   -wihqeht-

wihqehtuwan (DOV) he takes it away from him

wihqimal (TA) he calls him to him
stem 1:   -wihqim-
Pawaliyeq, ktokehkimoloniyahc eli wihqimiyeq. If you want me, I will teach you how to call me.

wihqintuwamal (TA) he calls him by singing
'Tolintuwatomon motewolonuwintuwakon, wihqintuwama putepiyi. He sings a song of great power, luring the whales with his song.

wihqintuwewakon (I) jolly song; calling song
plural: wihqintuwewakonol

wihqipkotehtamike (AI) he inhales smoke from a pipe over and over
stem 1:   -wihqipkotehtamik(e)-

wihqipkotehtamu (AI) he inhales smoke from a pipe
stem 1:   -wihqipkotehtam(i)-

wihqipkotenike (AI) he inhales smoke from a pipe, puffing slowly
stem 1:   -wihqipkotenik(e)-

wihqiye (AI) he faints
plural: wihqiyawolotuwok, wihqiyawotuwok, wihqiyahtuwok
stem 1:   -wihqiy(a)-: nwihqi I faint; wihqiyat when he fainted

wihqonal (TA) he takes hold of him
stem 1:   -wihqon-

wihqonomon (TI) he takes it
stem 1:   -wihqonom-

wihqonomuwan (DOV) he takes it from him (the person it belongs to)

wihton (I) (dep.) his nose; his (a bird's) bill, beak
loc: wihtonok

wihtonaloq (I) nostril
plural: wihtonalokul

wihtuwiw (AI) he has a beard

wihtuwol (I) (dep. pl.) his beard
loc: wihtuwihkuk in his beard
(literally, "his whiskers"; wiht, "his whisker")

wik (I) his house; his home
plural: wikol
loc: wikok
dim: wiksis

wikhike (AI) he writes, paints, draws, takes a picture, etc.
plural: wikhikhotuwok

stem 1a: -uwikhik(e)-: ntuwikhik I write
stem 1b: wikhik(e)-
stem 2:   ewikhik(e)-: ewikhiket when he wrote
stem 3:   -uwikhik(e)-: toluwikhike he is writing

kotuwuwikhike (AI) he wants to write

But: 'tawwikhike (AI) he knows how to write

wikhikon (I) book; letter; any written material
  plural: wikhikonol
  poss: 'tuwikhikon, 'tahtuwikhikon

wikhikoney (I) pencil
  plural: wikhikoneyal

wikhikonikuwam (I) library
  plural: wikhikonikuwamol
  loc: wikhikonikuwamok

wikihtun (TI) he likes to make it
  stem 1:   -wikiht-

wikitahamal (TA) he desires her; he desires it (an.)
  stem 1:   -wikitaham-

wikitahatomon (TI) he desires it
  stem 1:   -wikitahatom-

wikitahatomuwan (DOV) he desires something of his (someone else's)

wikkiskot (II) it is always storming
  stem 1:   wikkiskot(o)-

wikossomu (AI) he likes to drink; he is a drunkard
  stem 1:   -wikossom(i)-

wikossomuwin (A) drunkard; alcoholic

wikossu (AI) he plays (said of children)
  stem 1:   -wikoss(i)-

wikp (A) brown ash; basket ash
  plural: wikpiyik, wikpihik

wikpolahsal (TA) he smokes it (an., food)
  stem 1:   -wikpolahs-

wikpolastike (AI) he smokes (meat)
  stem 1:   -wikpolastik(e)-

wikpolastikon (I) ham

wikpolastun (TI) he smokes it (food)
  stem 1:   -wikpolast-

wiku (AI) he lives (dwells) (in a place)
  plural: wikultuwok, wikuhtuwok, wikihtuwok
  stem 1a: -wik(i)-, -uwik(i)-
  stem 1b: wik(i)-
  stem 2:   wik(i)-, ewik(i)-

Eci wolinaqqopon wikiyanpon. It was pretty where I used to live.

Musuwok wikultuwok kcihkuk naka ma te wikultimok oliyawolotiwiyik. Moose live in the woods and they do not go where people live.

wikuwacehtun (TI) he likes to do it

Nwikuwacehtunen nkomoqotqihinen. We (nilun, dual) like to dive.

Wikuwacehtaq na nekom 'komoqotqihin. He too likes to dive.

wikuwam (I) house; building
  plural: wikuwamol
  poss: (none: see wik "his house")

loc: wikuwamok
dim: wikuwamsis little house; outhouse

Ma te ihiw elacimok wikuwamihkuk. There are no furnishings in the houses.

wikuwossol (A) (dep.) his mother
  dim: wikuwossis
  abs: wikuwosskol, wikuwoss
  nikuwoss my mother
  kikuwoss your (sg.) mother

Wikuwossol not wasis wolomahtuwol. That child's mother is nice.

wilitpan (I) brain
  plural: wilitpanol

wilol (I) (dep.) his tongue
  loc: willok
  willuwal their tongues

wiloss (I) (dep.) his navel

winas (A) stomach (of a cow)
  plural: winasok

winasey (I) tripe
  plural: winaseyal

winis (I) bone marrow
  plural: winisol

winitehe (AI) he is afraid
  plural: winitahawolotuwok
  stem 1:   -winit_h(a)-

winiyal (TA) he pins him to the ground
  stem 1:   -winiy-

wiphun (A) feather
  plural: wiphunok
  poss: wiphunomol
  loc: wiphunok
  dim: wiphunis

'Toli woliya sipsis wiphunom. The bird is cleaning its feathers.

wiphunhasu (II) it is feathered; it has a feather (or feathers) on it

wipit (I) (dep.) his tooth
  plural: wipitol
  poss: wipit
  loc: wipitok
  dim: wipitsis

Nkosinuhkan nipit. My tooth hurts.

wipitine (AI) he has a toothache
  plural: wipitinhotuwok
  stem 1:   -wipitin(e)-; but: nipitin I have a toothache; kipitin you have a toothache; etc.
  stem 2:   wipitin(e)-: wipitiniyin when you (sg.) had a toothache

wipitiw (AI) he has teeth
  stem 1:   -uwipit(i)-: type B: nuwipit I have teeth
  stem 2:   ewipit(i)-

wiqhopaltuwok (AI) they feast

wiqqot (II) the tide goes out

wiqsonehtasit (A) cigarette

wiqsonehtomon (TI) he inhales it

wiqsonepal (TA) he inhales it (an.)

-wis(i)- be named
  (forms AI verb stems)
  li macewisu (AI) his first name is...
  li mehciwisu (AI) his last name is...

Li macewisu Piyel. His first name is Peter.
Tan 'toli mehciwisin? What is his last
name?

wisa (wisay-) (PV) in a hurry
(See wiwisa "in a great hurry.")

wisahkawotuwok (AI) they (dual) walk fast
stem 1:   -wisahkawot(i)-
(dual forms only)

wisahulal (TA) he takes him by boat in a
hurry

wisaluhke (AI) he works hurriedly
plural: wisalukhotuwok
stem 1:   -wisaluhk(e)-

wisanaqsu (AI) he is in a hurry
plural: wisanaqsultuwok,
              wisanaqsuhtuwok
stem 1:   -wisanaqs(i)-

wisawahpukeku (AI) it (an.) is dented
stem 1:   -wisawahpukek(i)-

wisawahq (I) brass

wisawaqsit (A) carrot
plural: wisawaqsicik

wisawatpe (AI) he has blond hair
stem 1:   -wisawatp(a)-

wisaweyu (AI, II) he, it is yellow
plural: wisaweyultuwok,
              wisaweyuhtuwok (AI)
stem 1:   wisawey(i)-

Nehtaw nomiyot wisaweyihtit oposihik,
kosicihtun oc eli toqakuwik. If you (sg.) see
yellow trees, you will know that it is fall.

Tokec kutoput wisaweyik, ma te
npawatomuwon. If the chair is yellow, I
don't want it.

wisawi (wisaw-) (PV, PN) yellow
wisawi man gold
Nomihtunol wisawi pehsuwahsuweskil. I
see yellow flowers.

wisawiye (AI, II) he, it turns yellow
plural: wisawiyahtuwok,
              wisawiyawolotuwok (AI)
poss: -wisawiy(a)-

Oposihik mace wisawiyawolotuwok. The
trees are starting to turn yellow.

Eci pehsuwahsuwehsok wisawiyak, nit tehc
kisikon. When the flower turns yellow, it will
be full-grown.

wisawse (AI) he walks fast
plural: wisayapasuwok
stem 1:   -wisaws(e)-

wisayahkan (AI, AI+OBJ) he throws it hard
stem 1:   -wisayahk(e)-

wisayapasuwok (AI) they (pl.) walk fast
stem 1:   -wisayapas(i)-

wisayu (AI) he hurries
stem 1:   -wisay(i)-

wisiyelomu (AI) he bursts out crying

wisoki nihkaniw (P) way ahead
Yut ntihinehpon wisoki nihkaniw. I was
here way ahead (of everyone else).

wisoki (wisok-) (PV) very

wisokiluwehe (AI) he is angry
plural: wisokiluwahawolotuwok
stem 1:   -wisokiluw_h(a)-

wisokiluwehehtuwal (TA) he is mad at him
stem 1:   -wisokiluwehehtuw-

wisokiluwehenaqsu (AI) he looks angry

wisokiluwehtuwal (TA) he is mad at him
stem 1:   -wisokiluwehtuw-

Neke wisokiluwehtask, eci nokatom
kpeskhukun. When he was mad at you (sg.),
I was afraid that he would shoot you.

Ksikte wisokiluwehtawotuhtipon. We
(kilun, pl.) are terribly angry with one
another.

wisokiluweyuwal (TA) he makes him mad

wisokitahamal (TA) he likes him a lot

wisokitahatomon (TI) he likes it a lot

wisokolamson (II) the wind blows very
strongly
stem 1:   wisokolamson(o)- type A

wisokolate (II) it is very hot
stem 1:   wisokolat(e)-

wisoss (I) gall

wissekhal (TA) he covers him (with a blanket,
etc.)
stem 1:   -wissekh-

wisuwacu (AI) he breaks camp
stem 1:   -wisuwac(i)-

witahke, witanahke (AI) he joins in
plural: witakhotuwok
stem 1:   -witahk(e)-: nwitahkepon we
(nilun, dual) join in

witanahkewakon (I) joint activity
plural: witanahkewakonol

witapehkamal (TA) he makes friends with
him; he is friendly to him
stem 1:   -witapehkam-
Ktoluhkewolonen naka
kwitapehkamolonen. Let us work for you
and be your friends.

witapehkanol (AI, AI+OBJ) he makes friends
with him
plural: witapekhotiniyal,
              witapehkahtiniyal
stem 1:   -witapehk(e)-
Nwitapehkanok nikk nil skicinuwok. I
made friends with those Indians.

witapehkatomon (TI) he gets to like it
Kwitapehkatomon na kil etoli skuhutasik?
Are you getting to like what is being
discussed?

witapehkatomuwan (DOV) he gets to like
something of his
Ma te nkisi witapehkatomuwawon
elomahtaq. I can't get to like the way he is.

witapehkewal (TA) he makes friends for
someone
stem 1:   -witapehkew-

witapehtuwok (AI) they (dual) are friends
(with each other)

witapiyil, witapihil (A) (dep.) his friend
plural: witapiyi, witapihi, witapi
dim: witapehsisol
witapesqiyil his friend (female)
Ntotoli nisossominen kitap. I am drinking
with your (sg.) friend.

witawsumal (TA) he is related to him

witawsuwelomal (TA) he is related to him

witayyc, witahyc (AI) he plays with him
(See tolayye.)

witimiye (AI) he attends church
stem 1:   -witimiy(a)-: nwitimi I go to church
(Compare wicimiye.)

witkosuhtuwok (AI) they (dual) are sleeping together, one at the foot of the bed
plural: witkosuhtultuwok, witkosuhtuhtuwok

Cuwihc witkosuhtuhtu nican. Her children will have to share beds, some sleeping at the foot of the beds.

witkul (A) (dep.) his eyebrow
plural: witku
poss: witkul
loc: witkuk
nitq my eyebrow; nitkuk my eyebrows
kitq your (sg.) eyebrow

witsehkchsu (AI) she is a sister
stem 1:   -witsehkehs(i)-; but: nitsehkehs I am a sister; kitsehkehs you (sg.) are a sister; etc.
stem 2:   witsehkehs(i)-:

witsehkehsuwol (A) (dep.) her sister
nitsehkehs, nitsehkehsum my sister (woman speaking)

witsehkestuwok (AI) they (dual) are sisters to each other

wiwcossuwatpe, wiwcossatpe (AI) he has curly hair
plural: wiwcossuwatpawolotuwok, wiwcossatpawolotuwok
stem 1:   -wiwcossuwatp(a)-, -wiwcossatp(a)_

wiwilomcq (A) slug
plural: wiwilomeqok, wiwilomeqiyik
dim: wiwilomeqsis

wiwisa (wiwisay-) (PV) in a great hurry
(Compare wisa, "in a hurry.")

Tokec ntahcuwi wiwisa natsakiyak kotokik npomawsuwinumok, supekuk qihiw wikulticik. Now I must hurry away to visit others of my people, who live by the sea.

wiwisahulal (TA) he takes him away by canoe in a great hurry

wiwisanaqsu (AI) he is in a great hurry

wiwisayu (AI) he hurries
plural: wiwisayultuwok
stem 1:   -wiwisay(i)-

wiwonasiye (AI) he turns foolish; he turns crazy
plural: wiwonasiyahtuwok, wiwonasiyawolotuwok
stem 1:   -wiwonasiy(a)-

wiwoni (wiwon-) (PV) around in a circle; encircling
wiwonopu (AI) it (an.) encircles

wiwonihtahkusin (AI, AI + OBJ) he wears it around (his neck, ankle, etc.)
stem 1:   -wiwonihtahkus(i)-

Wiwonihtahkusinol psokossuhunol. She wears a necklace around her neck.

wiwonikapuwihtuwawal (TA) they stand around him
stem 1:   -wiwonikapuwihtuw-

wiwonimiye (AI) he goes around to the Stations of the Cross; he goes around (something) praying

wiwonituwiye (AI) he flies around in a circle
stem 1:   -wiwonituwiy(a)-
Nihikehs oqimuwi sakom wiwonituwiye qospemok. Three times the chief of the loons flies around the lake.

wiwoniw (P) around in a circle; encircling

-wiy- call by a name
(forms TA verb stems)
macewiyal he starts to call him (by a name)

wiyuhs (I) meat
dim: wiyuhsis a little piece of meat

wiyuhsuwapit (I) gum (without teeth)
plural: wiyuhsuwapitol

wo-
(See also: words beginning with u-.)

woc (A) mound; mountain; protruding lump
plural: wocuwok
poss: wocumol
loc: wocuk
dim: wocuhs, wocuhsis

wocawson (II) the wind blows
stem 1:   wocawson(o)- type A
stem 2:   wecawson(o)-: wecawsok when the wind blew
Neqt neke ehtahsikiskahkil wocawson, wisokolamson. Once, long ago, the wind blew every day; it blew strongly.
Kil nit kisihtuwon mecokiskahk, wecawsok, eliwehsek. You (sg.) are the one who has made the bad weather, the wind, the gusts.

wocemal
(See ucemal.)

wocopsq (I) root
plural: wocopskul

wokosiyil (A) (dep.) his fingernail; his claw, nail
plural: wokosiyi, wokosihi, wokosi
nokos my fingernail; nokosiyik my fingernails
kokos your (sg.) fingernail

wolahk (I) fish scale
plural: wolahkiyil

wolahqemihke (II) there is a good stand of trees (for wood)
stem 1:   wolahqemihk(e)-
stem 2:   welahqemihk(e)-

wolaku (P) yesterday; last night

wolakuk (P) tonight

wolalokosse (AI) he has good ears; he has good hearing
stem 1a: -ulalokoss(a)-
stem 1b: wolalokoss(a)-
stem 2:   welalokoss(a)-

wolamkisiye (II) there is a good sandy surface
Wolamkisiye lampeq. The bottom is nice and sandy under the water.
wolamsotomon, ulamsotomon (AI, AI+OBJ) he believes in it
  plural: wolamsotomultiniya, wolamsotomuhtiniya
  stem 1a: -wolamsotom(o)-, -ulamsotom(o)- type A
  stem 1b: wolamsotom(o)-: wolamsotok if he believes
  stem 2:   welamsotom(o)-: welamsotok one who believes
Ma te nikk skitapihik wolamsotomuhtiwoniyal Keluwosilicil. Those men (pl.) do not believe in God.
wolamsotuwal (TA) he believes him
wolanol (A) (dep.) his calf (of the leg); his muscle
  plural: wolan his calves; his muscles
nolan my calf; my muscle
kolan your (sg.) calf; your (sg.) muscle
wolapewiw (AI) he is handsome
  plural: wolapewultuwok
  stem 1a: -ulapew(i)-
  stem 1b: wolapew(i)-: wolapewiwok they (dual) are handsome
  stem 2:   welapew(i)-
Pilsqehsisok ntiyukunnuk nulapewultipon. The girls told us (nilun, pl.) that we are handsome.
wolapuwahte (II) it is a good-tasting soup; it is a good-tasting stew
Peci 'ci milaniya ktaqhomuhsol welapuwahtek ote otuhkey. They came to give the old man some tasty deer meat stew.
wolaqahqe (AI) he cooks supper
  plural: wolaqaqhotuwok, wolaqahqahtuwok
wolaqihik (AI) they (dual) are in bed
  plural: wolaqahtuwok
  stem 1a: -ulaq(e)-
  stem 1b: wolaq(e)-
  stem 2:   welaq(e)-: welaqehtit when they (dual) were in bed
(Note: There are no singular forms.)
wolaqihpuwakon (I) supper time
  plural: wolaqihpuwakonol
wolaqiw (P) this evening
wolaqiwiw (II) it is evening
  stem 1:   wolaqiw(i)- type B
  stem 2:   welaqiw(i)-: welaqiwik in the evening
wolaqosasu (AI) it (an.) is well done (food)
wolaqote (II) it is well done (food)
Wolastokuk St. John River (Locative); Maliseet country (Locative)
wolastoq (A) a Maliseet
wolatkuwe (II) it rides the waves well
wolatoke (II) it is straight
wolatokehlal (TA) he straightens it (an.) out
wolatqonokosu (AI) it (an.) is a tree with a nice shape

wolatqonokot (II) it is a tree with a nice shape
wolawtosson (II) it is a good road
  stem 1:   wolawtosson-
  stem 2:   welawtosson-: welawtossok when it was a good road
wolek (A) diaper; breechcloth
  plural: wolekiyik
wolekewhom (AI) he wears diapers (baby)
wolewolal, ulewolal (TA) he arranges him; he puts it (an.) away
wolewotun, ulewotun (TI) he arranges it he puts it away
woleyu (AI) he is well off; he lives well
woleyuwal (TA) he treats him well
Nit apc pesq yukt peciyacik unakessin, 'tolewestun, ulasuweltomon eli kisi woleyaht sakomal, eli wolomahtulit.
Then again one of the new-comers stands up, speaks, gives thanks for the good way the chief has treated them, for his good nature.
woli ehpituwiw (AI) she is a good woman
Wot yaq skitap eci mocikit, kenoq yaq olu woli ehpituwiwol nisuwihticil. This man, they say, was very bad; but his wife was a good woman.
woli (wol-) (PV, PN) good; well
  prefixed form: -uli (-ul-), -woli (-wol-)
  (-woli and -wol- used only with third person or obviative subjects)
  neke form: weli (wel-)
  woli paqahson (II) there is nice moonlight
  wolelomoqe (AI) something good happens to him
  wolopu (AI) he is seated comfortably
  woli ehpit (A) a good woman
wolicuwehtahsu (AI) he sets the table
wolihpukot (AI) it tastes good
wolikon (II) it is good (for use)
  stem 1:   wolikon(o)- type A
  stem 2:   welikon(o)-: welikok something good
  welikkopon something that was good
wolikossu (AI) she is pretty
  plural: wolikossultuwok
  stem 1a: -ulikoss(i)-
  stem 1b: wolikoss(i)-
  stem 2:   welikoss(i)-
Mali ma te tuci wolikossiwon tahalu Susan. Mary is not as pretty as Susan.
Nulikossultipon eci wolehlosultiyek. We (nilun, pl.) are pretty when we fix ourselves up.
woliku (AI) he is good (at what he does); it (an.) is good (for use)
  stem 1a: -ulik(i)-
  stem 1b: wolik(i)-
  stem 2:   welik(i)-
wolimahte (II) it smells good
  stem 1:   wolimaht(e)-
  stem 2:   welimaht(e)-
Etuci yaq wolimahtek otuhkey etolaqotek. The deer meat that was cooking smelled very good, they say.

wolinaqot (II) it looks good
   stem 1:   wolinaqot-
   stem 2:   welinaqot-: welinaqahk when
              it looked good
wolinaqsu (AI) he looks good
   plural: wolinaqsultuwok
   stem 1a: -ulinaqs(i)-
   stem 1b: wolinaqs(i)-
   stem 2:   welinaqs(i)-: welinaqsit when
              he looked good
wolinessu (II) it splits, well; it cracks well; it
tears well
wolinomon
   (See ulinomon.)
wolitahasin (AI, AI+OBJ) he forgets it
   plural: wolitahasultuwok
   (Maliseet)
   (See unitahasin "he forgets it.")
   Nulitahasin nmacahan. I forgot about
leaving.
wolitahasu (AI) he is happy
   plural: wolitahasultuwok
   stem 1a: -ulitahas(i)-
   stem 1b: wolitahas(i)-
   stem 2:   welitahas(i)-
   Ma te nulitahasultihpon 'sami kisi tqonak
nitapennuk. We (nikun, pl.) were not happy
because our friends got arrested.
wolitahatomon (TI) he is willing to do it; he
thinks well of it
woliw, woli (P) right away
wolkawotuwok (AI) they (dual) compliment
each other
wolkil (AI) he is nice and big
   Etuci wolkilulit yaq otuhkol nemiyahtit, on
yaq nehpahaniya. They saw a really nice big
deer, they say, and then they killed it.
wollamson (II) there is a nice breeze; there is
a breeze from a good direction, etc.
wolokasq (I) bark (of a tree)
wolokiskot (II) it is a good day
   stem 1a: wolokiskot-
   stem 1b: welokiskot-: welokiskahk it is
              a good day
   Tan al leyu welokiskahk. It's about time
there was a good day.
woloks (I) intestine
   plural: woloksiyil
wolomahtu (AI) he is good-natured
   plural: wolomahtultuwok,
              wolomahtuhtuwok
   stem 1a: -ulomaht(u)-
   stem 1b: wolomaht(u)-
   stem 2:   welomaht(u)-
wolomon (A) blood poisoning
wolomonhuke (AI) he has blood poisoning
wolomuwecuwapsq (I) coal (for burning)
   plural: wolomuwecuwapskul
wolomuwiqewu (AI) he smiles (a small smile)
woloposal, woloposumal (TA) he keeps him
warm
woloposu (AI) he is warm

wolopote (II) it is warm
wolopu (AI) he is sitting nicely, comfortably;
he is well off
woloq (I) (dep.) his armpit
   plural: woloqihil, woloqiyil
   noloq my armpit
   koloq your (sg.) armpit
wolukon (I) his hip
   plural: wolukonol
   nolukon my hip
   kolukon your (sg.) hip
woluwe (AI) he has nice hair; he has nice fur
   stem 1a: -uluw(a)-: kulu you (sg.) have
              nice hair
   stem 1b: woluw(a)-
   stem 2:   weluw(a)-
   Eci woluwayin. You (sg.) have very nice
hair.
woluwenal (TA) he fixes (sets, arranges, etc.)
his (someone else's) hair
woluwepu (AI) his hair is nicely fixed
woluwipon (II) the water is calm
wonakessu (AI) he gets up (from a sitting
position)
   stem 1a: -unakess(i)-
   stem 1b: wonakess(i)-
   stem 2:   wenakess(i)-
   Nit etuci Koluskap wonakessit. At that
point, Koluskap gets up.
wonaku (AI) he gets up
   plural: wonakultuwok,
              wonakiyahtuwok
   (esp., he gets up to dance)
woneyu (AI) he is living in sin
   stem 1a: -woney(i)-
   stem 1b: woney(i)-
   stem 2:   weney(i)-
woneyuwakon (I) adultery
wonhuke (AI, II) he is covered with snow
   plural: wonhukhotuwok (AI)
   stem 1a: -wonhuk(e)-
   stem 1b: wonhuk(e)-
   stem 2:   wenhuk(e)-: wenhuket silver
              fox (literally, "one who is
              covered with snow.")
woniyakon (I) (dep.) his head
   plural: woniyakonol
   loc: woniyakonok
   dim: woniyakonossis
   noniyakon my head
   koniyakon your (sg.) head
woniyakonine (AI) he has a headache
   stem 1:   -woniyakonin(e)-; but:
              noniyakonin I have a
              headache; koniyakonin you
              have a headache
   stem 2:   weniyakonin(e)-
wonosk (A) wing
   plural: wonoskihik
   poss: wonoskihil, unoskihil
   loc: wonoskek
   nunosk my wing
   kunosk your (sg.) wing

wonoskiyil (A) (dep.) his shoulder blade
nunosk my shoulder blade
wonoskewa their shoulder blades
wonpeq (I) mist over water
wontemal
(See untemal.)
wonu (I) (dep.) his cheek
plural: wonuwihil
nonu my cheek
konu your (sg.) cheek
woqon (I) (dep.) his heel
plural: woqonol
loc: woqonok
dim: woqonossis
noqon my heel
koqon your (sg.) heel
wosokehte (II) it (a building) is empty of
people; it is unoccupied
stem 1: wosokeht(e)-
stem 2: wesokeht(e)-: wesokehtek one
(a building) which is empty of
people
wosokesq (A) blister
plural: wosokesqihik
poss: wosokesqemol
loc: wosokesqek
dim: wosokesqehsis
wosokiyatop, wosokiyatp (I) skull
plural: wosokiyatpol, wosokiyatpiyil,
wosokiyatopiyil
wososs (I) nest
plural: wosossiyil
poss: wosossem
loc: wosossek
dim: wosossehsis
wosqon (I) (dep.) his elbow
plural: wosqonol
nosqon my elbow
kosqon your (sg.) elbow
wot (I) (dep.) his belly
plural: wotewal: their bellies
loc: wotek
dim: wotehsis
not my belly
kot your (sg.) belly
Tehsaqopu sipsis skinuhsisol wotek. The
bird is sitting on the boy's belly.
wot (A) (PRO) this (an.)
plural: yuktok, yukt, yukk these (an.)
obv: yuhtol (sg.); yuhuht (pl.)
(See yut "this (an.).")
wotaqol (A) (dep.) her sister's husband,
brother's wife, or husband's sister; his wife's
sister
notaq my sister's husband, brother's wife,
or husband's sister (woman speaking); my
wife's sister (man speaking)
wotaqtuwok (AI) they are related as brother's
wife and husband's sister or as sister's
husband and wife's sister (i.e. they call each
other notaq)
wotkul (A) (dep.) his knee
plural: wotku his knees
notq my knee

kotq your knee
wotoq (I) (dep.) his forehead
plural: wotoqewal their foreheads
notoq my forehead
kotoq your (sg.) forehead
wotqesit (I) (dep.) his toe
(Compare kotqesit, "toe.")
-ws(e)- walk
(forms AI verb stems after preverbs ending
in a or e; changes to -uhs(e)- after other
preverbs)
ksewse (AI) he walks in
kakawuhse (AI) he walks fast

Y

-y(a)- go
(forms AI verb stems; changes to -_h(a)-
after preverbs ending in e and some preverbs
ending in a)
kakawiye (AI) he goes swiftly
ksehe (AI) he goes in; he enters
sehtehe (AI) he goes backwards (from
sehta, "backwards")
wiwisaye (AI) he hurries
yaka (P) then (in the future)
Ma te apc yut nkotuhsomiwon, apc oc
yaka mawossomultihiq spomkik. I will not
drink this again until that time when we drink
together in heaven.
Peciyayin kikok, yaka kmicin. Eat it when
you (sg.) arrive at your house.
yaka, yakat, yakaw (A) (PRO) that (an.,
absent or dead, away from speaker and
person spoken to)
(=absentative form of yat "that (an.)."
See paradigms.)
yali (yal-) (PV) around; within an area;
(direction and location vague, unspecified or
uncertain)
prefixed form: -iyali (-iyal-)
neke form: yali (yal-)
yali nutaqsu (AI) he is heard of in the area
(See ali "around; within an area.")
yalipokomu (AI) he rides around on a bicycle;
he skates around
Ma te tepikotonhotiwiyik wasisok
'tiyalipokomultiniya. The children are not
old enough to ride bikes.
yaluhse (AI) he walks around
plural: yalapasuwok
stem 1a: -iyaluhs(e)-: ntiyaluhs I walk
around
stem 1b: yaluhs(e)_
stem 2: yaluhs(e)-: yaluhset when he
walked around
yap, iyap (A) buck deer
plural: yapiyik, yapihik
poss: yapimol, yapemol
dim: yapehsis

yaq (P) they say (or said); he says (or said); it is said

    Pesq yaq skicin. One, they say, is an Indian.

    Wisanaqs yaq. He says to hurry.

yaqa (P) that's why

    Nmihtaqs yaqa kisokehkimit. My father taught me, that's why.

yat (A) (PRO) that (an., away from speaker and person spoken to)

    plural: yektok, yekt, yekk those

    obv: yehtol (sg.); yeheht (pl.)

    (See yet, "that (inan.).")

yet (I) (PRO) that (inan., away from speaker and person spoken to)

    plural: yehtol

    (See yat "that (an.).")

yet (P) there; then

    (See yet "that (inan.).")

yut (P) here; now

    (See yut "this (inan.).")

yut (I) (PRO) this (inan.)

    plural: yuhtol

    (See wot "this (an.).")

ENGLISH

AND

PASSAMAQUODDY - MALISEET

A

able
kisi (kis-) (PV) can; be able to
about
'ciw, uhc (P) about; for
above
ewepi (ewep-) (PV) upward; up above
ewepiw (P) up; up above
spomok (P) up; above
tehsahqiw (P) above; on top
absence
pehqiye (AI) he comes back (to friends or family) after a long absence
accessible
'komasopu (AI) he is accessible (physically); it (an.) is easy to get at
accident
kistehsin (AI) he fell; he got into an accident
kistehsu (AI) he fell; he got into an accident
molomahkonoma (AI) his gun goes off by accident
nospiptun (TI) he takes it by accident; he takes it along
'poccipilal (TA) he hooks him by accident
qolopihtahasu (II) it is moved a little by accident
accidentally
kespiw (P) accidentally
'pottahal (TA) he hits him accidentally
'pottaqosal (TA) he burns him accidentally
'pottaqosomon (TI) he burns it accidentally
'pottehmon (TI) he hits it accidentally
'potteluwal (TA) he shoots him accidentally
ptosusu, potsusu (AI) he cuts himself accidentally
accompany
wiciyemal (TA) he goes around with him; he goes out with her (or she... with him); he accompanies him
account
akonutomakon (I) story; account; narrative
accurately
miyawteluwal (TA) he shoots him accurately; he shoots him and hits him; he wounds him
ace
neqtuwikhikon (A) ace (in cards)
ache
't-olamhokewine (AI) he has a stomach ache
acorn
asahqahahsis (A) acorn
acrobatics
amalhotokku (AI) he jumps fancily; he does acrobatics
across
ksoka (ksokay-) (PV) across
ksokawse (AI) he walks across
ksokayaskutew (P) across a field
ksokayiw (P) across
okamok (P) across (i.e., on the other side)
'qosokahsinon (AI, AI+OBJ) he lies across it

act
olomahtu (AI) he acts thus; he has such and such a nature
-omaht(u)- act; be of a nature; behave
activity
witanahkewakon (I) joint activity
adam's apple
't-ahcikonemol (A) his apple; his adam's apple
adultery
woneyuwakon (I) adultery
afraid
nokasu (AI) he is afraid
winitehe (AI) he is afraid
again
apc (P) again; else; next
again and again
ahtoli (ahtol-) (PV) over and over;' again and again; keeps on...
against
ksatokihtehsin (AI) it (an., a string-like object) strikes sharply against something; it (an., a string-like object) pounds against something
sasokuhqepu (AI) he half stands; he half sits; he is leaning against something
ahead
nihkaniw (P) ahead; in front
wisoki nihkaniw (P) way ahead
aim
motkayakhom (AI) he aims (a gun) straight up
't-olaksuhutun, 't-oliqsuhutun (TI) he aims at it
't-olaksuhutuwal, 't-oliqsuhutuwal (TA) he aims at him
alcoholic
wikossomuwin (A) drunkard; alcoholic
alder
tuhp (I) (Maliseet A) alder
tuhpiyahtoq (I) alder pole
alewife
siqonomeq (A) alewife, gaspereau (Maliseet)
alike
kcoci (P) all alike; nothing but
alive
pomawsu (AI) he lives; he is alive
all
mehtonaskiye (II) it is all over; it is all finished
msi, msiw (P) all; every
nokkahlal (TA) he eats it (an.) all
nokkahtun (TI) he eats it all
nokkalahtomon (TI) he licked it all
nokkanal (TA) he takes it (an.) all
nokkayahpal (TA) he licked it (an.) all
pehki (pehk-, pek-) (PV) all; completely
'pektahal (TA) he hits all of it (an.)
'pektehmon (TI) he gets it all; he hits it all
psi, psiw (P) all, every
all at once
sesolahkiw, sesolahki (P) suddenly; all at once
all day
'kekiw (P) all day
'kekoluhke (AI) he works all day
all of a sudden
kamotu (P) all of a sudden
komotu, kamotu (P) all of a sudden

nanakiw (P) suddenly; all of a sudden; immediately

all right

saphome, saphoma (AI) he gets by; he does all right

all the time

nehkayiw, nehkayi (P) all the time

alligator

akotalahq (A) alligator

allow

'kiseltomuwal (TA) he lets him; he allows him; he permits him

almost

eluwe (P) almost; nearly (indicates final state, activity completed)

keka (P) almost, nearly; soon; practically, all but

alone

'cikihtomon (TI) he leaves it alone

'cikihtuwal (TA) he leaves him alone

'qoci ('qoc-, 'qot-) (PV) one; alone

'qotuhkanu (AI) he lives alone

'qotuhkayiw, 'qotuhkayi; kotuhkayiw (P) alone

'qotulom (AI) he is in a canoe alone; he has one point (in the traditional dice game, altestakon)

'silom (AI) he is paddling alone

along

olomomomqot (II) it feels like it is going along (something)

pomasuke (AI) he wades along

pomehloqe (AI) he floats along

pomi (pom-) (PV) along in space or time

pomi suku (AI) he paddles (or rows) along

pomicuwon (II) it flows along

pomiqehe (AI, II) it rolls along

pomituwiye (AI) he flies along

pomkawotuwok (AI) they (dual) walk along

pomoka, pomoke, pomka, pomke (AI) he dances (along)

pomotomhe (AI) he slides along

pomuhse (AI) he walks along

along (location)

sonutaskutew (P) along the edge of a field

sonutasokiw (P) along the edge of a floor

sopayahkiw (P) along a hill

sopayakom (P) along a lake

sopayakomiw (P) along a lake

sopayawtiw (P) along (or by) the edge of a road

sopayiw (P) by way of; along the edge

along (with)

wiciye (AI) he receives communion; he goes along

already

kis (P) already; yet

also

na, ona (P) also, besides; for his part; here (when handing something to someone)

altar boy

nutonahket (A) altar boy; one who tends (something)

although

apeq (P) although

always

alitahasu (AI) he is always thinking

ihtolahte (II) it is always there

mecimi (P) always

mecimihponoltuwok (AI) they (dual) are always fighting (each other)

mecimihponosu (AI) he is always fighting

milehtakesku (AI) he is a joker; he is always getting into mischief

'tomihkesku (AI) he is always in the way

'tomiye (AI) he is always on the go

wikkiskot (II) it is always storming

ambidextrous

ehetuwosqone (AI) he can pitch (in baseball) with either arm (literally, with either elbow); he is ambidextrous

American

malihkin (A) an American

among

nawiw (P) among

anchor

cuhponapsqakon (I) anchor

and

ayut (P) and even; and besides; including even

cel (P) and besides; and even

naka (P) and; with

on, an (P) and; and then

angle

asuwi psihkomon (TI) he wears it at an angle

asuwiw (P) crooked; at an angle; obliquely

angrily

nikcahke (AI) it (an., an animal) digs up the ground noisily and angrily

angry

naskahtaqsu (AI) he is loud and angry, obnoxious

peciluwehe (AI) he becomes angry

'qayu (AI) he is angry

'qolapomal (TA) he won't look at him (because he is angry with him)

wisokiluwehe (AI) he is angry

wisokiluwehenaqsu (AI) he looks angry

animal

weyossis (A) animal

weyossisuwiwisu (AI) he has an animal name

ankle

kolaqhikon (I) ankle

announce

kinuwehlosuwiw (II) it announces itself

'kinuwehtun (TI) he announces it; he does it in his own special way

annoying

'siktehtaqsuwamal (TA) he talks about him annoyingly often

answer

't-asitehmuwal (TA) he replies to him; he answers him

't-asitemal (TA) he answers him

asitewtom (AI) he answers

't-asitewtomon (TI) he answers it

't-asitewtomuwan (DOV) he answers something of his

ant

eniqs (A) ant

antler

kinahqisomuwe (AI) he has big antlers

anymore
aqamok, aqamk (P) more; more than; anymore
apart
cepiw, cocepiw (P) separately; apart
'cepsomon, 'cocepsomon (TI) he cuts it apart
cocepi (cocep-) (PV) separately; apart
mitacaskekapuhu, mitacaskekapuwu (AI) he
  stands with his legs spread apart
'paskinehtun (TI) he tears it apart
appear
messuwessu (AI) he appears
apple
't-ahcikonemol (A) his apple; his adam's apple
cikon (A) apple
cikoniyahqemus (A) apple tree
approach
ckuhtaqot, ckuwihtaqot (II) it sounds as if it is
  coming toward here; it (a sound) approaches
ckuwapon (II) it is dawn; dawn approaches; dawn
  arrives
approximation
al (P) (indicates uncertainty, vagueness;
  approximation)
apron
lekopisuwon (I) apron
argue
'kolulal (TA) he argues with him; he scolds him
'kolultiniyal (AI, AI+OBJ) he argues with him
arm
'kolinskenal (TA) he takes his (someone else's)
  arm
molihkiptine (AI) he has strong arms (or hands)
'pihtinahqem (I) (dep.) his arm (excluding the
  hand)
armpit
woloq (I) (dep.) his armpit
around
amoniw (P) detouring (avoiding something);
  around (circling)
lahkalusonohom (AI) it (an.) has a ring around it
wiwoni (wiwon-) (PV) around in a circle;
  encircling
wiwonihtahkusin (AI, AI+OBJ) he wears it
  around (his neck, ankle, etc.)
wiwonikapuwihtuwawal (TA) they stand around
  him
wiwoniw (P) around in a circle; encircling
around (turning)
qolopessu (AI) he turns around
around (vague location)
alakomasu (AI) he snowshoes around
alamkuhusu (AI) he poles himself around (in a
  boat)
alapasuwok (AI) they (pl.) walk around
't-alaphal ('t-iyalaphal) (TA) he tracks him
  around
alaptahsu (AI) he tracks (an animal) around
alasuke (AI) he wades around
alhom (AI) he swims around
't-alhulal (TA) he guides him around in a boat
ali (al-) (PV) around; within an area; (direction
  and location vague, unspecified or uncertain)
alihpu (AI) he eats around (in various places)

alikhahsu (AI) he looks around (for something)
alinaqsu (AI) he is seen around (in various places
  within an area)
't-aliphal (TA) he carries him around; he drives
  him around in a vehicle
alossin (AI) he lies around
alqepu (AI) he sits around
altehkasu (AI, II) it is kicked around
't-altehkomon (TI) he kicks it around
't-altehkuwal (TA) he kicks him around; he kicks
  it (an.) around
aluhse (AI) he walks around
yali (yal-) (PV) around; within an area;
  (direction and location vague, unspecified or
  uncertain)
yalipokomu (AI) he rides around on a bicycle; he
  skates around
yaluhse (AI) he walks around
arrange
-ewot- arrange
't-olewotun (TI) he arranges it
wolewolal, ulewolal (TA) he arranges him; he puts
  it (an.) away
wolewotun, ulewotun (TI) he arranges it he puts
  it away
arrest
'peci tqonal (TA) he comes and arrests him
tahqonahke (AI) he arrests
'tahqonal (TA) he arrests him
tqonke (AI) he arrests
arrive
peciye (AI, II) he, it arrives
arrow
pahq (I) arrow
arrowhead
sikuwan (I) arrowhead
as
kesq (P) while; as
tahalu, talu (P) as; like
as... as
tan ote, tan te however; in whatever way; as... as
as for
olu, lu (P) but; however; as for (focuses on
  preceding word)
as if
cess (P) as if
stehpal, sehpal (P) as if
as many as
akim (P) as many as; exactly
as much as possible
memhuwi (memhuw-) (PV) as much as possible
as soon as
tan etuci when; as soon as
ash
akomahq (A) white ash
ankuwaqtihikon (A) second length of
  pounding-ash (from a single tree)
kahkakomahq (A) brittle white ash (tree)
likpehtihike (AI) he pounds ash
wikp (A) brown ash; basket ash
ashamed
'toqesiktun (TI) he is ashamed of it

ashes
sosq, ososq (I) stove ashes mixed with water; mud
sqotewamq (I) ashes
ask
't-aluwimal (TA) he asks (or tells) him in vain to do something
't-okelhal (TA) he asks him to stay
't-oqecimal (TA) he asks him
't-oqecimulal, 'qecimulal (TA) he asks him
asleep
kuhu (AI) he sleeps; he falls asleep
assemble
maqehhik, maqeyhik (AI) they (pl.) assemble
mawehhik, maweyyik (AI) they (pl.) assemble
assist
enuwaqhomuwal (TA) he assists him
at
tuci (tuc-, tut-) (PV) (going) past, by; very, extremely; at a certain point
at last
malom (P) finally; at last; eventually
mamote (P) finally; at last; eventually
at night
nipawse (AI) he goes out at night; he walks at night
nipehe (AI) he goes out at night
at that point
etuci (etuc-, etut-) (PV) very; to an extreme; at that point
at that time
oli (ol-) (PV) in that way; to that place, there; at that time
attend
witimiye (AI) he attends church
aunt
'kisisol (A) (dep.) his aunt
automobile
atomupil (I) car, automobile
'tapakon (I) car; sled; wagon
awake
spasu (AI) he is awake
away
'komuciptun (TI) he sneaks it away
macehkuwal (TA) he forces him to go home by following him; he chases him away
macekuhuke (AI) he floats away
macephuwe (AI) he runs away
maceptasu (II) it is taken away
maciyehloqe (AI) he drifts away
mehcikonahsin (AI) he is wasting away
miluwan (AI, AI+OBJ) he gives it away
olomamu (AI, II) he, it falls away; he, it flies by
olomi (olom-) (PV) away (direction of motion or extension or orientation)
olomiye (AI, II) he, it goes away
pektahasu (II) everything is taken away
'qasahkan (AI, AI+OBJ) he throws it away
wolewolal, ulewolal (TA) he arranges him; he puts it (an.) away
wolewotun, ulewotun (TI) he arranges it he puts it away

awesome
'samitposu (AI) he has awesome power
'samitpot (II) it has awesome power
awl
cossakon (I) awl
axe
tomhikon (I) axe
tomhikonahtoq (I) axe handle

B

baby
pileyahsis (A) new baby
back
apacuhse (AI) he walks back
't-asitehtahal (TA) he hits him back
wesuwe (wesuwiy-) (PV) back; going back
wesuwessu (AI) he goes back
back and forth
esuwapilom (AI) he goes back and forth fetching water
esuwessu (AI, II) he, it goes back and forth
esuwi (esuw-) (PV) back and forth
esuwiw (P) back and forth
ewot-, awot- (PV) back and forth
ewotapilom, awotapilom (AI) he goes back and forth fetching water
't-ewotewolal (TA) he goes back and forth bringing it (an.) out
't-ewotewotun (TI) he goes back and forth bringing it out
ewotonike (AI) he goes back and forth fetching (or bringing out) wood
't-ewotuhulal (TA) he goes back and forth ferrying him
sahsessu (AI, II) it goes back and forth quickly
back (body part)
mosop (I) region across the back at the waist
'pahkam (I) his back
'pahkamine (AI) he has a back ache
'susqihtahal (TA) he knocks him flat on his back
back (in back of)
akuwi (akuw-) (PV) behind (something); in back; out of view
akuwiw (P) behind; in back; out of view
back of the hand
pahkamilc (I) back of the hand
backbone
wawikon (I) backbone
backwards
apuckoliye (AI) he falls over backwards
sehta (sehtay-) (PV) backwards
sehtapasuwok (AI) they (pl.) walk backwards
sehtatkuhu (AI) he jumps backwards
sehtawse (AI) he walks backwards
sehtawtahapiye (AI) he paddles backwards
sehtayapasuwok, sehtapasuwok (AI) they (pl.) walk backwards
sehtehe (AI) he goes backwards

bad

ktomakiku (AI) he is in bad shape; he is not well off

mocawtosson (II) it is a bad road

moci (moc-) (PV, PN) bad, evil; "dirty"; sexy

mocihpukot (II) it tastes bad

mocihpuksu (AI) it (an.) tastes bad

mocihtaqot (II) it sounds bad

mociku (AI) he is bad (bad at what he does, evil, etc.)

mocimahsu (AI) he, it (an.) smells bad

mocimahte (II) it smells bad

mocinaqot (II) it looks bad

mocinaqsu (AI) he looks bad

mocokiskot (II) it is a bad day (bad weather, bad events, etc.)

polhikesku (AI) he is a bad shot

'tomakiku (AI) he is in bad shape

bad luck

asihtuwal (TA) he brings bad luck by magic

bad weather

mocokiskot (II) it is a bad day (bad weather, bad events, etc.)

mocolamson (II) the wind is blowing from a bad direction, in bad weather, etc.

bag

ptoqap (I) bag

bait

wakon (I) bait

bald

apolahsatpe (AI) he is bald

ball

epeskomakon (A) ball

epeskome (AI) he plays ball

ball of fire

wesqotewit (A) ball of fire

bandage

wiccickep (I) bandage

bang

'koppotiyahkan (AI, AI+OBJ) he bangs it closed

barber

musawe (AI) he cuts hair; he barbers

barefoot

ahsaksitehe, sahsaksitehe (AI) he is barefoot

barely

nemq (P) barely

wahk, wahka, wahkac (P) barely; hardly

bark

monhiqe (AI) he peels off bark

pqonhike (AI) he peels bark off

wolokasq (I) bark (of a tree)

basin

kossicuwenikon (A, I) dish rag (I); basin to wash dishes in (A)

bask

ksalosuhke (AI) he sweats; he basks in the sun

basket

't-oposonut (I) his basket

posonut (I) basket

posonutehke (AI) he makes baskets

wikp (A) brown ash; basket ash

bass

mokahk (A) striped bass; sea bass

mokahkehke (AI) he spears bass

bat (animal)

motekoniyehs (A) bat (animal)

bat (baseball)

tokotikon (I) something to hit with; bat

tokotom (AI) he hits; he bats

be

'ciye (AI) he comes back from there; he has been there

cuwitpot (II) it should be

elinaqsit (AI) there is a lot of it (an.); there are a lot of them (an.)

iyu (AI, II) he, it is there (or is here)

kat cipotu, kat cipotuk, kat cuwitpotu (II (?)) it should not be; it had better not be

be... -ing

toli (tol-) (PV) is... -ing

totoli (totol-) (PV) is... -ing

bead

wenucqapsis (I) bead

beak

wihton (I) (dep.) his nose; his (a bird's) bill, beak

bean

eskitaqotek (I) bean cooked on stove top

malsqosit, masqosit (I) bean

peskotehsok (I) firecracker; bean (slang)

bear

minkasu (AI) it (an.) bears fruit

muwin (A) bear

muwinesq (A) she-bear

muwinewey (I) bear meat

muwinuhke, muwinehke (AI) he hunts bear

wapsq (A) polar bear

beard

wihtuwiw (AI) he has a beard

wihtuwol (I) (dep. pl.) his beard

beat

mattahal (TA) he beats him

beaver

pqapit, qapit (A) beaver

because

ipocol (P) because; because of course

'sami (P) because

become

weci (wec-, wet-) (PV) in order that; so that; because

ceposkehtehson, coceposkehtehson (II) it becomes dislocated (of a bone)

ceposkessu, coceposkessu (II) it becomes dislocated (of a bone)

peci (pec-, pet-) (PV) come; become

peciluwehe (AI) he becomes angry

bed

kuhut (I) bed

naskuwal (TA) he shares a bed with him

naskuwaniyal (AI, AI+OBJ) he sleeps with him (in the same bed or in the same house)

opun (I) bed

'topun (I) (dep.) his spot (where he usually hides or rests, where he stays when not doing something); his bed

wolaqihik (AI) they (dual) are in bed

bee
amuwes (A) bee
beef
kuhusey (I) beef
beetle
sikusq (A) widow; pear; beetle species
before
mesq (P) not yet; before
beg
'tutomesku (AI) he begs
begin
mace (maciy-) (PV) start, begin go away or start off while doing go along while doing
macehkawotuwok (AI) they (dual) start out on foot; they (dual) start to walk (toddlers)
macehkot (II) the tide is starting to go out
maciyapasuwok (AI) they (pl.) leave on foot; they start to walk (toddlers)
behave
-omaht(u)- act; be of a nature; behave
behind
akuwi (akuw-) (PV) behind (something); in back; out of view
akuwiw (P) behind; in back; out of view
asit (P) behind, in back; at the rear;
nokothal (TA) he leaves him behind (by leaving in a vehicle, a boat, in a race, etc.)
nokothomon (TI) he leaves it behind (by leaving in a vehicle, a boat, etc.)
believe
wolamsotomon, ulamsotomon (AI, AI + OBJ) he believes in it
wolamsotuwal (TA) he believes him
bell
suwahqihikon (I) bell
belly
wot (I) (dep.) his belly
belongings
leyuwakon (I) personal belongings; gear
below
poneqiw (P) down; below; downward
belt
kospisun, kspisun (I) belt
bend
cituwessu (AI) he bends over
pehkuwoske (AI) he bends
pehkuwoskot (II) it bends
bent
ckuwahkuhucin (AI) he is bent over (rear end facing this way)
olomahkuhucin (AI) he is bent over (rear end facing away)
besides
na, ona (P) also, besides
tuciw (P) moreover; besides; right away
bestow
olelomal (TA) he bestows a gift, a talent on him
better
kamot op (P) it would be better...
mewiyawiw (AI) he is feeling better
better not
kat cipotu, kat cipotuk, kat cuwitpotu (II (?)) it should not be; it had better not be

between
niktuhkomon (TI) he holds it between his legs
beyond
ankuwi- (ankuw-) (PV) further; a little further; beyond
big
kci (kc-, kt-) (PV, PN) big; great; old
kinalokiqe (AI) he has big eyes
kini (kin-) (PV) big
'kinikonomon (TI) he grows it bigger
kinkihqon (II) it is big
kinkil (AI) he is big
kinskute (II) it is a big field
kinskutenoma (AI) he has a big field
ksatqin (II) the waves are big
ktonukot (II) something big happens
natomaskute (II) it is quite a big field
natomokihqon (II) it is fairly big
natomokil (AI) he is fairly big
olkihqon (II) it is big (by so much); it is of a (certain) size
olkil (AI) he is big (by so much); he is of a (certain) size
tutkihqon (II) it is big to such an extent
tutkil (AI) he is big to such an extent
wolkil (AI) he is nice and big
bike
alipokomu, alikopomu (AI) he skates; he rides a bike
bill
wihton (I) (dep.) his nose; his (a bird's) bill, beak
binoculars
alaputihike (AI) he looks around with a telescope; he looks around with binoculars
laputihike (AI) he looks with a telescope, binoculars, etc.
birch
masq (I) birchbark
masqemus (A) birch tree
masqewuloq (I) birchbark canoe
natonihiqe (AI) he goes (or comes) to get birchbark
bird
sips (A) bird (esp. duck)
sipsuhke (AI) he hunts birds (esp. ducks)
birthday
tetomaskuwikotone (AI) his birthday falls on the day of the week on which he was born
bishop
muhsilepehk (A) bishop
bit
lalokihikon (I) bit (of a drill)
bitch
sqehsomuhs (A) bitch
bite
'tommal (TA) he bites him in two
'tomotomon (TI) he bites it in two
bittern
cimqaha (A) bird species (American bittern?)
black
mokosewalokiqe (AI) he has a black eye
mokosewaluhkiye (II) there are black clouds
mokosewatpe (AI) he has black hair
mokoseweyu (AI, II) he, it is black

mokosewi (mokosew-) (PV) dark; black
mokosewiye (AI) he turns black
mokosewocossu (AI) he, it (an.) is colored black; he is black and blue
black fly
sipun (A) black fly
blackberry
saqtemin (A) blackberry
saqteminimus (A) blackberry bush
blacksmith
kolaptan (A) blacksmith
nutahkuhket (A) blacksmith
blanket
ahsuhun, ahsuwun (I) blanket
wissekhal (TA) he covers him (with a blanket, etc.)
blaspheme
nipskatuwe (AI) he swears; he blasphemes
blaze
ksamkole (II) it blazes up
bleed
mehciqqiye (AI, II) he, it stops bleeding
nuciqqiyat (A) hemophiliac bleeder
pokahkoniw (II) it is bloody, bleeding
blind
khapu, 'kapu (AI) he is blind
blink
piskiqehpusu (AI) he blinks repeatedly
blister
pupukhawihq (A) balsam fir blister (with pitch inside)
wosokesq (A) blister
bloat
putawiyapskessu (AI) he is bloated
block and tackle
kuhkukhahs (A) owl species; moth (diminutive only); block and tackle (Pleasant Point, Maine)
blocked
sonikpoputon (II) the view is blocked (by fallen snow) through the trees
blond
wisawatpe (AI) he has blond hair
blood
pokahkon (I) blood
wolomon (A) blood poisoning
wolomonhuke (AI) he has blood poisoning
bloody
'pehkehkihtonehtahal (TA) he bloodies his (someone else's) nose
pokahkonaptu (AI) he leaves bloody tracks
pokahkonekon (II) it (e.g. cloth, garment) is bloody
'pokahkonihtahal (TA) he bloodies him; he hits him, drawing blood
pokahkoniptine (AI) he has bloody hands
pokahkoniw (II) it is bloody, bleeding
bloom
psqahsuwe (II) it blooms
psqahsuwe (AI) she blooms
blow
liwehse (II) the wind is blowing from there
monolamson (II) the wind blows something off

pomolamson (II) the wind blows along
putuwe (AI) he blows
soniku (AI) he blows his nose
wisokolamson (II) the wind blows very strongly
wocawson (II) the wind blows
blow up
peskote (II) it shoots off; it blows up
blue
mokosewocossu (AI) he, it (an.) is colored black; he is black and blue
sinpisiye (AI) he turns blue
wapalokiqe (AI) he has blue (or white) eyes
blueberry
saht (I) blueberry
sahtewi (PN) blueberry
bluejay
tihtiyas (A) bluejay
board
't-olawsikhal (TA) he boards him
psiksoq (I) piece of wood; board
boat
macehulal (TA) he carries him away by boat
macehutun (TI) he carries it away by boat
oposuloq (I) wooden boat
pusu (AI) he leaves by boat
'tul (I) (dep.) his canoe; his boat
'tuliw (AI) he has a boat or canoe
'tuloq (I) (dep.) his boat
wisahulal (TA) he takes him by boat in a hurry
bob sled
suwhewik (I) moose sled; bob sled; pack sled
bobcat
posu (A) bobcat
body
hok (I) body
bog
elomocokek (I) bog
boil
anqotuwa (A) boil; carbuncle
't-olakomitehlal (TA) he boils it (an.)
't-olakomitehtun (TI) he boils it
'pakolapsqehlal (TA) he boils it (an.)
'pakolapsqesal (TA) he boils it (an.); he broils it (an.)
pakolapsqesu (AI) it (an.) is boiled
tolakomitehe (AI) it (an.) is boiling
boiler
lakomitehtikon (A) boiler
bone
skonis (I) bone
book
wikhikon (I) book; letter; any written material
born
nomihqosu (AI) he is born.
both
ehetuwiw (P) on both sides
toqiw, toqi (P) both
bother
'peci 'tomeyuwal (TA) he comes and bothers him
utomeyuwal (TA) he bothers him
bothersome
cossinaqsu (AI) he is bothersome; he is a nuisance

bottle
puhtay (A) bottle
bottom
puhkonikciyepu (AI) only the bottom of it (an.)
    is covered (e.g. a cup with only a few berries
    inside)
bow
't-ahtapiyil (A) his bow
tap (A) bow (for shooting arrows)
bowl
walot (A) plate; dish; bowl
box
paksis (I) box
boxer
nucinseqemat (A) boxer
boy
skinuhsis (A) boy
brace
pimonikon (I) brace (of a drill)
braid
't-otolatokonomewal (TA) he braids someone
    else's hair; he ties someone else's hair with a
    ribbon, string, etc.
brain
wilitpan (I) brain
branch out
niktuwikonehe (AI) it (an.) forks out into a V; it
    (an.) branches out into a V
brass
wisawahq (I) brass
brave
kinapiw (AI) he is brave
bread
kcitqihikon (A) bread cooked directly in coals
opan (A) bread; piece of bread; loaf of bread
opanke (AI) he mixes bread dough
putawehtikon (A) raised bread
skawey, skawey opan (A) bread cooked in the
    oven
break
'paskocokonal (TA) he breaks it (an., something
    soft) by hand
'paskocokonomon (TI) he breaks it (something
    soft) by hand
'paskonal (TA) he breaks it (an.) by hand
'paskonomon (TI) he breaks it by hand
pomoloqihton (II) the ice is breaking up and
    floating downstream
'poqqenal (TA) he breaks a piece off of it (an.)
    with his hand
psikiye (AI, II) it breaks up
suhkacu (AI) he breaks camp
'tomehtuwan (DOV) he breaks something of his
    (someone else's) in two
tomesson (II) it breaks
tomessu (AI, II) it breaks
tomi (tom-) (PV) cut, break into two separate
    pieces
'tomihkuwal (TA) he breaks it (an.) by stepping
    on it
'tomtahal (TA) he chops it down (of a tree); he
    hits it (an.) and makes it break into two pieces

'tomtehmon, 'tomihtehmon (TI) he hits it and
    breaks it apart
tomtehson (II) it strikes something and breaks
ucikpenal (TA) he breaks a piece off of it (an.)
    by hand
wekehtun (TI) he breaks it
wekihtun (TI) he breaks it
wekihtuwan (DOV) he breaks something of his
    (someone else's)
wekiyal (TA) he breaks it (an.)
wekoluhke (AI) he breaks something
wisuwacu (AI) he breaks camp
break out
muskessu (AI, II) he, it comes out; he breaks out
    in a rash
breast
nusakon (A) breast
breast-feed
nunuwal (TA) she breast-feeds him
breath
nehsewon (I) breath
breathe
nehse (AI) he breathes
-olatom- breathe
tollatom (AI) he is breathing
wehqalamuhsuhke (AI) he cannot breathe; he
    smothers, suffocates
breechcloth
wolek (A) diaper; breechcloth
breeze
nulomolamson (II) there is a slight breeze
wollamson (II) there is a nice breeze; there is a
    breeze from a good direction, etc.
bridge
soqasuwakon (I) bridge, trestle
bring
ankuwacomu (AI) he relays a message; he brings
    a report of; he interprets (translates)
't-asihtuwal (TA) he brings bad luck by magic
't-ewotewolal (TA) he goes back and forth
    bringing it (an.) out
't-ewotewotun (TI) he goes back and forth
    bringing it out
'peciptun (TI) he brings it
'peciptuwan (DOV) he brings it to, for him
brittle
kahkeyu (II) it is brittle
broil
'pakolapsqesal (TA) he boils it (an.); he broils it
    (an.)
broken
paskeyu (AI, II) it is broken
broom
cihkihikon (A) (I for some speakers) broom
brother
hesis (A) older brother
hesisuwiw (AI) he is an older brother
'siwehsol (A) (dep.) his brother
'siwestuwok (AI) they (dual) are brothers
wotaqtuwok (AI) they are related as brother's
    wife and husband's sister or as sister's husband
    and wife's sister (i.e. they call each other
    notaq)

brother-in-law
makotem (A) a man's brother-in-law
makotemtuwok (AI) they are brothers-in-law to
  each other
brother or sister
uhsimisol (A) (dep.) his (or her) younger brother
  (or sister)
wicikitihticil (A) his (or her) brother or sister; his
  family member
buck
't-otkumol (A) (dep.) his buck (deer)
yap, iyap (A) buck deer
bucket
wapahkuhs (A) pail; bucket
build
tolotutuwe (AI) he is building a fire
wihke (AI) he builds a house
wihkosu (AI) he builds a house for himself
building
wikuwam (I) house; building
bullet
cossuwan (I) bullet
skolunsq (I) bullet lead
bum
motutomesku (AI) he bums
motutomuwan (DOV) he bums it from him
'tutomesku (AI) he bums
bumpy
milapskihke (II) it is bumpy
bundle
qiwosun (I) bundle
burdock
kawis (A) burdock (plant or seed pod)
burn
't-ahtolotutuwatomon (TI) he keeps it burning
-aqos- cook; burn
ehqamkole (II) it stops burning
kcoskuwesu (AI) his hair burns off
kcoskuwete (II) its hair burns off
'kihkaqosu (AI) he burns himself
'kihkaqote (II) it gets burned
'kihkayaqosu (AI) it (an.) burns up
'kihkayaqote (II) it burns up
mehtamkole (AI, II) it stops burning; it burns out
motutuwalal (TA) he starts it (an.) burning; he
  kindles it (an.)
motutuwatomon (TI) he starts it burning; he
  kindles it
nokkapkiksomon (TI) he burns it up
nokkayaqosal (TA) he burns it (an.) completely
  in cooking it
nokkayaqosomon (TI) he burns it completely in
  cooking it
't-olaqosal (TA) he cooks it (an.); he burns it
  (an.)
pkiksu (AI) it (an.) is burned; it (an.) is scorched
pkikte (II) it is burned; it is scorched
'pokkiksal (TA) he burns it (an.)
'pottaqosal (TA) he burns him accidentally
'pottaqosomon (TI) he burns it accidentally
'samamkole (II) it burns too much
siktiyaqosu (AI) he is very hot; he burns to death
tolamkole (II) it is burning
tolaqote (II) it is burning, cooking

burst
paskesson (II) it bursts
paskessu (AI) he, it (an.) bursts
psqentu (AI) he bursts into song
psqolessu (AI) it (an.) bursts into flames
psqotemu (AI) he bursts into tears
wisiyelomu (AI) he bursts out crying
bury
'puskonal (TA) he buries him
puskonasu (II) it is buried
'puskonomon (TI) he buries it
bushy
piqonewatpe (AI) he has bushy hair
but
kahk (P) but; however (emphatic; singles out the
  preceding word)
kenoq, kenuk, qenoq (P) but; however
olu, lu (P) but; however; as for (focuses on
  preceding word)
butt
cahahq (A) butt of a tree
butter
molaqsipom (I) butter
butterfly
amakehs (A) butterfly
buttocks
't-ahkuhkol (A) (dep.) his buttocks
kuhk (A) buttocks
buy
ankusu (AI) he buys; he sells
'kisonuhmon (TI) he bought it
'kisonuhmuwewan (DOV) he bought it for him;
  he can buy it for him
monuhmon (TI) he buys it
monuhmuwan (DOV) he buys it from him; he
  buys something of someone else's
monuhmuwewan (DOV) he buys it for him
monuwal (TA) he buys it (an.)
-onuhm- buy
-onuw- buy
't-otolonuhmon (TI) he is buying it
by
qihiw (P) near; by
sopayiw (P) by way of; along the edge

C

cable
olonahqey ahpap (A) cable
cake
sukolopan (A) cake (pastry)
Calais
Kelisk Calais, Maine (Locative)
calf
wolanol (A) (dep.) his calf (of the leg); his muscle
calf (animal)
kuhusis (A) calf (See kuhus.)
call
'kakaluwamal (TA) he calls him; he yells to him
kakaluwe (AI) he hollers; he calls out
'kossekimal (TA) he calls him into the house

liwihtasu (II) it is called, named
liwisu (AI) he is named; he is called
't-oliwihtomon (TI) he calls it (by a name); he names it
't-oliwiyal (TA) he calls him (by a name); he names him
wihqimal (TA) he calls him to him
wihqintuwamal (TA) he calls him by singing
-*wiy*- call by a name

calm
mimuwipon (II) the water is perfectly calm
woluwipon (II) the water is calm

calmly
sankewimiye (AI) he prays quietly; he prays calmly
sankewiw (P) slow and easy; calmly

camp
suhkacu (AI) he breaks camp
wisuwacu (AI) he breaks camp

Campobello
Wapikonok Campobello, New Brunswick (Locative)

can
'kisehtun (TI) he did it; he can do it
kisi (kis-) (PV) can; be able to
'kisihtun (TI) he made it; he can make it
'kisiyal (TA) he made it (an.); he can make it (an.)
kisotemu (AI) he cried; he can cry
memonal (TA) he can and does reach him, it (an.) with his hand

candy
sukolis (I) piece of candy

cane
apotuhun (I) cane; walking stick
pomapotuhusu (AI) he walks with a cane
'sesomitahamal (TA) he does not know about him; he cannot imagine about him

cannot
wehqalamuhsuhke (AI) he cannot breathe; he smothers, suffocates

canoe
oqehe (AI) he runs his canoe up on shore
oqiton (I) canoe
'qotulom (AI) he is in a canoe alone; he has one point (in the traditional dice game, altestakon)
tepuloq (I) the inside of a canoe
'tul (I) (dep.) his canoe; his boat
tuliw (AI) he has a boat or canoe

canopy
akuwahtihikon (I) umbrella; sun shade (e.g. a roof supported by four poles) canopy

capable
koluwosu (AI) he is capable, useful for something; he is good for something; it (an.) is good for use

capsize
'kuskahtehkuwal (TA) he capsizes him

car
atomupil (I) car
'tapakon (I) car; sled; wagon

carbuncle
anqotuwa (A) boil; carbuncle

care
't-ankeyutomon (TI) he takes care of it

careful
nossawalal (TA) he is careful with him; he watches out for him
nossawatomon (TI) he is careful with (or about) it; he watches out for it
'sawatom, nsawatom (AI) he is careful

caribou
mokalip (A) caribou (Maliseet)

carrot
wisawaqsit (A) carrot

carry
't-aliphal (TA) he carries him around; he drives him around in a vehicle
macehulal (TA) he carries him away by boat
macehutun (TI) he carries it away by boat
petonike (AI) he carries firewood
'pomiphal (TA) he carries him; he gives him a ride in a vehicle
'pomumqamal (TA) he carries him on his back
'poqanal (TA) he can lift and carry him

carve
'kisaqsal (TA) he carved it (an.)

carver
nutaqsawet (A) carver

casket
puskonikon (I) casket

cast
tolatokihtesta (AI) he is casting (a fishing line)

cat
psuwis (A) cat

catch
keckuluwiw (AI) he has a cold; he catches a cold
mosonal (TA) he catches him; he gets it (an.)
nihtuphal (TA) he catches him, it (an.)
nihtuptun (TI) he catches it
nokosantuphal, nokosahtuphal (TA) he catches it (an.) quickly
ptihike (AI) he catches fish
'tetomihkuwal (TA) he catches up with him (on foot)
'tuptahsu (AI) he catches (esp. in baseball)

caterpillar
akawhu (A) tent caterpillar
atpahqonikehs (A) caterpillar; inch-worm

catfish
motepehs (A) catfish

caught
kolomu (AI, II) he, it sticks he, it is stuck, caught

cause
milluhke (AI) he does many things; he causes many kinds of trouble

cease
chqi (ehq-, eq-) (PV) stop; cease

cedar
kakskus (A) cedar

cellar
lahkap (I) cellar

certain
kinuwosu (AI) he is a certain one; he is a particular one
chain
olonahqap (I) chain; wire
chair
kùtoput (I) chair
qotoput (I) chair
challenge
enkamhal (TA) he challenges him (to a race)
chamber pot
tuwiskut (A) chamber pot; toilet
change
accossu (AI) he changes color; he turns red
't-acehlal (TA) he changes him
't-acehtun (TI) he changes it
atpe (II) the water level changes
atpehe (II) the tide changes
naci (nac-, nat-) (PV) change location; go (or come) to...
nenehsawte (II) it could go either way; it could be changed, knocked off, etc., easily; it is precarious
'qolopehlal (TA) he turns him over; he makes him change his mind
'qolopitahamal (TA) he changes his mind about him
qolopitahasu (AI) he changes his mind
'qolopitahatomon (TI) he changes his mind about it
qolopiye (AI) he changes the direction he is facing; he goes in the wrong direction (as a result of not following directions); he changes his mind
chase
macehkuwal (TA) he forces him to go home by following him; he chases him away
nuhsuhkuwal (TA) he chases him
nuhsuphoqalal (TA) he chases him
'tahsihpulal (TA) he "chases" her (or she... him)
check
tolsoqe (AI) he is checking traps
cheek
wonu (I) (dep.) his cheek
cherish
'qossihtun (TI) he pays reverence to it; he follows the proper observances with respect to it; he cherishes it
chest
kaskimikikone (AI) he has chest pains
mikikon (I) chest (body part)
mosqon (I) chest (body part)
chew
moscehtun (TI) he swallows it whole; he swallows it without chewing it
nukcokotamu (AI) he chews
chickadee
kocokikilahs (A) chickadee
chicken
ehem (A) chicken
ehemuhke (AI) he hunts chickens
ehemuwikuwam (I) chicken coop

chief
sakom (A) chief; tribal governor
child
ksiyaqsu (AI) he loves children
nicaniw (AI) she has a child
nicanol (A) (dep.) his child
'samcuwe (AI) she has too many children
sawecuwe (AI) she has children often
was (A) child (archaic except as a term used in addressing a child)
wasis (A) child
chin
tapehkikon (I) chin
chip
piyaqtihikon (I) wood chip
piyaqtihikonihke (AI) he gathers wood chips
chipmunk
asakuwahq (A) chipmunk
choke
neqotom (AI) he chokes (on liquid)
'patosikhal (TA) he makes him choke on smoke
patosu (AI) he chokes on smoke
chop
't-apsihtahal (TA) he chops it (an.) into small pieces
't-apsihtehmon (TI) he chops it into small pieces
-ht_h-, -t_h- hit; strike; chop
-htehm-, -tehm- hit; strike; chop
-htihik(e)-, -tihik(e)- hit; strike; chop
'kettahal (TA) he chops it (an.) off
'kettehmon (TI) he chops it off
'kuwhal (TA) he chops it (an.) down
psketqonhike (AI) he chops limbs off a tree
'tomapskihtahal (TA) he chops it (an.) into sections
'tomapskihtehmon (TI) he chops it into sections
'tomtahal (TA) he chops it down (of a tree); he hits it (an.) and makes it break into two pieces
tomtihike (AI) he chops
tomtihikon (I) chopping tool
choppy
milatqihton (II) the water is choppy
Christian
papahtok (A) a Christian; a religious person
chub
ponapsqehs (A) chub (fish)
church
imiyewikuwam (I) church
witimiye (AI) he attends church
cigarette
psqolehtoma, psqolehtome (AI) he lights up (a cigarette)
'tome, 'toma (AI) he smokes (cigarettes etc.)
wapaqsit (A) cigarette
wiqsonehtasit (A) cigarette
circle
wiwonituwiye (AI) he flies around in a circle
clam
ess (A) clam
tolonesse (AI) he is digging clams
claw
wokosiyil (A) (dep.) his fingernail; his claw, nail

clean
'*pehkihtun* (TI) he cleans it
pehkikon (II) it is clean
'*pehkiyal* (TA) he cleans him

clear
musqiye (II) it (weather) clears off

clearing
pankomike (II) there is a clearing
panskute (II) there is a clearing

climb
-atuw(e)- climb
latuwe (AI) he climbs

close (near)
wecuwawkomon (TI) he gets closer to it; he nears it
wecuwawtaqot (II) it sounds close
wecuwawtaqsu (AI) he sounds close (talking, etc.)

close (shut)
'*koppihtonenal* (TA) he holds his (someone else's) nose closed
'*koppotiyahkan* (AI, AI+OBJ) he bangs it closed
piskiqewu (AI) he closes his eyes

clot
paht (A) blood clot

clothes
ewepaqhikon (A) clothes pole
kostokonike (AI) he washes clothes; he does laundry

clothing
loqtewakon (I) piece of clothing
mocehs (I) article of clothing
oloqotewakon (I) article of clothing

cloud
aluhk (I) cloud
mokosewaluhkiye (II) there are black clouds
pomalukte (II) there is a stretch of cloud

cloudy
aluhkot (II) it is cloudy

clown
cipuhtes (A) clown

club
pokomakon (I) club (used in splitting wood into strips)
psqocis (I) war club
siktihikon (I) club (for killing)

coal
mokos (I) soot; dead coal
pukset (I) live coal
sqotes (I) spark; ember; glowing coal
wolomuwecuwapsq (I) coal (for burning)

coat
opsqons (I) man's coat

cod
nuhkomeq (A) cod
nuhkomeqotekon (I) codfish skin

coffee
kahpe (I) coffee
kahpehsis (A) coffee pot

cold
keckuluwiw (AI) he has a cold; he catches a cold
tkeyu (AI) he is cold (to the touch)
tkeyu (II) it is cold (to the touch); it (weather) is cold

tki (tk-) (PV, PN) cold
tkokiskot (II) it is a cold day
tuhkikuwocu (AI) he wakes up cold
tukocu (AI) he wakes up cold

collapse
suhkessu (II) it collapses

collect
maqenasu (II) it is collected

color
accossu (AI) he changes color; he turns red
mokosewocossu (AI) he, it (an.) is colored black; he is black and blue

comb
nasqahal (TA) he combs his (someone else's) hair

come
ckuwye (AI, II) he, it comes toward here
ksehe (AI) he comes in; he goes in
ksehkawotuwok (AI) they (dual) come in; they (dual) go in
ksiyapasuwok (AI) they (pl.) come in, they (pl.) go in
maqehe (II) it comes together
mihqaphal (TA) he comes to his tracks
muskessu (AI, II) he, it comes out; he breaks out in a rash
pecessu (AI) he comes and then leaves again immediately
peci (pec-, pet-) (PV) come; become
peci suku (AI) he comes paddling
'*peci 'tomeyuwal* (TA) he comes and bothers him
'*peci tqonal* (TA) he comes and arrests him
peci wiciye (AI) he comes with others
'*peci wikuwamkomal* (TA) he comes to visit him
peci wolaqihpu (AI) he comes and eats supper
'*peci yahal* (TA) he comes and tells him
pecitihkessu (II) the shock of it (impact, explosion, etc.) comes to here
peciwehse (II) a gust of wind comes
'*peciyamal* (TA) he comes to him
pecuhse (AI) he comes walking
petamoqessu (II) a storm comes
petapasuwok (AI) they (pl.) come walking
petapeku (AI) he comes crawling
petkawotuwok (AI) they (dual) come walking
'*pettomimal* (TA) he comes to hire him
sakhiye (AI) he comes into view

come back
apaci (apac-, apat-) (PV) coming back; returning
apatawsu (AI) he comes back to life
'*ciye* (AI) he comes back from there; he has been there
pehqiye (AI) he comes back (to friends or family) after a long absence

come from
'*tamoqesson* (II) the storm is coming from there
'*tamoqessu* (II) the storm is coming from there

come in
upiye (AI) he comes in over and over

come out
nute (nutiy-) (PV) out; going out; coming out
nutew (P) coming out; going out
pskelute (II) smoke is coming out (of it) because it cannot escape through a flue, stovepipe, etc.

come to
enuwiye (AI) he comes to; he regains
consciousness

come together
maqe (maqiy-) (PV) coming together
mawe (mawiy-) (PV) coming together (of more
than two or of a mass)
mawe putuwosuwok (AI) they (pl.) come together
and hold a council meeting
mawehe (II) it comes together
mawekak (AI) they (pl.) come together dancing

come up
ckuwinuwe (II) the wind is coming up over the
water

come upon
'keskuhtehkuwal (TA) he comes upon him

comfortably
wolopu (AI) he is sitting nicely, comfortably; he
is well off

communion
wiciye (AI) he receives communion; he goes along

completely
'kihkane (AI) it (an.) is completely dead; he dies
completely
nokka (nokkay-) (PV) completely; entirely; to
completion
nokkayaqosal (TA) he burns it (an.) completely
in cooking it
nokkayaqosomon (TI) he burns it completely in
cooking it
pehki (pehk-, pek-) (PV) all; completely
sesomi, (sesom-) (PV) completely

compliment
wolkawotuwok (AI) they (dual) compliment each
other

conscious
enuwiye (AI) he comes to; he regains
consciousness

constantly
costaqsu (AI) he talks constantly; he talks and
talks
stiti (P) constantly

constipated
tpahqonoqce (AI) he is constipated

contain
tuhpe (AI) it (an.) contains liquid

continue
apcituwiye (AI) he is flying; he is on the wing; he
continues to fly

continuous
'qotatokot (II) it is one continuous length (in
space or time)

cook
-aqos- cook; burn
nuhkaqosu (AI) it (an.) is cooked tender
nuhkaqote (II) it is cooked tender
nutahqet (A) cook
't-olaqosal (TA) he cooks it (an.); he burns it
(an.)
't-olaqosomon (TI) he cooks it
pasqiyahqe (AI) he cooks dinner (noon meal)
suksahqe (AI) he cooks
tolahqe (AI) he is cooking

tolaqosu (AI) it (an.) is cooking
tolaqote (II) it is burning, cooking
wapaqosal (TA) he cooks it (an.) until it is white
wapaqosu (AI) he cooks something until it is
white
wolaqahqe (AI) he cooks supper

cool off
tkahsomu, tahkahsomu (AI) he swims (to cool off)

corbie
skonoqoss (A) corbie

cormorant
oqons (A) shag, cormorant

corn
piyeskomon (I) ear of corn; grain of corn

corner
kikociw (P) in the corner; at the corner

corpse
puwin (A) corpse

Corpus Christi
pomuhse imiyan Corpus Christi

correct
't-ihkaskuwal (TA) he does not correct him (a
child); he does not discipline him (a child)

correctly
wewi (wew-) (PV) correctly; knowledgeably;
perceivably

cough
neqhom (AI) he coughs

council member
litposuwin (A) office holder; tribal council
member

counsel
mihkumal (TA) he preaches to him; he lectures
to him; he counsels him

counter
okitomakon (I) counter; counting stick

cove
walineyu (II) there is a cove

cover
'koppektehmon (TI) he covers it by hitting
(something 2-dimensional: cloth, paper, etc.)
'koptunenal (TA) he covers his (someone else's)
mouth with his hand
kpihikon (I) lid; cover; dam
psonekte (II) it (something sheet-like) covers
puhkonikciyepu (AI) only the bottom of it (an.)
is covered (e.g. a cup with only a few berries
inside)
wissekhal (TA) he covers him (with a blanket,
etc.)
wonhuke (AI, II) he is covered with snow

cow
kuhus (A) cow

crab
nomocinuhsehs, nomocinuhsehsit (A) crab

crack
paskoloqessu (AI) he is moving across the ice as
it cracks
psikapskiye (II) there is a crack in the rock
psikipahsu (AI) it (an.) cracks because it is dry
wolinessu (II) it splits, well; it cracks well; it tears
well

cranberry
sun (I) cranberry
crash
siktehsin (AI) he dies from a fall; he dies from a
  crash
crave
kotuhtamu (AI) he craves some kind of food
crawl
nutiyapeku (AI) he crawls out
petapeku (AI) he comes crawling
crazy
amuwye (AI) he is crazy
amuwyessu (AI) he goes crazy
epahsiyahsu (AI) he is a little crazy
epahsiye (AI) he is foolish; he is crazy
wiwonasiye (AI) he turns foolish; he turns crazy
cricket
sikiliyem (A) cricket
cripple
mamatuwiku (AI) he is crippled
crooked
asuwikon (I) crooked
asuwiw (P) crooked; at an angle; obliquely
crooked knife
lihkahkonikon (I) crooked knife (a wood-working
  tool)
pkahkonikon (I) crooked knife
cross
cipiyahtoq (A) cross; crucifix
crow
kahkakuhs (A) crow
crucifix
cipiyahtoq (A) cross; crucifix
crush
nukcokhal (TA) he crushes him up
nukcokonomon (TI) he crushes it by hand
cry
eqotemu (AI) he stops crying
kisotemu (AI) he cried; he can cry
mesotemit (AI) why is he crying?
mettemu (AI) he finishes crying
motetemu (AI) he is heard crying
-otem(i)- cry
pskotemu (AI) he cries himself to sleep
sasotemu (AI) he cries
sehsoluhke (AI) he works so hard he is ready to
  cry
sespayu (AI) he cries out of fear
'sestahal (TA) he makes him cry
tolotemu (AI) he is crying
wisiyelomu (AI) he bursts out crying
cup
tuwapuwakon (A) cup
tuwossomut (A) cup
curly
topuwepu (AI) he has curly hair
wiwcossuwatpe, wiwcossatpe (AI) he has curly
  hair
curtain
ahsuwekopolikon (I) window shade; curtain
curved
pkuwakiye (II) it is curved

cut
'cepsomon, 'cocepsomon (TI) he cuts it apart
'kessal (TA) he cuts so much of it (an.); he cuts
  it (an.) into so many pieces
'kessomon (TI) he cuts so much of it; he cuts it
  into so many pieces
'kocoskeksomon (TI) he nearly cuts it (a part of
  his body), but misses
musal (TA) he cuts his (someone else's) hair
musawe (AI) he cuts hair; he barbers
't-olekisomon (TI) he cuts it (sheet-like object)
't-olsal, 't-olosal (TA) he cuts it (an.) with a knife
't-olsomon, 't-olosomon (TI) he cuts it with a
  knife
't-otoliksomon (TI) he is cutting it
potsusu (AI) he cuts himself accidentally
ptosusu, potsusu (AI) he cuts himself accidentally
-s-, -os- cut
-som-, -osom- cut
'soqskosal (TA) he cuts him up into pieces
'sosqihtahal (TA) he cuts him, it (an.) up (with
  a knife, fist, etc.)
'tetpekisomon (TI) he cuts it (sheet-like object)
  straight; he trims it to the same length
tolasksawe (AI) he is cutting grass with a scythe
  or sickle
tolsusu, tolosusu (AI) he is cutting himself
  (deliberately)
'tomeksomon (TI) he cuts a slice off of it (with a
  knife)
tomi (tom-) (PV) cut, break into two separate
  pieces
'tomikosiyesal (TA) he cuts his (someone else's)
  fingernails
'tomosal (TA) he cuts it (an.) in two
'tomsomon, 'tomosomon (TI) he cuts it in two
uteksal, 'teksal (TA) he cuts a slice from it (an.)
uteksomon, 'teksomon (TI) he cuts a slice from it
utsal (TA) he cuts a piece from it
utsomon (TI) he cuts a piece from it
utsomuwan (DOV) he cuts a piece from
  something of his (someone else's); he cuts a
  piece of it for him

D

dam
kpihikon (I) lid; cover; dam
dance
astuwokak (AI) they (dual) dance toward each
  other and then apart (part of the welcome
  dance)
eqqa (AI) he stops dancing
mawekak (AI) they (pl.) come together dancing
metka (AI) he stops dancing
miltehkasu it is danced in various ways
pomoka, pomoke, pomka, pomke (AI) he dances
  (along)
sakomawka (AI) he does a governor's dance
skicinuwoka, skicinuwoke (AI) he does an Indian
  dance

dance hall
qanotuwan (I) (?) dance hall (archaic)
dancer
nutkat (A) dancer
dangerous
'sanaqot (II) it is dangerous
dark
mokosewi (mokosew-) (PV) dark; black
piski psan (II) it is snowing so hard that it's dark or it's hard to see
piskolan (II) it is raining so hard that it's dark or it's hard to see
tuccossu (AI) he is dark
daughter
'tusol (A) (dep.) his daughter
dawn
cehqoniw (P) at dawn
cehqonoluhke (AI) he works until dawn
ckuwapon (II) it is dawn; dawn approaches; dawn arrives
day
amsqahsukonohom (II) it is the first day of the month
cilkokiskot (II) it is a short day
ehtahsikiskot (II) it is once a day
kisq (I) day
nisukonokkiwiw (II) it is two days
spote, (spotiy-) (PV) during the day
spotew (P) in the daytime; during the day
tkokiskot (II) it is a cold day
wolokiskot (II) it is a good day
daytime
spotew (P) in the daytime; during the day
spotewi (PN) of the daytime
dead
'kihkane (AI) it (an.) is completely dead; he dies completely
mehcine (AI) he dies; he is dead
deaf
enehtawe (AI) he is deaf and dumb
kokepse (AI) he is deaf
okepse (AI) he is deaf
death
'siktehpawolal (TA) he scares him to death (literally or figuratively)
siktiyaqosu (AI) he is very hot; he burns to death
death rattle
nopuwakon (I) death rattle
decide
'kisitahatomon (TI) he decides on it
'kisolumal (TA) he decided about him
decorate
't-amalhuwikhomon (TI) he writes it fancily; he makes it with fancy designs or colors; he decorates it
deep
spaqahte (II) the snow is deep
deer
iyap, yap (A) buck deer
niktuwahqonehc (A) spike-horn deer
otuhk (A) deer
otuhkatop (I) deer head
otuhkew (A) deer skin
otuhkey (I) deer meat

otuhki, (otuhk-) (PN) deer; deer's
otukke (AI) he hunts deer
degree
qasqomehe (AI) it (an.) melts by degree
deliver
kinuwehtahsu (AI) he delivers a message
dent
wisawahpukeku (AI) it (an.) is dented
design
amalhuwikhomon (TI) he writes it fancily; he makes it with fancy designs or colors; he decorates it
desire
wikitahamal (TA) he desires her; he desires it (an.)
wikitahatomon (TI) he desires it
wikitahatomuwan (DOV) he desires something of his (someone else's)
detour
amoniw (P) detouring (avoiding something); around (circling)
deuce
nisuwikhikon (A) deuce
devil
kinahant (A) devil; fearless person
mocahant (A) devil
wahant (A) devil
devil diver
asups (A) devil diver (bird species)
diamond
kaluhs (A) diamond (in cards)
diaper
wolek (A) diaper; breechcloth
wolekewhom (AI) he wears diapers (baby)
diarrhea
sapessu (AI) he has diarrhea
dice game
altestakon (A) wooden dish used in a traditional dice game; die (pl. dice) the traditional dice game
die
'kihkane (AI) it (an.) is completely dead; he dies completely
mehcine (AI) he dies; he is dead
mehtatom (AI) he dies of old age
piluwessu (AI) he is going to die
'sikine (AI) he dies horribly
siktehsin (AI) he dies from a fall; he dies from a crash
sipine (AI) he dies hard
toline (AI) he is dying
die (dice)
amkakon (A) die
different
militahasu (AI) he thinks of many different things
piluwi (piluw-) (PV, PN) different
piluwitposu (AI) he has a different position or office; he has extraordinary power
difficult
motuweyu (II) it is difficult, hard to deal with
sakoleyu (AI, II) it is hard to the touch; it is difficult
sakoli (sakol-) (PV, PN) hard (to the touch); difficult; tough

dig
kehsalke (AI) he digs so much
monkehtun (TI) he digs it out with its roots
nikcahke (AI) it (an., an animal) digs up the
    ground noisily and angrily
nutiyalkatomon (TI) he digs it out
tolalke (AI) he is digging
tolonesse (AI) he is digging clams
walke (AI) he digs
dinner
pasqihihpu (AI) he eats dinner (noon meal)
pasqiyahqe (AI) he cooks dinner (noon meal)
direction
ali (al-), yali (yal-) (PV) around; within an area;
    (direction and location vague, unspecified or
    uncertain)
't-oloqaphal (TA) he tracks him in that direction
oloqi (oloq-) (PV) in that direction; over that
    way
oloqiw (P) in that direction; over that way
qolopiye (AI) he changes the direction he is
    facing; he goes in the wrong direction (as a
    result of not following directions); he changes
    his mind
sisse (sissiy-) (PV) in all directions; scattering
tett, tetta (P) in that direction
wollamson (II) there is a nice breeze; there is a
    breeze from a good direction, etc.
directly
natkuwal (TA) he goes right to him
dirt
mocacomuwakon (I) false statement; libel; dirty
    story
mocalokotune (AI) he has a dirty mouth (uses
    dirty language)
mocatuwe (AI) he talks dirty
moccoke (II) it is dirty
moccokiptinehlal (TA) he gets his (someone
    else's) hand dirty
moci (moc-) (PV, PN) bad, evil; "dirty"; sexy
qaqeyu (AI) he is dirty
tupqan (I) soil; dirt
disappointed
peqositahasu (AI) he feels discouraged; he feels
    disappointed; he feels unconvinced
disassembled
cepte, cocepte (II) it is separate; it is disassembled
discipline
't-ihkaskuwal (TA) he does not correct him (a
    child); he does not discipline him (a child)
discourage
naskahtaqsuwamal (TA) he hollers at him
    discouragingly
naskaluwemal (TA) he discourages him
discouraged
naskatahamal (TA) he is discouraged about him
naskatahasu (AI) he feels discouraged
peqositahasu (AI) he feels discouraged; he feels
    disappointed; he feels unconvinced
disease
ksinuhkewakon (I) sickness; disease
mosiyal (TA) he gives him a disease; he infects
    him

disgust
cokahk (P) (interjection indicating surprise,
    shock, disgust)
dish
altestakon (A) wooden dish used in a traditional
    dice game; the traditional dice game
kahsicukhike (AI) he wipes dishes
kossicuwenike (AI) he washes dishes
'tephomuwal (TA) he dishes out food to him
walot (A) plate; dish; bowl
waltestakon (A) wooden dish used in a traditional
    dice game
dish rag
kossicuwenikon (A, I) dish rag (I); basin to wash
    dishes in (A)
dish water
kossicuwenikonap, kossicuwenikonop (I) dish
    water
disinclined
'kihtomatomon (TI) he does not feel like doing it;
    he is disinclined to do it
disk
noskomakon (A) metal disk worn as an ornament
dislocated
ceposkehtehson, coceposkehtehson (II) it becomes
    dislocated (of a bone)
ceposkessu, coceposkessu (II) it becomes
    dislocated (of a bone)
disobey
'polsotuwal (TA) he misunderstands him; he
    disobeys him
disperse
sissessu (II) it spreads out; it disperses; it scatters
distance
tokkopu (AI) he sits up to some point; he sits at
    some distance; he sits until some time
distract
untemal, wontemal (TA) he distracts him while
    he is talking
dive
komoqotkuhu (AI) he dives
dizzy
kehtahqehe (AI) he is dizzy
do
-ehl- do to
'kihtomatomon (TI) he does not feel like doing it;
    he is disinclined to do it
'kinuwehtun (TI) he announces it; he does it in
    his own special way
'kisehtun (TI) he did it; he can do it
'kisehtuwan (DOV) he made him do it
'komaseyu (II) it is easy to do
luhke (AI) he works; he does (something)
nisoluhke (AI) he works with someone; he does
    two jobs
nuci (nuc-, nut-) (PV) do something on a regular
    basis or as an occupation
't-olehlal (TA) he does something to him
't-olokimal (TA) he tells him to do thus
saphome, saphoma (AI) he gets by; he does all
    right
sikeyu (II) it is hard to do
't-uwapolehtun (TI) he messes it up; he does it
    wrong

wewoluhke (AI) he knows what to do
wikuwacehtun (TI) he likes to do it
wolitahatomon (TI) he is willing to do it; he
   thinks well of it

doe
el (A) doe

dog
olomuss (A) dog
otuhkewahsom (A) deer-hunting dog

doll
amsqocehkan (A) doll

dollar
'qotakisu (A) one dollar

don't!
mus, musa, musahk (P) not; don't

door
'kahakonum (I) his door
khakon (I) door

doubt
koluhtom (AI) he doubts

douse
nokkahsuwiyapawotun (TI) he douses it

dove
poles (A) pigeon; dove

down
apuckolopu (AI) he is upside down
apuckolte (II) it is upside down
ekhute (II) it hangs down
'kuwhal (TA) he chops it (an.) down
lossin (AI) he lies down; he is lying down
olqehsin, luhkehsin (AI) he lays his head down
pokossin (AI) he falls down; it (an.) falls; he, it
   (an.) lands
pomossin (AI) he is lying down
'poneqahkan (AI, AI + OBJ) he throws it down
'poneqehlal (TA) he gets him down; he puts him
   down
poneqi (poneq-) (PV) down, downward
poneqiw (P) down; below; downward
poneqotokku (AI) he jumps down
'tomtahal (TA) he chops it down (of a tree); he
   hits it (an.) and makes it break into two pieces

down and out
ktomakiqewu (AI) he looks down and out

down below
emehkew (P) down below; downstairs
emekte (II) it is down below

downhill
cikcahkehe (AI) he goes downhill
cikcahkiw (P) downhill
motape (motapiy-) (PV) downhill
motapeqehe (AI, II) it rolls downhill
motapetomehe (AI, II) he, it goes downhill on
   wheels
motapetomhe (AI, II) he, it goes downhill with a
   gliding motion
motapew (P) downhill
motapiyahkiw (P) downhill

downriver
papkiw (P) downriver (See also: downstream.)
papkiye (AI) he goes downriver

downstairs
emehkew (P) down below; downstairs

downstream
papkehloqe (AI) he floats downstream (See also:
   downriver.)

downward
poneqiw (P) down; below; downward

dragonfly
apuciqaha (A) dragonfly

draw
wikhike (AI) he writes, paints, draws, takes a
   picture, etc.

draw blood
'pokahkonihtahal (TA) he bloodies him; he hits
   him, drawing blood

draw knife
lihkutolakon (I) draw knife (for shaving wood)

dream
puwihta (AI) he dreams
puwihtu (AI) he dreams
'puwihtun (TI) he dreams about it
'puwiyal (TA) he dreams about him

dress
mahkut (I) dress
nassewe (AI) he gets dressed
nassewhutolal (TA) he dresses him
't-olahsewhutolal (TA) he dresses him
pqeku (AI) he is dressed in red

drift
maciyehloqe (AI) he drifts away

driftwood
qanusq (I) piece of driftwood

drink
kotuhsomu (AI) he drinks (an alcoholic beverage)
kotuwapuwe (AI) he wants a drink (of anything);
   he wants to eat soup, stew, etc.
mawossominiyal (AI, AI + OBJ) they drink with
   him
nisossominiyal (AI, AI + OBJ) he drinks with him
nopim (I) (dep.) his liquid; his drink (water, etc.)
't-osihmuwal (TA) he gives him a drink
't-otolapuwewan (DOV) he drinks something of
   his (someone else's)
tolapuwe (AI) he is drinking (anything); he is
   eating liquid food (soup, stew, etc.)
wikossomu (AI) he likes to drink; he is a
   drunkard

drive
't-aliphal (TA) he carries him around; he drives
   him around in a vehicle
-hkom-, -kom- drive
milkomon (TI) he moves it every which way; he
   drives it (e.g., a car) erratically
't-olkomon (TI) he drives it there
'pomkomon (TI) he drives it
tolomomtihike (AI) he is driving something (e.g.
   stakes) into the ground

drop
-ahke- throw; drop; release
't-olahkan (AI, AI + OBJ) he throws it; he lets go
   of it; he drops it
'tepahkan (AI, AI + OBJ) he throws it in; he
   pushes it in; he drops it in

drop by
nimskehe (AI) he drops by to visit
drop (liquid)
sukonalokiqe (AI) he puts drops in his eyes
'sukoniqewal (TA) he puts drops in his (someone else's) eyes
drown
komoqiye (AI) he drowns
pucokossu, pucoqossu (AI) he drowns
drum
kotuhmahsinuwintuwakon (I) drum song
kotuhmahsu (AI) he plays the drum
pokuhulakon (I) drum
drunkard
wikossomu (AI) he likes to drink; he is a drunkard
wikossomuwin (A) drunkard; alcoholic
dry
ekhucuwole (AI) he hangs clothes out to dry
'kahsihpulal (TA) he dries him off; he wipes him dry
'kahsihputun (TI) he dries it off; he wipes it dry
'kahsihputun (TI) he dries it off; he wipes it dry
psikipahsu (AI) it (an.) cracks because it is dry
duck
kathucin (AI) he ducks (to hide)
kathucu (AI) he ducks (to hide)
duck (bird)
lontoqiyehs (A) wood duck
motehehsim (A) duck (especially black duck)
dump
sukayewotahsu (AI) he dumps (liquid)
during
qoni (qon-) (PV) through or during a length of space or time
spotewse (AI) he walks during the day
dye
cossikon (I) dye

E

each other
makotemtuwok (AI) they are brothers-in-law to each other
'qayihtawotuwok (AI) they (du.) are mad at each other
tolihponoltuwok (AI) they (dual) are fighting each other
wolkawotuwok (AI) they (dual) compliment each other
ear
calokoss (I) ear
'kolonalokossenal (TA) he holds his (someone else's) ear
piyeskomon (I) ear of corn; grain of corn
wolalokosse (AI) he has good ears; he has good hearing
earache
'calokossewine (AI) he has an earache

earring
sokossuhun (I) earring
earth
ktahkomiq (I) land; ground; earth
easily
'komasi ('komas-) (PV) easy; easily
nenehson (II) it flips over easily
nokomasiw (P) easily
easy
'komaseyu (II) it is easy to do
'komasi ('komas-) (PV) easy; easily
'komasopu (AI) he is accessible (physically); it (an.) is easy to get at
'komaste, nkomaste (II) it is easy to get at
eat
alihpu (AI) he eats around (in various places)
kotuwapuwe (AI) he wants a drink (of anything); he wants to eat soup, stew, etc.
lawsu (AI) he lives there; he eats there
mahal (TA) he eats it (an.)
mehsihpit (AI) why is he eating?
memihpu (AI) he has eaten enough; he is full
micin (TI) he eats it
mitsu (AI) he eats
nimcokonike (AI) he eats with his fingers; he eats with his (own) hand
nokkahlal (TA) he eats it (an.) all
nokkahtun (TI) he eats it all
't-otolomal (TA) he is eating it (an.)
pasqihihpu (AI) he eats dinner (noon meal)
peci wolaqihpu (AI) he comes and eats supper
'saputiyalokotomon (TI) he eats through it
tolapuwe (AI) he is drinking (anything); he is eating liquid food (soup, stew, etc.)
'tuwalokotomon (TI) he "eats" into it (makes a hole into it by gnawing, dissolving away material, etc.)
echo
pokotahqewiye (II) it echoes
eclipse
seqqe (II) there is an eclipse
edge
kecalokiqat (AI) the edge of his eye
'kocalokiqawon (I) (dep.) the edge of his eye
sonuciw (P) on (or along) the edge
sonucuhse (AI) he walks along the edge
sonutasuke (AI) he wades along the edge
eel
kat (A) eel
egg
ksossiyehsin (AI) she (a bird) sits on her eggs
pokhutike (AI) she hatches her eggs
ponatom (AI) she lays an egg (or eggs)
wawon (I) egg
eight
ukomolcin, oqomolcin (P) eight
either
ehetuwosqone (AI) he can pitch (in baseball) with either arm (literally, with either elbow); he is ambidextrous
either way
nenehsawte (II) it could go either way; it could be changed, knocked off, etc., easily; it is precarious

elbow

wosqon (I) (dep.) his elbow

else

apc (P) again; else; next

ember

sqotes (I) spark; ember; glowing coal

emphasis

ehta (P) (emphatic)

te, ote (P) (emphatic)

empty

siqehe (AI, II) it is emptying

siqepu (AI) it (an.) is empty

siqeyawiw (AI, II) it is empty

siqeyu (AI, II) it is empty

'sukahtestun (TI) he pours it out; he empties it; he spills it (because it's too full or because he's not paying attention to it)

wosokehte (II) it (a building) is empty of people; it is unoccupied

encircling

wiwoni (wiwon-) (PV) around in a circle; encircling

wiwoniw (P) around in a circle; encircling

encourage

nihkaskuwal (TA) he encourages him

end

eqtokot (II) it ends (said of the length of something)

mehcikoton (II) the year ends

mehtapeksu (AI) that is the end of him

mettokot (II) it is over; it comes to an end

English

ikolisomanatuwe (AI) he speaks English

Englishman

Ikolisoman (A) white man; Englishman

enough

memihpu (AI) he has eaten enough; he is full

miskot (II) there is enough to go around

nutaqsu (AI) he has not slept enough

tepi (tep-) (PV) enough

'tepitahatomon (TI) he thinks enough of it (to do such and such); he thinks well of it

entirely

nokka (nokkay-) (PV) completely; entirely; to completion

epilepsy

cipilqe, 'cipilqe (AI) he has epilepsy

'cipiluwehs (A) pleurisy; epilepsy; muscle spasms

erect

'kisikapuwehlal (TA) he stood him; he erected it (an.)

errand

'kolonomahsin (AI, AI+OBJ) he goes on an errand to get it

erratically

milkomon (TI) he moves it every which way; he drives it (e.g., a car) erratically

especially

pciliw (P) especially

even

peciw, peci (P) even

even if

cika (P) even if

evening

wolaqiw (P) this evening

wolaqiwiw (II) it is evening

evenly

tetpi (tetp-) (PV) to the same extent as (something else); evenly

eventually

malom (P) finally; at last; eventually

mamote (P) finally; at last; eventually

ever

tan + Pronoun -ever; the one who, the one which; which one of... (these, those, them)?

tan tehpu (P) -ever; however

ever since

tanehk, tanek, tane (P) from the first time; ever since

every

ehtahs (P) every; every time; time after time

ehtahs (P) every; every time; time after time

milkomon (TI) he moves it every which way; he drives it (e.g., a car) erratically

msi, msiw (P) all; every

psi, psiw (P) all, every

everything

sahsomahtu (AI) he does everything fast

everywhere

noluwiw (P) everywhere

evil

mocitahasuwamal (TA) he thinks evil thoughts about him

evil-looking

cipi (cip-) (PV,PN) ugly; evil-looking; hideous

exactly

akim (P) as many as; exactly

miyaw (P) exactly; just the one

papehk (P) exactly the same

exaggerate

koluskapiw (AI) he exaggerates or lies a lot; he tells tall tales

example

kete (P) for example he threw it for him

excessively

'sami (sam-) (PV) too much; excessively

express

wewehsimal (TA) he expresses sorrow about a death to him

extent

tutkihqon (II) it is big to such an extent

tutkil (AI) he is big to such an extent

extract

'ketapitehlal (TA) he extracts his (someone else's) tooth

extraordinary

motewolon, ptewolon (A) person with extraordinary power; witch (contemporary usage)

piluwapiyuwakon (I) extraordinary power

piluwitposu (AI) he has a different position or office; he has extraordinary power

extreme
etuci (etuc-, etut-) (PV) very; to an extreme; at that point

eye
apskapu (AI) his eyes are open
kecalokiqat (AI) the edge of his eye
mokosewalokiqe (AI) he has a black eye
piskiqewu (AI) he closes his eyes
pqalokiqe (AI) he has red eyes
psuhutolosu (AI) he has something in his eye
sisoq (I) face; eye
'sisqine (AI) his eye (or eyes) hurts (hurt)
tomoliqawon (I) hardened eye secretion
wapalokiqe (AI) he has blue (or white) eyes

eyebrow
witkul (A) (dep.) his eyebrow

eyeglasses
sisqeyal (I) (pl.) eyeglasses

eyelash
moshawapun, mushawapun, nossawapun (A)
    eyelash

F

face
apsiqe (AI) he has a small face
'kossiqenal (TA) he washes his (someone else's) face
noskiqetutom (AI) he has a sour look on his face
sisoq (I) face; eye

facing
ckuhqepu (AI) he sits facing this way

fade
kahsiye (II) it fades
wapaqosu (AI) it (an.) fades; it (an.) is bleached

faint
wihqiye (AI) he faints

fairly
natomokihqon (II) it is fairly big
natomokil (AI) he is fairly big

fall
apuckoliye (AI) he falls over backwards
cuhpiye (AI, II) he, it falls into the water
kipiye (AI) he falls over
kistehsin (AI) he fell; he got into an accident
kistehsu (AI) he fell; he got into an accident
ksihtehsin (II) he is hurt in a fall (or crash)
motehtehsin (AI) he is heard falling with a crash
nutiyamu (AI, II) he, it falls out (of a window, basket, etc.)
olomamu (AI, II) he, it falls away; he, it flies by
'pisamin (AI, AI+OBJ) he falls into it
pistehsin (AI) he falls in
pokossin (AI) he falls down; it (an.) falls; he, it (an.) lands
pokossin (AI) he falls down; it (an.) falls; he, it (an.) lands
siktehsin (AI) he dies from a fall; he dies from a crash
'tehsaqtehsinon (AI, AI+OBJ) he falls on it
tkiqtehsin (AI) he falls and hits heavily

fall (season)
toqakiw (II) it is fall
toqakuwiw (P) in the fall
toqakuwiw (II) it is fall

false
'koluskakonutomuwal (TA) he tells someone something false about him; he lies about him
mocacomuwakon (I) false statement; libel; dirty story
piluwikemosku (AI) he spreads false stories a lot; he is a jealous person
'pisuwahqimal (TA) he tells false information about him

family member
wicikitihticil (A) his (or her) brother or sister; his family member

fan
awahsihikon (I) small hand-held fan
't-ewahsehmon (TI) he fans it (a fire)

fancily
amalhotokku (AI) he jumps fancily; he does acrobatics
amalhuwikhomon (TI) he writes it fancily; he makes it with fancy designs or colors; he decorates it

fancy
amalhi (amalh-) (PV) fancy
seskoqone (AI) he has a fancy heel (on his shoe)

far
nawtaqsu (AI) sounds far away
'pihcehtahal (TA) he hits it (an.) far
pihceqehe (II) rolls far
pihcetu (P) far away
pihciye (AI, II) he, it goes far
tutopu (AI) he is far along (in rank, etc.; of a woman, in pregnancy); he is sitting a long way off
waht (P) far away; over there; far off

fast
'kakawahkan (AI, AI+OBJ) he throws it fast
kakawessu (AI, II) he, it goes fast
kakawi- (kakaw-) quickly; fast
kakawiw (P) quickly; fast
kakawiyewiw (II) it goes fast
monuhsehkasu (AI) he fasts (does not eat)
pomessu (AI) he goes along fast
sahsewestu (AI) he talks fast
sahsimiye (AI) he prays fast
sahsomahtu (AI) he does everything fast
wisahkawotuwok (AI) they (dual) walk fast
wisawse (AI) he walks fast
wisayapasuwok (AI) they (pl.) walk fast

fat
kinapskosu (AI) he is fat

father
mihtaqs (A) father; priest
tatat (A) father (but not priest)

favor
munsayuwal (TA) he does things to gain his favor

fear
nokalal (TA) he fears him
nokatomon (TI) he fears it
sespayu (AI) he cries out of fear

fearless
kinahant (A) devil; fearless person
feast
wiqhopaltuwok (AI) they feast
feather
wiphun (A) feather
wiphunhasu (II) it is feathered; it has a feather (or feathers) on it
feed
't-ahsomal (TA) he feeds him
'kisahsomal (TA) he fed him
'somal (TA) he feeds him
utsomal (TA) he feeds him with something
feel
koskimkasuwiw (II) it (a part of the body) goes to sleep; it feels like pins and needles (sensation in skin)
mewiyawiw (AI) he is feeling better
mocomolsu (AI) he feels ill
naskatahasu (AI) he feels discouraged
olomolsu (AI) he feels thus
olomomomqot (II) it feels as if it is going along (something)
olomomqot (II) it feels thus
-omols(i)- feel
peqositahasu (AI) he feels discouraged; he feels disappointed; he feels unconvinced
female
sqehkiqs (A) female animal
fence
lahkaluson (I) high fence; high wall
lahkalusonihikon (I) fence
't-olahkalusonahal (TA) he fences him out (or in)
ferry
ewotuhulal (TA) he goes back and forth ferrying him
fetch
esuwapilom (AI) he goes back and forth fetching water
ewotapilom, awotapilom (AI) he goes back and forth fetching water
ewotonike (AI) he goes back and forth fetching (or bringing out) wood
tolapilom (AI) he is fetching water
fib
'pak (I) fib
fiddlehead
mahsus (I) fiddlehead (young fern)
mahsuske (AI) he picks fiddleheads
fiddler
nutapektuhusit (A) musician who plays a stringed instrument; fiddler
field
apsaskute (II) it is a small field
epahsaskutew (P) right in the middle of a field
kinskute (II) it is a big field
kinskutenoma (AI) he has a big field
olomaskute (II) there is a long field
pemskutek (I) field
pomskute (II) there is a field
suwaskutew (P) out in the middle of a field

fight
matonal (TA) he fights him
mecimihponoltuwok (AI) they (dual) are always fighting (each other)
mecimihponosu (AI) he is always fighting
mikahke (AI) he fights
tolihponoltuwok (AI) they (dual) are fighting each other
tolihponosu (AI) he is fighting
ucihponoltiniya (AI, AI+OBJ) they fight (each other) over (or about) it
fighter
nucihponosit (A) fighter
file
kittakon (A) file (for working wood or metal)
fill
pitsone (AI) he fills his (own) pipe
'pitsonewal (TA) he fills his pipe for him
psonpewse (AI) it (an.) fills up
'tuhpolal (TA) he fills it (an.)
fin
sekonoss (A) porpoise fin
finally
malom (P) finally; at last; eventually
mamote (P) finally; at last; eventually
find
moskomon (TI) he finds it
moskuwal (TA) he finds him
find out
'papehcimal (TA) he finds out the truth from him
'papehcimanol (AI, AI+OBJ) he finds out the truth from him
wewcoskuwimal (TA) he finds out the truth from him
wewcoskuwimanol (AI, AI+OBJ) he finds out the truth from him
finger
nimcokonike (AI) he eats with his fingers; he eats with his (own) hand
puskiyelcan (I) finger
fingernail
'tomikosiyesal (TA) he cuts his (someone else's) fingernails
wokosiyil (A) (dep.) his fingernail; his claw, nail
finish
mehtewestu (AI) he finishes speaking
mettemu (AI) he finishes crying
finished
kiste (II) it is finished; it is ready
mehtonaskiye (II) it is all over; it is all finished
mehtonaskiye (II) it is all over; it is all finished
fir
stahqon (A) fir (Peter Dana Point, Maine); tree (Pleasant Point, Maine)
stahqoney (I) something made of fir
fire
't-ewahsehmon (TI) he fans it (a fire)
motutuwe (AI) he builds a fire
nattutuwe (AI) he goes (or comes) to build a fire
peskuwotasu (II) it is fired (of a gun, a cannon, etc.)
'posqolehlal (TA) he ignites it (an.); he fires him (from a job)
sqot (I) fire

'tawtutuwe (AI) he knows how to build a fire
tolotutuwe (AI) he is building a fire

firecracker
peskotehsok (I) firecracker; bean (slang)

firefly
possaqhessoss (A) firefly

firewood
petonike (AI) he carries firewood
piwsokuhke (AI) he gathers firewood
piwsoq (I) firewood

first
amsqahs (P) first; at first
amsqahsewey (A, I) first; the first one
amsqahsukonohom (II) it is the first day of the
    month
pol (P) first (indicating priority of action)
tanehk, tanek, tane (P) from the first time; ever
    since
tomk (P) first (before others)

fish
ame (AI) he fishes
aneqehsuhke (AI) he spears flounder; he fishes for
    flounder
nomehs (A) fish
ptahma, ptahme (AI) he hooks a fish; he "hooks"
    a girl
ptihike (AI) he catches fish
ptohom (AI) he hooks a fish
punamuhke (AI) he fishes for whitefish
sihtomuhke (AI) he fishes in a weir

fish hawk
isomeqehs A fish hawk; osprey

fish hook
mkihkon (I) fish hook
pkihkon (I) fish hook

fish net
ahp (A) fish net

fish scale
wolahk (I) fish scale

fisher
pokomk (A) fisher (animal)

fisherman
amewin (A) fisherman

fishing line
tolatokihtesta (AI) he is casting (a fishing line)

fishing pole
pkihkonahtoq (I) fishing pole

fist
ptoqilc (I) fist

five
nan (P) five (in counting)
nanuhsalqot (II) it is five miles

fix
woluwenal (TA) he fixes (sets, arranges, etc.) his
    (someone else's) hair

flag
motewahqem (A) flag pole
motewekon (I) flag
motewekonahasu (II) it has a flag on it

flake
misuwes (I) flake of dry skin

flame
psqolessu (AI) it (an.) bursts into flames

flap
tolekihpute (II) it (sheet-like object) is flapping,
    waving, etc.

flash
tutahtuwessu (AI, II) he, it goes by flashing a
    light

flat
opokekon (II) it is flat
opokeku (AI) it (an.) is flat
sokotiyapske (II) it is a flat rock
tetpahkomike (II) it is flat land

flick
'peskhikosamal (TA) he flicks him

flint
malsapsq (I) flint

flip
nenehson (II) it flips over easily

float
macekuhuke (AI) he floats away
papkehloqe (AI) he floats downstream
pomehloqe (AI) he floats along
tolokuhuke (AI) he is floating

floor
epahsasokiw (P) right in the middle of the floor
kospahtahsu (AI) he washes the floor
pemsokhas (I) floor
pomsokhasu (II) the floor is on (stage in building
    a house); it is on another part of the same floor
suwasokiw (P) out in the middle of the floor

flop
asuwocokahte (II) it has slid over to one side; it
    has flopped over to one side

flounder
aneqehs (A) flounder
aneqehsuhke (AI) he spears flounder; he fishes for
    flounder

flour
nukhomon (I) flour
nukhomoniw (II) it has flour on it
nukhomonumiw (AI) he has flour

flow
pomicuwon (II) it flows along
tolicuwon (II) it is flowing
tucicuwon (II) it flows by

flower
pehsuwahsuwehsok, pesqahsuwehsok (I) flower

fly
apcituwiye (AI) he is flying; he is on the wing; he
    continues to fly
cinituwiye (AI) he flies low
'cinituwiyemuhtuwal (TA) he flies low at him
nucituwiye (AI) he flies (a plane) on a regular
    basis; he pilots
olomamu (AI, II) he, it falls away; he, it flies by
pomituwiye (AI) he flies along
sasokamu (AI) it (an.) flies straight
tolituwiye (AI) he is flying
wiwonituwiye (AI) he flies around in a circle

fly (insect)
amucalu (A) fly

fog

pahkuwon (II) the fog lifts

pahqonuwiye (II) the fog is lifting

piskuwon (I) fog

soni piskuwon (II) there is a thick fog

foggy

piskuwon (II) it is foggy

uwon (II) it is foggy; it is misty

fold

nisekopisu (AI) it (an.) is folded twice; it (an.) is wrapped twice

oloqekte (II) it is folded back thus

'pakikpenómon (TI) he folds over the standers (vertical splints) of it (a basket)

panekte (II) it is folded open

follow

macehkuwal (TA) he forces him to go home by following him; he chases him away

't-oliphoqalal (TA) he follows him there

't-oliphoqatomon (TI) he follows it there

-phoqal- follow

-phoqatom- follow

fond

muhsacin (AI, AI+OBJ) he is fond of it

food

kolike (AI) he hogs food

kotuhtamu (AI) he craves some kind of food

micuwakon (I) food

'tephomuwal (TA) he dishes out food to him

foolish

epahsiye (AI) he is foolish; he is crazy

wiwonasiye (AI) he turns foolish; he turns crazy

foot

maskosite (AI) his feet stink

panuwosite (AI) his feet point out (when he walks)

'sit (I) (dep.) his foot

tolikonahtehsin (AI) he is tapping his foot

wewtuhkesite (AI) his feet point in when he walks

foot of the bed

witkosuhtuwok (AI) they (dual) are sleeping together, one at the foot of the bed

foot wrap

tosikon (I) foot wrap (worn under stockings)

for his part

na, ona (P) also, besides; for his part; here (when handing something to someone)

for sure

'cikawi nutehlal (TA) he forces him to go out

cu (P) yes, why yes; for sure; (when the answer "no" is expected or disbelief expressed) on the contrary; for sure

pehkiw, pehki (P) for sure

force

'cikawi nutehkuwal (TA) he forces him to move out

macehkuwal (TA) he forces him to go home by following him; he chases him away

forearm

'pihtin (I) (dep.) his hand; his forearm (including the hand)

forehead

wotoq (I) (dep.) his forehead

forest

kcihq (I) woods; forest

forever

askomawsu (AI) he lives forever

askomi (askom-) (PV) forever

askomiw (P) forever

forget

unitahasin (AI, AI+OBJ) he forgets it

wolitahasin (AI, AI+OBJ) he forgets it

fork

mitsut (I) fork (utensil)

niktuwikonehe (AI) it (an.) forks out into a V; it (an.) branches out into a V

form

qaskewoton (II)_ ice is forming

formerly

meciniw (P) formerly; used to; in the past

fort

wahkaluson (I) fort

foul up

nihluwehtun (TI) he fouled it up by tinkering with it

four

new (P) four (in counting)

newuhsalqot (II) it is four miles

newukoniw (P) for four days; after four days

fox

qaqsoss (A) fox

wenhuket (A) silver fox

freckle

puhpuhkomiqe (AI) he has freckles

Fredericton

Sitansisk Fredericton, New Brunswick (Locative)

freeze

'kolocomulal (TA) he freezes it (an.)

'kolocomutun (TI) he freezes it

kolocu (AI) he, it (an.) freezes

koloton (II) it freezes

freezer

kolocomutikon (A) refrigerator; freezer

French

polecomonatuwe (AI) he speaks French

Frenchman

Polecomon (A) Frenchman

frequently

molihkiw (P) frequently

fresh water

lontoq (I) fresh water

Friday

Kci Skehewahtoq (I) Good Friday

skehewahtoq (I) Friday

friend

witapehkamal (TA) he makes friends with him; he is friendly to him

witapehkanol (AI, AI+OBJ) he makes friends with him

witapehkewal (TA) he makes friends for someone

witapehtuwok (AI) they (dual) are friends (with each other)

witapiyil, witapihil (A) (dep.) his friend

frog
coqols (A) frog
coqolsuwi (coqolsuw-) (PN) frog; frog's
from
'cey (A) someone from there
'ci ('c-, 't-) (PV, PN) from; out of; on account of
from...on (time)
'cimaciw, 'cimacihiw (P) from...on (time)
from place to place
ankuwotkuhu (AI) he jumps from place to place
from then on
-hk from then on
from there
'ciye (AI) he comes back from there; he has been there
liwehse (II) the wind is blowing from there
'tamihkessu (AI) he gets up from there
front
nihkaniw (P) ahead; in front
nihkanke (AI) he paddles in the front of a canoe
frost fish
punam (A) frost fish (tomcod)
frozen
kpoton (II) it is frozen over; it is frozen shut (e.g., a faucet)
fruit
minkasu (AI) it (an.) bears fruit
fry
'sisolapsqehlal (TA) he fries it (an.)
'sisolapsqehtun (TI) he fries it
sisolastike (AI) he fries pork
fry bread
alahket (A) fry bread
tumahsis (A) Tom Francis (fry bread)
tumahsisey (A) fry bread
frying pan
sisolapsqehtikon (A) frying pan
full
memihpu (AI) he has eaten enough; he is full
psoni (pson-) (PV) full; fully
psonpe (AI) it (an.) is full of liquid
psonte (II) it is full
full grown
kisikon (II) it is full grown; it is mature
kisiku (AI) he is full grown
funeral
puskonike (AI) he goes to a funeral
fungus
wapi latuwan (A) fungus species
fur
woluwe (AI) he has nice hair; he has nice fur
further
ankuwi- (ankuw-) (PV) further; a little further; beyond

G

gall
wisoss (I) gall
game
amkakon (I) game
amke (AI) he plays a game; he runs for an office
pehqey (I) meat obtained by hunting, wild meat
game warden
kukec (A) game warden
garden
't-ahkihkan (I) his garden
kihkan (I) garden
gaspereau
siqonomeq (A) alewife, gaspereau (Maliseet)
gather
maqenike (AI) he takes people into his home; he gathers (food, clothing) for some worthy cause
mawona (TA) he gathers them (an.)
piwsokuhke (AI) he gathers firewood
piyaqtihikonihke (AI) he gathers wood chips
pupukhawihqe (AI) he gathers balsam fir pitch
gauge
likpesawakon (I) gauge for cutting ash splints
gauze
cossuwewekon (I) mosquito net; gauze
gear
leyuwakon (I) personal belongings; gear
get
ikahawqe (AI) he gets sick
'kihkaqote (II) it gets burned
kiskatom (AI) he got married
'kolonomuwewal (TA) he gets something for him
mosonal (TA) he catches him; he gets it (an.)
mosonomon (TI) he gets it
nassewe (AI) he gets dressed
natewotuwan (DOV) he comes (or goes) and gets it for him
'pektehmon (TI) he gets it all; he hits it all
petonom (AI) he gets there
'pitkotomuwewan (DOV) he gets it ready for him
'pitkotuwatomon (TI) he gets it ready
sikopu (AI) he, it (an.) is hard to get at
sikte (II) it is hard to get to; it is hard to get at
get by
saphome, saphoma (AI) he gets by; he does all right
get down
'poneqehlal (TA) he gets him down; he puts him down
get into
kistehsin (AI) he fell; he got into an accident
kistehsu (AI) he fell; he got into an accident
tepessu (AI) he gets into a vehicle or boat
get off
kahpotassu (AI) he steps out; he gets off
mehtoluhke (AI) he gets off work; he stops working
monessu (AI) it (an.) peels off; he gets off, gets out of a trap

get out
kahtopassu (AI) he gets out of the water
nattokaphuwe (AI) he gets out and runs away
nutehlal, nutelal (TA) he gets him out, he lets him out; he puts him out
piluhse (AI) he gets out of the way
get there
petonome (AI) he gets there
get to
'sipkihkomon (AI, AI+OBJ) it takes him a long time to get to it
witapehkatomon (TI) he gets to like it
witapehkatomuwan (DOV) he gets to like something of his
get up
amihkessu (AI) he gets up (from a sitting position)
'tamihkessu (AI) he gets up from there
wonakessu (AI) he gets up (from a sitting position)
wonaku (AI) he gets up
ghost
kehtaqs (A) ghost
nisekopisit (A) ghost
gift
olelomal (TA) he bestows a gift, a talent on him
girl
pilsqehsis (A) girl
ptahma, ptahme (AI) he hooks a fish; he "hooks" a girl
give
't-ahsihpilal (TA) he gives him medicine
milan (DOV) he gives it to him
miluwan (AI, AI+OBJ) he gives it away
mosiyal (TA) he gives him a disease; he infects him
't-osihmuwal (TA) he gives him a drink
'pomiphal (TA) he carries him; he gives him a ride in a vehicle
glance
sahsapu (AI) he glances quickly
gland
cehcoloqs (A) gland
muwikasu (AI) he has a swollen gland
glide
alaku (AI) he glides (on wings)
motapetomhe (AI, II) he, it goes downhill with a gliding motion
go
amuwyessu (AI) he goes crazy
cikcahkehe (AI) he goes downhill
esuwessu (AI, II) he, it goes back and forth
-h(a)- go
kakawessu (AI, II) he, it goes fast
kakawiyewiw (II) it goes fast
'kolonomahsin (AI, AI+OBJ) he goes on an errand to get it
mace (maciy-) (PV) start, begin; go away or start off while doing go along while doing
menakaciye (AI) he goes slowly
neqiye
oliye (AI) he goes there
pihciye (AI, II) he, it goes far

pithawiye (AI) he goes upriver
qolopiye (AI) he changes the direction he is facing; he goes in the wrong direction (as a result of not following directions); he changes his mind
saputessu (AI, II) he, it goes through
sehtehe (AI) he goes backwards
sipkiye (AI) he is gone for a long time
toliye (II) it is going; it is running
tuciye (AI, II) he, it goes by; he, it goes fast
wewciye (AI) he goes somewhere and returns without stopping over: he makes a home run (in baseball)
wiciye (AI) he receives communion; he goes along
-y(a)- go
go against
pihciqehe (AI) he goes against the wind
go along
pomaptu (AI) he goes along leaving tracks
pomessu (AI) he goes along fast
pomoqotehe (AI) he goes along underwater
go around
miskot (II) there is enough to go around
wiciyemal (TA) he goes around with him; he goes out with her (or she... with him); he accompanies him
wiwonimiye (AI) he goes around to the Stations of the Cross; he goes around (something) praying
go away
mace (maciy-) (PV) start, begin; go away or start off while doing go along while doing
olomiye (AI, II) he, it goes away
go back
wesuwe (wesuwiy-) (PV) back; going back
wesuwessu (AI) he goes back
go by
akomihom (AI) he goes by snowshoe
tuci (tuc-, tut-) (PV) (going) past, by; very, extremely; at a certain point
tuciye (AI, II) he, it goes by; he, it goes fast
tutahtuwessu (AI, II) he, it goes by flashing a light
go in
ksehe (AI) he comes in; he goes in
ksehkawotuwok (AI) they (dual) come in; they (dual) go in
ksiyapasuwok (AI) they (pl.) come in, they (pl.) go in
pisessu (AI) he goes in
go into
cuwahpiye (AI, II) he, it goes (or falls) into the water
go on
pomikoton (II) the year is not over yet; the year is going on
tolonukot (II) it is happening, going on
go onto
nahsiye (AI, II) it goes onto (something)
nastahal (TA) he hits it (an.) to make it go on (e.g. a ring over a post)
nastehmon (TI) he hits it to make it go on

go out
'cikawi nutehlal (TA) he forces him to go out
macehkot (II) the tide is starting to go out
nipawse (AI) he goes out at night; he walks at night
nipehe (AI) he goes out at night
nute (nutiy-) (PV) out; going out; coming out
nutew (P) coming out; going out
olomihkot (II) the tide goes out
wiciyemal (TA) he goes around with him; he goes out with her (or she... with him); he accompanies him
wiqqot (II) the tide goes out
go to
koskimkasuwiw (II) it (a part of the body) goes to sleep; it feels like pins and needles (sensation in skin)
makasanke (AI) he goes to the store (archaic)
naci (nac-, nat-) (PV) change location; go (or come) to...
nacossin (AI) he goes (or comes) and lies down
natassihkuwal (TA) he goes to meet him
natkuwal (TA) he goes right to him
natolasihkuwal (TA) he goes (or comes) to greet him
natonihiqe (AI) he goes (or comes) to get birchbark
nipayimiye (AI) he goes to midnight mass
puskonike (AI) he goes to a funeral
go under
neqiye (AI) he goes under
God
Keluwosit, Kelusit (A) God
gone
api (ap-) (PV) having gone to do X and returned; be back from doing X
good
akun (P) it's a good thing
koluwosu (AI) he is capable, useful for something; he is good for something; it (an.) is good for use
ksalokosse (AI) he has good hearing
'tawi ('taw-) (PV) know how; be good at
ulankeyuwal (TA) he takes good care of him
wolahqemihke (II) there is a good stand of trees (for wood)
wolalokosse (AI) he has good ears; he has good hearing
wolapuwahte (II) it is a good-tasting soup; it is a good-tasting stew
wolawtosson (II) it is a good road
woli ehpituwiw (AI) she is a good woman
woli (wol-) (PV, PN) good; well
wolihpukot (AI) it tastes good
wolikon (II) it is good (for use)
woliku (AI) he is good (at what he does); it (an.) is good (for use)
wolimahte (II) it smells good
wolinaqot (II) it looks good
wolinaqsu (AI) he looks good
wolokiskot (II) it is a good day

Good Friday
Kci Skehewahtoq (I) Good Friday
good-natured
wolomahtu (AI) he is good-natured
goose
waptoq (A) Canada goose
gossip
tpolukemosku (AI) he gossips a lot
tpolukemu (AI) he gossips
governor
sakom (A) chief; tribal governor
sakomawikuwam (I) governor's house
sakomawka (AI) he does a governor's dance
grab
'pokkikalal (TA) he grabs him
'pokkikatomon (TI) he grabs it
gradually
ahaciw (P) gradually; more and more
grain
piyeskomon (I) ear of corn; grain of corn
Grand Manan Island
Monahnuk Grand Manan Island, New Brunswick (Locative)
grandchild
qenoss (A) grandchild
grandfather
muhsums (A) grandfather
grandmother
uhkomossol (A) (dep.) his grandmother
grass
pisokonike (AI) he walks into high grass, brush, etc.
pskihq (I) blade of grass
puspekihke (II) the grass is wet
grass-cutter
nutasksawet (A) grass-cutter (person)
grasshopper
cals (A) grasshopper
gravel
ponapsqisamq (I) gravel
gray
wapqe (AI) he has gray hair
grease
mimey (I) grease; oil
great
kci (kc-, kt-) (PV, PN) big; great; old
wiwisanaqsu (AI) he is in a great hurry
greet
natolasihkuwal (TA) he goes (or comes) to greet him
skawewintuwakon (I) greeting song
grip
molihkapocu (AI) he has a strong grip
ground
ktahkomiq (I) land; ground; earth
nuhkahkomike (II) the ground is soft
tolomomtihike (AI) he is driving something (e.g. stakes) into the ground
walkomike (II) the ground is uneven (hills and valleys)
ground hemlock
toqonastoq (A) ground hemlock

groundhog
munimqehs (A) woodchuck; groundhog
group
mawi (maw-) (PV) together; in a group
mawiw (P) together (of more than two or of a mass); in a group
grow
'kinikonomon (TI) he grows it bigger
maceku (AI) he grows up
growth
kcimkatoke (II) there is thick growth
guide
't-alhulal (TA) he guides him around in a boat
nuthutahsit (A) guide (e.g. for a hunting trip)
gull
kiyahq (A) seagull
gum
wiyuhsuwapit (I) gum (without teeth)
gun
ketkosewe (AI) he unloads a gun
molomahkonoma (AI) his gun goes off by accident
'pitkatomuwan (DOV) he loads his (someone else's) gun
'pitkosewan (AI, AI+OBJ) he loads it (a gun)
gunpowder
psew (I) gunpowder
gust
peciwehse (II) a gust of wind comes

H

haddock
cilonasit (A) haddock
hair
atuwe (AI) he (an animal) sheds his hair
kcoskuwesu (AI) his hair burns off
kcoskuwete (II) its hair burns off
konasisuwatpe (AI) he has nits in his hair
'kossatpenal (TA) he washes his (someone else's) hair
mawwenal (TA) he holds back (someone else's) hair
mehtuwehe (AI) his hair is falling out
mocuwe (AI) he has messy hair
mokosewatpe (AI) he has black hair
musal (TA) he cuts his (someone else's) hair
musawe (AI) he cuts hair; he barbers
nasqahal (TA) he combs his (someone else's) hair
't-otolatokonomewal (TA) he braids someone else's hair; he ties someone else's hair with a ribbon, string, etc.
piqonewatpe (AI) he has bushy hair
piyehs (I) (single) hair
possetokahmuwal (AI) he parts his (someone else's) hair
possetoqahal (TA) he parts his (someone else's) hair
pqatpe (AI) he has red hair

pskuwhe (AI) he sheds (his hair)
pskuwhetul (II) hairs fall out (when a person is losing hair or an animal is shedding)
topuwepu (AI) he has curly hair
wapatpe (AI) he has white hair
wisawatpe (AI) he has blond hair
wiwcossuwatpe, wiwcossatpe (AI) he has curly hair
woluwe (AI) he has nice hair; he has nice fur
woluwenal (TA) he fixes (sets, arranges, etc.) his (someone else's) hair
woluwepu (AI) his hair is nicely fixed
hake
qolopapehkikonoss (A) silver hake
half
epahsahkiw (P) halfway up (or down) a hill
epahsahsu (AI) it (an.) is half-illuminated
epahsi (epahs-, epas-) (PV) half, halfway; in the middle; in two, in half
't-epahsiksal (TA) he saws it (an.) in two; he saws it (an.) in half
't-epahsiksomon (TI) he saws it in two; he saws it in half
epahsiw (P) halfway; in the middle
epaspe (AI, II) it is half full (of liquid)
sasokuhqepu (AI) he half stands; he half sits; he is leaning against something
half dollar
epahsakisu (A) half dollar
ham
wikpolastikon (I) ham
hammer
maltuhsis (A) hammer
hand
'ciptinessu (AI) he makes a hand print
'koliptinenal (TA) he holds his (someone else's) hand
'kossiptinenal (TA) he washes his (someone else's) hand(s)
moccokiptinehlal (TA) he gets his (someone else's) hand dirty
nimcokonike (AI) he eats with his fingers; he eats with his (own) hand
nukcokonomon (TI) he crushes it by hand
't-olonomuwan (DOV) he hands it to him
'paskocokonal (TA) he breaks it (an., something soft) by hand
'paskocokonomon (TI) he breaks it (something soft) by hand
'paskonal (TA) he breaks it (an.) by hand
'paskonomon (TI) he breaks it by hand
'pihtin (I) (dep.) his hand; his forearm (including the hand)
pokahkoniptine (AI) he has bloody hands
-ptine- hand
'sokiptinenal (TA) he shakes hands with him
uckuhnomuwan, uckuwonomuwan (DOV) he hands it to him
handful
psonopulce (AI) he has a handful
handsome
wolapewiw (AI) he is handsome

hang
ekhucuwole (AI) he hangs clothes out to dry
ekhute (II) it hangs down
happen
kinuwitpiye (II) it happens sometimes
ktonukot (II) something big happens
lelomoqe (AI) something happens to him
leyu (II) it happens; it is true
olonukot (II) it happens thus
-onukot(o)- happen
tolonukot (II) it is happening, going on
-tpiy(a)- happen
happy
ulitahasuwehlal (TA) he makes him happy
wolitahasu (AI) he is happy
hard
checinaqsu (AI) he is hard to see
motuweyu (II) it is difficult, hard to deal with
sakoleyu (AI, II) it is hard to the touch; it is difficult
sakoli (sakol-) (PV, PN) hard (to the touch); difficult; tough
sikeyu (II) it is hard to do
sikopu (AI) he, it (an.) is hard to get at
sikte (II) it is hard to get to; it is hard to get at
sipine (AI) he dies hard
wisayahkan (AI, AI+OBJ) he throws it hard
hardly
wahk, wahka, wahkac (P) barely; hardly
hardwood
sakoli opos (A) hardwood tree; witch hazel
harness
ahahs elsewet (I) harness
lapekhasu (AI) he (a horse) is harnessed
lapekhikon (I) harness
hat
ahsusuwon (I) hat
hatch
pokhu, pokhuwe (AI) it (an.) hatches
pokhutike (AI) she hatches her eggs
hate
musqitahamal (TA) he hates him
nacitahamal (TA) he hates him
haunt
cilomomal (TA) he receives a sign from him; he is haunted by him
cilomotome, cilomotoma (AI) he receives a sign; he is haunted; he receives an omen
cilomotomon (TI) he receives a sign through it; he is haunted through it
have
't-ihin (TI) he has it
't-ihmuwan (DOV) he has something of his (someone else's)
't-iywal (TA) he has him; he has it (an.)
kinahqisomuwe (AI) he has big big antlers
manimiw, manimu (AI) he has money
matsehkessu (AI) he has an infection
nihkoskawe (AI) he has a nightmare (of being unable to move)
nukhomoniw (AI) he has flour; he has flour on him
pahkamine (AI) he has a back ache
psonopulce (AI) he has a handful

puhpuhkomiqe (AI) he has freckles
have to
cuwi, ahcuwi (ehcuwi) (PV) must; should; have to
hazy
pkotewqiw (II) it is hazy
he
nekom (A) (PRO) he, she
not (A) (PRO) that ((an.) near person spoken to); that (location unspecified); he, him, it (an.)
head
kciqaha (A) head (of a business, office, etc.)
nihkanatpe (AI) he heads (an organization)
olomatqin (II) the waves are heading away (i.e. the wind is blowing from behind on the water)
't-opqehsimuhtuwal (TA) he lays his head on him
't-opqehsinon (AI, AI+OBJ) he lays his head on it
'paskatpehtahal (TA) he hits him on the head and wounds him
woniyakon (I) (dep.) his head
head first
olonomtehsin (AI) he strikes head first (making a dent)
headache
woniyakonine (AI) he has a headache
heal
'kikahal (TA) he heals him
kikehtahsu (AI) he heals (someone)
kikehtasu (II) it is healed
'kikehtun (TI) he heals it
kikihike (AI) he heals (someone)
healthy
sakolomtu (AI) he is healthy
hear
nutomon (TI) he hears it
nutuwal (TA) he hears him
heard
mote (motiy-) (PV) be heard ...ing
motehtehsin (AI) he is heard falling with a crash
moteqsu (AI) he is heard sleeping; he snores
motetemu (AI) he is heard crying
motiyaqasokonike (AI) he is heard walking in high bushes
motiyewestu (AI) he is heard speaking
nutaqsu (AI) he is heard
hearing
ksalokosse (AI) he has good hearing
wolalokosse (AI) he has good ears; he has good hearing
heart
psuhun (I) heart
psuhun, psuhunsis (A) heart (in cards)
psuhunine, moshunine (AI) he has heart trouble
heart-wood
lamahqem (A) heart-wood of a tree
heartless
wihkukelkesku (AI) he is unfeeling, heartless, uncharitable, etc.
wihkukelomal (TA) he is unfeeling, heartless, uncharitable, etc. toward him
wihkukeltomon (TI) he is heartless, unfeeling, uncharitable, etc. toward it

heat
matsehkiye (AI) she is in heat; he is rutting
heath
pkuwahq (I) heath (open, boggy land)
heaven
spomk (I) heaven
heavily
tkiqtehsin (AI) he falls and hits heavily
heavy
tkiqol (AI) he is heavy
tkiqon (II) it is heavy
tutatqin (II) there is a heavy sea; the waves are very high
heed
'ciksotomon (TI) he listens to it; he heeds it
'ciksotuwal (TA) he listens to him; he heeds him
heel
maskoqone (AI) she has sexy shoes; she has high heels
seskoqone (AI) he has a fancy heel (on his shoe)
woqon (I) (dep.) his heel
hell
lamk hell
help
ktomakelke (AI) he helps out because he is sympathetic
wicuhkekemu (AI) he helps out
wicuhkemal (TA) he helps him
hemlock
ksiwsk (A) hemlock
hemophiliac
nuciqqiyat (A) hemophiliac bleeder
hemorrhage
'cehtu (AI) he hemorrhages through the nose and mouth
here
coke (P) here; let me see (indicates interest in something near the person spoken to); hmm, let me think; well, now...
na, ona (P) also, besides; for his part; here (when handing something to someone)
yut (P) here; now
hesitate
ehetsu (AI) he hesitates
hey!
ipa (P) hey!; listen!; look!
hiccup
kehtepsulu (AI) he hiccups
hidden
kaciw (P) secretly; hidden
katte (II) it is hidden
hide
'kaciptun (TI) he takes it by hiding it
'kalal (TA) he hides him
'katun (TI) he hides it
'katuwan (DOV) he hides it from him; he hides something of his (someone else's)
hideous
cipi (cip-) (PV,PN) ugly; evil-looking; hideous
hiding place
'toputoss (I) (αep.) his (an animal's) hiding place

high
ksakuwiye (II) the tide is at its highest (in its monthly cycle)
psonpehe (II) it is high tide
spekopu (AI) he, it (an., a sheet-like object) is high
spopu (AI) he sits up high
'tehsahqaphal (TA) he tracks him on high ground
hill
cikcahkew (P) at the bottom of a hill
hilly
milahkomike (II) it is hilly land
hip
mosopine (AI) he has hip pain
wolukon (I) his hip
hire
't-ahcuwyal, 'cuwyal (TA) he hires him
't-aptomimal (TA) he went to hire him (and came back)
'cuwyal (TA) he hires him
nattomimal (TA) he goes (or comes) to hire him
'pettomimal (TA) he comes to hire him
hit
't-ahtoptahal (TA) he hits him by luck
't-ahtoptehmon (TI) he hits it by luck
't-ahtoptelomon (TI) he shoots at it and hits it by luck
't-ahtopteluwal (TA) he shoots at him and hits him by luck
-ht_h-, -t_h- hit; strike; chop
-htehm-, -tehm- hit; strike; chop
-htihik(e)-, -tihik(e)- hit; strike; chop
miyawtahal (TA) he hits him with a well-aimed blow
miyawtehmon (TI) he hits it with a well-aimed blow
miyawteluwal (TA) he shoots him accurately; he shoots him and hits him; he wounds him
't-oltahal (TA) he hurts him thus by hitting
't-otolihtehmon (TI) he is hitting it
'paskatpehtahal (TA) he hits him on the head
'pektahal (TA) he hits all of it (an.)
'pektehmon (TI) he gets it all; he hits it all
'pokahkonihtahal (TA) he bloodies him; he hits him, drawing blood
'pottahal (TA) he hits him accidentally
'pottehmon (TI) he hits it accidentally
'tokan (AI, AI+OBJ) he hits him, it
'tokomal (TA) he hits him (usually implies intention)
tokotikon (I) something to hit with; bat (baseball)
tokotom (AI) he hits; he bats (baseball)
'tokotomon (TI) he hits it (usually implies intention); he strikes at it
'tomtahal (TA) he chops it down (of a tree); he hits it (an.) and makes it break into two pieces
'tomtehmon, 'tomihtehmon (TI) he hits it and breaks it apart
hit back
't-asitehtahal (TA) he hits him back
hit (do by hitting)
'koppektahal (TA) he shuts him in by hitting (something 2-dimensional: cloth, paper, etc.)

'*koppektehmon* (TI) he covers it by hitting (something 2-dimensional: cloth, paper, etc.)

'*qolopihtahal* (TA) he turns him around by hitting him, knocking against him, etc.

'*tuwalokihtahal* (TA) he puts a hole through it (an.) by hitting it

'*tuwalokihtehmon* (TI) he puts a hole through it by hitting it

hit far

'*pihcehtahal* (TA) he hits it (an.) far

hit on

nastahal (TA) he hits it (an.) to make it go on (e.g. a ring over a post)

nastehmon (TI) he hits it to make it go on

hmm

coke (P) here; let me see (indicates interest in something near the person spoken to); hmm, let me think; well, now...

hoarse

kpocale (AI) he is hoarse

hoe

lahkihikon (I) hoe

hog

'*kolikatomon* (TI) he hogs it (food)

kolike (AI) he hogs food

hold

ewepikonatutom (AI) he has his leg propped up; he holds his leg up

ewepikonawu (AI) he holds his (own) leg up

'*t-eweponal* (TA) he holds him up; he lifts him up

'*t-eweponomon* (TI) he holds it up; he lifts it up

'*kolikonatenal* (TA) he holds him by the leg(s)

'*koliptinenal* (TA) he holds his (someone else's) hand

'*kolonalokossenal* (TA) he holds his (someone else's) ear

niktuhkomon (TI) he holds it between his legs

'*sakolonomon* (TI) he holds it tight

hold back

mawwenal (TA) he holds back (someone else's) hair

hold onto

'*kolonal* (TA) he holds onto him

'*kolonomuwan* (DOV) he holds onto something of his (someone else's); he holds onto it for him

hole

apsalokosu (AI) it (an.) has a small hole in it

'*tuwalokihkomon* (TI) he puts a hole through it by stepping on it

'*tuwalokihkuwal* (TA) he puts a hole through it (an.) by stepping on it

'*tuwalokihtahal* (TA) he puts a hole through it (an.) by hitting it

'*tuwalokihtehmon* (TI) he puts a hole through it by hitting it

waloq, aloq (I) hole

holler

kakaluwe (AI) he hollers; he calls out

naskahtaqsuwamal (TA) he hollers at him discouragingly

hollow

piqeku (AI) it (an.) is hollow

holy water

imiyewp (I) holy water

home

nemaht (P) to, at my home

wik (I) his house; his home

home run

wewciye (AI) he goes somewhere and returns without stopping over; he makes a home run (in baseball)

hook

'*poccipilal* (TA) he hooks him by accident

'*pothal* (TA) he hooks him

'*pothomon* (TI) he hooks it

ptahma, ptahme (AI) he hooks a fish; he "hooks" a girl

ptohom (AI) he hooks a fish

wihqaqhal (TA) he pulls it (an.) with a hook

wihqaqhomon (TI) he pulls it with a hook

hoop

lahqostikon (I) hoop

horribly

'*sikine* (AI) he dies horribly

horse

ahahs (A) horse

pomumqe (AI) he rides a horse

horse whip

ahahsuwipis (I) horse whip

horsefly

psosahq (A) horsefly

horseshoe

wekososs (A) horseshoe

host

ustiwin, hustiwin (A) host (altar bread)

hot

ksate (II) it is very hot

ksihposu (AI) he is hot

ksihpote (II) it is hot

ksopote (II) it is hot

siktiyaqosu (AI) he is very hot; he burns to death

sqotewahkosu (AI) it (an.) is red hot

sqotewahkote (II) it is red hot

wisokolate (II) it is very hot

house

'*kossekimal* (TA) he calls him into the house

naskuwamal (TA) he sleeps in the same house with him

wihke (AI) he builds a house

wihkosu (AI) he builds a house for himself

wik (I) his house; his home

wikuwam (I) house; building

how

tan (P) how; where; thus

however

kahk (P) but; however (emphatic; singles out the preceding word)

kenoq, kenuk, qenoq (P) but; however

olu, lu (P) but; however; as for (focuses on preceding word)

tan ote, tan te however; in whatever way; as... as

tan tehpu (P) -ever; however

tepot (P) nevertheless; however

howl
tolewehtu (AI) he (a dog) is howling
hug
ehkosqenal (TA) he hugs him
hungry
kotuhpu (AI) he is hungry
hunt
ahkiqqe (AI) he hunts seals
ahkiqsiske (AI) he hunts pup seals
cuspeske (AI) he hunts porpoise
ehemuhke (AI) he hunts chickens
kiwhosuhke (AI) he hunts muskrats; he traps
   muskrats
kotunke (AI) he hunts
'kotunolal (TA) he hunts him; he is out to get him
mociyehsuhke (AI) he hunts partridges
musuhke (AI) he hunts moose
muwinuhke, muwinehke (AI) he hunts bear
neqskihqessuhke (AI) he hunts woodcock
otukke (AI) he hunts deer
sipsuhke (AI) he hunts birds (esp. ducks)
hunter
kotunkewin (A) hunter
hurriedly
wisaluhke (AI) he works hurriedly
hurry
wisa (wisay-) (PV) in a hurry
wisanaqsu (AI) he is in a hurry
wisayu (AI) he hurries
wiwisa (wiwisay-) (PV) in a great hurry
wiwisanaqsu (AI) he is in a great hurry
wiwisayu (AI) he hurries
hurt
'kosehlal (TA) he hurts him (physically)
'kosehtun (TI) he hurts it
'kosehtuwan (DOV) he hurts something of his
   (someone else's) (physically)
'kosonal (TA) he hurts him
ksihtehsin (II) he is hurt in a fall (or crash)
't-oltahal (TA) he hurts him thus by hitting
'sisqine (AI) his eye (or eyes) hurts (hurt)

I

I
nil (A) (PRO) I, me; my; mine
ice
neqoloqessu (AI) he goes under the ice
pomoloqihton (II) the ice is breaking up and
   floating downstream
posson (A) reef of ice
pqom (A) ice
pqomuwessu (II) it is turning into ice
qaskewoton (II)_ ice is forming
ice skate
olonahqakom (A) ice skate
if
tokec (P) now; if

if not
ska, skat (P) not; if not
if only
nopal (P) I wish; if only
ignite
'posqolehlal (TA) he ignites it (an.); he fires him
   (from a job)
'posqolehtun (TI) he ignites it
ill
mocomolsu (AI) he feels ill
imagine
'sesomitahamal (TA) he does not know about
   him; he cannot imagine about him
immediately
nanakiw (P) suddenly; all of a sudden;
   immediately
implement
wehkewakon (I) implement
impound
'tahqonomon (TI) he impounds it
'tahqonomuwan (DOV) he impounds something
   of his
improperly
't-uwapolitahamal (TA) he thinks about him
   improperly; he thinks there is something wrong
   with him
wapoli (wapol-) (PV) wrong; improperly
in
ckuhpehe (II) the tide is coming in
'kossehlal (TA) he lets him in
kse (ksiy-) (PV) in; inward; into
pisessu (AI) he goes in
'tepahkan (AI, AI+OBJ) he throws it in; he
   pushes it in; he drops it in
in order that
weci (PV) in order that; so that
inch-worm
atpahqonikehs (A) caterpillar; inch-worm
included
wiciye (II) it is included
including
ayut (P) and even; and besides; including even
Indian
skicin (A) Indian
skicinuwatuwe (AI) he speaks an Indian lanuage;
   he speaks Maliseet-Passamaquoddy
skicinuwi (skicinuw-) (PN, PV) Indian
skicinuwoka, skicinuwoke (AI) he does an Indian
   dance
Indian Island
Panuwapskek Indian Island, Maine (Locative)
infect
mosiyal (TA) he gives him a disease; he infects
   him
infection
matsehkessu (AI) he has an infection
inform
'kinuwehtuwal (TA) he informs him
'tahkinuwehtuwal (TA) he informs him
inhale
wihqipkotehtamike (AI) he inhales smoke from a
   pipe over and over
wihqipkotehtamu (AI) he inhales smoke from a
   pipe

wihqipkotenike (AI) he inhales smoke from a
  pipe, puffing slowly
wiqsonehtomon (TI) he inhales it
wiqsonepal (TA) he inhales it (an.)
inject
'saphomuwan (DOV) he pokes, injects something
  of his (someone else's)
injection
saphutin (AI) there are injections being given
inquire
papehcikesu (AI) he inquires
wewisu (AI) he inquires
inside
lamatqoniw (AI) it (an.) is knotty inside
lamiw (P) inside; underneath
tepiw (P) inside
tepuloq (I) the inside of a canoe
instead
awonehe (P) instead
instrument
lapektuhusu (AI) he plays a stringed instrument
interpret
ankuwacomu (AI) he relays a message; he brings
  a report of; he interprets (translates)
't-ankuwacomuwewal (TA) he interprets for him
intestine
woloks (I) intestine
into
ehpituwehlosu (AI) he turns himself into a woman
kse (ksiy-) (PV) in; inward; into
maqena (TA) he takes them into his home
maqenike (AI) he takes people into his home; he
  gathers (food, clothing) for some worthy cause
petute (AI) he moves (his household) into...
'pisamin (AI, AI+OBJ) he falls into it
pisi (pis-) (PV) into, out (through a boundary in
  either direction)
pisiw (P) into, out (through a boundary in either
  direction)
into view
sakhahte (II) it sticks out into view
sakhalokittiyhe (AI) (intensive or angry form of
  sakhiye "he comes into view")
sakhi (sakh-) (PV) into view; unexpectedly
sakholiqehe (AI) (intensive or angry form of
  sakhiye "he comes into view")
inward
kse (ksiy-) (PV) in; inward; into
Irishman
elisomen (A) Irishman
iron
olonahkuloq (I) iron ship
olonahq (I) iron
island
monihq (I) island
monossapsq (I) rock island
nit (I) (PRO) that (inanimate, near person spoken
  to); that (location unspecified); it
itch
kikcokiye (AI) he itches

J

jacket
cehkit (A) jacket
jam
suwonap (I) jam; jelly
jealous
'coskuwalal (TA) he is jealous of him
coskuwe (AI) he is jealous
'kocoskuwalal (TA) he is jealous of him
piluwikemosku (AI) he spreads false stories a lot;
  he is a jealous person
piluwikemu (AI) he is jealous
'piluwimal (TA) he is jealous of him
jelly
suwonap (I) jam; jelly
jellyfish
sahsap (A) jellyfish
Jesus
Sesuhs (A) Jesus
Jew
lehsuwis (A) Jew
join
witahke, witanahke (AI) he joins in
joker
milehtakesku (AI) he is a joker; he is always
  getting into mischief
jug
pukcinsqehs (A) jug; name of an evil character in
  legends
jump
amalhotokku (AI) he jumps fancily; he does
  acrobatics
amikotokku (AI) he jumps up
ankuwotkuhu (AI) he jumps from place to place
cipqam (AI) he has a nightmare of falling; he
  jumps in his sleep or when dozing
cuwapotokku (AI) he jumps into the water
eqotokku (AI) he stops jumping
ewepotokku (AI) he jumps up
kisamikotokku (AI) he jumped up; he can jump
  up
olotokku (AI) he jumps there
't-oqehtuwal (TA) he sets him up for a jump (in
  checkers)
-otoqq(i)-, -otq_h(i)- jump
poneqotokku (AI) he jumps down
sakhotkuhu (AI) he jumps into view
sasotokku (AI) he jumps up and down quickly
sehtatkuhu (AI) he jumps backwards
tehsaqotokku (AI) he jumps on top
just
tehpu, tehpukt (P) only (restrictive); just; all; the
  only thing
just a minute
temonu, temonuk (P) later; just a minute
just the one
miyaw (P) exactly; just the one

K

keep

ahtoli (ahtol-) (PV) over and over;' again and again; keeps on...

't-ahtolotutuwatomon (TI) he keeps it burning

'kolahman (AI+OBJ) he keeps anyone from using it

mec (P) still; yet; keep(s) on

woloposal, woloposumal, uloposal (TA) he keeps him warm

kelp

kaskolosihil (I) (pl.) kelp

key

apqasokihikon (I) key

kick

altehkasu (AI, II) it is kicked around

't-altehkomon (TI) he kicks it around

't-altehkuwal (TA) he kicks him around; he kicks it (an.) around

kidnap

'komutonalal (TA) he steals him, it (an.); he kidnaps him

kidney

puhkiluwan (A) kidney

kill

nehpahal (TA) he kills him

nehpahtun (TI) he kills it

'siktehkuwal (TA) he kills him by running into (or over) him with a vehicle

kind

-k(i)- look; be of a kind or nature

likon (II) it looks thus; it is of such and such a kind

liku (AI) he looks thus; he is of such and such a kind or nature

kindle

motutuwalal (TA) he starts it (an.) burning; he kindles it (an.)

motutuwatomon (TI) he starts it burning; he kindles it

'posqolenomon (TI) he kindles it

kinship

lakutuwakon (I) relationship; kinship

kiss

ucemal, wocemal (TA) he kisses him

knee

wotkul (A) (dep.) his knee

kneel

petkupu (AI) he kneels

knife

mihkutan (I) knife

mihqotakon (I) knife

't-olsal, 't-olosal (TA) he cuts it (an.) with a knife

't-olsomon, 't-olosomon (TI) he cuts it with a knife

knock

eqtihike (AI) he stops pounding; he stops knocking

'kotqihtahal (TA) he knocks him over

monapitehtahal (TA) he knocks his (someone else's) teeth out

'susqihtahal (TA) he knocks him flat on his back

knock-kneed

toqolukheku (AI) he is knock-kneed

knot

psketqon (I) knot (in wood)

knotty

lamatqoniw (AI) it (an.) is knotty inside

know

'kocicihtun (TI) he knows it

'kocicihtuwan (DOV) he knows something of his; he knows something about him

'kociciyal (TA) he knows him; he knows (someone else) what he is like

'kosicihtun (TI) he knows it

'kosiciyal (TA) he knows him

nonuwal (TA) he knows him; he recognizes him

'sesomitahamal (TA) he does not know about him; he cannot imagine about him

'sesomitahatomon (TI) he does not know about it; he cannot imagine about it

wewewestu (AI) he knows what he is talking about

wewoluhke (AI) he knows what to do

know how

'tawe (II) he knows how to talk

'tawi ('taw-) (PV) know how; be good at

'tawokisu (AI) he knows how to read

'tawtutuwe (AI) he knows how to build a fire

knowledgeably

wewi (wew-) (PV) correctly; knowledgeably; perceivably

L

ladder

latuwakon (I) ladder

lady

motaqs (A) lady; older woman (primarily a term of address)

lady's slipper (flower)

wihpulakson (A) lady's slipper

lake

kuspem (I) lake

pihtakome (II) it is a long lake

qonakome (II) the lake is long by so much

qospem (I) lake

land

ktahkomiq (I) land; ground; earth

milahkomike (II) it is hilly land

pokossin (AI) he falls down; it (an.) falls; he, it (an.) lands

tetpahkomike (II) it is flat land

language

latuwewakon (I) language

mocalokotune (AI) he has a dirty mouth (uses dirty language)

piluwatuwe (AI) he speaks a different language

lap
'tahsomeluk in his lap (Locative)
large
aqamkihqon (II) it is larger
last
peossolewey (A, I) last one
last night
welaqik (P) last night
wolaku (P) yesterday; last night
last winter
pun (I) winter; last winter
late
metsoqsu (AI) he sleeps late
later
temonu, temonuk (P) later; just a minute
laugh
-elom(i)- laugh, smile
siktiyelomu (AI) he laughs very hard
laundry
kostokonike (AI) he washes clothes; he does
   laundry
lay
olqehsin, luhkehsin (AI) he lays his head down
't-opqehsimuhtuwal (TA) he lays his head on him
't-opqehsinon (AI, AI+OBJ) he lays his head on
   it
ponatom (AI) she lays an egg (or eggs)
layer
nisekopu (AI) it (an.) has two layers
nisekte (II) it has two layers
'sekopu (AI) it (an.) has three layers
lazy
maleyu (AI) he is lazy
lead
piltal (I) lead (metal)
leaf
mip (I) leaf
leak
ciweiye (AI) it (an.) leaks
lean
apote (apotiy-) (PV) leaning
't-apotehsinon (AI, AI+OBJ) he stands leaning
   against it; he leans on it
't-apotepin (AI, AI+OBJ) he sits leaning against
   it
sasokuhqepu (AI) he half stands; he half sits; he
   is leaning against something
leave
alaptu (AI) he leaves tracks around
'cikihtomon (TI) he leaves it alone
'cikihtuwal (TA) he leaves him alone
macehe (AI) he leaves
macewse (AI) he starts out on foot; he leaves on
   foot; he starts to walk (toddler)
maciyapasuwok (AI) they (pl.) leave on foot;
   they start to walk (toddlers)
nokolal (TA) he leaves him
nokothal (TA) he leaves him behind (by leaving
   in a vehicle, a boat, in a race, etc.)
nokothomon (TI) he leaves it behind (by leaving
   in a vehicle, a boat, etc.)
nokotomon (TI) he leaves it
pecessu (AI) he comes and then leaves again
   immediately

pokahkonaptu (AI) he leaves bloody tracks
pomaptu (AI) he goes along leaving tracks
pusu (AI) he leaves by boat
'taptu (AI) he leaves tracks from there
lecture
mihkumal (TA) he preaches to him; he lectures
   to him; he councils him
left
pahtanom (AI) he is left-handed
'pahtat (I) (dep.) his left hand
leg
ewepikonatutom (AI) he has his leg propped up;
   he holds his leg up
ewepikonawu (AI) he holds his (own) leg up
kat (I) leg (including the foot)
tomikonatessu (AI) he breaks his (own) leg
legend
atkuhkakon (I) story; legend
atkuhke (AI) he tells an old story; he tells a
   legend
length
qoni (qon-) (PV) through or during a length of
   space or time
sasokatokot (II) it is a long straight length
let
't-apqasokahal (TA) he lets him out by unlocking
   a door, etc.
coke (P) here; let me see (indicates interest in
   something near the person spoken to); hmm,
   let me think; well, now...
'kiseltomuwal (TA) he lets him; he allows him;
   he permits him
'kocoskehlal (TA) he lets him loose
'kossehlal (TA) he lets him in
nutehlal, nutelal (TA) he gets him out, he lets him
   out; he puts him out
't-olahkan (AI, AI+OBJ) he throws it; he lets go
   of it; he drops it
letter
tpaskutikon (A) letter (of the alphabet); numeral
wikhikon (I) book; letter; any written material
lever stick
enuwaqhomakon (I) lever stick (placed over one
   shoulder and under a log one is carrying over
   the other shoulder, thus helping to distribute
   the log's weight)
libel
mocacomuwakon (I) false statement; libel; dirty
   story
library
wikhikonikuwam (I) library
lice
'tahqomiw (AI) he has lice
lick
nokkalahtomon (TI) he licked it all
nokkayahpal (TA) he licked it (an.) all
'sapolahtomon (TI) he licks through it
lid
kpihikon (I) lid; cover; dam
lie
alossin (AI) he lies around
-hsin(o)- lie down; be lying down
'koluskakonimal (TA) he lies about him

'koluskakonutomuwal (TA) he tells someone
  something false about him; he lies about him
kolusku (AI) he lies
lossin (AI) he lies down; he is lying down
nacossin (AI) he goes (or comes) and lies down
nopakotuwal (TA) he lies to him
-ossin(o)- lie down; be lying down
'pakotahsu (AI) he tells a lie
'pakotahsuwakon (I) lie
'pakotuwal (TA) he lies to him
pomaqte (II) it (something stick-like) lies there
pomossin (AI) he is lying down
'qosokahsinon (AI, AI+OBJ) he lies across it
'tehsahqossinon (AI, AI+OBJ) he lies on top of
  it

lieutenant governor
leptanet (A) lieutenant governor

life
apatawsu (AI) he comes back to life
pomawsuwakon (I) life

lift
't-ewepehlal (TA) he lifts him
't-ewepehtun (TI) he lifts it
't-eweponal (TA) he holds him up; he lifts him
  up
't-eweponomon (TI) he holds it up; he lifts it up
pahkuwon (II) the fog lifts
pahqonuwiye (II) the fog is lifting
'poqanal (TA) he can lift and carry him
'tehsahqehlal (TA) he lifts him up and puts him
  on top

light
lipkotenoma (AI) he lights a smudge
nokkahsuwehtun (TI) he puts it (fire, light) out
'posqolehtomon (TI) he lights it (something to
  smoke)
'posqolepal (TA) he lights it (an., something to
  smoke)
psqolehtoma, psqolehtome (AI) he lights up (a
  cigarette)

lightning
monomeqe (AI) lightning strikes

like
ansa (P) like; truly; really
'koselomal (TA) he likes him; he loves him
'koseltomon (TI) he likes it
'kosi ihin (TI) he likes it
'kosi iywal (TA) he likes him
'kositahamal (TA) he likes him
ksatke (AI) he likes the place so much that he
  stays longer
muhsalal (TA) he likes him very much
muhsaltomon (TI) he likes it very much
tahalu, talu (P) as; like
ulinomon, wolinomon (TI) he likes the way it
  looks
wikihtun (TI) he likes to make it
wikossomu (AI) he likes to drink; he is a
  drunkard
wikuwacehtun (TI) he likes to do it
wisokitahamal (TA) he likes him a lot
wisokitahatomon (TI) he likes it a lot
witapehkatomon (TI) he gets to like it

limb
psketqonhike (AI) he chops limbs off a tree

lime
akiyahq (A) stucco; plaster; lime

limp
alahkahamu (AI) he limps

line
lamkikapuwuwok (AI) they are standing in a line

lion
pihtal (A) lion

liquid
nopim (I) (dep.) his liquid; his drink (water, etc.)
psonpe (AI) it (an.) is full of liquid
tolapuwe (AI) he is drinking (anything); he is
  eating liquid food (soup, stew, etc.)
tuhpe (AI) it (an.) contains liquid

liquor
puktewick (I) liquor

listen
'ciksotomon (TI) he listens to it; he heeds it
'ciksotuwal (TA) he listens to him; he heeds him
ipa (P) hey!; listen!; look!

lit
possaqhe (AI, II) it is lit up

little
amuwyahsu (AI) he acts a little bit crazy
ankuwi- (ankuw-) (PV) further; a little further;
  beyond
ankuwiw (P) a little further
kekesk (P) a little; slightly
wahkathoma, wahkathome (AI) he has little sense

live
askomawsu (AI) he lives forever
-aws(i)- live
lawsu (AI) he lives there; he eats there
niseyiniyal (AI, AI+OBJ) he is living as married
  with her (or she...with him)
nisininiyal (AI, AI+OBJ) he lives with him
pomawsu (AI) he lives; he is alive
'qotuhkanu (AI) he lives alone
utawsin (AI, AI+OBJ) he survives it; he lives by
  means of it
wiku (AI) he lives (dwells) (in a place)
woleyu (AI) he is well off; he lives well
woneyu (AI) he is living in sin

liver
sqon (I) liver

load
pithasu (II) it is stuffed; it is loaded
'pitkatomuwan (DOV) he loads his (someone
  else's) gun
'pitkosewan (AI, AI+OBJ) he loads it (a gun)

loaf
opan (A) bread; piece of bread; loaf of bread
pqesikon (A) loaf of unsliced bread

lobster
'sak, sak (A) lobster

lock
'koppasokahmon (TI) he locks it
kpahasu (AI) he is locked up
kpahasu (II) it is locked

lodge
'possulin (AI, AI + OBJ) he has it lodged in his throat

log
ktuwan (A) big log for a fire
ku (A) log

log cabin
kuwehkewikuwam (I) log cabin

lonely
'kiwacehlal (TA) he makes him lonely
kiwacinaqot (II) it looks lonely
kiwaciye (AI) he is lonely
olomaskute (II) there is a long field

long
pihceyu (AI) it (an.) is long and inflexible
pihtahqot (II) it is long and stick-like
pihtakome (II) it is a long lake
pihtaqsu (AI) it (an.) is long and stick-like; it (an.) is tall and stick-like
pihtatokosu (AI) he is long (horizontally); it (an.) is long (said of something string-like)
pittokot (II) it is long (said of something string-like, or a film, story, etc.)
pittoksu (AI) it (an.) is long (said of something string-like)
qonakome (II) the lake is long by so much
qonatokosu, qontoksu (AI) he, it (an.) is long by so much
qonatokot, qontokot (II) it is long by so much

long ago
neke, neket (P) then, at that time (past); long ago
pihce (P) long ago

long time
'sipkaskuwyal (TA) he waits for him for a long time
sipki (sipk-) (PV) for a long time
sipkiw (P) for a long time
sipkiye (AI) he is gone for a long time

long way
tutopu (AI) he is far along (in rank, etc,; of a woman, in pregnancy); he is sitting a long way off

longingly
wewehsitahasu (AI) he thinks sympathetically, longingly, etc. about someone who has died

look
ipa (P) hey!; listen!; look!
-k(i)- look; be of a kind or nature
kiwacinaqot (II) it looks lonely
ksinuhkawinaqsu, ksinuhkewinaqsu (AI) he looks sick
ktomakiqewu (AI) he looks down and out
likon (II) it looks thus; it is such and such a kind
liku (AI) he looks thus; he is of such and such a kind or nature
mocinaqot (II) it looks bad
mocinaqsu (AI) he looks bad
't-olapomal (TA) he looks at him
't-olapotomon (TI) he looks at it
paliqewu (AI) he looks proud; he looks stuck up
paliqewu (AI) he looks proud; he looks stuck up
psahkeyuwinaqot (II) it looks regrettable; it looks tragic

psahkeyuwinaqot (II) it looks regrettable; it looks tragic
wapinaqot (II) it looks white
wewehsinaqot (II) it looks sorrowful (after a death)
wisokiluwehenaqsu (AI) he looks angry
wolinaqot (II) it looks good
wolinaqsu (AI) he looks good

look at
-apom- look at
-apotom- look at
'kikimapomal TA he looks at him secretly
lapomal (TA) he looks at him
't-olapotomuwan (DOV) he looks at it for him; he looks at something of his (someone else's)
't-osakihtun (TI) he looks at it
't-osakiyal (TA) he looks at him
qolapomal (TA) he won't look at him (because he is angry with him)

look back
qolopapessu (AI) he looks back quickly over his shoulder

look for
alikhahsu (AI) he looks around (for something)
'qiluwahal, 'kiluwahal (TA) he looks for him
'qiluwahtun, 'kiluwahtun (TI) he looks for it
'qiluwapomal, 'kiluwapomal (TA) he looks for him (specifically by vision)

look (watch)
alaputihike (AI) he looks around with a telescope; he looks around with binoculars
-ap(i)- look
lapu (AI) he looks (there)
laputihike (AI) he looks with a telescope, binoculars, etc.

loon
oqim (A) loon

loop
cokiqis (A) wart; decorative loop woven into the side of a basket

loose
'kocoskehlal (TA) he lets him loose

lose
'koskahtan (AI, AI + OBJ) he loses it
'koskahtun (TI) he loses it
'putoman (AI + OBJ) he loses it

lost
ksihkehe (AI) he is lost

lot
cossuwewihke (II) there are a lot of mosquitoes out
elinaqahk (II) there is a lot of it; there are a lot of them (inan.)
elinaqsit (AI) there is a lot of it (an.); there are a lot of them (an.)
kceyawiw (AI, II) there is a lot of it
koluskapiw (AI) he exaggerates or lies a lot; he tells tall tales
skuweyu (AI) he often spends a lot of time (there)
tpolukemosku (AI) he gossips a lot
wisokitahamal (TA) he likes him a lot
wisokitahatomon (TI) he likes it a lot

loud
cipoki (cipok-) (PV) loud
cipokihtaqot (II) it is noisy; it is loud
naskahtaqsu (AI) he is loud and angry, obnoxious
loud-mouth
cipokalokotune (AI) he is a loud-mouth
louse
oqom (A) louse
love
'koselomal (TA) he likes him; he loves him
ksiyaqsu (AI) he loves children
low
cinituwiye (AI) he flies low
kiskot (II) it is low tide
lowest
ksihkot (II) the tide is at its lowest (in its monthly cycle); it is neap tide
luck
't-ahtoptahal (TA) he hits him by luck
't-ahtoptehmon (TI) he hits it by luck
lump
woc (A) mound; mountain; lump
lunch
nimawonikhal (TA) he packs a lunch for him
lynx
apiqosikon (A) lynx

M

mackerel
amalomeq (A) mackerel
mad
'qayihtawotuwok (AI) they (du.) are mad at each other
uhkayihtuwal (TA) he is mad at him
wisokiluwehehtuwal (TA) he is mad at him
wisokiluwehtuwal (TA) he is mad at him
wisokiluweyuwal (TA) he makes him mad
maggot
puhkes (A) maggot
magnet
skonahq (A) magnet
make
't-aluwihtun (TI) he tries to make it and fails; he tries in vain to make it
't-amalhuwikhomon (TI) he writes it fancily; he makes it with fancy designs or colors; he decorates it
'cihtasu (II) it is made of (something)
'ciptinessu (AI) he makes a hand print
'kinuwehlal (TA) he notifies him; he makes it (an.) in his own special way
'kisihtun (TI) he made it; he can make it
'kisiyal (TA) he made it (an.); he can make it (an.)
kotuwihtasu (II) it is going to be made
nisihtuniyal (TI) they (two) make it together
't-olapuhkewal (TA) he makes soup (stew, etc.) for him
't-otolapuwhal (TA) he is making soup (stew, etc.) for him

posonutehke (AI) he makes baskets
'qecihtun, 't-oqecihtun (TI) he tries to make it
ucihtun (TI) he makes it (of something)
wikihtun (TI) he likes to make it
make (cause)
'kiwacehlal (TA) he makes him lonely
'kosinuhkuwal (TA) he makes him sick
miyawiluweyuwal (TA) he makes him very happy
nihluweyuwal (TA) he makes trouble for him
'patosikhal (TA) he makes him choke on smoke
'pecimal (TA) he makes him come by talking or calling to him
'sestahal (TA) he makes him cry
'siktehkomon (TI) he makes it (a part of the body) go to sleep (e.g. he makes his leg go to sleep by the way he is sitting)
'siktehkomuwan (DOV) he makes it (a part of the body) go to sleep on him (e.g. a child making his mother's leg go to sleep by the way he is sitting on her lap)
ulitahasuwehlal (TA) he makes him happy
usikiyal (TA) he makes him suffer; he punishes him
wisokiluweyuwal (TA) he makes him mad
make (force to)
'kisehtuwan (DOV) he made him do it
'koptunahal (TA) he makes him shut up
't-oluhkekhal (TA) he makes him work; he puts him to work
'qolopehlal (TA) he turns him over; he makes him change his mind
make friends
witapehkamal (TA) he makes friends with him; he is friendly to him
witapehkanol (AI, AI+OBJ) he makes friends with him
witapehkewal (TA) he makes friends for someone
make fun
malikikemosku (AI) he is someone who makes fun of people
malikikemu (AI) he makes fun of (someone)
malikimal (TA) he makes fun of him
male
napehsom (A) male animal
Maliseet
Wolastokuk St. John River (Locative); Maliseet country (Locative)
Wolastoq (A) a Maliseet
Maliseet-Passamaquoddy
skicinuwatuwe (AI) he speaks an Indian lanuage; he speaks Maliseet-Passamaquoddy
mallet
lakomakon (A) round-headed mallet
man
skitap (A) man
skitapewehlosu (AI) he (e.g., an animal) turns himself into a man; she turns herself into a man
tqesuwapiw, tqesuwapihiw (AI) he is a shy man
many
kakehsukoniw (P) for many days; for several days
kceyawi (kceyaw-) (PV) much; many
kehsi (kehs-, kes-) (PV) X much; X many

ktanaqsuwok, ktenaqsuwok (AI) there are many of them (an.)

mili (mil-) (PV) many; various; in a variety of ways

milluhke (AI) he does many things; he causes many kinds of trouble

many times

sawe (sawiy-) PV often; many times

maple syrup

mahqan (I) sap of the sugar maple; maple syrup (or sugar); anything sweet

marker

toqoss (A) marker (in a game)

marrow

winis (I) bone marrow

marry

copkatom (AI) he is married

cpahkatom, copkatom (AI) he is married

kiskatom (AI) he got married

nipuwamal (TA) he marries her (or she...him)

nipuwikhal (TA) he marries him (performs the wedding ceremony)

nisuwiniyal (AI, AI + OBJ) he is married to her (or she...to him)

nutiyahkatom (AI) he is married out of his group

pilkatom (AI) he is newly married

Mary

Sakomawi Mali (A) the Virgin Mary

mass

olomeske (AI) he says mass

mat

nekosun (A, I) sleeping mat (blanket, animal skin, etc.)

't-onekosunol, 't-onekosun (A, I) his sleeping mat

mature

kisikon (II) it is full grown; it is mature

maul

nukcoktihikon (A) a maul; pounding tool

maybe

cipotu, cipotuk (II (?)) it is possible; maybe; perhaps

eluwehkal (P) of course; must be; maybe

me

nil (A) (PRO) I, me

means

utawsin (AI, AI + OBJ) he survives it; he lives by means of it

measure

tpaskutike (AI) he measures

measuring stick

tpaskutikon (I) measuring stick

meat

pehqey (I) meat obtained by hunting; wild meat

wiyuhs (I) meat (See also: animal names.)

medal

imiyewissul (A) religious medal

medicine

't-ahsihpilal (TA) he gives him medicine

'kissihpilal (TA) he gave him medicine

paqolus (A) medicinal plant species (ginseng?)

'pisun, npisun (I) medicine

meet

assihkawe (AI) he meets someone

assihkawotuwok (AI) they (dual) meet

't-assihkuwal (TA) he meets him

natassihkuwal (TA) he goes to meet him

meeting

mawe putuwosuwok (AI) they (pl.) come together and hold a council meeting

melt

qasomiye (AI) it (an.) melts

qasqomehe (AI) it (an.) melts by degree

'qasqomesomon (TI) he melts it

qasqomessu (AI) it (an.) melts

mention

nostuhmon (TI) he reveals it by saying it; he mentions it

nostuwal (TA) he understands him; he mentions him

'sotuwa (TA) he is understood, mentioned

mess

't-uwapolehtun (TI) he messes it up; he does it wrong

message

ankuwacomu (AI) he relays a message; he brings a report of; he interprets (translates)

kinuwehtahsu (AI) he delivers a message

messenger

kinuwehtahsuwin (A) messenger

messy

mocuwe (AI) he has messy hair

Micmac

mihkom (A) Micmac Indian

Mihkomahkik Micmac territory (Locative)

mihkomasqehs (A) Micmac woman

middle

epahsakom (P) in the middle of a lake (See also: suwaskutew, suwasokiw, suwawtiw.)

epahsi (epahs-, epas-) (PV) half, halfway; in the middle; in two, in half

epahsitpuhkot (II) it is midnight; it is the middle of the night

epahsiw (P) halfway; in the middle

midge

sipunis (A) midge, no-see-um

midnight

epahsitpuhkot (II) it is midnight; it is the middle of the night

midnight mass

nipayimiye (AI) he goes to midnight mass

mile

kehsuhsalqot (II) it is so many miles (land measure)

nanuhsalqot (II) it is five miles

newuhsalqot (II) it is four miles

nisuhsalqot (II) it is two miles

'qotuhsalqot (II) it is one mile

'suhsalqot (II) it is three miles

milk

molaqs (A) milk

molaqsinut (A) milk container

million

kehsalokamqahk (P) millions

'qotalokamqahk (P) one million

mind

'qolopitahamal (TA) he changes his mind about
  him

'qolopitahatomon (TI) he changes his mind about
  it

mine

nil (A) (PRO) I, me; my; mine

mink

ciyahkehs (A) mink

ciyahkehsuhke (AI) he hunts (or traps) mink

mirror

nucahkomasut (pinucahkomkat, penucahkomat,
  pinucahkomat) (I) mirror

miscarriage

putoma (AI) she has a miscarriage

mischief .

milehtakesku (AI) he is a joker; he is always
  getting into mischief

mischievous

milomahtu (AI) he is mischievous

miss

'polaphal (TA) he misses his tracks

'polhal (TA) he misses him (with a shot)

polhike (AI) he misses his target (with a shot)

polosehta (AI) he (a nursing baby) misses the
  nipple when nursing

'poltahal (TA) he misses him (with a blow)

mist

pkotewpiw (II) there is mist over the water

wonpeq (I) mist over water

misty

pkotete (II) it is smoky, misty

uwon (II) it is foggy; it is misty

misunderstand

'polsotuwal (TA) he misunderstands him; he
  disobeys him

mitten

mulcess (A) mitten

mix

opanke (AI) he mixes bread dough

wawikehtun, 't-uwawikehtun (TI) he mixes it

wawikiw (P) mixed together with

moccasin

olonakson (A) moccasin

Mohawk

meqiyik, meqihik (A) Mohawks

mold

tupankakon (A) mold for making bread

mole

posokiyan (I) mole (on skin)

money

man (I) money

manimiw, manimu (AI) he has money

month

kisuhs (A) sun; moon; month

moon

kisuhs (A) sun; moon; month

nipawset (A) the moon

paqahson (II) the moon is shining

moose

mus (A) moose

musuhke (AI) he hunts moose

moose call

putuwakon (I) whistle; moose-call (or anything
  one makes noise with by blowing)

more

aqami (aqam-) (PV) more

aqamok, aqamk (P) more; more than; anymore

more and more

ahaciw (P) gradually; more and more

moreover

tuciw (P) moreover; besides; right away

morning

sepay (P) this morning (past only)

spasuwiw (P) in the morning

mosquito

cossu (A) mosquito

cossuwewekon (I) mosquito net; gauze

cossuwewihke (II) there are a lot of mosquitoes
  out

most

piyemi (piyem-) (PV) the most

moth

kuhkukhahsis (A) moth (See kuhkukhahs.)

mother

mamam (A) mother

nika mother (term of address)

wikuwossol (A) (dep.) his mother

mound

woc (A) mound; mountain; protruding lump

mountain

ktoton (A) mountain

woc (A) mound; mountain; protruding lump

mourn

nihtakihtomuwal (TA) he is in mourning for him

nihtakihtuwal, 'takihtuwal (TA) he mourns for
  him

'taku (AI) he is in mourning

mouse

apiqsehsis (Passamaquoddy) (A) mouse (See
  apiqsehs.)

tuhkis (A) mouse (Maliseet)

mouth

'koptunenal (TA) he covers his (someone else's)
  mouth with his hand

lamaqtun (I) inside of the mouth

popu (AI) he (a child) has a rash on his tongue
  and inside his mouth

'tun (I) (dep.) his mouth

move

acessu (AI, II) he, it moves to a different location

aciye (AI) he moves to a different location

aciye (II) it moves to a different location; it is...
  o'clock

ewepamu (AI) he moves rapidly upward
  (involuntarily)

kikimskahsu (AI) he moves along without making
  any noise

macehlal (TA) he moves him

macessu (AI, II) he, it moves

maciyamkessu (II) it moves in a mass of pieces

maciyessu (II) it starts to move; it moves along

milkomon (TI) he moves it every which way; he
  drives it (e.g., a car) erratically

'panekonal (TA) he uncovers it (an.) by moving
  something sheet-like aside with his hand

paskoloqessu (AI) he is moving across the ice as it cracks

poli (pol-) (PV) moving away; moving out of the way

sasokiye (AI) he moves in a straight line

tolotomhe (AI, II) he, it is moving (sliding, rolling, etc.) with a smooth, gliding motion

move (household)

petute (AI) he moves (his household) into...

tolute (AI) he is moving (changing residence)

move out

'cikawi nutehkuwal (TA) he forces him to move out

moved

qolopihtahasu (II) it is moved a little by accident

much

kceyawi (kceyaw-) (PV) much; many

kehsi (kehs-, kes-) (PV) X much; X many

muck

mosson (I) muck

mucus

cahlak (A) nasal mucus

cahlakiw (AI) he has nasal mucus on him

mud

sosq, ososq (I) stove ashes mixed with water; mud

muscle

wolanol (A) (dep.) his calf (of the leg); his muscle

musician

nutapektuhusit (A) musician who plays a stringed instrument; fiddler

muskrat

kiwhos (A) muskrat

kiwhosuhke (AI) he hunts muskrats; he traps muskrats

must

cuwi, ahcuwi (ehcuwi) (PV) must; should; have to

must be

eluwehkal (P) of course; must be; maybe

possaqal (P) must be

my

nil (A) (PRO) I, me; my; mine

N

nail

cossokhikon (I) nail

wokosiyil (A) (dep.) his fingernail; his claw, nail

name

liwihtasu (II) it is called, named

liwisu (AI) he is named; he is called

't-oliwihtomon (TI) he calls it (by a name); he names it

't-oliwiyal (TA) he calls him (by a name); he names him

weyossisuwiwisu (AI) he has an animal name

-wis-(i) be named

narrative

akonutomakon (I) story; account; narrative

nature

liku (AI) he looks thus; he is of such and such a kind or nature

olomahtu (AI) he acts thus; he has such and such a nature

-omaht(u)- act; be of a nature; behave

navel

wiloss (I) (dep.) his navel

neap tide

ksihkot (II) the tide is at its lowest (in its monthly cycle); it is neap tide

sincokkot (II) the tide is at its lowest in its monthly cycle it is neap tide

near

qihiw (P) near; by

wecuwawkomon (TI) he gets closer to it; he nears it

wecuwawsu (AI) he is near

nearly

eluwe (P) almost; nearly (indicates final state, activity completed--compare keka)

'kocoskeksomon (TI) he nearly cuts it (a part of his body), but misses

neck

topskuhk (A) neck

necklace

pokossuhunol (I) (pl.) necklace

psihkuwosuwon (I) necklace

need

nituwin (AI, AI+OBJ) he needs it

pawalqot (II) it is needed

needle

sahkat (A) needle

nest

ksossiyehsu (AI) it (an.) nests

wososs (I) nest

net

nihtaphal (TA) he nets it (an., a fish)

nevertheless

tepot (P) nevertheless; however

new

pili (pil-) (PV, PN) new

newly

pilkatom (AI) he is newly married

news

akonutome (AI) he talks; he tells a story; he reports news

next

apc (P) again; else; next

macekotok next year

nice

wolkil (AI) he is nice and big

wollamson (II) there is a nice breeze; there is a breeze from a good direction, etc.

woluwe (AI) he has nice hair; he has nice fur

nickname

amalhiwisu (AI) he has a nickname

't-amalhiwiyal (TA) he nicknames him

night

epahsitpuhkot (II) it is midnight; it is the middle of the night

nightmare
cipqahsin (AI) he has a nightmare
cipqam (AI) he has a nightmare of falling; he jumps in his sleep or when dozing
nihkoskawe (AI) he has a nightmare (of being unable to move)
nine
esqonatek (P) nine
nit
konasis (A) nit
konasisuwatpe (AI) he has nits in his hair
no
konotiri (P) no (slang, Indian Township, Maine)
kotama, katama (P) no; not
ma (P) not; no
nama (P) no
ne (P) no (sassy)
no-see-um
sipunis (A) midge, no-see-um
noise
eqtaqsu (AI) he stops making noise (by mouth)
kikimskahsu (AI) he moves along without making any noise
nikcahkehtun (TI) he (e.g. a rutting animal) tears it (e.g. the ground) up noisily and angrily
noisy
cipokihtaqot (II) it is noisy; it is loud
noon
pasqe (II) it is noon
north
lahtoqehsonuk north (Locative)
northern lights
nipayapon (II) the northern lights are shining
nose
'koppihtonenal (TA) he holds his (someone else's) nose closed
pehkehkihtone (AI) he has a nosebleed
'pehkehkihtonehtahal (TA) he bloodies his (someone else's) nose
qonasqihtone, qinusqihtone (AI) he has a pointed nose
soniku (AI) he blows his nose
wihton (I) (dep.) his nose; his (a bird's) bill, beak
nose and mouth
'cehtu (AI) he hemorrhages through the nose and mouth
nostril
wihtonaloq (I) nostril
not
kat (P) not (used to deny an identification; compare ma, kotama "not")
kotama, katama (P) no; not
ma (P) not; no
mus, musa, musahk (P) not; don't
ska, skat (P) not; if not
not at all
katekon (P) not at all
not even
muck (P) (not) even
not well off
ktomakiku (AI) he is in bad shape; he is not well off

not yet
mesq (P) not yet; before
nothing but
kcoci (P) all alike; nothing but
notify
'kinuwehlal (TA) he notifies him; he makes it (an.) in his own special way
now
toke (P) now
tokec (P) now; if
yut (P) here; now
nuisance
cossinaqsu (AI) he is bothersome; he is a nuisance
numeral
tpaskutikon (A) letter (of the alphabet); numeral
nun
sistoss (A) nun, religious sister
nurse
polosehta (AI) he (a nursing baby) misses the nipple when nursing (See breast-feed.)

obliquely
asuwiw (P) crooked; at an angle; obliquely
obnoxious
naskahtaqsu (AI) he is loud and angry, obnoxious
observance
'qossihtun (TI) he pays reverence to it; he follows the proper observances with respect to it he cherishes it
'qossiyal (TA) he follows the proper observances with respect to him
ocean
supeq (I) salt water; ocean
o'clock
aciye (II) it moves to a different location; it is... o'clock
of course
coqahk, cu kahk (P) sure; of course
eluwehkal (P) of course; must be; maybe
kat olu (P) of course
off
't-amihkuhtuwal (TA) he throws him off (in wrestling)
'kahsihputun (TI) he dries it off; he wipes it dry
ketolaskessu (AI) it (an.) slips off
'kettahal (TA) he chops it (an.) off
'kettehmon (TI) he chops it off
'kisamihkuhtuwal (TA) he threw him off (in wrestling); he can throw him him off (in wrestling)
monessu (AI) it (an.) peels off; he gets off, gets out of a trap
monhomon (TI) he skims it off
moniptinephal (TA) he pulls his (someone else's) hand quickly off (something)
monnomon (TI) he peels it off
peskote (II) it shoots off; it blows up

office
amke (AI) he plays a game; he runs for an office
litposuwakon (I) office, position (in an organization, government, etc.)
litposuwin (A) office holder; tribal council member
piyemitposu (AI) he has more power than anyone else; he is in a higher office than anyone else

often
puskiw (P) sometimes; often
sawe (sawiy-) PV often; many times
sawecuwe (AI) she has children often
sawew (P) often

oil
mimey (I) grease; oil

old
kci (kc-, kt-) (PV, PN) big; great; old
kcikotone (AI) he is old
mehtatom (AI) he dies of old age

old maid
mehtatomi naksq (A) old maid

old man
ktaqhomuhs (A) old man

old person
'kansuhs (A) old person; person who lived long ago

omen
cilomotome, cilomotoma (AI) he receives a sign; he is haunted; he receives an omen

on
nahsehtun (TI) he puts it (clothing) on
naste (II) it (clothing) is on; it (clothing) is being worn
'posokapecin (AI, AI+OBJ) he scratches himself on it
'possahtuwehtun (TI) he puts it (a light) on
'sicihqehmon (TI) he pastes it on
skitpeq (P) on the water
'tapotehsinon (AI, AI+OBJ) he stands leaning against it; he leans on it
'tehsaqtehsinon (AI, AI+OBJ) he falls on it
toqci (toqc-, toqt-) (PV) on
'toqtopin (AI, AI+OBJ) he sits on it
wiphunhasu (II) it is feathered; it has a feather (or feathers) on it

on foot
macehkawotuwok (AI) they (dual) start out on foot; they (dual) start to walk (toddlers)
macewse (AI) he starts out on foot; he leaves on foot; he starts to walk (toddler)
maciyapasuwok (AI) they (pl.) leave on foot; they start to walk (toddlers)

on the contrary
cu (P) yes, why yes; for sure; (when the answer "no" is expected or disbelief expressed) on the contrary; for sure

on the go
'tomiye (AI) he is always on the go

on top
tehsahqi (tehsahq-, tehsaq-) (PV) on top of
tehsahqiw (P) above; on top
'tehsaqopin (AI, AI+OBJ) he sits on top of it
tehsaqotokku (AI) he jumps on top
uskitewolal (TA) he puts it (an.) on top

on top of that
nihluwinaw, nihluwinaq (P) to make matters worse; on top of that

once
ehtahsikiskot (II) it is once a day
neqt (P) one (in counting); once

one
neqt (P) one (in counting); once
peskuhs (A) one; one of them; one of them in particular
pesq (P) one (in counting)
pesq (A) one
'qoci ('qoc-, 'qot-) (PV) one; alone
'qocikoton (II) it is one year
'qotakisu (A) one dollar
'qotalokamqahk (P) one million
'qotatokiye (II) it is one string (e.g. of beads); it has one strand
'qotatokot (II) it is one continuous length (in space or time)
'qotuhsalqot (II) it is one mile
'qotulom (AI) he is in a canoe alone; he has one point (in the traditional dice game, altestakon)

one who
tan + Pronoun -ever; the one who, the one which; which one of... (these, those, them)?

onion
psehpon (A) onion

only
onote (P) only (sense of disappointment)
tehpu, tehpukt (P) only (restrictive); just; all; the only thing

open
't-apqotehmuwan (DOV) he opens it for him
't-apqotehtun (TI) he opens it
apskapu (AI) his eyes are open
panekopu (AI) it (an.) is open
panekte (II) it is folded open

operate
'tusal (TA) he operates on him

or
kosona (P) or

orange
alonocis, alinocis (I) orange (fruit)

orphan
kiposs (A) orphan (one or both parents dead)

osprey
isomeqehs A fish hawk; osprey

otter
kiwonik (A) otter

ouch!
okiya, okeya (P) ouch!

our
kilun (A) (PRO) we, us; our, ours (including you)
nilun (A) (PRO) we, us; our, ours (not including you)

out
'kisekehlal (TA) he spread (an., sheetlike) it out
milawiw (P) out in the water; out on the ice
muskiye (AI, II) he, it comes out
nute (nutiy-) (PV) out; going out; coming out
nutehlal, nutelal (TA) he gets him out, he lets him out; he puts him out

nutiyamu (AI, II) he, it falls out (of a window, basket, etc.)

't-olahkalusonahal (TA) he fences him out (or in)

pisi (pis-) (PV) into, out (through a boundary in either direction)

pisiw (P) into, out (through a boundary in either direction)

out of

akuwi (akuw-) (PV) behind (something); in back; out of view

akuwiw (P) behind; in back; out of view

'ci ('c-, 't-) (PV) from; out of; on account of

kahtopassu (AI) he gets out of the water

koloqesson, koloqoskesson (II) it is twisted out of joint (of a bone)

koloqessu (II) it is twisted out of joint (of a bone)

out of the way

piluhse (AI) he gets out of the way

out to get

'kotunolal (TA) he hunts him; he is out to get him

outdoors

qocom (I) the outdoors

oven

'pisacqehtun (AI) he puts it into the oven

over

cituwessu (AI) he bends over

kipiye (AI) he falls over

'kotqihtahal (TA) he knocks him over

kpoton (II) it is frozen over; it is frozen shut (e.g., a faucet)

mehtonaskiye (II) it is all over; it is all finished

mettaqot (II) it stops playing (radio, record, etc.); it is over; the sound stops

mettokot (II) it is over; it comes to an end

napisqahman (AI, AI+OBJ) he trips over it

pasici (pasic-, pasit-) (PV) over; on (or to) the other side; passing over

pasiciw (P) over; on the other side;

pomikoton (II) the year is not over yet; the year is going on

'qolopehlal (TA) he turns him over; he makes him change his mind

ucihponoltiniya (AI, AI+OBJ) they fight (each other) over (or about) it

over and over

ahtoli (ahtol-) (PV) over and over; again and again; keeps on...

upiye (AI) he comes in over and over

over-sexed

maskap (A) stud; over-sexed man

maskapiw (AI) he is over-sexed

over that way

oloqi (oloq-) (PV) in that direction; over that way

oloqiw (P) in that direction; over that way

over the water

ckuwinuwe (II) the wind is coming up over the water

pkotewpiw (II) there is mist over the water

over there

waht (P) far away; over there; far off

over to one side

asuwocokahte (II) it has slid over to one side; it has flopped over to one side

oversleep

kespoqsu (AI) he oversleeps

owe

ucanomuwan (DOV) he owes it to him

owl

kamkamoss (A) barn owl

kuhkukhahs (A) owl species; moth (diminutive only); block and tackle (Pleasant Point, Maine)

tihtokol (A) owl species (great horned owl?)

own

'topelomal (TA) he owns it (an.)

'topeltomon (TI) he owns it

tpeltom (AI) he owns

P

pace

elomelkimok (II) so many yards; so many paces (land measure)

olomelku (AI) he paces off so much

pack

nimawonikhal (TA) he packs a lunch for him

'pitkatomon (TI) he packs it (puts it in a pack, a bag, etc.)

'pitkoman (AI, AI+OBJ) he packs it; he makes preparations with it

'pitkomewal (TA) he packs for him; he makes preparations for him

'pitkotomon (TI) he packs it (a pack, a bag, etc.)

'pitkotomuwan (DOV) he packs it for him

'pitkotomuwewal (TA) he packs for him; he makes preparations (e.g. winterizing a house) for him

pack basket

pomutewey (I) pack basket

pack down

skihkipolasu (AI) it (an.) is packed down by tramping

pack sled

suwhewik (I) moose sled; bob sled; pack sled

paddle

cihcihke (AI) he paddles in the back of a canoe (steers)

nihkanke (AI) he paddles in the front of a canoe

peci suku (AI) he comes paddling

pomi suku (AI) he paddles (or rows) along

sehkehepiye, sehkahapiye (AI) he paddles standing up

sehtawtahapiye (AI) he paddles backwards

'silom (AI) he is paddling alone

'tahakon (I) paddle

tolisuku (AI) he is paddling

pail

sihpac (A) pail

wapahkuhs (A) pail; bucket

pain

'kosinuhkan (AI, AI + OBJ) he is sick; he has pain in it

mosopine (AI) he has hip pain

petahkemolsu (AI) he has a sharp pain (from pleurisy)

paint

lilomonhikon (I) paint

wikhike (AI) he writes, paints, draws, takes a picture, etc.

palm

lamiptin (I) palm (of the hand)

't-olamilc (I) (dep.) his palm (of the hand)

paper

pilasq (I) paper

pilasqhike (AI) he papers (a wall)

par-boil

puskolahqe (AI) he par-boils something

'puskolaqosal (TA) he par-boils it (an.)

'puskolaqosomon (TI) he par-boils it

park

conte (II) it is parked (of a vehicle)

part

possetokahmuwal (AI) he parts his hair

'possetokahmuwan (DOV) he parts it (his hair) for him

possetoqahal (TA) he parts his (someone else's) hair

particular

kinuwosu (AI) he is a certain one; he is a particular one

kinuwot (II) it is a particular one

partition

tomsokhasu (II) it is divided by a partition (e.g., a room)

partridge

mociyehs (A) partridge

mociyehsuhke (AI) he hunts partridges

Passamaquoddy

peskotomuhkat, pestomuhkat (A) a Passamaquoddy

pestomuhkati (PN) Passamaquoddy

Pestomuhkatik Passamaquoddy territory (Locative)

passing over

pasici (pasic-, pasit-) (PV) over; on (or to) the other side; passing over

past

asitiw (P) in the distant past

kisi (kis-) (PV) (indicates completion or past time)

mecimiw (P) formerly; used to; in the past

paste

'sicihqehmon (TI) he pastes it on

path

awt (I) road; path

pay

apenke (AI) he pays

't-apenkotuwewal (TA) he pays (for something) for him

't-apenkuwal (TA) he pays him

't-apenkuwan (DOV) he pays him with it

'qossihtun (TI) he pays reverence to it; he follows the proper observances with respect to it; he cherishes it

pear

sikusq (A) widow; pear; beetle species

peel

monessu (AI) it (an.) peels off; he gets off, gets out of a trap

monhiqe (AI) he peels off bark

monnomon (TI) he peels it off

'poqqonahqehlal (TA) he peels it (an., something stick-like)

'poqqonahqehtun (TI) he peels it (something stick-like)

'poqqonaskehtun (TI) he peels it

'poqqonhal (TA) he peels it (an.)

'poqqonomon (TI) he peels it

pqonahqehtasu (AI, II) it (something stick-like) is peeled

pqonhike (AI) he peels bark off

pencil

wikhikoney (I) pencil

Penobscot

panuwapskew (A) a Penobscot

Penobscot River

Panuwapskewtoq (I) Penobscot River

pepper

tehpisewey (I) pepper (ground black pepper, green pepper, etc.)

perceivably

wewi (wew-) (PV) correctly; knowledgeably; perceivably

perch

acaqaluhs, aqacaluhs (A) yellow perch

puhkakon (A) white perch

perhaps

cipotu, cipotuk (II (?)) it is possible; maybe; perhaps

periwinkle

pukocalahs (A) periwinkle

permit

'kiseltomuwal (TA) he lets him; he allows him; he permits him

Perry

Wehqapiqek Perry, Maine (Locative)

person

alitahasuwinuwiw (AI) he is a wise person; he is a thinker

'kansuhs (A) old person; person who lived long ago

Motahkomiqew (A) a person from Peter Dana Point, Maine

piluwikemosku (AI) he spreads false stories a lot; he is a jealous person

Sipayikew (A) person from Pleasant Point, Maine

pet

utuwheminol (AI, AI + OBJ) he has it (an.) as a pet

uwhem (A) pet

Peter Dana Point

Motahkokmikuk Peter Dana Point, Maine (Locative)

physic
sapossomu (AI) he takes a physic
pick
mahsuske (AI) he picks fiddleheads
mokonal (TA) he picks him out
pickerel
qonus (A) pickerel
pickle
salawehtasu (II) it is pickled in salt; it is salted
piece
't-apseksal (TA) he slices it (an.) into thin pieces
't-apseksomon (TI) he slices it into small pieces
't-apsihtahal (TA) he chops it (an.) into small pieces
't-apsihtehmon (TI) he chops it into small pieces
'kessal (TA) he cuts so much of it (an.); he cuts it (an.) into so many pieces
'kessomon (TI) he cuts so much of it; he cuts it into so many pieces
maciyamkessu (II) it moves in a mass of pieces
nukcoktahal (TA) he smashes it (an.); into small pieces; he smashes it (an.) (something soft)
nukcoktehmon (TI) he smashes it into small pieces; he smashes it (something soft)
'poqqenal (TA) he breaks a piece off of it (an.) with his hand
'poqqesal (TA) he slices a piece off of it
'soqskosal (TA) he cuts him up into pieces
ucikpenal (TA) he breaks a piece off of it (an.) by hand
utsal (TA) he cuts a piece from it
utsomon (TI) he cuts a piece from it
utsomuwan (DOV) he cuts a piece from something of his (someone else's); he cuts a piece of it for him
pig
piks (A) pig
pigeon
poles (A) pigeon; dove
pile
laqe (II) it is piled up
matayamkahte (II) a pile reaches its end
pillow
opqehsimutiyey (I) pillow case
puhkehsimut, opqehsimut (I) pillow
pilot
nucituwiye (AI) he flies (a plane) on a regular basis; he pilots
pimple
meqehsis (A) pimple
pin
winiyal (TA) he pins him to the ground
pine
kuwes (A) pine
pins and needles
koskimkasuwiw (II) it (a part of the body) goes to sleep; it feels like pins and needles (sensation in skin)
pipe
pitsone (AI) he fills his (own) pipe
'pitsonewal (TA) he fills his pipe for him
pitsonosu (AI) he stuffs his (own) pipe
ponapsqahson (A) stone pipe
'tomakon (A) pipe (for smoking)

'tomakonahtoq (A) pipe stem stove pipe
wihqipkotehtamu (AI) he inhales smoke from a pipe
pistol
lamsewey (I) pistol
pitch
kuwesihq (A) pine pitch
pupukhawihqe (AI) he gathers balsam fir pitch
pitch (in baseball)
ehetuwosqone (AI) he can pitch (in baseball) with either arm (literally, with either elbow); he is ambidextrous
pitcher
nutahket (A) pitcher (in baseball)
pity
'kotomakitahamal (TA) he pities him
plaintain
sekotepokahtek (I) plaintain leaf
plan
pahtawe (AI) his plans are not to work out
plant
kihke (AI) he plants
't-okihkan (AI+OBJ) he plants with it
't-okihkatomon (TI) he plants it
plaster
akiyahq (A) stucco; plaster; lime
akiyaqhasu (II) it is stuccoed, plastered
akiyaqhike (AI) he stuccoes; he plasters
't-akiyaqhomon (TI) he stuccoes it; he plasters it
plate
walot (A) plate; dish; bowl
play
amke (AI) he plays a game; he runs for an office
epeskome (AI) he plays ball
nisayye, nisahye (AI) he plays with someone
'pahpiyal (TA) he plays with him
pahpu (AI) he plays
tolayye, tolahye (AI) he is playing
wikossu (AI) he plays (said of children)
witayye, witahye (AI) he plays with him
play (music)
-apektuhus(i)- play a stringed instrument
kotuhmahsu (AI) he plays the drum
lapektuhusu (AI) he plays a stringed instrument
mettaqot (II) it stops playing (radio, record, etc.); it is over; the sound stops
playing card
tolehp (A) playing card
Pleasant Point
Sipayik Pleasant Point, Maine (Locative)
pleasantly
ulimal (TA) he talks to him pleasantly
please
mecopal (P) please; would it be possible?
'palitahasikhal (TA) he pleases him
palitahasu (AI) he is pleased; he is proud
ulasuwiyal (TA) he pleases him
pleurisy
'cipiluwehs (A) pleurisy; epilepsy; muscle spasms
plow
lahkesawakon (I) plow
't-otolahkesal (TA) he is plowing it (an.)
't-otolahkesomon (TI) he is plowing it
tolahkesawe (AI) he plows

pocket

pitsonakon (I) pocket

point

'qotulom (AI) he is in a canoe alone; he has one point (in the traditional dice game, altestakon)

point in

wewtuhkesite (AI) his feet point in when he walks

point out

panuwosite (AI) his feet point out (when he walks)

pointed

qinuskeyu, qonusqeyu (AI, II) it is sharp; it is pointed

qonasqihtone, qinusqihtone (AI) he has a pointed nose

poisoning

wolomon (A) blood poisoning

wolomonhuke (AI) he has blood poisoning

poke

'saphomuwan (DOV) he pokes, injects something of his (someone else's)

pole

alamkuhusu (AI) he poles himself around (in a boat)

opos (I) stick; pole

policeman

nuci tqonket (A) policeman

pollock

peskotom (A) pollock

pond

qotasq (I) pool of water; pond

poor

ktomakeyu (AI) he is poor

ktomaki (ktomak-) (PV, PN) poor; unfortunate

poplar

mit (I) poplar

porcupine

matuwehs (A) porcupine

pork

piksey (I) pork

sisolastike (AI) he fries pork

porpoise

cuspes (A) porpoise

cuspeske (AI) he hunts porpoise

position

litposuwakon (I) office, position (in an organization, government, etc.)

opu (AI) he sits; it (an.) is in position

ote (II) it is in position

piluwitposu (AI) he has a different position or office; he has extraordinary power

possible

cipotu, cipotuk (II (?)) it is possible; maybe; perhaps

possibly

pal (P) (indicates possibility and uncertainty; = op + al)

pot

katkuhk (A) cooking pot

potato

pekkiktehsok (I) potato slice cooked on stove top

pocetes (I) potato

tahkitom (A) wild potato

pound

eqtihike (AI) he stops pounding; he stops knocking

-kpehtihik(e)- pound ash logs (to obtain basket splints)

ksatokihtehsin (AI) it (an., a string-like object) strikes sharply against something; it (an., a string-like object) pounds against something

likpehtihike (AI) he pounds ash

nukcoktihikon (A) a maul; pounding tool

tolatokihtehson (II) it is pounding, throbbing (e.g., a pulse)

pour

'sukahtestun (TI) he pours it out; he empties it; he spills it (because it's too full or because he's not paying attention to it)

sukolan (II) it pours (rain)

power

piluwitposu (AI) he has a different position or office; he has extraordinary power

piluwitposuwakon (I) extraordinary power

piyemitposu (AI) he has more power than anyone else; he is in a higher office than anyone else

'samitposu (AI) he has awesome power

'samitpot (II) it has awesome power

powerful

tutsonu (AI) he is very strong; he is very powerful

practically

keka (P) almost, nearly; soon; practically, all but;

pray

imiye (AI) he prays

macemiye (AI) he starts to pray

sahsimiye (AI) he prays fast

sankewimiye (AI) he prays quietly; he prays calmly

wicimiye (AI) he prays with others

wiwonimiye (AI) he goes around to the Stations of the Cross; he goes around (something) praying

wiwonimiye (AI) he goes around to the Stations of the Cross; he goes around (something) praying

prayer

imiyewakon, imiyakon (I) prayer

papahtomuwakon (I) religion; prayer

'papahtomuwewal (TA) he says prayers for him

preach

mihkumal (TA) he preaches to him; he lectures to him; he councils him

precarious

nenehsawte (II) it could go either way; it could be changed, knocked off, etc., easily; it is precarious

pregnant

kinhoke (AI) she is pregnant

tupu (AI) she is pregnant (said of animals)

preparation

'pitkoman (AI, AI+OBJ) he packs it; he makes preparations with it

'pitkomewal (TA) he packs for him; he makes preparations for him

'pitkotomuwewal (TA) he packs for him; he makes preparations (e.g. winterizing a house) for him

press
'colokehlal (TA) he presses it (an.)
pretend
ksinuhkehkalsu (AI) he pretends to be sick
pretty
wolikossu (AI) she is pretty
previously
ewecitu (P) previously
priest
mihtaqs (A) father; priest
pahtoliyas (A) priest
pahtoliyasuwiw (AI) he is a priest
Princeton
Nolomok Princeton, Maine. (Locative)
problem
mamselessu (AI, II) he, it has many problems
prong
niktuwiku (AI) it (an.) has two prongs, branches, extensions, etc.
prop
't-apqotiyaqhomon (TI) he props it open with a stick
ewepikonatutom (AI) he has his leg propped up; he holds his leg up
proud
palapiw (AI) he is proud
palapuwitahasu (AI) he thinks proudly
paliqewu (AI) he looks proud; he looks stuck up
palitahasu (AI) he is pleased; he is proud
pucker
suwonhuke (AI) he puckers up from eating something sour
puddle
walcopekuhs (I) puddle
pull
moniptinephal (TA) he pulls his (someone else's) hand quickly off (something)
wihqahkan (AI, AI+OBJ) he pulls it (sharply)
wihqaqhal (TA) he pulls it (an.) with a hook
wihqaqhomon (TI) he pulls it with a hook
punish
usikiyal (TA) he makes him suffer; he punishes him
pupil
uskicinuhsisomol (A) (dep.) his pupil (of the eye)
pus
pimolehsun (I) pus
pimolehsuniw (AI) he has pus on him
push
'kosomahkalal (TA) he pushes him
'kosomahkan (AI, AI+OBJ) he pushes it
'kosomonal (TA) he pushes him
'kosomonomon (TI) he pushes it
'tepahkan (AI, AI+OBJ) he throws it in; he pushes it in; he drops it in
put
't-oluhkekhal (TA) he makes him work; he puts him to work
'pitkatomon (TI) he packs it (puts it in a pack, a bag, etc.)
'punal (TA) he puts him, it (an.) (somewhere)
'punomon (TI) he puts it (somewhere)
'saputehtun (TI) he puts it through

put away
wolewolal, ulewolal (TA) he arranges him; he puts it (an.) away
wolewotun, ulewotun (TI) he arranges it he puts it away
put down
'poneqehlal (TA) he gets him down; he puts him down
put in
sukonalokiqe (AI) he puts drops in his eyes
'sukoniqewal (TA) he puts drops in his (someone else's) eyes
put into
'pisacqehtun (AI) he puts it into the oven
put on
nahsehtun (TI) he puts it (clothing) on
put on top
'tehsahqehlal (TA) he lifts him up and puts him on top
uskitewolal (TA) he puts it (an.) on top
put out
nokkahsuwehtun (TI) he puts it (fire, light) out
nutehlal, nutelal (TA) he gets him out, he lets him out; he puts him out
'possahtuwehtun (TI) he puts it (a light) on

Q

quarter
kaltolu (A) quarter dollar
quick
nokosanome (AI) he is quick
quickly
kakawi- (kakaw-) quickly; fast
kakawiw (P) quickly; fast
nokosa (nokosay-) (PV) quickly; without delay
nokosantuphal, nokosahtuphal (TA) he catches it (an.) quickly
'panahkalal (TA) he uncovers him quickly
sahsapu (AI) he glances quickly
sahsessu (AI, II) it goes back and forth quickly
sasotokku (AI) he jumps up and down quickly
quiet
cikte (II) it is quiet it is silent
quietly
menakaciw (P) quietly; slowly
sankewimiye (AI) he prays quietly; he prays calmly
quill
kaw (A) porcupine quill
kawihuke (AI) he has porcupine quills on him
quite
natomaskute (II) it is quite a big field
qasi (PV) quite

R

rabbit
mahtoqehs (A) rabbit
raccoon
espons (A) raccoon
esponsuwehlosu (AI) he turns himself into raccoon
race
enkamhal (TA) he challenges him (to a race)
rag
ahtulhawekon (I) rag
rain
kisolan (II) it rained
komiwon (II) it rains
ksqopehsan (II) it rains and snows at the same time
macelan (II) it starts to rain
piskolan (II) it is raining so hard that it's dark or it's hard to see
sukolan (II) it pours (rain)
tollan (AI) it is raining
rainbow
monoqan (A) rainbow
rash
muskessu (AI, II) he, it comes out; he breaks out in a rash
popu (AI) he (a child) has a rash on his tongue and inside his mouth
raspberry
minsoss (A) raspberry
minsossimus (A) raspberry bush
rat
apiqsehs (A) rat
raven
kci kakak (A) raven
razor
psqihtuhusut (I) razor
psqihtuwewakon (I) razor
reach
matayamkahte (II) a pile reaches its end
petkil (AI) he reaches a size (in growth)
read
't-okitomuwan (DOV) he reads it to him
't-okitomuwewan (DOV) he reads it for him
'tawokisu (AI) he knows how to read
ready
kiste (II) it is finished; it is ready
'pitkotomuwewan (DOV) he gets it ready for him
'pitkotuwatomon (TI) he gets it ready
really
ansa (P) like; truly; really
qin (P) really
rear
asit (P) behind, in back; at the rear;
rear end
ckuwahkuhucin (AI) he is bent over (rear end facing this way)
olomahkuhucin (AI) he is bent over (rear end facing this way)

recall
mihqitahamal (TA) he recalls him; he thinks of him
receive
'cilomomal (TA) he receives a sign from him; he is haunted by him
cilomotome, cilomotoma (AI) he receives a sign; he is haunted; he receives an omen
'cilomotomon (TI) he receives a sign through it; he is haunted through it
wiciye (AI) he receives communion; he goes along
recognize
nonuwal (TA) he knows him; he recognizes him
red
accossu (AI) he changes color; he turns red
pqalokiqe (AI) he has red eyes
pqatpe (AI) he has red hair
pqeku (AI) he is dressed in red
pqeyu, mqeyu (AI, II) he, it is red
sqotewahkosu (AI) it (an.) is red hot
sqotewahkote (II) it is red hot
Red Beach
Mehqamkesk Red Beach, Maine (Locative)
red willow
nepskihkamq (I) red willow; squaw bush
refrigerator
kolocomutikon (A) refrigerator; freezer
regain
enuwiye (AI) he comes to; he regains consciousness
regrettable
psahkeyuwinaqot (II) it looks regrettable; it looks tragic
regularly
nucituwiye (AI) he flies (a plane) on a regular basis; he pilots
reins
napolup (I) one of the reins for a horse
related
lakutuwok (AI) they (dual) are related
witawsumal (TA) he is related to him
witawsuwelomal (TA) he is related to him
wotaqtuwok (AI) they are related as brother's wife and husband's sister or as sister's husband and wife's sister (i.e. they call each other notaq)
relationship
lakutuwakon (I) relationship; kinship
relative
'siwiyil (A) (dep.) his relative
'tolonapemol (A) (dep.) his relative
relay
ankuwacomu (AI) he relays a message; he brings a report of; he interprets (translates)
release
-ahke- throw; drop; release
religion
papahtomuwakon (I) religion; prayer
religious
papahtok (A) a Christian; a religious person
papahtom (AI) he is religious

remember
mihqitahatomon (TI) he remembers it (suddenly)
sipitahasu (AI) he remembers very well
wewitahamal (TA) he remembers him
wewitahasu (AI) he remembers
wewitahatomon (TI) he remembers it

reminisce
pehqitahasu (AI) he reminisces

repeatedly
piskiqehpusu (AI) he blinks repeatedly

reply
asitehmuwal (TA) he replies to him; he answers him

report
akonutome (AI) he talks; he tells a story; he reports news
ankuwacomu (AI) he relays a message; he brings a report of; he interprets (translates)

reprimand
musqelomal (TA) he reprimands him

return
apaci (apac-, apat-) (PV) coming back; returning
apaciye (AI) he returns
wewciye (AI) he goes somewhere and returns without stopping over; he makes a home run (in baseball)

reveal
nostuhmon (TI) he reveals it by saying it; he mentions it

reverence
'qossihtun (TI) he pays reverence to it; he follows the proper observances with respect to it he cherishes it

rib
pik (A) rib

ribbon
't-otolatokonomewal (TA) he braids someone else's hair; he ties someone else's hair with a ribbon, string, etc.

rice
aptelomultineweyal (I) (pl.) rice

ride
alipokomu, alikopomu (AI) he skates; he rides a bike
'pomiphal (TA) he carries him; he gives him a ride in a vehicle
pomumqe (AI) he rides a horse
'tawatkuwe (II) it rides the waves well
wolatkuwe (II) it rides the waves well
yalipokomu (AI) he rides around on a bicycle; he skates around

ridge
pomotone (II) a ridge runs along

rifle
peskuwat (I) rifle

right
'tinahkat (I) (dep.) his right hand
tinahkatuwey (A, I) the one on the right

right away
tuciw (P) moreover; besides; right away
woliw, woli (P) right away

ring
lahkalusonohom (AI) it (an.) has a ring around it
nahsahqehtakon (I) ring
nipuwilcuhun (I) wedding ring

rinse
'kahsapawolal (TA) he rinses it (an.)

rip
't-olkinehlal (TA) he splits it, rips it (e.g., ripping a jacket by catching it on something)
't-olokinehkomon (TI) he rips it (clothing) by wearing it when it is too small for him
't-olokinehkomuwan (DOV) he rips something (clothing) of his (someone else's) by wearing it when it is too small for him
't-olokinehkuwal (TA) he rips it (an., clothing) by wearing it when it is too small for him

rise
motkapkotete (II) smoke rises straight up;
putawehe (AI) it rises (e.g. bread)

river
sip (I) river

road
awt (I) road; path
mocawtosson (II) it is a bad road
suwawtiw, suwawtihiw (P) out in the middle of the road
wolawtosson (II) it is a good road

robin
ankuwiposehehs, ankuwiposiyehs (A) robin

rock
ponapsq (I) rock
psikapskiye (II) there is a crack in the rock
sokotiyapske (II) it is a flat rock

roll
liqehe (II) it rolls thus, there
motapeqehe (AI, II) it rolls downhill
motapetomehe (AI, II) he, it goes downhill on wheels
pomiqehe (AI, II) it rolls along
-q_h(a)- roll

roof (of the mouth)
celkahq (A) roof of the mouth

room
wahsiw, wahsi (P) in (or into) the other room: on the other side (of a hill or other barrier)

rooster
napaha (A) rooster

root
monkehtun (TI) he digs it out with its roots
wocopsq (I) root

rope
ahpap (A) rope

rosary
imiyakonok (A (pl.)) rosary beads

rough
kakawatqin (II) the water is rough
kaweyu (AI, II) it is rough

round
ptoqakin (II) it is round
ptoqakisu (AI) it (an.) is round (e.g., a coin)

ruler
tpahqonikon (I) ruler; yardstick

run

amke (AI) he plays a game; he runs for an office

ksephuwe (AI) he runs in

macehpayu (AI) he runs away because he is scared

macephuwe (AI) he runs away

nattokaphuwe (A) he gets out and runs away

pomotone (II) a ridge runs along

qasku (AI) he runs

'siktehkuwal (TA) he kills him by running into (or over) him with a vehicle

toliye (II) it is going; it is running

run ashore

oqehe (AI) he runs his canoe up on shore

rust

caqahk (I) rust

caqahkiye (AI, II) it is rusty

rut

matsehkiye (AI) she is in heat; he is rutting

S

sable

nimaqsuwehs (A) sable (animal)

sad

tucitahasu (AI) he is sad

sail

lekhikon (A) sail

sailor

pokuwoss (A) sailor

St. Andrews

Qonasqamkuk St. Andrews, New Brunswick (Locative)

St. George

Mekikatewik St. George, New Brunswick (Locative)

St. John

Menahqesk St. John, New Brunswick (Locative)

St. John River

Wolastokuk St. John River (Locative); Maliseet country (Locative)

Ste.-Anne-de-Beaupré

Sitank Ste.-Anne-de-Beaupré, Québec (Locative)

saliva

sossoq (I) saliva

salmon

polam (A) Atlantic salmon

taqanan (A) land-locked salmon

salt

salawehtasu (II) it is pickled in salt; it is salted

salawey (I) salt

salt pork

sikusas (A) fried sliced salt pork

salt water

supeq (I) salt water; ocean

salty

salawehpuko: (II) it tastes salty

salawehpuksu (AI) it (an.) tastes salty

same

'tetpekisomon (TI) he cuts it (sheet-like object) straight; he trims it to the same length

tetpi (tetp-) (PV) to the same extent as (something else); evenly (Compare papehk "exactly the same.")

sandy

wolamkisiye (II) there is a good sandy surface

sap

mahqan (I) sap of the sugar maple; maple syrup (or sugar); anything sweet

saw

't-epahsiksal (TA) he saws it (an.) in two; he saws it (an.) in half

't-epahsiksomon (TI) he saws it in two; he saws it in half

liksawakon (I) saw

liksawe (AI) he saws

toliksawe (AI) he is sawing

say

itom (AI) he says

't-itomon (TI) he says it

nostuhmon (TI) he reveals it by saying it; he mentions it

olomeske (AI) he says mass

yaq (P) they say (or said); he says (or said); it is said

scab

mok (I) scab

mokis (I) scab

scale

tpapekhikon (I) scale (for weighing)

scarce

notuwot (II) it is scarce

scare

'siktehpawolal (TA) he scares him to death (literally or figuratively)

scared

macehpayu (AI) he runs away because he is scared

seksu (AI) he is scared

scatter

sisse (sissiy-) (PV) in all directions; scattering

sissessu (II) it spreads out; it disperses; it scatters

scissors

'tomosponhunol (I) (pl.) scissors

scold

'kolulal (TA) he argues with him; he scolds him

scorch

pkiksu (AI) it (an.) is burned; it (an.) is scorched

pkikte (II) it is burned; it is scorched

scrape

'cishal (TA) he scrapes him

scratch

maciyapenike (AI) he starts to scratch around

't-otolapehlal (TA) he is scratching him

'posokapecin (AI, AI+OBJ) he scratches himself on it

scream

masqolamu (AI) he screams

sculpin

kikcokapskotiyehputikon (A) sculpin

scythe

lasksawakon (I) scythe; sickle

tolasksawe (AI) he is cutting grass with a scythe or sickle

sea

tutatqin (II) there is a heavy sea; the waves are very high

sea urchin

musahkuhs (A) sea urchin

seal

ahkiq (A) seal (animal)

ahkiqewi (PN) seal; seal's

ahkiqqe (AI) he hunts seals

ahkiqsiske (AI) he hunts pup seals

second

nisewey (A, I) second (in number)

secretly

kaciw (P) secretly; hidden

'kikimapomal TA he looks at him secretly

kikimi (kikim-) (PV) secretly; stealthily; silently

komuci (komuc-, komut-) (PV) secretly

section

'tomapskihtahal (TA) he chops it (an.) into sections

'tomapskihtehmon (TI) he chops it into sections

see

ehecinaqsu (AI) he is hard to see

esansu (AI) she wears something one can see through

nomihtu (AI) he sees

nomihtun (TI) he sees it

nomiyal (TA) he sees him

see-saw

apuciyaskuwakon (I) see-saw

seed

skonimin (I) seed

tahkomons (I) seed

seen

alinaqsu (AI) he is seen around (in various places within an area)

sell

ankusu (AI) he buys; he sells

't-ankuwehtun (TI) he sells it

't-ankuwekhal (TA) he sells it (an.)

send

'pocitahkan (AI, AI+OBJ) he sends it

'pocitahkewan (DOV) he sends it to him

sense

wahkathoma, wahkathome (AI) he has little sense

separate

cepiye, cocepiye (AI) he is separated from his spouse

cepte, cocepte (II) it is separate; it is disassembled

separately

cepi (cep-) (PV) separately; apart

cepiw, cocepiw (P) separately; apart

cocepi (cocep-) (PV) separately; apart

set

mulatomuwehe (II) it (a boat) sets deep in the water .

oltokopu (AI) it (an.) is set (in a direction) (e.g., rope)

oltokte, latokahte (II) it is set (in a direction) (e.g., wire)

't-oqehtuwal (TA) he sets him up for a jump (in checkers)

punawe (AI) he sets traps

wolicuwehtahsu (AI) he sets the table

seven

oluwikonok (P) seven (in counting)

several

kakehsukoniw (P) for many days; for several days

severe

tutamoqesson (II) there has been a severe storm

tutamoqessu (II) there is a severe storm

sew

toliqahsu (AI) he is sewing

sexy

moci (moc-) (PV, PN) bad, evil; "dirty"; sexy

shadow

pokotahsu (AI) casts a shadow

shag

oqons (A) shag, cormorant

shake

'puwehlal (TA) he shakes him

'sokiptinenal (TA) he shakes hands with him

shall

oc (P) will; shall (indicates future)

shape

milapskosu (AI) it (an.) comes in many shapes; it (an.) sticks out in one or more places

wolatqonokosu (AI) it (an.) is a tree with a nice shape

wolatqonokot (II) it is a tree with a nice shape

shark

sikolat (A) shark

sharp

ksikihin (II) it is sharp

petahkemolsu (AI) he has a sharp pain (from pleurisy)

qinuskeyu, qonusqeyu (AI, II) it is sharp; it is pointed

shave

'posqihtuwahal (TA) he shaves him

psqihtuhusu (AI) he shaves (himself)

she

nekom (A) (PRO) he, she

shed

atuwe (AI) he (an animal) sheds his hair

mehtuwehe (AI) his hair is falling out

pehke (I) shed (behind a house)

pskuwhe (AI) he sheds (his hair)

pskuwhetul (II) hairs fall out (when a person is losing hair or an animal is shedding)

tuhsan (I) shed

sheet

lamokut (I) sheet (for a bed)

psekon (II) it is like a sheet

pseku (AI) it (an.) is like a sheet

sheldrake

sihku (A) sheldrake

shelf

tehsaqtihikon (I) shelf

shine

nipayapon (II) the northern lights are shining

't-olahsenomuwal (TA) he shines a light there for him

paqahson (II) the moon is shining

possahtuwe (II) it shines
tolahsu (II) it is shining
ship
motapekuloq (I) ship; warship
shirt
ahtulhaw (A) shirt
shock
cokahk (P) (interjection indicating surprise, shock, disgust)
pecitihkessu (II) the shock of it (impact, explosion, etc.) comes to here
shoe
-akson-, -koson- shoe
maksonol (A) his shoe
maskoqone (AI) she has sexy shoes; she has high heels
pkoson (A) shoe
shoelace
pkosonap (I) shoelace
shoot
't-ahtoptelomon (TI) he shoots at it and hits it by luck
't-ahtopteluwal (TA) he shoots at him and hits him by luck
eqhike (AI) he stops shooting
kishike (AI) he shot
miyawtelasu (AI) he wounds himself (by shooting)
montelomuwan (DOV) he shoots off something of his (someone else's) (e.g. he shoots his hand off)
nokkahteluwa (TA) he shot them (an.) all
'peskhal (TA) he shoots him
peskote (II) it shoots off; it blows up
'potteluwal (TA) he shoots him accidentally
shop
utenehke (AI) he goes shopping in town
shore
sitom (I) shore
short
cilkatokosu (AI) it (an.) is short (said of something string-like)
cilkatokot (II) it is short (said of something string-like) it is short (said of a story, film, etc.)
cilkenskosu (AI) he is short (standing up)
cilkeyu (AI, II) it is short
cilkokiskot (II) it is a short day
shortcut
kskomihike (AI) he takes a shortcut
shortstop
nekosantuphat (A) shortstop (in baseball)
shot
polhikesku (AI) he is a bad shot
should
cuwi, ahcuwi (ehcuwi) (PV) must; should; have to
cuwitpot (II) it should be
should not
kat cipotu, kat cipotuk, kat cuwitpotu (II (?)) it should not be; it had better not be
shoulder
qolopapessu (AI) he looks back quickly over his shoulder
tolomakon (I) shoulder

shoulder blade
wonoskiyil (A) (dep.) his shoulder blade
shovel
akalhike, okalhike (AI) he shovels snow
't-okalhomon (TI) he shovels snow off it
sapol (I) shovel
'sapolahal (TA) he shovels it (an.)
'sapolatomon (TI) he shovels it
show
messunal (TA) he shows him (to someone)
messunom (AI) he shows (something)
messunomon (TI) he shows it
messunomuwan (DOV) he shows it to him
shower
petakolan (II) there is a thunder shower
shut
'kophomon, 'koppahmon (TI) he shuts it
'koppektahal (TA) he shuts him in by hitting (something 2-dimensional: cloth, paper, etc.)
'koptunahal (TA) he makes him shut up
kpoton (II) it is frozen over; it is frozen shut (e.g., a faucet)
shy
tqesusqihiw, tqesusqiw (AI) she is a shy woman
tqesuwapiw, tqesuwapihiw (AI) he is a shy man
sick
ikahawqe (AI) he gets sick
'kosinuhkan (AI, AI+OBJ) he is sick; he has pain in it
'kosinuhkuwal (TA) he makes him sick
ksinuhka, ksinuhke (AI) he is sick
ksinuhkawinaqsu, ksinuhkewinaqsu (AI) he looks sick
ksinuhkehkalsu (AI) he pretends to be sick
ksiyawqe (AI) he is very sick;
sickle
lasksawakon (I) scythe; sickle
sickness
ksinuhkewakon (I) sickness; disease
side
isikoni- (isikon-) (PV) on one side (only)
isikoniw (P) on one side (only)
nomocini (nomocin-) (PV) sideways; to the side
nomociniw (P) on the side
nomocinuhse (AI) he walks sideways
pasici (pasic-, pasit-) (PV) over; on (or to) the other side; passing over
pasiciw (P) over; on the other side;
wahsiw, wahsi (P) in (or into) the other room; on the other side (of a hill or other barrier)
sign
'cilomomal (TA) he receives a sign from him; he is haunted by him
cilomotome, cilomotoma (AI) he receives a sign; he is haunted; he receives an omen
'cilomotomon (TI) he receives a sign through it; he is haunted through it
silent
cikopu (AI) he is silent; he sits silently
cikte (II) it is quiet it is silent
silently
kikimi (kikim-) (PV) secretly; stealthily; silently

sin

lahkomiksuwakon (I) sin

olkomiksu (AI) he sins thus

woneyu (AI) he is living in sin

sing

kehsintu (AI) he sings so much

lintu (AI) he sings

mehcintu (AI) he stops singing

-nt(u)- sing

't-olintuwatomon (TI) he sings it

pihcintu (AI) he sings far

tolintu (AI) he is singing

wihqintuwamal (TA) he calls him by singing

singer

nucintaq (A) singer

sink

ktapehe (AI, II) he, it sinks

sinner

lahkomiksu (AI) he is a sinner

sister

mossis (A) older sister

'pehenomumol (A) (dep.) his sister (archaic)

sistoss (A) nun, religious sister

witsehkehsu (AI) she is a sister

witsehkehsuwol (A) (dep.) her sister

witsehkestuwok (AI) they (dual) are sisters to each other

wotaqol (A) (dep.) her sister's husband, brother's wife, or husband's sister; his wife's sister

sit

alqepu (AI) he sits around

amihkessu (AI) he gets up (from a sitting position)

't-apotepin (AI, AI + OBJ) he sits leaning against it;

't-apotukonapin (AI + OBJ) he sits against it with his knees raised

ckuhqepu (AI) he sits facing this way

cuppu (AI) he sits in the water

eqopu (AI) he stops being able to sit up

eweppu (AI) he sits up

ksossiyehsin (AI) she (a bird) sits on her eggs

nospopin (AI, AI + OBJ) he sits down with something he should have taken off or put down (e.g. knapsack, coat, pocketbook)

olqepu (AI) he sits thus

opu (AI) he sits; it (an.) is in position

-qep(i)-, -uhkep(i)- sit, be sitting

sankewopu (AI) he sits still

sasokuhqepu (AI) he half stands; he half sits; he is leaning against something

spopu (AI) he sits up high

'tehsaqopin (AI, AI + OBJ) he sits on top of it

tokkopu (AI) he sits up to some point; he sits at some distance; he sits until some time

'toqtopin (AI, AI + OBJ) he sits on it

tutopu (AI) he is far along (in rank, etc.; of a woman, in pregnancy); he is sitting a long way off

wolopu (AI) he is sitting nicely, comfortably; he is well off

six

kamahcin (P) six

size

olkihqon (II) it is big (by so much); it is of a (certain) size

olkil (AI) he is big (by so much); he is of a (certain) size

petkil (AI) he reaches a size (in growth)

skate

alipokomu, alikopomu (AI) he skates; he rides a bike

yalipokomu (AI) he rides around on a bicycle; he skates around

skeleton

kukonasikon (A) skeleton

skim

monhomon (TI) he skims it off

skin

maspotekone (AI) he has thick skin

motekon (I) skin

-otekon- skin

'possehlal (TA) he skins him

skinny

apsatokosossu (AI) he is thin (said of a snake, a string, etc.); he is skinny (said of a person)

skull

wosokiyatop, wosokiyatp (I) skull

skunk

apikcilu (A) skunk

skunk spruce

kawatoq (A) skunk spruce

sky

spemuk sky (Locative)

sled

suwhewik (I) moose sled; bob sled; pack sled

'tapakon (I) car; sled; wagon

sleep

cipqam (AI) he has a nightmare of falling; he jumps in his sleep or when dozing

koskimkasuwiw (II) it (a part of the body) goes to sleep; it feels like pins and needles (sensation in skin)

kuhu (AI) he sleeps; he falls asleep

kuwimkewey (A,I) something that helps one sleep

metsoqsu (AI) he sleeps late

moteqsu (AI) he is heard sleeping; he snores

naskuwamal (TA) he sleeps in the same house with him

naskuwaniyal (AI, AI + OBJ) he sleeps with him (in the same bed or in the same house)

natqahsu (AI) he goes somewhere to sleep

nutaqsu (AI) he has not slept enough

pskotemu (AI) he cries himself to sleep

'siktehkomon (TI) he makes it (a part of the body) go to sleep (e.g. he makes his leg go to sleep by the way he is sitting)

'siktehkomuwan (DOV) he makes it (a part of the body) go to sleep on him (e.g. a child making his mother's leg go to sleep by the way he is sitting on her lap)

toloqahsu (AI) he is sleeping

toloqsu (AI) he is sleeping

witkosuhtuwok (AI) they (dual) are sleeping together, one at the foot of the bed

slice
't-apseksal (TA) he slices it (an.) into thin pieces
't-apseksomon (TI) he slices it into small pieces
-eks- slice
't-oleksal (TA) he slices it (an.)
't-oleksomon (TI) he slices it
'poqqesal (TA) he slices a piece off of it
toleksawe (AI) he is slicing
'tomeksomon (TI) he cuts a slice off of it (with a knife)
uteksal, 'teksal (TA) he cuts a slice from it (an.)
uteksomon, 'teksomon (TI) he cuts a slice from it
slick
sashoma (AI) he slips on something slick
slide
asuwocokahte (II) it has slid over to one side; it has flopped over to one side
pomotomhe (AI) he slides along
slight
nulomolamson (II) there is a slight breeze
slightly
kekesk (P) a little; slightly
slip
ketolaskessu (AI) it (an.) slips off
sashoma (AI) he slips on something slick
simis (A) slip (garment)
slippery
sahseyu (II) it is slippery
sloppy
moconome (AI) he is sloppy
noskonoma (AI) he is sloppy
slow
sankewiw (P) slow and easy; calmly
slowly
menakaciw (P) quietly; slowly
menakaciye (AI) he goes slowly
menakacuhse (AI) he walks slowly
menakatapasuwok (AI) they (pl.) walk slowly
menakatkawotuwok (AI) they (dual) walk slowly
slug
wiwilomeq (A) slug
small
apsalokosu (AI) it (an.) has a small hole in it
apsaskute (II) it is a small field
apsiqe (AI) he has a small face
apsokil (AI) he is small
siktelomuwiqewu (AI) he smiles a small smile
wolomuwiqewu (AI) he smiles (a small smile)
smart
wawapiw (AI) he is smart
smash
nukcoktahal (TA) he smashes it (an.); into small pieces; he smashes it (an.) (something soft)
nukcoktehmon (TI) he smashes it into small pieces; he smashes it (something soft)
smell
mocimahsu (AI) he, it (an.) smells bad
mocimahte (II) it smells bad
'possahal (TA) he smells him
'possehtun (TI) he smells it
wolimahte (II) it smells good

smelly
maski (mask-) (PV) smelly
maskosit (I) smelly foot
smile
-elom(i)- laugh, smile
lelomu (AI) he smiles (in some way)
't-olelomuhtuwal (TA) he smiles at him
siktelomu (AI) he smiles
siktelomuwiqewu (AI) he smiles a small smile
wolomuwiqewu (AI) he smiles (a small smile)
smoke
patosu (AI) he chokes on smoke
pkot (I) smoke
pkotesawe (AI) he smokes (meat, fish, etc.)
pskelute (II) smoke is coming out (of it) because it cannot escape through a flue, stovepipe, etc.
siktepskelusu (AI) he smothers in smoke
tolipkotesu (AI) it (an.) is smoking
wihqipkotehtamike (AI) he inhales smoke from a pipe over and over
wihqipkotenike (AI) he inhales smoke from a pipe, puffing slowly
wikpolahsal (TA) he smokes it (an., food)
wikpolastike (AI) he smokes (meat)
wikpolastun (TI) he smokes it (food)
smoke (tobacco)
'tome, 'toma (AI) he smokes (cigarettes etc.)
utomektun (TI) he smokes it (tobacco, etc.)
smoky
pkotete (II) it is smoky, misty
smooth
supeyu (II) it is smooth
tolotomhe (AI, II) he, it is moving (sliding, rolling, etc.) with a smooth, gliding motion
smother
siktepskelusu (AI) he smothers in smoke
wehqalamuhsuhke (AI) he cannot breathe; he smothers, suffocates
smudge
lipkotenoma (AI) he lights a smudge
lipkotenomakon (I) smudge
snake
athusoss (A) snake
snare
lapektuwakon (I) snare
sneak
'komuciphal (TA) he sneaks him away
'komuciptun (TI) he sneaks it away
sneeze
eksku (AI) he sneezes
snore
ciqoleqsu (AI) he snores
moteqsu (AI) he is heard sleeping; he snores
snow
akalhike, okalhike (AI) he shovels snow
alalikonike (AI) he walks around in deep snow (without snowshoes)
't-okalhomon (TI) he shovels snow off it
piski psan (II) it is snowing so hard that it's dark or it's hard to see
psan (II) it snows
spaqahte (II) the snow is deep
wast (A) snow (on the ground; fallen snow)
wonhuke (AI, II) he is covered with snow

snowshoe
akom (A) snowshoe
akomawt (I) snowshoe path
akomihom (AI) he goes by snowshoe
akomohom (AI) he wears snowshoes
alakomasu (AI) he snowshoes around
'takomiw, akomiw (AI) he has snowshoes
so
saku (P) so; therefore
so long
kehsatokot (II) it is so long (said of something string-like)
kestokot (II) it is so long (said of something string-like)
so many
kehsahqonasu (II) it is so many yards (cloth measure)
kehsikotonewiw (II) it is so many years old
kehsuhsalqot (II) it is so many miles (land measure)
so much
kehsalke (AI) he digs so much
kehsintu (AI) he sings so much
'kessal (TA) he cuts so much of it (an.); he cuts it (an.) into so many pieces
'kessomon (TI) he cuts so much of it; he cuts it into so many pieces
olomelku (AI) he paces off so much
qonatokosu, qontoksu (AI) he, it (an.) is long by so much
qonatokot, qontokot (II) it is long by so much
qonenskosu (AI) he is tall by so much
so that
weci (PV) in order that; so that; because
soak
't-oqithal (TA) he soaks it (an.)
ptoqcokpe (AI) he is soaked to the skin
soap
kostokonikon (I) soap
soft
nuhkahkomike (II) the ground is soft
nuhkeyu (AI, II) it is soft, tender
soil
tupqan (I) soil; dirt
soldier
'somakonoss (A) soldier
sole
lamsitawon (I) sole of the foot
't-olamsitawon (I) his sole
someone
wen (A) (PRO) who, what (an.); someone, something (an.)
something
keq, keqoss, keqsey (I) (PRO) what?; something
sometimes
anqoc (P) sometimes
kinuwitpiye (II) it happens sometimes
puskiw (P) sometimes; often
somewhere
tama (P) where; somewhere
son
'qossol (A) (dep.) his son

song
lintuwakon (I) song
motewolonuwintuwakon (I) song of great magical power
psqentu (AI) he bursts into song
wihqintuwewakon (I) jolly song; calling song
soon
keka (P) almost, nearly; soon; practically, all but;
nokosayiw (P) soon
soot
mokos (I) soot; dead coal
qaqopos (A) soot
sore
'qotakonine (AI) he has a sore throat; he has throat trouble
sorrow
wewehsimal (TA) he expresses sorrow about a death to him
sorrowful
wewehsinaqot (II) it looks sorrowful (after a death)
sorrowfully
wewehsitahamal (TA) he thinks about him (someone who has died) sorrowfully, with sympathy for his family, etc.
sorry
moskeyin (AI, AI+OBJ) he is sorry about it
sound
ckuhtaqot, ckuwihtaqot (II) it sounds as if it is coming toward here; it (a sound) approaches
mettaqot (II) it stops playing (radio, record, etc.); it is over; the sound stops
mocihtaqot (II) it sounds bad
nawtaqsu (AI) sounds far away
oltaqot (II) it sounds thus
wecuwawtaqot (II) it sounds close
wecuwawtaqsu (AI) he sounds close (talking, etc.)
soup
ksap (I) soup; stew
't-olapuhkewal (TA) he makes soup (stew, etc.) for him
't-otolapuwhal (TA) he is making soup (stew, etc.) for him
wolapuwahte (II) it is a good-tasting soup; it is a good-tasting stew
sour
noskiqetutom (AI) he has a sour look on his face
suwonhuke (AI) he puckers up from eating something sour
south
sawonehson (II) the wind is blowing from the south
sawonehsonuk south (Locative)
southwest
sonutsekotonuk southwest (Locative)
spade
piks (A) spade (in cards)
spark
sqotes (I) spark; ember; glowing coal
spasm
'cipiluwehs (A) pleurisy; epilepsy; muscle spasms

speak
-atuw(e)- speak a language
-ewest(u)- speak; talk
ikolisomanatuwe (AI) he speaks English
'koluluwewal (TA) he speaks for him
mehtewestu (AI) he finishes speaking
motiyewestu (AI) he is heard speaking
piluwatuwe (AI) he speaks a different language
polecomonatuwe (AI) he speaks French
skicinuwatuwe (AI) he speaks an Indian lanuage; he speaks Maliseet-Passamaquoddy
tolewestu (AI) he is speaking
spear
aneqehsuhke (AI) he spears flounder; he fishes for flounder
mokahkehke (AI) he spears striped bass
spend
skuweyu (AI) he often spends a lot of time (there)
spider
amushopihk (A) spider
spill
'sukahtehmon (TI) he spills it (by hitting it)
'sukahtestun (TI) he pours it out; he empties it; he spills it (because it's too full or because he's not paying attention to it)
spirit woman
sqewtomuhs (A) spirit woman
spit
sumsqe (AI) he spits
splash
tolpektihike (AI) he is splashing
splinter
moskuwecinon (AI, AI+OBJ) he gets a splinter from it
split
't-olkinehlal (TA) he splits it, rips it (e.g., ripping a jacket by catching it on something)
psikessu (AI) it (an.) splits
wolinessu (II) it splits, well; it cracks well; it tears well
Split Rock
Pessikapskiyak Split Rock (place on the shore near Pleasant Point, Maine)
spoil
mocikon (II) it is spoiled, no good
spoon
emqan (A) spoon
spot
'topun (I) (dep.) his spot (where he usually hides or rests, where he stays when not doing something); his bed
spread
'kisekehlal (TA) he spread (an., sheetlike) it out
piluwikemosku (AI) he spreads false stories a lot; he is a jealous person
sissessu (II) it spreads out; it disperses; it scatters
spring
kisuwupeq (I) warm spring (of water)
ktopeqon (II) there is a cold spring of water
siqon (II) it is spring
siqoniw (P) in the spring

sprinkle
'kispekehlal (TA) he sprinkled him; he can sprinkle him
komiwonisiye (II) it sprinkles (rain)
macelanisiye (II) it starts to sprinkle (rain)
't-olpekehtun (TI) he sprinkles (something) with it
spruce
supeqatoq (A) white spruce
spruce beer
kawatokup (I) spruce beer
squaw bush
nepskihkamq (I) red willow; squaw bush
squeeze
'colokonal (TA) he squeezes him, it (an., something soft)
squint
puhkalokiqewu (AI) he squints
squirrel
mihku (A) squirrel
stand
-kapuw(i)- stand
'kisikapuwehlal (TA) he stood him; he erected it (an.)
lamkikapuwuwok (AI) they are standing in a line
mehsikapuwit (AI) why is he standing?
mitacaskekapuhu, mitacaskekapuwu (AI) he stands with his legs spread apart
sankewikapuwu, sankewikapuhu (AI) he stands still
sasokuhqepu (AI) he half stands; he half sits; he is leaning against something
sehke (AI) he stands
sehkehepiye, sehkahapiye (AI) he paddles standing up
'sehkehlal (TA) he stands him up
sehkomu (AI, II) it stands
'sehkomutun (TI) he stands it up
'tapotehsinon (AI, AI+OBJ) he stands leaning against it; he leans on it
'tehsahqikapuwin (AI, AI+OBJ) he stands on top of it
wiwonikapuwihtuwawal (TA) they stand around him
stander
'pakikpenomon (TI) he folds over the standers (vertical splints) of it (a basket)
star
possesom (A) star
start
mace (maciy-) (PV) start, begin; go away or start off while doing go along while doing
macelan (II) it starts to rain
macelanisiye (II) it starts to sprinkle (rain)
macemiye (AI) he starts to pray
macewse (AI) he starts out on foot; he leaves on foot; he starts to walk (toddler)
maciyapenike (AI) he starts to scratch around
maciyaphal (TA) he starts to track him
maciyessu (II) it starts to move; it moves along
motutuwalal (TA) he starts it (an.) burning; he kindles it (an.)
motutuwatomon (TI) he starts it burning; he kindles it

startle

'cipimal (TA) he startles him by talking

starve

siktelamu (AI) he starves; he is starving (literally or figuratively)

statement

acomuwakon (I) story-telling; story; statement

Stations of the Cross

wiwonimiye (AI) he goes around to the Stations of the Cross; he goes around (something) praying

stay

ksacessu (AI) he stays too long on a visit

ksatke (AI) he likes the place so much that he stays longer

ktoqonu (AI) he stays over (at someone's house)

't-okelhal (TA) he asks him to stay

't-oqetokelhal (TA) he tries to get him to stay

steal

'komutonalal (TA) he steals him, it (an.); he kidnaps him

'komutonan (AI, AI+OBJ) he steals it

'komutonatomon (TI) he steals it

'komutonomal (TA) he steals from him

komutse (AI) he steals wood

stealthily

kikimi (kikim-) (PV) secretly; stealthily; silently

steel

skonahq (I) piece of steel

steer

cihcihke (AI) he paddles in the back of a canoe (steers)

step

kahpotassu (AI) he steps out; he gets off

'tomihkuwal (TA) he breaks it (an.) by stepping on it

'tuwalokihkomon (TI) he puts a hole through it by stepping on it

'tuwalokihkuwal (TA) he puts a hole through it (an.) by stepping on it

stew

ksap (I) soup; stew

wolapuwahte (II) it is a good-tasting soup; it is a good-tasting stew

stick

't-apqotiyaqhomon (TI) he props it open with a stick

kolomu (AI, II) he, it sticks he, it is stuck, caught

opos (I) stick; pole

stick-like

pihtahqot (II) it is long and stick-like

pihtaqsu (AI) it (an.) is long and stick-like; it (an.) is tall and stick-like

stick out

milapske (AI, II) it comes in many shapes; it sticks out in one or more places

milapskosu (AI) it (an.) comes in many shapes; it (an.) sticks out in one or more places

sakhahte (II) it sticks out into view

still

mec (P) still; yet; keep(s) on

sankewikapuwu, sankewikapuhu (AI) he stands still

sankewopu (AI) he sits still

stingy

sikinaqsu (AI) he is stingy

stink

maskosite (AI) his feet stink

stir

't-awskahqahal (TA) he stirs it (an.)

't-awskahqehmon (TI) he stirs it

nihluwacomin (AI, AI+OBJ) he stirs up trouble by talking about it

stomach

't-olamhok (I) (dep.) his stomach

't-olamhokewine (AI) he has a stomach ache

winas (A) stomach (of a cow)

stop

ankuwakhucu (AI) he stops for a while (ends a stage in a trip)

'conehlal (TA) he stops him

conehtasu (II) it is stopped

'conehtun (TI) he stops it

conesson (II) it stops; it comes to a stop

conessu (AI) he stops; he comes to a stop

conpekiw (II) the motion of the tide stops (when it is about to change)

ehqamkole (II) it stops burning

ehqi (ehq-, eq-) (PV) stop; cease

eqhike (AI) he stops shooting

eqopu (AI) he stops being able to sit up

eqotemu (AI) he stops crying

eqotokku (AI) he stops jumping

eqqa (AI) he stops dancing

eqtaqsu (AI) he stops making noise (by mouth)

eqtihike (AI) he stops pounding; he stops knocking

'kolahmuwal (TA) he stops him (from doing something)

mehcintu (AI) he stops singing

mehciqqiye (AI, II) he, it stops bleeding

mehtamkole (AI, II) it stops burning; it burns out

mehtoluhke (AI) he gets off work; he stops working

metka (AI) he stops dancing

mettaqot (II) it stops playing (radio, record, etc.); it is over; the sound stops

store

makasanikuwam (I) store (archaic)

makasanke (AI) he goes to the store (archaic)

store-keeper

malsanhok (A) store-keeper

storm

monomeqalal (TA) he storms at him

monomeqatomon (TI) he storms at it

petamoqessu (II) a storm comes

'tamoqesson (II) the storm is coming from there

'tamoqessu (II) the storm is coming from there

tutamoqesson (II) there has been a severe storm

tutamoqessu (II) there is a severe storm

wikkiskot (II) it is always storming

story

acomu (AI) he tells (a story)

acomuwakon (I) story-telling; story; statement

akonutomakon (I) story; account; narrative

akonutome (AI) he talks; he tells a story; he reports news

't-akonutomon (TI) he tells it (e.g., a story)

't-akonutomuwal (TA) he tells him a story
atkuhkakon (I) story; legend
atkuhke (AI) he tells an old story; he tells a
    legend
story-telling
acomuwakon (I) story-telling; story; statement
stove
papskot (I) stove
stove pipe
'tomakonahtoq (A) pipe stem; stove pipe
straight
kiyahqiw (P) straight
motkapkotete (II) smoke rises straight up;
motkayakhom (AI) he aims (a gun) straight up
sasokamu (AI) it (an.) flies straight
sasokatokot (II) it is a long straight length
sasokiye (AI) he moves in a straight line
'tetpekisomon (TI) he cuts it (sheet-like object)
    straight; he trims it to the same length
wolatoke (II) it is straight
straighten
wolatokehlal (TA) he straightens it (an.) out
strand
'qotatokiye (II) it is one string (e.g. of beads); it
    has one strand
strange
assokeyu (AI) he has strange ways
strawberry
pskihqimins (A) strawberry
stretch
pomalukte (II) there is a stretch of cloud
'sasokatokehlal (TA) he stretches it (an.) out
siptoku (AI) he stretches
strike
-ht_h-, -t_h- hit; strike; chop
-htehm-, -tehm- hit; strike; chop
-htihik(e)-, -tihik(e)- hit; strike; chop
ksatokihtehsin (AI) it (an., a string-like object)
    strikes sharply against something; it (an., a
    string-like object) pounds against something
molomeqalal, monomeqalal (TA) it (lightning)
    strikes him
molomeqatomon, monomeqatomon (TI) it
    (lightning) strikes it
monomeqe (AI) lightning strikes
olonomtehsin (AI) he strikes head first (making a
    dent)
'qolopihtehmon (TI) he turns it by striking it
'tokotomon (TI) he hits it (usually implies
    intention); he strikes at it
tomtehson (II) it strikes something and breaks
string
'qotatokiye (II) it is one string (e.g. of beads); it
    has one strand
strong
kinsonu (AI) he is strong
molihkapocu (AI) he has a strong grip
molihkikone (AI) he is strong
molihkiptine (AI) he has strong arms (or hands)
moliksonu (AI) he is strong
tutsonu (AI) he is very strong; he is very powerful

strong-willed
sakolitehe (AI) he is strong-willed
stucco
akiyahq (A) stucco; plaster; lime
akiyaqhasu (II) it is stuccoed, plastered
akiyaqhike (AI) he stuccoes; he plasters
't-akiyaqhomon (TI) he stuccoes it; he plasters it
stuck
kolocoqe (AI) he is stuck
kolomu (AI, II) he, it sticks he, it is stuck, caught
mecimtehsinon (AI, AI+OBJ) he gets stuck in it
stuck up
paliqewu (AI) he looks proud; he looks stuck up
'palitahamal (TA) he thinks he (someone else) is
    stuck up
palitahamsu (AI) he is stuck up; he thinks highly
    of himself
stud
maskap (A) stud; over-sexed man
stuff
pithasu (II) it is stuffed; it is loaded
'pithotuhkatomon (TI) he stuffs it
'pitkomalal (TA) he stuffs it (an., e.g. pipe,
    chicken)
pitsonosu (AI) he stuffs his (own) pipe
sturgeon
pasokos (A) sturgeon
stutter
nokhoma, nokhome (AI) he stutters
such and such
likon (II) it looks thus; it is such and such a kind
liku (AI) he looks thus; he is of such and such a
    kind or nature
olomahtu (AI) he acts thus; he has such and such
    a nature
suddenly
nanakiw (P) suddenly; all of a sudden;
    immediately
sesolahkiw, sesolahki (P) suddenly; all at once
suffer
usikiyal (TA) he makes him suffer; he punishes
    him
suffocate
wehqalamuhsuhke (AI) he cannot breathe; he
    smothers, suffocates
sugar
sukol (I) sugar
sumac
solanimus (A) sumac
summer
niponahkik region where it is always like summer
    (Locative)
niponiw (P) in the summer
sun
kisuhs (A) sun; moon; month
ksalosuhke (AI) he sweats; he basks in the sun
sun dog
oposenta (A) sun dog
sun shade
akuwahtihikon (I) umbrella; sun shade (e.g. a roof
    supported by four poles) canopy

sunfish
sikonoss (A) sunfish
supper
wolaqahqe (AI) he cooks supper
wolaqihpuwakon (I) supper time
sure
coqahk, cu kahk (P) sure; of course
haw (P) sure; yes, go ahead
surface
skitoqotehe (AI) he swims under water near the surface
wolamkisiye (II) there is a good sandy surface
surprise
cokahk (P) (interjection indicating surprise, shock, disgust)
survive
utawsin (AI, AI+OBJ) he survives it; he lives by means of it
swallow
epeskocossis (A) barn swallow
koloqehtamu (AI) he swallows
moscehtun (TI) he swallows it whole; he swallows it without chewing it
swear
nipskatuwe (AI) he swears; he blasphemes
nipskatuwesku (AI) he swears all the time
sweat
alosu (AI) he sweats
ksalosuhke (AI) he sweats; he basks in the sun
sweep
'cihkehmon (TI) he sweeps it away
cihkihike (AI) he sweeps
sweet
mahqan (I) sap of the sugar maple; maple syrup (or sugar); anything sweet
swell
moqin (II) it swells; it is swollen
moqisu (AI) he swells; he is swollen
swim
alamehe (AI) he zigzags through the water; he swims around underwater
alhom (AI) he swims around
ckuwoqotehe (AI) he swims toward here under the water
-hom(o)-, -ohom(o)- swim
komoku (AI) he swims down under the water
olhom (AI) he swims to that place
oloqoqotehe (AI) he swims in that direction under the water
skitoqotehe (AI) he swims underwater near the surface
tehsaqhom (AI) he swims on top of something which is under the water
tkahsomu, tahkahsomu (AI) he swims (to cool off)
toloqotehe (AI) he is swimming underwater
tuthom (AI) he swims by
switch
ipis (I) switch (slender, flexible stick); whip
swollen
moqin (II) it swells; it is swollen
moqisu (AI) he swells; he is swollen
muwikasu (AI) he has a swollen gland

sympathetic
ktomakelke (AI) he helps out because he is sympathetic
sympathetically
wewehsitahasu (AI) he thinks sympathetically, longingly, etc. about someone who has died
sympathy
likew (P) (expresses sympathy)
wewehsitahamal (TA) he thinks about him (someone who has died) sorrowfully, with sympathy for his family, etc.

T

table
tuwihput (I) table
wolicuwehtahsu (AI) he sets the table
take
'kaciptun (TI) he takes it by hiding it
'kolinskenal (TA) he takes his (someone else's) arm
kskonihike (AI) he takes a shortcut
maceptuwan (DOV) he takes it to him
monipqotatomon (TI) he takes the ashes out of it
nima, nime (AI) he takes his lunch with him
nokkanal (TA) he takes it (an.) all
nospiptun (TI) he takes it by accident; he takes it along
'pehkonomuwan (DOV) he takes all of it from him; he takes all of something of his
'pehkonomuwan (DOV) he takes all of it from him; he takes all of something of his
sapossomu (AI) he takes a physic
'sipkihkomon (AI, AI+OBJ) it takes him a long time to get to it
wihqehtun (TI) he takes it
wihqehtuwan (DOV) he takes it away from him
wihqonomon (TI) he takes it
wihqonomuwan (DOV) he takes it from him (the person it belongs to)
wikhike (AI) he writes, paints, draws, takes a picture, etc.
wisahulal (TA) he takes him by boat in a hurry
wiwisahulal (TA) he takes him away by canoe in a great hurry
take care
't-ankeyutomon (TI) he takes care of it
't-ankeyuwal (TA) he takes care of him
ulankeyuwal (TA) he takes good care of him
take hold
wihqonal (TA) he takes hold of him
take in
'kossewsolal (TA) he takes her in (for her wedding)
maqena (TA) he takes them into his home
maqenike (AI) he takes people into his home; he gathers (food, clothing) for some worthy cause
taken
maceptasu (II) it is taken away
pektahasu (II) everything is taken away

talk

akonutome (AI) he talks; he tells a story; he reports news

'cipinal (TA) he startles him by talking

'cipokihtaqsuwamal (TA) he talks very loudly to him

costaqsu (AI) he talks constantly; he talks and talks

-ewest(u)- speak; talk

mocatuwe (AI) he talks dirty

'pecimal (TA) he makes him come by talking or calling to him

sahsewestu (AI) he talks fast

'siktehtaqsuwamal (TA) he talks about him annoyingly often

'tawe (II) he knows how to talk

'topolumal (TA) he talks about him

ulimal (TA) he talks to him pleasantly

uskuhutomon (TI) he talks about it

uskuhutomuwan (DOV) he talks about it for him; he talks to him about it

uskuwimal (TA) he talks about him

wewewestu (AI) he knows what he is talking about

talker

nutewestaq (A) talker

tall

pihtaqsu (AI) it (an.) is long and stick-like; it (an.) is tall and stick-like

pihtenskosu (AI) he is tall (said of people only)

qonenskosu (AI) he is tall by so much

tall tale

koluskapiw (AI) he exaggerates or lies a lot; he tells tall tales

tangle

ciqolatokopu (AI) it (an.) is tangled up

tap

tolikonahtehsin (AI) he is tapping his foot

target

polhike (AI) he misses his target (with a shot)

taste

mocihpukot (II) it tastes bad

mocihpuksu (AI) it (an.) tastes bad

't-oqetomal, 'qetomal (TA) he tests the taste of it (an.)

salawehpukot (II) it tastes salty

salawehpuksu (AI) it (an.) tastes salty

wolihpukot (AI) it tastes good

tea

ti (I) tea

teach

kehkimsu (AI) he teaches himself

't-okehkimal (TA) he teaches him

teacher

nutokehkikemit (A) teacher

tear

nikcahkehtun (TI) he (e.g. a rutting animal) tears it (e.g. the ground) up noisily and angrily

't-olokinehtun (TI) he tears it; he cracks it

'paskinehtun (TI) he tears it apart

psqotemu (AI) he bursts into tears

sopiqon (I) tear (teardrop)

wolinessu (II) it splits, well; it cracks well; it tears well

tease

'cikawiyal (TA) he teases him

teeth

kikcokapitehe (AI) he is teething (See also: tooth.)

monapitehtahal (TA) he knocks his (someone else's) teeth out

wipitiw (AI) he has teeth

telephone

telihpum (I) telephone

telescope

alaputihike (AI) he looks around with a telescope; he looks around with binoculars

laput (I) instrument for looking (telescope, microscope, etc.; pl., binoculars)

laputihikon (I) instrument for looking (telescope, microscope, etc.)

tell

acomu (AI) he tells (a story)

akonutome (AI) he talks; he tells a story; he reports news

't-akonutomon (TI) he tells it (e.g., a story)

't-akonutomuwal (TA) he tells him a story

atkuhke (AI) he tells an old story; he tells a legend

't-iyal (TA) he tells him

'koluskakonutomuwal (TA) he tells someone something false about him; he lies about him

koluskapiw (AI) he exaggerates or lies a lot; he tells tall tales

nostuhmuwan (DOV) he tells him about it

't-olokimal (TA) he tells him to do thus

'pakotahsu (AI) he tells a lie

'peci yahal (TA) he comes and tells him

'pisuwahqimal (TA) he tells false information about him

ten

'qotinsk (P) ten

tend

nutonahket (A) altar boy; one who tends (something)

tender

nuhkaqosu (AI) it (an.) is cooked tender

nuhkaqote (II) it is cooked tender

nuhkeyu (AI, II) it is soft, tender

test

't-oqetomal, 'qetomal (TA) he tests the taste of it (an.)

than

katok (P) than

piyemitposu (AI) he has more power than anyone else; he is in a higher office than anyone else

that

litahasu (AI) he thinks that...

neke, neket, nekew (I) (PRO) that (in., absent or dead, near person spoken to)

nit (I) (PRO) that (inanimate, near person spoken to); that (location unspecified); it

nita (I) (PRO) that one (inan.)

not (A) (PRO) that ((an.) near person spoken to); that (location unspecified); he, him, it (an.)

yaka, yakat, yakaw (A) (PRO) that (an., absent or dead, away from speaker and person spoken to) *yat* (A) (PRO) that (an., away from speaker and person spoken to)

yet (I) (PRO) that (inan., away from speaker and person spoken to)

that's why

yaqa (P) that's why

thaw

qasqomete (II) it thaws

then

neke, neket (P) then, at that time (past); long ago

nit (P) then; there; thus, so

yaka (P) then (in the future)

there

ihtolahte (II) it is always there

nit (P) then; there; thus, so

oliye (AI) he goes there

yet (P) there; then

therefore

saku (P) so; therefore

thick

kcimkatoke (II) there is thick growth

maspotekone (AI) he has thick skin

pahseyu (AI, II) he, it is thick

pahsi (pahs-, pas-) (PV) thick

soni piskuwon (II) there is a thick fog

thief

komutonesku (AI) he is a thief

thigh

wihq (I) thigh

thin

apsatokosossu (AI) he is thin (said of a snake, a string, etc.); he is skinny (said of a person)

pipuwi (pipuw-) (PV) thin (said of a layer)

thing

milluhke (AI) he does many things; he causes many kinds of trouble

munsayuwal (TA) he does things to gain his favor

think

alitahasu (AI) he is always thinking

litahasu (AI) he thinks that...

mihqitahamal (TA) he recalls him; he thinks of him

siwi tpitahasu (AI) he is tired of thinking

-tahas(i)- think

tolitahasu (AI) he is worrying; he is thinking

'topitahatomon (TI) he thinks about it

tpitahasu (AI) he thinks

tpitahatasu (II) it is thought about (by a lot of people)

tpitahatom (AI) he thinks

utomitahamal (TA) he thinks about him

think (have an opinion of)

militahasu (AI) he thinks of many different things

mocitahamal (TA) he thinks badly of him

mocitahamtuwok (AI) they (dual) think badly of each other

mocitahasuwamal (TA) he thinks evil thoughts about him

nutatahamal (TA) he thinks poorly of him

palapuwitahasu (AI) he thinks proudly

'palitahamal (TA) he thinks he (someone else) is stuck up

palitahamsu (AI) he is stuck up; he thinks highly of himself

'tepitahatomon (TI) he thinks enough of it (to do such and such); he thinks well of it

't-uwapolitahamal (TA) he thinks about him improperly; he thinks there is something wrong with him

wewehsitahamal (TA) he thinks about him (someone who has died) sorrowfully, with sympathy for his family, etc.

wewehsitahasu (AI) he thinks sympathetically, longingly, etc. about someone who has died

wolitahatomon (TI) he is willing to do it; he thinks well of it

thinker

alitahasuwin (A) wise person; thinker

alitahasuwinuwiw (AI) he is a wise person; he is a thinker

third

nuhuwewey (A, I) third; third one

thirsty

kotuwossomu (AI) he is thirsty

thirteen

'sanku (P) thirteen

thirty

'sinsk (P) thirty

this

wot (A) (PRO) this (an.)

yut (I) (PRO) this (inan.)

thorn

mikut (A) thorn

mikutimus (A) thorn tree

thread

nashutasu (AI) it (an.) is threaded

sqasuntoq (A) thread (for sewing)

three

nihi (P) three (in counting)

nuhuwok (AI) there are three of them (an.)

nuwwiwok (AI) there are three of them (an.)

'satq (P) three hundred

'sekopu (AI) it (an.) has three layers

'sis, (P) three (in counting)

'suhsalqot (II) it is three miles

'suwikhikon (A) three (in cards)

throat

'possulin (AI, AI + OBJ) he has it lodged in his throat

'qotakon (I) (dep.) his throat

'qotakonine (AI) he has a sore throat; he has throat trouble

throb

tolatokihtehson (II) it is pounding, throbbing (e.g., a pulse)

through

alamehe (AI) he zigzags through the water; he swims around underwater

pisi (pis-) (PV) into, out (through a boundary in either direction)

pisiw (P) into, out (through a boundary in either direction)

qoni (qon-) (PV) through or during a length of space or time

sapi (sap-) (PV) through

sapiw (P) through

'sapolahtomon (TI) he licks through it

sapute (saputiy-) (PV) through

'saputehtun (TI) he puts it through
saputessu (AI, II) he, it goes through
'saputiyalokotomon (TI) he eats through it
soni kpoputon (II) the view is blocked (by fallen snow) through the trees

throw
-ahke- throw; drop; release
't-amihkuhtuwal (TA) he throws him off (in wrestling)
'kakawahkan (AI, AI+OBJ) he throws it fast
'kisahkan (AI, AI+OBJ) he threw it; he can throw it
'kisahkewan (DOV) he threw it for him
'kisamihkuhtuwal (TA) he threw him off (in wrestling); he can throw him him off (in wrestling)
't-olahkan (AI, AI+OBJ) he throws it; he lets go of it; he drops it
't-olahkewan (DOV) he throws it to him
'poneqahkan (AI, AI+OBJ) he throws it down
'tepahkan (AI, AI+OBJ) he throws it in; he pushes it in; he drops it in
uckuwahkan (AI, AI+OBJ) he throws it toward here
wisayahkan (AI, AI+OBJ) he throws it hard

throw away
'qasahkan (AI, AI+OBJ) he throws it away

thumb
cihcin (I) thumb

thunder
petakiw (II) it thunders
petakiyik (A) thunder (pl.)
petakolan (II) there is a thunder shower

thus
nit (P) then; there; thus, so
tan (P) how; where; thus

tide
atpehe (II) the tide changes
ckuhpehe (II) the tide is coming in
conpekiw (II) the motion of the tide stops (when it is about to change)
kiskot (II) it is low tide
ksihkot (II) the tide is at its lowest (in its monthly cycle); it is neap tide
olomihkot (II) the tide goes out
psonpehe (II) it is high tide
sincokkot (II) the tide is at its lowest in its monthly cycle it is neap tide
wiqqot (II) the tide goes out

tie
't-otolatokonomewal (TA) he braids someone else's hair; he ties someone else's hair with a ribbon, string, etc.

tight
ksewulqe (AI) he is tight (with his money, his tools, etc.)
'sakolonomon (TI) he holds it tight

time after time
ehtahs (P) every; every time; time after time

tinker
nihluwehtun (TI) he fouled it up by tinkering with it

tired
mettehsin (AI) he is tired
siktehsonu (AI) he is tired
siwi (siw-) (PV) be tired of...
siwi tpitahasu (AI) he is tired of thinking
siwoluhke (AI) he is tired of working
siwskuwasu (AI) he is tired waiting
'siwskuwyal (TA) he is tired of waiting for him

to
tokkiw, tokki (P) until; up to; to

to make matters worse
nihluwinaw, nihluwinaq (P) to make matters worse; on top of that

to that place (there)
oli (ol-) (PV) in that way; to that place, there; at that time

tobacco
'tomawey (I) tobacco

Tobique
Neqotkuk Tobique, New Brunswick (Locative)

toe
kci kotqesit (I) big toe
kotqesit (I) toe
kotqesitsis (I) little toe
wotqesit (I) (dep.) his toe

together
maqehe (II) it comes together
mawehe (II) it comes together
mawi (maw-) (PV) together; in a group
mawiw (P) together (of more than two or of a mass); in a group
nisihtuniyal (TI) they (two) make it together
nisiw (P) together; with (of two things, people, etc.)
niskawotuwok (AI) they (two) are walking together
wiciw (P) together with

toilet
tuwiskut (A) chamber pot; toilet

tomcod
punam (A) frost fish (tomcod)
'samcuwe (AI) she has too many children

tomorrow
sepawonu (P) tomorrow

tongue
wilol (I) (dep.) his tongue

tonight
wolakuk (P) tonight

too
possa (P) too

too much
'samamkole (II) it burns too much
'sami (sam-) (PV) too much; excessively

tool
luhkewakon (I) work; tool

tooth
'ketapitehlal (TA) he extracts his (someone else's) tooth
wipit (I) (dep.) his tooth

toothache
pokehloqe (AI) he has a toothache
wipitine (AI) he has a toothache

top

'tehsahqikapuwin (AI, AI+OBJ) he stands on top of it

'tehsahqossinon (AI, AI+OBJ) he lies on top of it

tehsaqkom (AI) he swims on top of something which is under the water

tough

sakoli (sakol-) (PV, PN) hard (to the touch); difficult; tough

toward

astuwokak (AI) they (dual) dance toward each other and then apart (part of the welcome dance)

toward here

ckuwi (ckuw-, ckuh-) (PV) toward here

ckuwoqotehe (AI) he swims toward here under the water

ckuwye (AI, II) he, it comes toward here

petolamsuke (II) the wind blows toward here

uckuwahkan (AI, AI+OBJ) he throws it toward here

town

uten (I) town

utenehke (AI) he goes shopping in town

toy

layektakon (I) toy

track

't-alaphal ('t-iyalaphal) (TA) he tracks him around

alaptahsu (AI) he tracks (an animal) around

alaptu (AI) he leaves tracks around

't-apaphal (TA) he went and tracked him (and came back)

apaptahsu (AI) he has been out tracking

ksiyaptu (AI) he tracks in

maciyaphal (TA) he starts to track him

mihqaphal (TA) he comes to his tracks

nutiyaphal (TA) he tracks him out

't-oloqaphal (TA) he tracks him in that direction

'polaphal (TA) he misses his tracks

pomaptahsu (AI) he tracks

'taptu (AI) he leaves tracks from there

'tehsahqaphal (TA) he tracks him on high ground

tolaptahsu (AI) he is tracking

tragic

psahkeyuwinaqot (II) it looks regrettable; it looks tragic

tramp

skihkipolasu (AI) it (an.) is packed down by tramping

trample

't-ahskihkipolomon, uskihkipolomon (TI) he tramples it

translate

ankuwacomu (AI) he relays a message; he brings a report of; he interprets (translates)

trap

ciyahkehsuhke (AI) he hunts (or traps) mink

kiwhosuhke (AI) he hunts muskrats; he traps muskrats

kolhikon (I) trap

monessu (AI) it (an.) peels off; he gets off, gets out of a trap

punawe (AI) he sets traps

tolsoqe (AI) he is checking traps

treats

woleyuwal (TA) he treats him well

tree

opos (A) tree

stahqon (A) fir (Peter Dana Point, Maine); tree (Pleasant Point, Maine)

wolahqemihke (II) there is a good stand of trees (for wood)

wolatqonokosu (AI) it (an.) is a tree with a nice shape

wolatqonokot (II) it is a tree with a nice shape

trestle

soqasuwakon (I) bridge, trestle

trim

'tetpekisomon (TI) he cuts it (sheet-like object) straight; he trims it to the same length

trip

napisqahman (AI, AI+OBJ) he trips over it

tripe

winasey (I) tripe

trouble

nihluwacomin (AI, AI+OBJ) he stirs up trouble by talking about it

nihluweyuwal (TA) he makes trouble for him

psuhunine, moshunine (AI) he has heart trouble

'qotakonine (AI) he has a sore throat; he has throat trouble

true

leyu (II) it happens; it is true

truly

ansa (P) like; truly; really

trump

lahtu (A) trump (in cards)

truth

'papehcimal (TA) he finds out the truth from him

'papehcimanol (AI, AI+OBJ) he finds out the truth from him

wewcoskuwimal (TA) he finds out the truth from him

wewcoskuwimanol (AI, AI+OBJ) he finds out the truth from him

try

'kiluwapomal (TA) he looks for him (with his eyes); he tries to catch sight of him

't-oqetokelhal (TA) he tries to get him to stay

'qecihtun, 't-oqecihtun (TI) he tries to make it

qecuhse (AI) he tries to walk

try in vain

't-aluwihtun (TI) he tries to make it and fails; he tries in vain to make it

tuberculosis

nucomuwiw (AI) he has tuberculosis

tuna

otuhkomeq (A) tuna

turkey

nem, nehm (A) turkey

turn

'qolopehlal (TA) he turns him over; he makes him change his mind

qolopessu (AI) he turns around

'qolopihtahal (TA) he turns him around by hitting him, knocking against him, etc.

'qolopihtehmon (TI) he turns it by striking it
turn into
accossu (AI) he changes color; he turns red
ehpituwehlosu (AI) he turns himself into a woman
esponsuwehlosu (AI) he turns himself into a
  raccoon
mokosewiye (AI) he turns black
pqomuwessu (II) it is turning into ice
sinpisiye (AI) he turns blue
skitapewehlosu (AI) he (e.g., an animal) turns
  himself into a man; she turns herself into a
  man
wisawiye (AI, II) he, it turns yellow
wiwonasiye (AI) he turns foolish; he turns crazy
turnip
wenuhcuwihpon (A) turnip
twenty
nisinsk (P) twenty
twice
nisekopisu (AI) it (an.) is folded twice; it (an.) is
  wrapped twice
nisokehs (P) twice
twin
toqehs (A) twin
toqehsiscuwe (AI) she has twins
twinkle
tolahtuwessu (AI) it is twinkling
twist
koloqesson (II) it is twisted out of joint (of a
  bone)
koloqessu (II) it is twisted out of joint (of a bone)
two
epahsi (epahs-, epas-) (PV) half, halfway; in the
  middle; in two, in half
't-epahsiksal (TA) he saws it (an.) in two; he
  saws it (an.) in half
't-epahsiksomon (TI) he saws it in two; he saws
  it in half
niktuwiku (AI) it (an.) has two prongs, branches,
  extensions, etc.
nis (P) two (in counting)
nisekopu (AI) it (an.) has two layers
nisekte (II) it has two layers
nisikotone (AI) he is two years old
nisoluhke (AI) he works with someone; he does
  two jobs
nisuhsalqot (II) it is two miles
nisukoniw (P) for two days; after two days
nisukonokkiwiw (II) it is two days
tapu (P) two (in counting)
'tomehtuwan (DOV) he breaks something of his
  (someone else's) in two
tomi (tom-) (PV) cut, break into two separate
  pieces
'tommal (TA) he bites him in two
'tomosal (TA) he cuts it (an.) in two
'tomotomon (TI) he bites it in two
'tomsomon, 'tomosomon (TI) he cuts it in two

U

ugly
cipi (cip-) (PV, PN) ugly; evil-looking; hideous
uh-oh!
nita (P) well, then; uh-oh!
umbrella
akuwahtihikon (I) umbrella; sun shade (e.g. a roof
  supported by four poles); canopy
akuwahtuhusut (I) umbrella
uncertain
al (P) (indicates uncertainty, vagueness;
  approximation)
uncharitable
wihkukelkesku (AI) he is unfeeling, heartless,
  uncharitable, etc.
wihkukelomal (TA) he is unfeeling, heartless,
  uncharitable, etc. toward him
wihkukeltomon (TI) he is heartless, unfeeling,
  uncharitable, etc. toward it
uncle
nicalkul (A) (dep.) his (or her) uncle (father's
  brother)
'tolamuksisol, 'kolamuksisol (A) (dep.) his uncle
  (esp. his mother's brother)
uncomfortable
mocomomqosu (AI) it (an.) is uncomfortable (of
  clothing: too tight, scratches the skin, etc.)
mocomomqot (II) it is uncomfortable (of clothing:
  too tight, scratches the skin, etc.)
unconvinced
peqositahasu (AI) he feels discouraged; he feels
  disappointed; he feels unconvinced
uncover
'panahkalal (TA) he uncovers him quickly
'panahkewan (DOV) he uncovers something on
  him (i.e. against his wishes)
'panehtun (TI) he uncovers it
'panekonal (TA) he uncovers it (an.) by moving
  something sheet-like aside with his hand
under
neqasuke (AI) he wades under (something, e.g.,
  a bridge)
neqiye (AI) he goes under
neqoloqessu (AI) he goes under the ice
underneath
lamiw (P) inside; underneath
neqiw (P) underneath
understand
nostomon (TI) he understands it
nostuwal (TA) he understands him; he mentions
  him
'sotom, nostom (AI) he understands (what is said)
'sotuwa (TA) he is understood, mentioned
underwater
alamehe (AI) he zigzags through the water; he
  swims around underwater
alamehe (AI) he zigzags through the water; he
  swims around underwater
komoku (AI) he swims down under the water
lampeq (P) underwater

oloqoqotehe (AI) he swims in that direction under the water

pomoqotehe (AI) he goes along underwater

toloqotehe (AI) he is swimming underwater

underwear

'tolasol (I) (pl.) his underwear

undress

ketsewe (AI) he undresses

'ketsewhutolal (TA) he undresses him

uneven

walkomike (II) the ground is uneven (hills and valleys)

unexpectedly

sakhi (sakh-) (PV) into view; unexpectedly

unfeeling

wihkukelkesku (AI) he is unfeeling, heartless, uncharitable, etc.

wihkukelomal (TA) he is unfeeling, heartless, uncharitable, etc. toward him

wihkukeltomon (TI) he is heartless, unfeeling, uncharitable, etc. toward it

unfortunate

ktomaki (ktomak-) (PV, PN) poor; unfortunate

unload

ketkosewe (AI) he unloads a gun

unlock

't-apqasokahmon (TA) he unlocks it

apqasokihike (AI) he unlocks (something)

unoccupied

wosokehte (II) it (a building) is empty of people; it is unoccupied

until

tokkiw, tokki (P) until; up to; to

tokkopu (AI) he sits up to some point; he sits at some distance; he sits until some time

up

ewepi (ewep-) (PV) upward; up above

ewepiw (P) up; up above

't-eweponal (TA) he holds him up; he lifts him up

't-eweponomon (TI) he holds it up; he lifts it up

ewepte (II) it is up

kisamikotokku (AI) he jumped up; he can jump up

'sehkehlal (TA) he stands him up

'sehkomutun (TI) he stands it up

spomok (P) up; above

wonakessu (AI) he gets up (from a sitting position)

up to

tokkiw, tokki (P) until; up to; to

tokkopu (AI) he sits up to some point; he sits at some distance; he sits until some time

uphill

kisahqew (P) uphill

upriver

pithawiw (P) upriver

pithawiye (AI) he goes upriver

pithawopu (AI) he is upriver

uproot

'keccopskahal (TA) he uproots it (an.)

'keccopskehlal (TA) he uproots it (an.)

'keccopskehtun (TI) he uproots it

upside down

apuckolopu (AI) he is upside down

apuckolte (II) it is upside down

upward

ewepamu (AI) he moves rapidly upward (involuntarily)

spiqi (spiq-) (PV) upward

urinate

-sk(i)- urinate

soku (AI) he urinates

urine

skiwon (I) urine

us

kilun (A) (PRO) we, us; our, ours (including you)

nilun (A) (PRO) we, us our, ours (not including you);

use

't-uwehkahal (TA) he uses him, it (an.)

't-uwehkan (TI) he uses it

used to

mecimiw (P) formerly; used to; in the past

uvula

ekhucaloss (A) uvula

ekhucossit (A) uvula

V

vague

al (P) (indicates uncertainty, vagueness; approximation)

vain

't-aluwimal (TA) he asks (or tells) him in vain to do something

various

mili (mil-) (PV) many; various; in a variety of ways

miltehkasu it is danced in various ways

veal

kuhusisey (I) veal

vehicle

tepessu (AI) he gets into a vehicle or boat

vein

cehcis (A) vein

venison

otuhkey (I) deer meat

pehqey (I) meat obtained by hunting; wild meat

very

eci (PV) very; when

etuci (etuc-, etut-) (PV) very; to an extreme; at that point

komac (P) very much

miyawiluweyuwal (TA) he makes him very happy

muhsalal (TA) he likes him very much

muhsaltomon (TI) he likes it very much

siktehpayu (AI) he is very scared

siktiyaqosu (AI) he is very hot; he burns to death

siktiyelomu (AI) he laughs very hard

sipitahasu (AI) he remembers very well

tuci (tuc-, tut-) (PV) (going) past, by; very, extremely; at a certain point *tutatqin* (II) there is a heavy sea; the waves are very high

tutsonu (AI) he is very strong; he is very powerful

wisoki (wisok-) (PV) very

wisokolate (II) it is very hot

vest

pikews (I) vest

view

sakhiye (AI) he comes into view

sakhotkuhu (AI) he jumps into view

visible

messuwiw (AI) he is visible

visit

ksacessu (AI) he stays too long on a visit

nimskehe (AI) he drops by to visit

'peci wikuwamkomal (TA) he comes to visit him

vomit

sokku (AI) he vomits

Wabanaki

Waponahkik Wabanaki territory (Locative)

wade

alasuke (AI) he wades around

neqasuke (AI) he wades under (something, e.g., a bridge)

pomasuke (AI) he wades along

sonutasuke (AI) he wades along the edge

tolasuke (AI) he is wading

wagon

'tapakon (I) car; sled; wagon

wait

't-askuwatomon (TI) he waits for it

't-askuwyal (TA) he waits for him

't-otolaskuwyal (TA) he is waiting for him

'qonaskuwyal (TA) he waits for him (through some period of time)

'sipkaskuwyal (TA) he waits for him for a long time

siwskuwasu (AI) he is tired waiting

'siwskuwyal (TA) he is tired of waiting for him

wake

tuhkikuwocu (AI) he wakes up cold

'tuhkimal (TA) he wakes him up

tuhkiye (AI) he wakes up

tukocu (AI) he wakes up cold

walk

alalikonike (AI) he walks around in deep snow (without snowshoes)

aluhse (AI) he walks around

apacuhse (AI) he walks back

-apas(i)- walk (pl. only)

-kawot(i)- walk (of two individuals)

ksewse (AI) he walks in

ksokawse (AI) he walks across

luhse (AI) he walks there, thus

macewse (AI) he starts out on foot; he leaves on foot; he starts to walk (toddler)

menakacuhse (AI) he walks slowly

motiyaqasokonike (AI) he is heard walking in high bushes

nipawse (AI) he goes out at night; he walks at night

nomocinuhse (AI) he walks sideways

pecuhse (AI) he comes walking

pisokonike (AI) he walks into high grass, brush, etc.

pomapotuhusu (AI) he walks with a cane

pomkawotuwok (AI) they (dual) walk along

pomuhse (AI) he walks along

qecuhse (AI) he tries to walk

sehtawse (AI) he walks backwards

sonucuhse (AI) he walks along the edge

spotewse (AI) he walks during the day

-uhs(e)- walk

wisawse (AI) he walks fast

-ws(e)- walk

yaluhse (AI) he walks around

walk (dual)

alapasuwok (AI) they (pl.) walk around

lapasuwok (AI) they (pl.) walk there; they (pl.) walk thus

macehkawotuwok (AI) they (dual) start out on foot; they (dual) start to walk (toddlers)

maciyapasuwok (AI) they (pl.) leave on foot; they start to walk (toddlers)

menakatapasuwok (AI) they (pl.) walk slowly

menakatkawotuwok (AI) they (du.) walk slowly

niskawotuwok (AI) they (two) are walking together

olkawotuwok, lihkawotuwok (AI) they (dual) walk there

petapasuwok (AI) they (pl.) come walking

petkawotuwok (AI) they (dual) come walking

sehtayapasuwok, sehtapasuwok (AI) they (pl.) walk backwards

wisahkawotuwok (AI) they (dual) walk fast

wisayapasuwok (AI) they (pl.) walk fast

walking stick

apotuhun (I) cane; walking stick

wall

lahkaluson (I) high fence; high wall

wallpaper

pilasqikon (I) wallpaper

wampum

wapap (I) wampum

want

'pawalal, 'puwalal (TA) he wants him

'pawatomon, 'puwatomon (TI) he wants it

'pawatomuwan (DOV) he wants him to ...; he wants something of his (someone else's)

want to

koti; kotuwi (kotuw-) (PV) want to...

kotuwapuwe (AI) he wants a drink (of anything); he wants to eat soup, stew, etc.

warm

woloposal, woloposumal (TA) he keeps him warm

woloposu (AI) he is warm

wolopote (II) it is warm

warrior

motapekuwin (A) warrior (archaic)

warship
motapekuloq (I) ship; warship
wart
cokiqis (A) wart; decorative loop woven into the side of a basket
wash
kospahtahsu (AI) he washes the floor
'kossatpenal (TA) he washes his (someone else's) hair
kossicuwenike (AI) he washes dishes
'kossiptinenal (TA) he washes his (someone else's) hand(s)
'kossiqenal (TA) he washes his (someone else's) face
kostokonike (AI) he washes clothes; he does laundry
waste away
mehcikonahsin (AI) he is wasting away
watch out
nossawalal (TA) he is careful with him; he watches out for him
nossawatomon (TI) he is careful with (or about) it; he watches out for it
water
atpe (II) the water level changes
cuhpi (cuhp-) (PV) in (or into) water
cuhpiye (AI, II) he, it falls into the water
cuppu (AI) he sits in the water
cuwahpi (cuwahp-) (PV) in (or into) water.
cuwahpiye (AI, II) he, it goes (or falls) into the water
cuwapotokku (AI) he jumps into the water
ktopeqon (II) there is a cold spring of water
milatqihton (II) the water is choppy
mimuwipon (II) the water is perfectly calm
mulatomuwehe (II) it (a boat) sets deep in the water
nossamaqan (I) his (or my) water
sakpe, sakhope (II) water is coming into view
'samaqan, samaqan (I) water
tkopeq (I) cold water
tolapilom (AI) he is fetching water
woluwipon (II) the water is calm
water-strider
atkuwessoss (A) wriggler (mosquito larva); water-strider
wave
ksatqin (II) the waves are big
olomatqin (II) the waves are heading away (i.e. the wind is blowing from behind on the water)
'tawatkuwe (II) it rides the waves well
toku (A) wave
tolekihpute (II) it (sheet-like object) is flapping, waving, etc.
tutatqin (II) there is a heavy sea; the waves are very high
wolatkuwe (II) it rides the waves well
way
mili (mil-) (PV) many; various; in a variety of ways
oli (ol-) (PV) in that way; to that place, there; at that time

ways
assokeyu (AI) he has strange ways
we
kilun (A) (PRO) we, us; our, ours (including you)
nilun (A) (PRO) we, us our, ours (not including you)
weak
malsonu (AI) he is weak
wear
akomohom (AI) he wears snowshoes
't-asuwi psihkomon (TI) he wears it at an angle
't-asuwihtahkusin (AI, AI+OBJ) he wears it over one shoulder and diagonally across his body to the opposite hip
esansu (AI) she wears something one can see through
naste (II) it (clothing) is on; it (clothing) is being worn
't-olokinehkomon (TI) he rips it (clothing) by wearing it when it is too small for him
't-olokinehkomuwan (DOV) he rips something (clothing) of his (someone else's) by wearing it when it is too small for him
't-olokinehkuwal (TA) he rips it (an., clothing) by wearing it when it is too small for him
'poskomon (TI) he wears it
'poskuwal (TA) he wears it (an.)
wiwonihtahkusin (AI, AI+OBJ) he wears it around (his neck, ankle, etc.)
wolekewhom (AI) he wears diapers (baby)
weasel
soqehs (A) weasel
weir
sihtomuhkakon (I) weir
sihtomuhke (AI) he fishes in a weir
well
woleyu (AI) he is well off; he lives well
woleyuwal (TA) he treats him well
woli (wol-) (PV, PN) good; well
wolinessu (II) it splits, well; it cracks well; it tears well
wolitahatomon (TI) he is willing to do it; he thinks well of it
well-aimed
miyawtahal (TA) he hits him with a well-aimed blow
miyawtehmon (TI) he hits it with a well-aimed blow
well done
wolaqosasu (AI) it (an.) is well done (food)
wolaqote (II) it is well done (food)
well off
woleyu (AI) he is well off; he lives well
wolopu (AI) he is sitting nicely, comfortably; he is well off
well, then
nita (P) well, then; uh-oh!
Welshpool
Wehqayik Welshpool, New Brunswick (Locative)
went
't-apaphal (TA) he went and tracked him (and came back)
't-aptomimal (TA) he went to hire him (and came back) (See also: go.)

West Grand Lake
Utoqehkakom (I) West Grand Lake, Maine

wet
-pus- wet
puscokpe, puccokpe (AI) he is wet
puspekihke (II) the grass is wet

whale
putep (A) whale
sapitimeq (A) killer whale

what
keq, keqoss, keqsey (I) (PRO) what?; something

what for
mehsi (PV) why; (what) for

whatever
tan ote, tan te however; in whatever way; as... as

wheel
wahkaliqs (A) wheel

when
eci (PV) very; when
tan etuci when; as soon as

where
tama (P) where; somewhere
tan (P) how; where; thus

which
tan + Pronoun -ever; the one who, the one
  which; which one of... (these, those, them)?

while
kesq (P) while; as
nahaht, nahahtew, nahahtiw (P) a little while ago
nahahtiwoss (P) a little while ago

whip
ipis (I) switch (slender, flexible stick); whip
't-osemahal, 't-osemhal (TA) he whips him

whirlpool
nomestuns (A) whirlpool

whirlwind
apolahsomuwehs (A) whirlwind

whisper
kikimuwasu (AI) he whispers

whistle
putuwakon (I) whistle; moose-call (or anything
  one makes noise with by blowing)

whistler
amoqalokehs (A) whistler (duck)

white
ikolisoman (A) white man; Englishman
'tutemisqiyil (A) (dep.) his white (female) friend
'tutemol (A) (dep.) his white (male) friend
wapaqosal (TA) it (an.) cooks until it is white;
  it (an.) fades; it (an.) is bleached
wapaqosu (AI) it (an.) cooks until it is white; it
  (an.) fades; it (an.) is bleached
wapatpe (AI) he has white hair
wapeyit (A) white man
wapeyu (AI, II) he, it is white
wapi (wap-) (PV, PN) white
wapinaqot (II) it looks white
wenuhc (A) white man

whitefish
punam (A) whitefish
punamuhke (AI) he fishes for whitefish

who
wen (A) (PRO) who, what (an.); someone,
  something (an.)

whole
moscehtun (TI) he swallows it whole; he swallows
  it without chewing it

whooping cough
mecimolamiye (AI) he has whooping cough

why
mehsi (PV) why; (what) for
mehsihpit (AI) why is he eating?
mehsikapuwit (AI) why is he standing?
mesotemit (AI) why is he crying?

wide
kskotqe (II) it is wide (of a brook)

widow
sikusq (A) widow; pear; beetle species

widower
sikuwit (A) widower

will
oc (P) will; shall (indicates future)

willing
wolitahatomon (TI) he is willing to do it; he
  thinks well of it

willow
konusehs (A) willow

win
'cihtihike (AI) he wins
tomhuwe (AI) he wins

wind
mocolamson (II) the wind is blowing from a bad
  direction, in bad weather, etc.
petolamsuke (II) the wind blows toward here
pihciqehe (AI) he goes against the wind
pomolamson (II) the wind blows along
sawonehson (II) the wind is blowing from the
  south
tkolamson (II) there is a cold wind
-wehs(e)- wind blows
wisokolamson (II) the wind blows very strongly
wocawson (II) the wind blows

window
possiyantehsok (I) window

window shade
ahsuwekopolikon (I) window shade; curtain

windpipe
'qotakonap (I) windpipe

wing
apcituwiye (AI) he is flying; he is on the wing; he
  continues to fly
wonosk (A) wing

wink
'qotalokiqessu (AI) he winks

winter
pecihpun (II) winter is coming
pun (I) winter; last winter
puniw (P) in the winter
punkik region where it is always winter (Locative)

wipe
kahsicukhike (AI) he wipes dishes
'kahsihpulal (TA) he dries him off; he wipes him
  dry
'kahsihputun (TI) he dries it off; he wipes it dry

wire
olonahqap (I) chain; wire
wise
alitahasuwin (A) wise person; thinker
alitahasuwinuwiw (AI) he is a wise person; he is a thinker
wish
nopal (P) I wish; if only
witch
motewolon, ptewolon (A) person with extraordinary power; witch (contemporary usage)
witch hazel
sakoli opos (A) hardwood tree; witch hazel
with
't-apenkuwan (DOV) he pays him with it
'kolulal (TA) he argues with him; he scolds him
'kolultiniyal (AI, AI+OBJ) he argues with him
mawossominiyal (AI, AI+OBJ) they drink with him
naka (P) and; with
naskuwal (TA) he shares a bed with him
nisayye, nisahye (AI) he plays with someone
niseyiniyal (AI, AI+OBJ) he is living as married with her (or she...with him)
nisininiyal (AI, AI+OBJ) he lives with him
nisiw (P) together; with (of two things, people, etc.)
nisoluhkamal (TA) he works with him
nisossominiyal (AI, AI+OBJ) he drinks with him
't-oluhkamal (TA) he works with him
'pahpiyal (TA) he plays with him
peci wiciye (AI) he comes with others
'tetomihkuwal (TA) he catches up with him (on foot)
wicimiye (AI) he prays with others
wiciyemal (TA) he goes around with him; he goes out with her (or she... with him); he accompanies him
witapehkamal (TA) he makes friends with him; he is friendly to him
witayye, witahye (AI) he plays with him
within
tepahkalusoniw (P) within the fence, the enclosure
tepi (tep-) (PV) in, within
yali (yal-) (PV) around; within an area; (direction and location vague, unspecified or uncertain)
without delay
nokosa (nokosay-) (PV) quickly; without delay
toqc, toqca (P) without further delay
wolf
malsom (A) wolf
wolverine
luks (A) wolverine (?); a malicious character in old stories
woman
ehpit (A) woman
motaqs (A) lady; older woman (primarily a term of address)
optan (A) woman's coat
tqesusqihiw, tqesusqiw (AI) she is a shy woman
wenuhcisqehs (A) white woman
woli ehpituwiw (AI) she is a good woman

wood
komutse (AI) he steals wood
pashaqe (AI) he collects wood for craft work
psiksoq (I) piece of wood; board
skitahqem (A) outer wood (of a tree)
wood-cutter
nutaqtihiket (A) wood-cutter
woodchuck
munimqehs (A) woodchuck; groundhog
woodcock
neqskihqessuhke (AI) he hunts woodcock
neqskiqessoss (A) woodcock
woodpecker
paqahqaha (A) woodpecker
woods
kcihq (I) woods; forest
work
cehqonoluhke (AI) he works until dawn
'kekoluhke (AI) he works all day
luhke (AI) he works; he does (something)
luhkewakon (I) work; tool
mehtoluhke (AI) he gets off work; he stops working
nisoluhkamal (TA) he works with him
nisoluhke (AI) he works with someone; he does two jobs
't-oluhkamal (TA) he works with him
't-oluhkatomon (TI) he works on it
't-oluhkatomuwan (DOV) he works on it for him
't-oluhkekhal (TA) he makes him work; he puts him to work
't-oluhkewal (TA) he works for him
sehsoluhke (AI) he works so hard he is ready to cry
siwoluhke (AI) he is tired of working
tolluhke (AI) he is working
wisaluhke (AI) he works hurriedly
work out
pahtawe (AI) his plans are not to work out
worker
luhkewin (A) worker
worm
wet (A) intestinal worm
wetihke (AI) he has worms
worry
tolitahasu (AI) he is worrying; he is thinking
worth
awotu (AI, II) he, it is worth something
would
mecopal (P) please; would it be possible?
op (P) would (indicates possibility)
wound
miyawtelasu (AI) he wounds himself (by shooting)
miyawteluwal (TA) he shoots him accurately; he shoots him and hits him; he wounds him
'tamuhteluwal (TA) he wounds him
'tokuhteluwal (TA) he wounds him (with a shot)
wrap
nisekopisu (AI) it (an.) is folded twice; it (an.) is wrapped twice

wriggler
atkuwessoss (A) wriggler (mosquito larva);
    water-strider
wrinkle
atkiqe (AI) he has wrinkles on his face
write
't-amalhuwikhomon (TI) he writes it fancily; he
    makes it with fancy designs or colors; he
    decorates it
wikhike (AI) he writes, paints, draws, takes a
    picture, etc.
wikhikon (I) book; letter; any written material
wrong
'kisamoqehlal (TA) he wronged him
't-uwapolehtun (TI) he messes it up; he does it
    wrong
't-uwapolitahamal (TA) he thinks about him
    improperly; he thinks there is something wrong
    with him
wapoli (wapol-) (PV) wrong; improperly

Y

yard
elomelkimok (II) so many yards; so many paces
    (land measure)
kehsahqonasu (II) it is so many yards (cloth
    measure)
yardstick
tpahqonikon (I) ruler; yardstick
yawn
ikotahma, ikotehma, ikotohom (AI) he yawns
year
kchsikotonewiw (II) it is so many years old
mehcikoton (II) the year ends
nisikotone (AI) he is two years old
pomikoton (II) the year is not over yet; the year
    is going on
'qocikoton (II) it is one year
yell
cipokihtaqsu (AI) he yells
'kakaluwamal (TA) he calls him; he yells to him
yellow
wisaweyu (AI, II) he, it is yellow
wisawi (wisaw-) (PV, PN) yellow
wisawiye (AI, II) he, it turns yellow
yes
aha (P) yes (indicates agreement: compare cu,
    haw)
cu (P) yes, why yes; for sure; (when the answer
    "no" is expected or disbelief expressed) on the
    contrary; for sure
haw (P) sure; yes, go ahead
yesterday
wolaku (P) yesterday; last night
yet
kis (P) already; yet
mec (P) still; yet; keep(s) on

you
kil (A) (PRO) you (sg.); your, yours (sg.)
kiluwaw (A) (PRO) you (pl.); your, yours (pl.)
young
naksq (A) young woman
skinuhs (A) young man (archaic)
wasisuwiw (AI) he is young
youngest
motehsan (A) youngest child
your
kil (A) (PRO) you (sg.); your, yours (sg.)
kiluwaw (A) (PRO) you (pl.); your, yours (pl.)

Z

zigzag
alamehe (AI) he zigzags through the water; he
    swims around underwater